"Precise . . . acutely perceptive . . . a revelation,
an opening up of knowledge too long buried."
—*Independent*

"[Reza Aslan] is among a growing number of Muslim writers and
intellectuals born or educated in the West who bring a rare intimacy,
born of experience, to their analysis of Islam in the world, and can also
translate it into terms comprehensible to their Western readers."
—Pankaj Mishra, *The New York Review of Books*

"Just the history of Islam I needed, judicious and truly illuminating."
—A. S. Byatt, *Guardian*

"Thought-provoking . . . At this fateful juncture, Aslan has provided a
masterful interpretative reading of Islam."
—*Globe and Mail*

"Sympathetic . . . engaging . . . sensitive and generous."
—*Financial Times*

"Fun to read . . . [Brings] each successive century to life with the
kind of vivid details and like-you-were-there, present-tense narration that
makes popular history popular. . . . An excellent overview
that doubles as an impassioned call to reform."
—*Booklist*

"Reza Aslan counters superficial notions of a clash of civilizations with a deep and exhilarating exploration of the fifteen-hundred-year-old clash within the civilization of Islam. Distinguishing concepts like faith and religion, Islamism and Islamic fundamentalism, in ways that shed vital new light on the morning's headlines, *No god but God* is a passionate argument for the shared history of the world's religions. An essential contribution to the most important issue of our time."

—TOM REISS,
author of *The Orientalist*

No god but God

DR. REZA ASLAN is an internationally acclaimed writer and scholar of religions. His first book, *No god but God: The Origins, Evolution, and Future of Islam*, was an international bestseller. Shortlisted for the *Guardian* First Book Award, it has been translated into thirteen languages and was named by Blackwells as one of the hundred most important books of the last decade. He is also the author of *How to Win a Cosmic War: Confronting Radical Religion*, as well as the editor of *Tablet & Pen: Literary Landscapes from the Modern Middle East*. Born in Iran, he now lives in Los Angeles, where he is associate professor of creative writing at the University of California, Riverside.

Also by Reza Aslan

How to Win a Cosmic War:
Confronting Radical Religion

No god but God

The Origins, Evolution, and Future of Islam

NEW EDITION, FULLY REVISED
AND UPDATED

REZA ASLAN

arrow books

Published by Arrow Books in 2011

9 10

Copyright © Reza Aslan, 2005, 2005, 2011

Maps copyright © 2011 David Lindroth, Inc.

Reza AsIan has asserted his right under the Copyright, Designs and Patents Act,
1988 to be identified as the author of this work.

First published in the United Kingdom in 2005 by William Heinemann

Arrow Books
The Random House Group Limited
20 Vauxhall Bridge Road, London, SW1V 2SA

Addressed for companies within the Random House Group Limited can be found at:
www.randomhouse.co.uk/offices.htm

Random House Group Limited Reg. No. 954009

www.randomhouse.co.uk

A CIP catalogue record for this book is available from the British Library

ISBN 9780099564324

The Random House Group Limited supports The Forest Stewardship Council
(FSC®), the leading international forest certification organisation. Our books
carrying the FSC label are printed on FSC® certified paper. FSC is the only forest
certification scheme endorsed by the leading environmental organisations,
including Greenpeace. Our paper procurement policy can be found at:
www.randomhouse.co.uk/environment

Book design by Meryl Sussman Levavi
Printed and bound by CPI Group (UK) Ltd, Croydon, CR0 4YY

For my mother, Soheyla,

and my father, Hassan

Acknowledgments

Thank you, Mom and Dad, for never doubting me; Catherine Bell, for getting me started; Frank Conroy, for giving me a shot; Elyse Cheney, for finding me; Daniel Menaker, for trusting me; Amanda Fortini, for fixing me; my teachers, for challenging me; and Ian Werrett, for absolutely everything else.

In the name of God, the Compassionate, the Merciful

Contents

❦

Preface to the Updated Edition

❦

Ten years after the attacks of 9/11, anti-Muslim sentiment is at an all-time high throughout Europe and North America, far higher than it was in the immediate aftermath of that tragic day in 2001. Polls show that nearly half the populations in the United States and Canada hold unfavorable views toward Islam. In Europe, the passage of laws curtailing the rights and freedoms of Muslims and the success of avowedly anti-Muslim politicians and political parties have led to an even greater sense of marginalization and disenfranchisement among Muslim communities.

Many reasons have been given to explain this sudden surge in anti-Muslim hysteria. Certainly the global financial crisis has played a role. In times of economic distress, it is only natural for people to look for a scapegoat upon whom to thrust their fears and anxieties. In many parts of Europe and North America, fear of Islam goes hand in hand with larger concerns over immigration and the increasingly border-less, increasingly heterogeneous world in which we live.

It is also true that, a decade after the start of the so-called war on terror, a sense of war weariness has descended upon the United States and its Western allies. Now that the patriotic fervor with which the conflicts in Afghanistan and Iraq were launched has dissipated and the architect of the 9/11 attacks—Osama bin Laden—killed, many are wondering what exactly has been achieved with the trillions of dollars spent and the thousands of lives lost fighting the so-called "war on terror." At the same time, a spate of "homegrown" terror attacks in Europe and North America has created a heightened sense of con-cern, even in the United States, where the economically prosperous, socially integrated, and upwardly mobile Muslim community is no longer thought to be immune to the kind of militant ideology that has found a foothold among some young Muslims in Europe.

But while these are all important determinants in explaining the tide of anti-Muslim sentiment that has washed over Europe and North America in recent years, there is another, more fundamental factor that must be addressed. It involves a 2010 poll showing that nearly a quarter of Americans continue to believe that President Barack Obama is himself a Muslim, a 10 percent jump from a similar survey taken in 2008. Among registered Republicans, the number is nearly 40 percent; among self-described Tea Party members, it is upward of 60 percent. In fact, polls consistently show that the more one disagrees with President Obama's policies on, say, healthcare or financial regulation, the more likely one is to consider him a Muslim.

Simply put, Islam in the United States has become *otherized*. It has become a receptacle into which can be tossed all the angst and appre-hension people feel about the faltering economy, about the new and unfamiliar political order, about the shifting cultural, racial, and reli-gious landscapes that have fundamentally altered the world. Across Europe and North America, whatever is fearful, whatever is foreign, whatever is alien and unsafe is being tagged with the label "Islam."

This is not an unexpected development, certainly not in the United States. Indeed, everything that is currently being said about America's diverse Muslim population—that they are foreign and exotic and un-American—was said about Catholic and Jewish immigrants nearly a century ago. Neither is the otherizing of Islam a new phenomenon in the Western world. On the contrary, from the Crusades to the clash of civilizations, Islam has always played a significant role as the West's quintessential other. Still, it is dispiriting to note that even in a country founded on the principle of religious freedom, a large swath of the population firmly believes that such freedoms do not apply to Muslims, that Muslims are somehow *different*.

When I published *No god but God* in 2005, my aim was to challenge this assumption. I wanted to demonstrate that there is nothing exceptional or extraordinary about Islam, that the same historical, cultural, and geographic considerations that have influenced the development of every religion in every part of the world have similarly influenced the development of Islam, transforming it into one of the most eclectic, most diverse faiths in the history of religions. And while that message is as important today as it was back then—perhaps even more so—we must recognize that greater knowledge about Islam is not enough to alter people's perceptions of Muslims. Minds are not changed merely through acquiring data or information (if that were the case it would take no effort to convince Americans that Obama is, in fact, a Christian). Rather, it is solely through the slow and steady building of personal relationships that one discovers the fundamental truth that all people everywhere have the same dreams and aspirations, that all people struggle with the same fears and anxieties.

Of course, such a process takes time. It may take another generation or so for this era of anti-Muslim frenzy to be looked back upon with the same shame and derision with which the current generation views the anti-Catholic and anti-Jewish hysterics of the past. But that day will no doubt come. Perhaps then we will recognize the intimate connections that bind us all together beyond any cultural, ethnic, or religious affiliations.

Inshallah. God willing.

Prologue

THE CLASH OF MONOTHEISMS

MIDNIGHT, AND FIVE hours to Marrakech. I have always had trouble sleeping on trains. There is something about the unrelenting rhythm and hum of the wheels as they roll over the tracks that always keeps me awake. It is like a distant melody that's too loud to ignore. Not even the darkness that inundates the compartments at night seems to help. It is worse at night, when the stars are the only lights visible in the vast, muted desert whizzing by my window.

This is an unfortunate quirk, because the best way to travel by train through Morocco is asleep. The trains are flooded with illegal *faux guides*, who shift from cabin to cabin searching for tourists with whom to share their recommendations for the best restaurants, the cheapest hotels, the cleanest women. The *faux guides* in Morocco speak half a dozen languages, which makes them difficult to ignore. Usually, my olive skin, thick brows, and black hair keep them at bay.

But the only way to avoid them completely is to be asleep, so that they have no choice but to move on to the next beleaguered traveler.

That is precisely what I thought was taking place in the compartment next to mine when I heard raised voices. It was an argument between what I assumed was a *faux guide* and a reluctant tourist. I could hear an inexorable cackle of Arabic spoken too quickly for me to understand, interrupted by the occasional piqued responses of an American.

I had witnessed this type of exchange before: in *grands-taxis*, at the bazaar, too often on the trains. In my few months in Morocco, I'd become accustomed to the abrupt fury of the locals, which can burst into a conversation like a clap of thunder, then—as you brace for the storm—dissolve just as quickly into a grumble and a friendly pat on the back.

The voices next door grew louder, and now I thought I grasped the matter. It wasn't a *faux guide* at all. Someone was being chastised. It was difficult to tell, but I recognized the garbled Berber dialect the authorities sometimes use when they want to intimidate foreigners. The American kept saying "Wait a minute," then, *"Parlez-vous anglais? Parlez-vous français?"* The Moroccan, I could tell, was demanding their passports.

Curious, I stood and stepped quietly over the knees of the snoring businessman slumped next to me. I slid open the door just enough to squeeze through and walked into the corridor. As my eyes adjusted to the light, I glimpsed the familiar red-and-black conductor's uniform flashing across the glass door of the adjoining compartment. I knocked lightly and entered without waiting for a response.

"Salaam alay-kum," I said. *Peace be with you.*

The conductor halted his diatribe and turned to me with the customary *"Walay-kum salaam." And to you, peace.* His face was flushed and his eyes red, though not, it seemed, from anger. His uncombed hair and the heavy creases in his uniform indicated he had only just awakened. There was an indolent quality to his speech that made him difficult to understand. He was emboldened by my presence.

"Dear sir," he said in clear and comprehensible Arabic, "this is not a nightclub. There are children here. This is not a nightclub."

I had no idea what he meant.

The American gripped my shoulders and turned me toward him. "Will you please tell this man we were sleeping?" He was young and remarkably tall, with large green eyes and a shock of blond hair that hung down over his face and that he kept combing back with his fingers. "We were only sleeping," he repeated, mouthing the words as though I were reading his lips. *"Comprendez-vous?"*

I turned back to the conductor and translated: "He says he was sleeping."

The conductor was livid and, in his excitement, dropped once more into an incomprehensible Berber dialect. He began gesticulating wildly, his movements meant to indicate his sincerity. I was to understand that he would not be in such a fit over a sleeping couple. He had children, he kept saying. He was a father; he was a *Muslim*. There was more, but I stopped listening. My attention had fallen completely on the other person in the cabin.

She was sitting directly behind the man, purposely obscured by him: legs crossed casually, hands folded on her lap. Her hair was disheveled and her cheeks radiated heat. She wasn't looking directly at us, but rather observing the scene through the bowed reflection we cast on the window.

"Did you tell him we were sleeping?" the American asked me.

"I don't think he believes you," I replied.

Though taken aback by my English, he was too shocked by the accusation to pursue it. "He doesn't believe me? Great. What's he going to do, stone us to death?"

"Malcolm!" the woman cried out, louder than it seemed she'd meant to. She reached up and pulled him down next to her.

"Fine," Malcolm said with a sigh. "Just ask him how much he wants to go away." He fumbled in his shirt pockets and took out a wad of tattered multicolored bills. Before he could fan them out, I stepped in front of him and put my arms out to the conductor.

"The American says he is sorry," I said. "He is very, very sorry."

Taking the conductor's arm, I led him gently to the door, but he would not accept the apology. He again demanded their passports. I pretended not to understand. It all seemed a bit histrionic to me. Perhaps he had caught the couple acting inappropriately, but that would have warranted little more than a sharp rebuke. They were young;

they were foreigners; they did not understand the complexities of social decorum in the Muslim world. Surely the conductor understood that. And yet he seemed genuinely disturbed and personally offended by this seemingly inoffensive couple. Again he insisted he was a father and a Muslim and a virtuous man. I agreed, and promised I would stay with the couple until we reached Marrakech.

"May God increase your kindness," I said, and slid open the door.

The conductor touched his chest reluctantly and thanked me. Then, just as he was about to step into the corridor, he turned back into the compartment and pointed a trembling finger at the seated couple. "Christian!" he spat in English, his voice brimming with contempt. He slid the doors closed and we heard him make his way noisily down the corridor.

For a moment, no one spoke. I remained standing by the door, gripping the luggage rack as the train tilted through a wide turn. "That was an odd thing to say," I said with a laugh.

"I'm Jennifer," the girl said. "This is my husband, Malcolm. Thanks for helping us. Things could have gotten out of hand."

"I don't think so," I said. "I'm sure he's already forgotten all about it."

"Well, there was nothing to forget," Malcolm said.

"Of course."

Suddenly, Malcolm was furious. "The truth is that man has been hovering over us ever since we boarded this train."

"Malcolm," Jennifer whispered, squeezing his hand. I tried to catch her eye but she would not look at me. Malcolm was shaking with anger.

"Why would he do that?" I asked.

"You heard him," Malcolm said, his voice rising. "Because we're Christians."

I flinched. It was an involuntary reaction—a mere twitch of the eyebrows—but Jennifer caught it and said, almost in apology, "We're missionaries. We're on our way to the Western Sahara to preach the gospel."

All at once, I understood why the conductor had been shadowing the couple; why he was so rancorous and unforgiving about having caught them in a compromising position. For the first time since entering the compartment I noticed a small, open cardboard box perched between two knapsacks on the luggage rack. The box was filled with green, pocket-sized New Testaments in Arabic translation. There were three or four missing.

"Would you like one?" Jennifer asked. "We're passing them out."

EVER SINCE THE ATTACKS of September 11, 2001, pundits, politicians, and preachers throughout the United States and Europe have argued that the world is embroiled in a "clash of civilizations," to use Samuel Huntington's now ubiquitous term, between the modern, enlightened, democratic societies of the West and the archaic, barbarous, autocratic societies of the Middle East. A few well-respected academics have carried this argument further by suggesting that the failure of democracy to emerge in the Muslim world is due in large part to Muslim culture, which they claim is intrinsically incompatible with Enlightenment values such as liberalism, pluralism, individualism, and human rights. It was therefore simply a matter of time before these two great civilizations, which have such conflicting ideologies, clashed with each other in some catastrophic way. And what better example do we need of this inevitability than the so-called war on terror?

But just beneath the surface of this misguided and divisive rhetoric is a more subtle, though far more detrimental, sentiment: that this is not so much a cultural conflict as a religious one; that we are not in the midst of a "clash of civilizations," but rather a "clash of monotheisms."

The clash-of-monotheisms mentality could be heard in the religiously polarizing, "good versus evil" rhetoric with which the United States launched the wars in Afghanistan and Iraq. It could be seen in the rising anti-Muslim vehemence that has become so much a part of the mainstream media's discourse about the Middle East. It could be read in the opinion columns of right-wing ideologues who insist that Islam represents a backward and violent religion and culture totally at odds with "Western" values.

Of course, there is no shortage of anti-Christian and anti-Jewish propaganda in Islam. In fact, it sometimes seems that not even the most moderate preacher or politician in the Muslim world can resist advancing the occasional conspiracy theory regarding "the Crusaders and Jews," by which most simply mean *them:* that faceless, colonialist, Zionist, imperialist "other" who is not *us.* So the clash of monotheisms is by no means a new phenomenon. Indeed, from the earliest days of the Islamic expansion to the bloody wars and inquisitions of the Crusades to the tragic consequences of colonialism and the cycle of violence in Israel/Palestine, the hostility, mistrust, and often violent intolerance that has marked relations among Jews, Christians, and Muslims has been one of Western history's most enduring themes.

Over the last few years, however, as international conflicts have increasingly been framed in apocalyptic terms and political agendas on all sides couched in theological language, it has become impossible to ignore the startling similarities between the antagonistic and uninformed rhetoric that fueled the destructive religious wars of the past, and that which drives the current conflicts of the Middle East. When the Reverend Jerry Vines, past president of the Southern Baptist Convention, calls the Prophet Muhammad "a demon-possessed pedophile," he sounds eerily like the medieval papal propagandists for whom Muhammad was the Antichrist and the Islamic expansion a sign of the Apocalypse. When the Republican senator from Oklahoma, James Inhofe, stands before the U.S. Congress and insists that the ongoing conflicts in the Middle East are not political or territorial battles but "a contest over whether or not the word of God is true," he speaks, knowingly or not, the language of the Crusades.

One could argue that the clash of monotheisms is the inevitable result of monotheism itself. Whereas a religion of many gods posits many myths to describe the human condition, a religion of one god tends to be monomythic; it not only rejects all other gods, it rejects all other explanations for God. If there is only one God, then there may be only one truth, and that can easily lead to bloody conflicts of irreconcilable absolutisms. Missionary activity, while commendable for providing health and education to the impoverished throughout the world, is nonetheless predicated on the belief that there is but one path to God, and that all other paths lead toward sin and damnation.

Malcolm and Jennifer, as I discovered on our way to Marrakech, were part of a rapidly growing movement of Christian missionaries who have increasingly begun to focus on the Muslim world. Because Christian evangelism is often bitterly reproached in Muslim countries—thanks in large part to the lingering memory of the colonial endeavor, when Europe's disastrous "civilizing mission" went hand in hand with a fervently anti-Islamic "Christianizing mission"—some evangelical institutions now teach their missionaries to "go undercover" in the Muslim world by taking on Muslim identities, wearing Muslim clothing (including the veil), even fasting and praying as Muslims. At the same time, the United States government has encouraged large numbers of Christian aid organizations to take an active role in rebuilding the infrastructures of Iraq and Afghanistan in the wake of the two wars, giving ammunition to those who seek to portray the occupation of those countries as another Crusade of Christians against Muslims. Add to this the perception, held by many in the Muslim world, that there is collusion between the United States and Israel against Muslim interests in general and Palestinian rights in particular, and one can understand how Muslims' resentment and suspicion of the West has only increased, and with disastrous consequences.

Considering how effortlessly religious dogma has become intertwined with political ideology, how can we overcome the clash-of-monotheisms mentality that has so deeply entrenched itself in the modern world? Clearly, education and tolerance are essential. But what is most desperately needed is not so much a better appreciation of our neighbor's religion as a broader, more complete understanding of religion itself.

Religion, it must be understood, is not faith. Religion is the *story* of faith. It is an institutionalized system of symbols and metaphors (read rituals and myths) that provides a common language with which a community of faith can share with each other their numinous encounter with the Divine Presence. Religion is concerned not with genuine history, but with sacred history, which does not course through time like a river. Rather, sacred history is like a hallowed tree whose roots dig deep into primordial time and whose branches weave in and out of genuine history with little concern for the boundaries of space and time. Indeed, it is precisely at those moments when sacred and genuine history collide that religions are born. The clash of monotheisms occurs when faith, which is mysterious and ineffable and which eschews all categorizations, becomes entangled in the gnarled branches of religion.

❦❦❦

THIS, THEN, IS the *story* of Islam. It is a story anchored in the memories of the first generation of Muslims and catalogued by the Prophet Muhammad's earliest biographers, Ibn Ishaq (d. 768), Ibn Hisham (d. 833), al-Baladhuri (d. 892), and al-Tabari (d. 922). At the heart of the story is the Glorious Quran—the divine revelations Muhammad received during a span of some twenty-three years in Mecca and Medina. While the Quran, for reasons that will become clear, tells us very little about Muhammad's life (indeed, Muhammad is rarely mentioned in it), it is invaluable in revealing the ideology of the Muslim faith in its infancy: that is, before the faith became a religion, before the religion became an institution.

Still, we must never forget that as indispensable and historically valuable as the Quran and the traditions of the Prophet may be, they are nevertheless grounded in *mythology*. It is a shame that this word, *myth*, which originally signified nothing more than stories of the supernatural, has come to be regarded as synonymous with falsehood, when in fact myths are always true. By their very nature, myths inhere both legitimacy and credibility. Whatever truths they convey have little to do with historical fact. To ask whether Moses actually parted the Red Sea, or whether Jesus truly raised Lazarus from the dead, or whether the word of God indeed poured through the lips of Muhammad, is to ask irrelevant questions. The only question that matters with regard to a religion and its mythology is "What do these stories mean?"

The fact is that no evangelist in any of the world's great religions would have been at all concerned with recording his or her objective observations of historical events. They would not have been recording observations at all! Rather, they were *interpreting* those events in order to give structure and meaning to the myths and rituals of their community, providing future generations with a common identity, a common aspiration, a common *story*. After all, religion is, by definition, interpretation; and by definition, all interpretations are valid. However, some interpretations are more reasonable than others. And as the Jewish philosopher and mystic Moses Maimonides noted so many years ago, it is reason, not imagination, which determines what is probable and what is not.

The way scholars form a reasonable interpretation of a particular religious tradition is by merging that religion's myths with what can be known about the spiritual and political landscape in which those myths arose. By relying on the Quran and the traditions of the Prophet, along with our understanding of the cultural milieu in which Muhammad was born and in which his message was formed, we can more reasonably reconstruct the origins and evolution of Islam. This is no easy task, though it is made somewhat easier by the fact that Muhammad appears to have lived "in the full view of history," to quote Ernest Renan, and died an enormously successful prophet (something for which his Christian and Jewish detractors have never forgiven him).

Once a reasonable interpretation of the rise of Islam in sixth- and seventh-century Arabia has been formed, it is possible to trace how Muhammad's revolutionary message of moral accountability and social egalitarianism was gradually reinterpreted by his successors into competing ideologies of rigid legalism and uncompromising orthodoxy, which fractured the Muslim community and widened the gap between mainstream, or *Sunni*, Islam and its two major branches, *Shi'ism* and *Sufism*. Although sharing a common sacred history, each group strove to develop its own interpretation of scripture, its own ideas on theology and the law, and its own community of faith. And each had different responses to the experience of colonialism in the eighteenth and nineteenth centuries. Indeed, that experience forced the entire Muslim community to reconsider the role of faith in modern society. While some Muslims pushed for the creation of an indigenous Islamic Enlightenment by eagerly developing Islamic alternatives to Western secular notions of democracy, others advocated separation from Western cultural ideals in favor of the complete "Islamization" of society. With the end of colonialism and the birth of the Islamic state in the twentieth century, these two groups have refined their arguments against the backdrop of the ongoing debate in the Muslim world over the prospect of forming a genuine Islamic democracy. But as we shall see, at the center of the debate over Islam and democracy is a far more significant internal struggle over who gets to define the Islamic Reformation that is already under way in most of the Muslim world.

The reformation of Christianity was a terrifying process, but it was not, as it has so often been presented, a collision between Protestant reform and Catholic intransigence. Rather, the Christian Reformation was an argument over the future of the faith—a violent, bloody argument that engulfed Europe in devastation and war for more than a century.

Thus far, the Islamic Reformation has proved no different. For most of the Western world, September 11, 2001, signaled the commencement of a worldwide struggle between Islam and the West—the ultimate manifestation of the clash of civilizations. From the Islamic perspective, however, the attacks on New York and Washington were part of an ongoing clash between those Muslims who strive to reconcile their religious values with the realities of the modern world, and those who react to modernism and reform by reverting—sometimes fanatically—to the "fundamentals" of their faith.

This book is not just a critical reexamination of the origins and evolution of Islam, nor is it merely an account of the current struggle among Muslims to define the future of this magnificent yet misunderstood faith. This book is, above all else, an argument for reform. There are those who will call it apostasy, but that is not troubling. No one speaks for God—not even the prophets (who speak *about* God). There are those who will call it apology, but that is hardly a bad thing. An apology is a defense, and there is no higher calling than to defend one's faith, especially from ignorance and hate, and thus to help shape the story of that faith, a story which, in this case, began fourteen centuries ago, at the end of the sixth century C.E., in the sacred city of Mecca, the land that gave birth to Muhammad ibn Abdallah ibn Abd al-Muttalib: the Prophet and Messenger of God. May peace and blessings be upon him.

Author's Note

While there is a widely recognized system for the transliteration of Arabic into English, along with specific diacritical markings to indicate long and short vowels, I have endeavored, for the sake of clarity and ease, to present all Arabic words in their simplest and most recognizable English rendering. The Arabic letter *hamza*, which is rarely vocalized, will occasionally be marked with an apostrophe. The letter *ain*—best pronounced as a glottal stop—will be marked with a *reverse* apostrophe, as in the word *bay'ah*, meaning "oath." Further, rather than pluralizing Arabic nouns according to their proper grammatical rules, I will simply add an *s:* thus, *Kahins*, instead of *Kuhhan*.

Unless otherwise indicated, all translations of the Quran are my own.

Chronology of Key Events

750–850 The Abbasid Dynasty

756 Last Umayyad prince, Abd al-Rahman, establishes rival Caliphate in Spain

874 The occultation of the Twelfth Imam, or the *Mahdi*

934–1062 Buyid Dynasty rules western Iran, Iraq, and Mesopotamia

969–1171 Fatimid Dynasty rules North Africa, Egypt, and Syria

977–1186 Ghaznavid Dynasty rules Khurasan, Afghanistan, and northern India

1095 Christian Crusades launched by Pope Urban II

1250–1517 Mamluk Dynasty rules Egypt and Syria

1281–1924 The Ottoman Empire

1501–1725 Safavid Dynasty rules Iran

1526–1858 Mughal Dynasty rules India

1857 The Indian Revolt against the British

1924 Creation of secular Turkish republic and the end of the Ottoman Caliphate

1925 Beginning of Pahlavi Dynasty in Iran

1928 The Society of Muslim Brothers founded by Hasan al-Banna in Egypt

1932 Kingdom of Saudi Arabia established

1947 Pakistan founded as first Islamic state

1948 State of Israel established

1952 Free Officers revolt in Egypt, led by Gamal Abd al-Nasser

1979 Soviets invade Afghanistan

1980 Iran Hostage Crisis

1987 First Intifada, or Palestinian Uprising

1988 Hamas founded

1989 Soviet army pulls out of Afghanistan

1991 The Persian Gulf War; al-Qaeda formed

1992 Algerian Civil War

2000 Second Intifada in Israel/Palestine

2001 Al-Qaeda attack on New York and Washington

2003 U.S.-led invasion of Iraq

2006 Hamas wins elections in Palestine

2008 Israeli invasion of Gaza

2009 Green Movement protests in Iran

2010 U.S. combat mission in Iraq officially ends

2011 Democratic protests erupt across North Africa

2011 Osama bin Laden killed in Pakistan

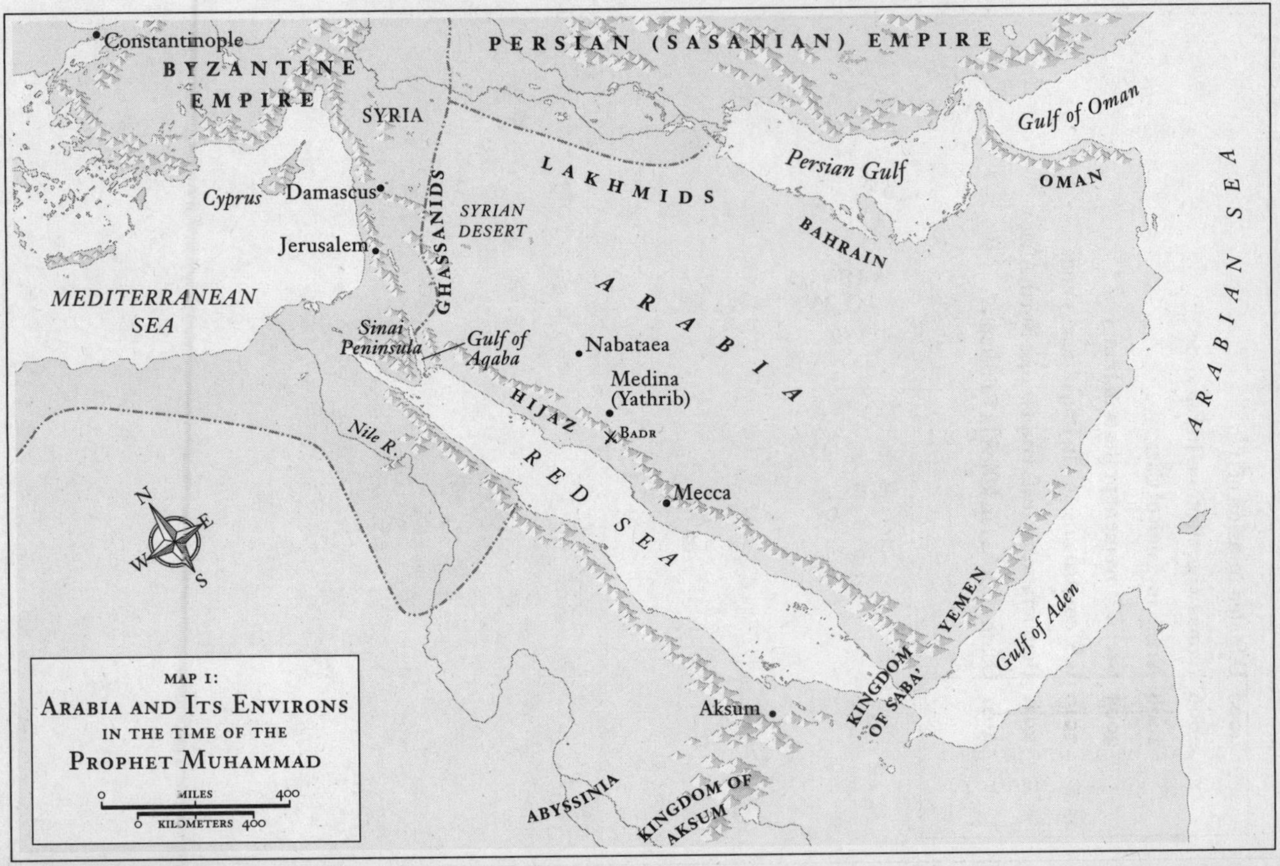

MAP 1:
ARABIA AND ITS ENVIRONS
IN THE TIME OF THE
PROPHET MUHAMMAD

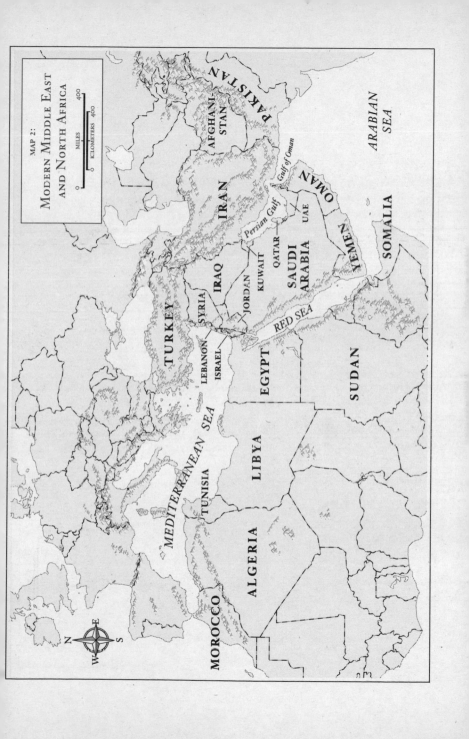

MAP 2:
MODERN MIDDLE EAST
AND NORTH AFRICA

MILES 400

KILOMETERS 400

PAKISTAN

AFGHANISTAN

IRAN

ARABIAN SEA

OMAN

Gulf of Oman

Persian Gulf

UAE

YEMEN

QATAR

KUWAIT

SAUDI ARABIA

IRAQ

SOMALIA

TURKEY

SYRIA

JORDAN

RED SEA

LEBANON

ISRAEL

EGYPT

SUDAN

MEDITERRANEAN SEA

LIBYA

TUNISIA

ALGERIA

MOROCCO

N
E
W
S

No god but God

1. The Sanctuary in the Desert

PRE-ISLAMIC ARABIA

Arabia. The Sixth Century C.E.

IN THE ARID, desolate basin of Mecca, surrounded on all sides by
the bare mountains of the Arabian desert, stands a small, nondescript
sanctuary that the pagan Arabs refer to as the *Ka'ba*: the Cube. The
Ka'ba is a squat, roofless edifice made of unmortared stones and sunk
into a valley of sand. Its four walls—so low it is said a young goat can
leap over them—are swathed in strips of heavy cloth dyed purple and
red. At its base, two small doors are chiseled into the gray stone,
allowing entry into the inner sanctum. It is here, inside the cramped
interior of the sanctuary, that the gods of pre-Islamic Arabia reside:
Hubal, the Syrian god of the moon; al Uzza, the powerful goddess the
Egyptians knew as Isis and the Greeks called Aphrodite; al-Kutba, the
Nabataean god of writing and divination; Jesus, the incarnate god of
the Christians, and his holy mother, Mary.

In all, there are said to be three hundred sixty idols housed in and around the Ka'ba, representing every god recognized in the Arabian Peninsula. During the holy months, when the desert fairs and the great markets envelop the city of Mecca, pilgrims from all over the Peninsula make their way to this barren land to visit their tribal deities. They sing songs of worship and dance in front of the gods; they make sacrifices and pray for health. Then, in a remarkable ritual—the origins of which are a mystery—the pilgrims gather as a group and rotate around the Ka'ba seven times, some pausing momentarily to kiss each corner of the sanctuary before being captured and swept away once more by the current of bodies.

The pagan Arabs gathered around the Ka'ba believe this sanctuary to have been founded by Adam, the first man. They believe that Adam's original edifice was destroyed by the Great Flood, then rebuilt by Noah. They believe that after Noah, the Ka'ba was forgotten for generations until Abraham rediscovered it while visiting his firstborn son, Ismail, and his concubine, Hagar, both of whom had been banished to this wilderness at the behest of Abraham's wife, Sarah. And they believe it was at this very spot that Abraham nearly sacrificed Ismail before being stopped by the promise that, like his younger brother, Isaac, Ismail would also sire a great nation, the descendants of whom now spin over the sandy Meccan valley like a desert whirlwind.

Of course, these are just stories intended to convey what the Ka'ba *means*, not where it came from. The truth is that no one knows who built the Ka'ba, or how long it has been here. It is likely that the sanctuary was not even the original reason for the sanctity of this place. Near the Ka'ba is a well called *Zamzam*, fed by a bountiful underground spring, which tradition claims had been placed there to nourish Hagar and Ismail. It requires no stretch of the imagination to recognize how a spring situated in the middle of the desert could become a sacred place for the wandering Bedouin tribes of Arabia. The Ka'ba itself may have been erected many years later, not as some sort of Arab pantheon, but as a secure place to store the consecrated objects used in the rituals that had evolved around Zamzam. Indeed, the earliest traditions concerning the Ka'ba claim that inside its walls was a pit, dug into the sand, which contained "treasures" (ritual objects) magically guarded by a snake.

It is also possible that the original sanctuary held some cosmological significance for the ancient Arabs. Not only were many of the idols in the Ka'ba associated with the planets and stars, but the legend that they totaled three hundred sixty in number suggests astral connotations. The seven circumambulations of the Ka'ba—called *tawaf* in Arabic and still the primary ritual of the annual *Hajj* pilgrimage—may have been intended to mimic the motion of the heavenly bodies. It was, after all, a common belief among ancient peoples that their temples and sanctuaries were terrestrial replicas of the cosmic mountain from which creation sprang. The Ka'ba, like the Pyramids in Egypt or the Temple in Jerusalem, may have been constructed as an *axis mundi*, sometimes called a "navel spot": a sacred space around which the whole of the universe revolves, the link between the earth and the solid dome of heaven. That would explain why there was once a nail driven into the floor of the Ka'ba that the ancient Arabs referred to as "the navel of the world." According to the traditions, the ancient pilgrims would sometimes enter the sanctuary, tear off their clothes, and place their own navels over the nail, thereby merging with the cosmos.

Alas, as with so many things about the Ka'ba, its origins are mere speculation. The only thing scholars can say with any certainty is that by the sixth century C.E., this small sanctuary made of mud and stone had become the center of religious life in pre-Islamic Arabia: that intriguing yet ill-defined era of paganism that Muslims refer to as the *Jahiliyyah*—"the Time of Ignorance."

TRADITIONALLY, THE JAHILIYYAH has been defined by Muslims as an era of moral depravity and religious discord: a time when the sons of Ismail had obscured belief in the one true God and plunged the Arabian Peninsula into the darkness of idolatry. But then, like the rising of the dawn, the Prophet Muhammad emerged in Mecca at the beginning of the seventh century, preaching a message of absolute monotheism and uncompromising morality. Through the miraculous revelations he received from God, Muhammad put an end to the paganism of the Arabs and replaced the "Time of Ignorance" with the universal religion of Islam.

In actuality, the religious experience of the pre-Islamic Arabs was far more complex than this tradition suggests. It is true that before the rise of Islam the Arabian Peninsula was dominated by paganism. But "paganism" is a somewhat meaningless and derogatory catchall term created by those outside the tradition to categorize what is in reality an almost unlimited variety of beliefs and practices. The word *paganus* means "a rustic villager" or "a boor," and was originally used by Christians as a term of abuse to describe those who followed any religion but theirs. In some ways, this is an appropriate designation. For unlike Christianity, paganism is not so much a unified system of beliefs and practices as it is a religious *perspective*, one that is receptive to a multitude of influences and interpretations. Often, though not always, polytheistic, paganism strives for neither universalism nor moral absolutism. There is no such thing as a pagan creed or a pagan canon. Nothing exists that could properly be termed "pagan orthodoxy" or "pagan heterodoxy."

What is more, when referring to the religious experience of the pre-Islamic Arabs, it is important to make a distinction between the nomadic Bedouin who wandered through the Arabian deserts and the sedentary tribes that had settled in major population centers like Mecca. Bedouin paganism in sixth-century Arabia may have encompassed a range of beliefs and practices—from fetishism to totemism to manism (ancestor cults)—but it was not as concerned with the more metaphysical questions that were cultivated in the larger sedentary societies of Arabia, particularly with regard to issues like the afterlife. This is not to say that the Bedouin practiced nothing more than a primitive idolatry. On the contrary, there is every reason to believe that the Bedouin of pre-Islamic Arabia enjoyed a rich and diverse religious tradition. However, the nomadic lifestyle is one that requires a religion to address immediate concerns: Which god can lead us to water? Which god can heal our illnesses?

In contrast, paganism among the sedentary societies of Arabia had developed from its earlier and simpler manifestations into a complex form of neo-animism, providing a host of divine and semi-divine intermediaries who stood between the creator god and his creation. This creator god was called *Allah*, which is not a proper name but a contraction of the word *al-ilah*, meaning simply "the god." Like his Greek counterpart, Zeus, Allah was originally an ancient rain/sky deity who had been elevated into the role of the supreme god of the pre-Islamic Arabs. Though a powerful deity to swear by, Allah's eminent status in the Arab pantheon rendered him, like most High Gods, beyond the supplications of ordinary people. Only in times of great peril would anyone bother consulting him. Otherwise, it was far more expedient to turn to the lesser, more accessible gods who acted as Allah's intercessors, the most powerful of whom were his three daughters, Allat ("the goddess"), al-Uzza ("the mighty"), and Manat (the goddess of fate, whose name is probably derived from the Hebrew word *mana*, meaning "portion" or "share"). These divine mediators were not only represented in the Ka'ba, they had their own individual shrines throughout the Arabian Peninsula: Allat in the city of Ta'if; al-Uzza in Nakhlah; and Manat in Qudayd. It was to them that the Arabs prayed when they needed rain, when their children were ill, when they entered into battle or embarked on a journey deep into the treacherous desert abodes of the *Jinn*—those intelligent, imperceptible, and salvable beings made of smokeless flame who are called "genies" in the West and who function as the nymphs and fairies of Arabian mythology.

There were no priests and no pagan scriptures in pre-Islamic Arabia, but that does not mean the gods remained silent. They regularly revealed themselves through the ecstatic utterances of a group of cultic officials known as the *Kahins*. The Kahins were poets who functioned primarily as soothsayers and who, for a fee, would fall into a trance in which they would reveal divine messages through rhyming couplets. Poets already had an important role in pre-Islamic society as bards, tribal historians, social commentators, dispensers of moral philosophy, and, on occasion, administrators of justice. But the Kahins represented a more spiritual function of the poet. Emerging from every social and economic stratum, and including a number of women, the Kahins interpreted dreams, cleared up crimes, found lost animals, settled disputes, and expounded upon ethics. As with their Pythian counterparts at Delphi, however, the Kahins' oracles were vague and deliberately imprecise; it was the supplicant's responsibility to figure out what the gods actually meant.

Although considered the link between humanity and the divine, the Kahins did not communicate directly with the gods but rather accessed them through the Jinn and other spirits who were such an integral part of the Jahiliyyah religious experience. Even so, neither the Kahins nor anyone else, for that matter, had access to Allah. In fact, the god who had created the heavens and the earth, who had fashioned human beings in his own image, was the only god not represented by an idol in the Ka'ba. Although called "the King of the Gods" and "the Lord of the House," Allah was not the central deity in the Ka'ba. That honor belonged to Hubal, the Syrian god who had been brought to Mecca centuries before the rise of Islam.

Despite Allah's minimal role in the religious cult of pre-Islamic Arabia, his eminent position in the Arab pantheon is a clear indication of just how far paganism in the Arabian Peninsula had evolved from its simple animistic roots. Perhaps the most striking example of this development can be seen in the processional chant that tradition claims the pagan pilgrims sang as they approached the Ka'ba:

> Here I am, O Allah, here I am.
> You have no partner,
> Except such a partner as you have.
> You possess him and all that is his.

This remarkable proclamation, with its obvious resemblance to the Muslim profession of faith—"There is no god but God"—may reveal the earliest traces in pre-Islamic Arabia of what the German philologist Max Müller termed *henotheism:* the belief in a single High God, without necessarily rejecting the existence of other, subordinate gods. The earliest evidence of henotheism in Arabia can be traced back to a tribe called the Amir, who lived near modern-day Yemen in the second century B.C.E., and who worshipped a High God they called *dhu-Samawi*, "The Lord of the Heavens." While the details of the Amirs' religion have been lost to history, most scholars are convinced that by the sixth century C.E., henotheism had become the standard belief of the vast majority of sedentary Arabs, who not only accepted Allah as their High God, but insisted that he was the same god as Yahweh, the god of the Jews.

* * *

The Jewish presence in the Arabian Peninsula can, in theory, be traced to the Babylonian Exile a thousand years earlier, though subsequent migrations may have taken place in 70 C.E., after Rome's sacking of the Temple in Jerusalem, and again in 132 C.E., after the messianic uprising of Simon Bar Kochba. For the most part, the Jews were a thriving and highly influential diaspora whose culture and traditions had been thoroughly integrated into the social and religious milieu of pre-Islamic Arabia. Whether Arab converts or immigrants from Palestine, the Jews participated in every level of Arab society. There were Jewish merchants, Jewish Bedouin, Jewish farmers, Jewish poets, and Jewish warriors throughout the peninsula. Jewish men took Arab names; Jewish women wore Arab headdresses. And while some of these Jews may have spoken Aramaic (or at least a corrupted version of it), their primary language was Arabic.

Although in contact with major Jewish centers throughout the Near East, Judaism in Arabia had developed its own variations on traditional Jewish beliefs and practices. The Jews shared many of the same religious ideals as their pagan Arab counterparts, especially with regard to what is sometimes referred to as "popular religion": belief in magic, the use of talismans and divination, and the like. For example, while there is evidence of a small yet formal rabbinical presence in some regions of the Arabian Peninsula, there also existed a group of Jewish soothsayers called the *Kohens* who, while maintaining a far more priestly function in their communities, nevertheless resembled the pagan Kahins in that they too dealt in divinely inspired oracles.

The relationship between the Jews and pagan Arabs was symbiotic in that not only were the Jews heavily Arabized, but the Arabs were also significantly influenced by Jewish beliefs and practices. One need look no further for evidence of this influence than to the Ka'ba itself, whose origin myths indicate that it was a Semitic sanctuary (*haram* in Arabic) with its roots dug deeply in Jewish tradition. Adam, Noah, Abraham, Moses, and Aaron were all in one way or another associated with the Ka'ba long before the rise of Islam, and the mysterious Black Stone that to this day is fixed to the southeast corner of the sanctuary seems to have been originally associated with the same stone upon which Jacob rested his head during his famous dream of the ladder (Genesis 28:11–19).

The pagan Arab connection to Judaism makes perfect sense when one recalls that, like the Jews, the Arabs considered themselves descendants of Abraham, whom they credited not only with rediscovering the Ka'ba, but also with creating the pilgrimage rites that took place there. So revered was Abraham in Arabia that he was given his own idol inside the Ka'ba, where he was depicted in traditional pagan fashion as a shaman casting divining rods. That Abraham was neither a god nor a pagan was as inconsequential to the Arabs as the association of their god, Allah, with the Jewish god, Yahweh. In sixth-century Arabia, Jewish monotheism was in no way anathema to Arab paganism, which, as mentioned, could easily absorb a cornucopia of disparate religious ideologies. The pagan Arabs would likely have perceived Judaism as just another way of expressing what they considered to be similar religious sentiments.

The same could be said with regard to Arab perceptions of Christianity, which, like Judaism, had an influential presence in the Arabian Peninsula. The Arab tribes were surrounded by Christians: from the Syrians in the northwest, to the Mesopotamian Christians in the northeast, to the Abyssinians in the south. By the sixth century C.E., Yemen had become the seat of Christian aspirations in Arabia; the city of Najran was widely considered to be the hub of Arab Christianity, while in Sana', a massive church had been constructed that, for a time, vied with Mecca as the primary pilgrimage site in the region.

As a proselytizing faith, Christianity was not content to remain at the borders of the Arab lands. Thanks to a concerted effort to spread the gospel throughout the peninsula, a number of Arab tribes had converted *en masse* to Christianity. The largest of these tribes was the Ghassanids, who straddled the border between the Roman and Arab worlds, acting as a buffer between the Christian Byzantine kingdom and the "uncivilized" Bedouin. The Ghassanids actively supported missionary efforts in Arabia, while at the same time the Byzantine emperors sent their bishops deep into the deserts to bring the rest of the pagan Arabs into their fold. And yet, the Ghassanids and the Byzantines were preaching two very different Christianities.

Ever since the first Council at Nicaea in 325 C.E.—which declared Jesus to be "fully God"—and the Council at Chalcedon in 451 C.E.—which entrenched the doctrine of the Trinity into Christian theology—Roman Orthodoxy had transformed a large portion of the Christian Near East into heretics. Because the concept of the Trinity is not explicitly mentioned in the New Testament (the term was coined by one of the oldest and most formidable church fathers, Tertullian of Carthage, early in the third century C.E.), it was neither widely adopted nor universally construed by the early Christian communities. Montanist Christians like Tertullian believed that Jesus possessed the same divine *quality* as God, but not in the same *quantity* as God. Modalist Christians conceived of the Trinity as representing God in three successive modes of being: first as the Father, then as the Son, and finally and forevermore as the Holy Spirit. Nestorian Christians argued that Jesus had two completely distinct natures—one human, the other divine—while Gnostic Christians, especially those called Docetists, claimed that Jesus only appeared to be human but was in fact fully God. And of course there were those like the Arians who rejected the Trinity altogether.

After Christianity became the imperial religion of Rome, all of these variations on Jesus' identity were replaced by the single orthodox position, most clearly presented by Augustine of Hippo (d. 430), that the Son was "of the same substance or being" as the Father—one God in three personae. All at once, the Montanists, the Modalists, the Nestorians, the Gnostics, and the Arians were declared heretics and their doctrines suppressed.

The Ghassanids, like so many Christians who lived beyond the ever-tightening grip of Constantinople, were Monophysites, meaning they rejected the Nicene doctrine confirming Jesus' dual nature. Instead, the Monophysites believed that Jesus had only one nature, simultaneously human and divine, though depending on the school of thought they tended to emphasize one over the other. In general, the Antiochians stressed Jesus' humanity, while the Alexandrians stressed his divinity. So while the Ghassanids may have been Christians, and while they may have acted as clients of the Byzantine Empire, they did not share the theology of their masters.

Once again, one need only look inside the Ka'ba to recognize which version of Christianity was taking hold in Arabia. According to the traditions, the image of Jesus residing in the sanctuary had been placed there by a Coptic (i.e., Alexandrian Monophysite) Christian named Baqura. If true, then Jesus' presence in the Ka'ba may be considered an affirmation of the Monophysite belief in the Christ as a fully divine god-man—a position that would have been perfectly acceptable to the pagan Arabs.

Christianity's presence in the Arabian Peninsula—in both its orthodox and heterodox incarnations—must have had a significant effect on the pagan Arabs. It has often been noted that the biblical stories recounted in the Quran, especially those dealing with Jesus, imply a familiarity with the traditions and narratives of the Christian faith. There are striking similarities between the Christian and Quranic descriptions of the Apocalypse, the Last Judgment, and the paradise awaiting those who have been saved. These similarities do not necessarily contradict the Muslim belief that the Quran was divinely revealed, but they do indicate that the Quranic vision of the Last Days may have been revealed to the pagan Arabs through a set of symbols and metaphors with which they were already familiar, thanks in some part to the wide spread of Christianity in the region.

While the Ghassanids protected the borders of the Byzantine Empire, another Arab tribe, the Lakhmids, provided the same service for the other great kingdom of the time, the Sasanians. As the imperial inheritors of the ancient Iranian kingdom of Cyrus the Great, which had dominated Central Asia for nearly a millennium, the Sasanians were Zoroastrians: followers of the seminal faith initiated by the Iranian prophet Zarathustra nearly fifteen hundred years earlier, whose ideas and beliefs had a formidable influence on the development of the other religions in the region, especially Judaism and Christianity.

More than a thousand years before Christ, Zarathustra preached the existence of a heaven and a hell, the idea of a bodily resurrection, the promise of a universal savior who would one day be miraculously born to a young maiden, and the expectation of a final cosmic battle that would take place at the end of time between the angelic forces of good and the demonic forces of evil. At the center of Zarathustra's theology was a unique monotheistic system based on the sole god,

Ahura Mazda ("the Wise Lord"), who fashioned the heavens and earth, the night and the day, the light and the darkness. Like most ancients, however, Zarathustra could not easily conceive of his god as being the source of both good and evil. He therefore developed an ethical dualism in which two opposing spirits, *Spenta Mainyu* ("the beneficent spirit") and *Angra Mainyu* ("the hostile spirit") were responsible for good and evil, respectively. Although called the "twin children" of Mazda, these two spirits were not gods, but only the spiritual embodiment of Truth and Falsehood.

By the time of the Sasanians, Zarathustra's primitive monotheism had transformed into a firmly dualistic system in which the two primordial spirits became two deities locked in an eternal battle for the souls of humanity. *Ohrmazd* (Ahura Mazda), the God of Light, and *Ahriman*, the God of Darkness and the archetype of the Christian concept of Satan. Although it was a non-proselytizing and notoriously difficult religion to convert to—considering its rigid hierarchical social structure and its almost fanatical obsession with ritual purity—the Sasanian military presence in the Arabian Peninsula had nonetheless resulted in a few tribal conversions to Zoroastrianism, particularly to its more amenable sects, Mazdakism and Manichaeism.

The picture that emerges from this brief outline of the pre-Islamic Arabian religious experience is that of an era in which Zoroastrianism, Christianity, and Judaism intermingled in one of the last remaining regions in the Near East still dominated by paganism, albeit a firmly henotheistic paganism. The relative distance that these three major religions enjoyed from their respective centers gave them the freedom to develop their creeds and rituals into fresh, innovative theologies. Especially in Mecca, the center of the Jahiliyyah religious experience, this vibrant pluralistic environment became a breeding ground for bold new ideas and exciting religious experimentation, the most important of which was an obscure Arab monotheistic movement called *Hanifism*, which arose sometime around the sixth century C.E. and which, as far as anyone is aware, existed nowhere else except in western Arabia, a region the Arabs called the *Hijaz*.

The legendary origins of Hanifism are recounted in the writings of one of Muhammad's earliest biographers, Ibn Hisham. One day, while the Meccans were celebrating a pagan festival at the Ka'ba, four men named Waraqa ibn Nawfal, Uthman ibn Huwairith, Ubayd Allah ibn Jahsh, and Zayd ibn Amr drew apart from the rest of the worshippers and met secretly in the desert. There they agreed "in the bonds of friendship" that they would never again worship the idols of their forefathers. They made a solemn pact to return to the unadulterated religion of Abraham, whom they considered to be neither a Jew nor a Christian, but a pure monotheist: a *hanif* (from the Arabic root *hnf*, meaning "to turn away from," as in one who turns away from idolatry). The four men left Mecca and went their separate ways preaching the new religion and seeking out others like them. In the end, Waraqa, Uthman, and Ubayd Allah all converted to Christianity, a fact that indicates the religion's influence over the region. But Zayd continued in the new faith, abandoning the religion of his people and abstaining from the worship of, in his words, "the helpless and harmless idols" in the sanctuary.

Standing in the shadow of the Ka'ba, his back pressed against its irregular stone walls, Zayd rebuked his fellow Meccans, shouting, "I renounce Allat and al-Uzza, both of them . . . I will not worship Hubal, though he was our lord in the days when I had little sense." Pushing through the crowded market, his voice raised over the din of the merchants, he would cry, "Not one of you follows the religion of Abraham but I."

Like all preachers of his time, Zayd was also a poet, and the verses that the traditions have ascribed to him contain extraordinary declarations. "To God I give my praise and thanksgiving," he sang. "There is no god beyond Him." And yet, despite his call for monotheism and his repudiation of the idols inside the sanctuary, Zayd maintained a deep veneration for the Ka'ba itself, which he believed was spiritually connected to Abraham. "I take refuge in that in which Abraham took refuge," Zayd declared.

By all accounts, the Hanif movement flourished throughout the Hijaz, especially in major population centers like Ta'if, where the poet Umayya ibn Abi Salt wrote verses extolling "the religion of Abraham," and Yathrib, the home of two influential Hanif tribal leaders, Abu Amir ar-Rahib and Abu Qais ibn al-Aslat. Other Hanif preachers included Khalid ibn Sinan, called "a prophet lost by his people," and Qass ibn Sa'idah, known as "the sage of the Arabs." It is impossible to say how many Hanif converts there were in pre-Islamic Arabia, or how large the movement had become. What seems evident, however, is that there were many in the Arabian Peninsula who were actively struggling to transform the vague henotheism of the pagan Arabs into what Jonathan Fueck has termed "a national Arabian monotheism."

But Hanifism seemed to have been more than just a primitive Arab monotheistic movement. The traditions present the Hanifs as preaching an active god who was intimately involved in the personal lives of his creation, a god who did not need mediators to stand between him and humanity. At the heart of the movement was a fervent commitment to an absolute morality. It was not enough merely to abstain from idol worship; the Hanifs believed one must strive to be morally upright. "I serve my Lord the compassionate," Zayd said, "that the forgiving Lord may pardon my sin."

The Hanifs also spoke in an abstract fashion about a future day of reckoning when everyone would have to answer for his or her moral choices. "Beware, O men, of what follows death!" Zayd warned his fellow Meccans. "You can hide nothing from God." This would have been a wholly new concept for a people with no firm notion of an afterlife, especially one based on human morality. And because Hanifism was, like Christianity, a proselytizing faith, its ideology would have spread throughout the Hijaz. Most sedentary Arabs would have heard Hanif preachers; the Meccans would surely have been familiar with Hanif ideology; and there can be little doubt that the Prophet Muhammad would have been aware of both.

There exists a little-known tradition recounting an astonishing meeting between Zayd, the Hanif, and a teen-aged Muhammad. The story seems to have been originally reported by Yunus ibn Bukayr on the authority of Muhammad's first biographer, Ibn Ishaq. And while it appears to have been expunged from Ibn Hisham's retelling of Muhammad's life, Professor M. J. Kister at Hebrew University has catalogued no fewer than eleven other traditions that recount nearly identical versions of the story.

It was, the chroniclers say, "one of the hot days of Mecca" when Muhammad and his childhood friend Ibn Haritha were returning home from Ta'if, where they had slaughtered and roasted a ewe in sacrifice to one of the idols (most likely Allat). As the two boys made their way through the upper part of the Meccan valley, they suddenly came upon Zayd, who was either living as a recluse on the high ground above Mecca or was in the midst of a lengthy spiritual retreat. Recognizing him at once, Muhammad and Ibn Haritha greeted the Hanif with "the greeting of the Jahiliyyah" (*in'am sabahan*) and sat down to rest next to him.

Muhammad asked, "Why do I see you, O son of Amr, hated by your people?"

"I found them associating divinities with God and I was reluctant to do the same," Zayd replied. "I wanted the religion of Abraham."

Muhammad accepted this explanation without comment and opened his bag of sacrificed meat. "Eat some of this food, O my uncle," he said.

But Zayd reacted with disgust. "Nephew, that is a part of those sacrifices of yours which you offer to your idols, is it not?" Muhammad answered that it was. Zayd became indignant. "I never eat of these sacrifices and I want nothing to do with them," he cried. "I am not one to eat anything slaughtered for a divinity other than God."

So struck was Muhammad by Zayd's rebuke that many years later, when recounting the story, he claimed never again to have "stroked an idol of theirs nor . . . sacrifice[d] to them until God honored me with his Apostleship."

The notion that a young pagan Muhammad could have been scolded for his idolatry by a Hanif flies in the face of traditional Muslim views regarding the Prophet's perpetual monotheistic integrity. It is a common belief in Islam that even before being called by God, Muhammad never took part in the pagan rituals of his community. In his history of the Prophet, al-Tabari states that God kept Muhammad from ever participating in any pagan rituals, lest he be defiled by them. But this view, which is reminiscent of the Catholic belief in Mary's perpetual virginity, has little basis in either history or scripture. Not only does the Quran admit that God found Muhammad "erring" and gave him guidance (93:7), but the ancient traditions clearly show Muhammad deeply involved in the religious customs of Mecca: circumambulating the Ka'ba, making sacrifices, and going on pagan devotional retreats called *tahannuth*. Indeed, when the pagan sanctuary was torn down and rebuilt (it was enlarged and finally roofed), Muhammad took an active part in its reconstruction.

All the same, the doctrine of Muhammad's monotheistic integrity is an important facet of the Muslim faith because it appears to support the belief that the Revelation he received came from a divine source. Admitting that Muhammad might have been influenced by someone like Zayd is, for some Muslims, tantamount to denying the heavenly inspiration of Muhammad's message. But such beliefs are based on the common yet erroneous assumption that religions are born in some sort of cultural vacuum; they most certainly are not.

All religions are inextricably bound to the social, spiritual, and cultural milieux from which they arose and in which they developed. It is not prophets who create religions. Prophets are, above all, reformers who redefine and reinterpret the existing beliefs and practices of their communities, providing fresh sets of symbols and metaphors with which succeeding generations can describe the nature of reality. Indeed, it is most often the prophet's successors who take upon themselves the responsibility of fashioning their master's words and deeds into unified, easily comprehensible religious systems.

Like so many prophets before him, Muhammad never claimed to have invented a new religion. By his own admission, Muhammad's message was an attempt to reform the existing religious beliefs and cultural practices of pre-Islamic Arabia so as to bring the God of the Jews and Christians to the Arab peoples. "[God] has established for you [the Arabs] the same religion enjoined on Noah, on Abraham, on Moses, and on Jesus," the Quran says (42:13). It should not be surprising, therefore, that Muhammad would have been influenced as a young man by the religious landscape of pre-Islamic Arabia. As unique and divinely inspired as the Islamic movement may have been, its origins are undoubtedly linked to the multiethnic, multireligious society that fed Muhammad's imagination as a young man and allowed him to craft his revolutionary message in a language that would have been easily recognizable to the pagan Arabs he was so desperately try-ing to reach. Because whatever else Muhammad may have been, he was without question a man of his time, even if one chooses to call that a "Time of Ignorance."

❧

MUHAMMAD WAS BORN, according to Muslim tradition, in 570 C.E., the same year that Abraha, the Christian Abyssinian ruler of Yemen, attacked Mecca with a herd of elephants in an attempt to destroy the Ka'ba and make the church at Sana' the new religious cen-ter in the Arabian Peninsula. It is written that when Abraha's army drew near the city, the Meccans, frightened at the sight of the massive elephants the Abyssinians had imported from Africa, retreated to the mountains, leaving the Ka'ba defenseless. But just as the Abyssinian army was about to attack, the sky darkened and a flock of birds, each carrying a stone in its beak, rained down the wrath of Allah on the invading army until it had no choice but to retreat back to Yemen.

In a society with no fixed calendar, "The Year of the Elephant," as it came to be known, was not only the most important date in recent memory, it was the commencement of a new Arab chronology. That is why the early biographers set Muhammad's birth in the year 570, so that it would coincide with another significant date. But 570 is neither the correct year of Muhammad's birth nor, for that matter, of the Abyssinian attack on Mecca; modern scholarship has determined that momentous event to have taken place around 552 C.E. The fact is that no one knows now, just as no one knew then, when Muhammad was born, because birthdays were not necessarily significant dates in pre-Islamic Arab society. Muhammad himself may not have known in what year he was born. In any case, nobody would have cared about Muhammad's birth date until long after he was recognized as a prophet, perhaps not even until long after he had died. Only then would his followers have wanted to establish a year for his birth in order to institute a firm Islamic chronology. And what more appropri-ate year could they have chosen than the Year of the Elephant? For better or worse, the closest our modern historical methods can come to determining the date of Muhammad's birth is sometime in the last half of the sixth century C.E.

As is the case with most prophets, Muhammad's birth was accompanied by signs and portents. Al-Tabari writes that while Muhammad's father, Abdallah, was on his way to meet his bride, he was stopped by a strange woman who, seeing a light shining between his eyes, demanded he sleep with her. Abdallah politely refused and continued to the house of Amina, where he consummated the marriage that would result in the birth of the Prophet. The next day, when Abdallah saw the same woman again, he asked her, "Why do you not make the same proposition to me today that you made to me yesterday?" The woman replied, "The light which was with you yesterday has left you. I have no need of you today."

Abdallah never had the chance to decipher the woman's words; he died before Muhammad was born, leaving behind a meager inheritance of a few camels and sheep. But the signs of Muhammad's prophetic identity continued. While she was pregnant, Amina heard a voice tell her, "You are pregnant with the Lord of this people, and when he is born, say, 'I put him in the care of the One from the evil of every envier'; then call him Muhammad." Sometimes Amina would see a light shining from her belly by which she could make out "the castles of Syria," a reference, perhaps, to Muhammad's prophetic succession to Jesus (Syria was an important seat of Christianity).

As an infant, Muhammad was placed in the care of a Bedouin foster mother to be nursed, a common tradition among Arabs of sedentary societies who wanted their children to be raised in the desert according to the ancient customs of their forefathers. Appropriately, it was in the desert that Muhammad had his first prophetic experience. While herding a flock of lambs, he was approached by two men, clothed in white, who carried with them a golden basin full of snow. The two men came to Muhammad and pinned him to the ground. They reached into his chest and removed his heart. After extracting a drop of black liquid from it, they washed the heart clean in the snow and gently placed it back into Muhammad's breast before disappearing.

When he was six years old, Muhammad's mother died as well, and he was sent to live with his grandfather, Abd al-Muttalib, who, as the man in charge of providing Zamzam water to the pilgrims, filled one of the most influential pagan posts in Meccan society. Two years later, Abd al-Muttalib also died, and the orphaned Muhammad was once again shuttled off to another relative, this time to the house of his powerful uncle, Abu Talib. Taking pity on the boy, Abu Talib employed him in his lucrative caravan business. It was during one of these trading missions, while the caravan made its way to Syria, that Muhammad's prophetic identity was finally revealed.

Abu Talib had prepared a large trading expedition to Syria when he decided, at the last moment, to take Muhammad along. As the caravan moved slowly across the scorched landscape, a Christian monk named Bahira caught sight of it passing by his monastery at Basra. Bahira was a learned man who possessed a secret book of prophecy passed down from generation to generation by the monks in his order. Crouched day and night in his cell, he had pored over the ancient manuscript and discovered within its weathered pages the coming of a new prophet. It was for this reason that he decided to stop the caravan. For he noticed that as the convoy balanced its way over the thin gray horizon, a small cloud hovered continuously over one member of the group, shielding only him from the heat of the merciless sun. When this person stopped, so did the cloud; and when he dismounted his camel to rest under a tree, the cloud followed him, overshadowing the tree's meager shade until its slender branches bent down to shelter him.

Recognizing what these signs could mean, Bahira sent an urgent message to the caravan leaders. "I have prepared food for you," the message read. "I should like you all to come, both great and small, bond and free."

The members of the caravan were startled. They had passed the monastery many times on their way to Syria, but Bahira had never before taken notice of them. Nevertheless, they decided to break for the evening and join the old monk. As they ate, Bahira noticed that the one he had seen in the distance, the one who was attended by the clouds and the trees, was not among them. He asked the men if every member of the caravan was present. "Do not let any of you remain behind and not come to my feast."

The men replied that everyone who ought to be was present; except, of course, for the young boy, Muhammad, whom they had left outside to watch over the baggage. Bahira was elated. He insisted the boy join them. When Muhammad entered the monastery the monk gave him a brief examination, and declared to everyone present that this was "the Messenger of the Lord of the Worlds."

Muhammad was nine years old.

If the childhood stories about Muhammad seem familiar, it is because they function as a prophetic *topos*: a conventional literary theme that can be found in most mythologies. Like the infancy narratives in the Gospels, these stories are not intended to relate historical events, but to elucidate the mystery of the prophetic experience. They answer the questions: What does it *mean* to be a prophet? Does one suddenly become a prophet, or is prophethood a state of existence established before birth, indeed before the beginning of time? If the latter, then there must have been signs foretelling the prophet's arrival: a miraculous conception, perhaps, or some prediction of the prophet's identity and mission.

The story of the pregnant Amina is remarkably similar to the Christian story of Mary, who, when pregnant with Jesus, heard the angel of the Lord declare, "You will be with child and will give birth to a son, and you are to give him the name Jesus. He will be great and will be called the Son of the Most High" (Luke 1:31–32). The story of Bahira resembles the Jewish story of Samuel, who, when told by God that one of Jesse's sons would be the next king of Israel, invited the entire family to a feast in which the youngest son, David, was left behind to tend the sheep. "Send for him," Samuel demanded when the rest of Jesse's sons were rejected. "We will not sit down until he arrives." The moment David entered the room, he was anointed king (1 Samuel 16:1–13).

Again, the historicity of these *topoi* is irrelevant. It does not matter whether the stories describing the childhood of Muhammad, Jesus, or David are "true." What matters is what these stories say about our prophets, our messiahs, our kings: that theirs is a holy and eternal vocation, established by God from the moment of creation.

Even so, when combined with what is known about pre-Islamic Arabian society, one can glean important historical information from these traditions. For example, we can reasonably conclude that Muhammad was a Meccan and an orphan; that he worked for his uncle's caravan from a young age; that this caravan made frequent trips throughout the region and would have encountered Christian, Zoroastrian, and Jewish tribes, all of whom were deeply involved in Arab society; and finally, that he must have been familiar with the religion and ideology of Hanifism, which pervaded Mecca and which very likely set the stage for Muhammad's own movement. Indeed, as if to emphasize the connection between Hanifism and Islam, the early Muslim biographers transformed Zayd into a John the Baptist character, attributing to him the expectation of "a prophet from the descendants of Ismail, in particular from the descendants of Abd al-Muttalib."

"I do not think that I shall live to see him," Zayd reportedly said, "but I believe in him, proclaim the truth of his message, and testify that he is a prophet."

Perhaps Zayd was wrong. Perhaps he did meet this prophet, though he could not have known that the young orphan boy he had instructed against sacrificing to the idols would one day stand where Zayd once stood, in the shadow of the Ka'ba, and raise his voice over the din of the spinning pilgrims to ask, "Have you considered Allat, al-Uzza, and Manat? . . . These are only names that you and your fathers invented . . . I prefer the religion of Abraham the Hanif, who was not one of the idolaters" (53:19, 23; 2:135).

2. The Keeper of the Keys

MUHAMMAD IN MECCA

WITH THE ARRIVAL of the pilgrimage season—the last two months and the first month of each year—ancient Mecca is transformed from a bustling desert metropolis into a city bursting at its borders with pilgrims, merchants, and caravans traveling to and from the great commercial fairs in neighboring towns like Ukaz and Dhu'l-Majaz. Whether originating in Mecca or not, all caravans wishing to enter the city must first halt at the outskirts of the Meccan valley so that their goods can be tallied and a record made of their trading mission. The camels are relieved of their burdens and placed in the custody of slaves while a Meccan official assesses the value of the textiles, or oils, or dates the caravan has brought back from the fairs. From this total, the official will collect Mecca's fee: a modest tax on all commerce that takes place in and around the sacred city. Only when this business is complete are the caravan workers free to strip off their dusty veils and make their way to the Ka'ba.

The ancient city of Mecca radiates concentrically from the sanctuary at its heart, its narrow dirt streets like arteries transporting pilgrims back and forth from the Ka'ba. The homes on the outer rings are made of mud and straw: impermanent structures inevitably swept away by the annual floods that inundate this valley. Closer to the city center, the homes are larger and more permanent, though still made of mud (only the Ka'ba is stone). This is Mecca's market quarter—the *suqs*—where the air is thick and pungent with smoke, and the stalls reek of blood and spices.

The caravan workers push their way wearily through the crowded market, past the sheep hearts and goat tongues roasting over open fires, past the boisterous merchants haggling with the pilgrims, past the dark women crouching in courtyards, until they finally arrive at the consecrated threshold of the sanctuary. The men cleanse themselves at the well of Zamzam, then announce their presence to "the Lord of the House" before joining the swarm of pilgrims circling the Ka'ba.

Meanwhile, inside the sanctuary, an old man in a spotless white tunic shuffles between the wood and stone idols, lighting candles and rearranging the altars. This man is no priest; he is not even a Kahin. He is someone far more important. He is a *Quraysh:* a member of the powerful, fabulously wealthy tribe that had settled in Mecca centuries earlier and who are now known throughout Arabia as *ahl Allah:* "the Tribe of God," the Wardens of the Sanctuary.

❧

THE QURAYSH'S DOMINANCE of Mecca began at the end of the fourth century C.E., when an ambitious young Arab named Qusayy managed to gain control of the Ka'ba by uniting a number of feuding clans under his rule. Clans in the Arabian Peninsula were primarily composed of large extended families that called themselves either *bayt* (house of) or *banu* (sons of) the family's patriarch. Muhammad's clan was known as Banu Hashim, "the Sons of Hashim." Through intermarriage and political alliances, a group of clans could merge to become an *ahl* or a *qawm:* a "people," more commonly called a tribe.

During the early settlement period of Mecca, a number of clans, some of whom shared a loose alliance, vied for control of the city. In essence, what Qusayy had managed to do was unite those clans who were nominally bound to each other through blood and marriage into a single dominant tribe: the Quraysh.

Qusayy's genius was his recognition that the source of Mecca's power rested in its sanctuary. Simply put, he who controlled the Ka'ba controlled the city. By appealing to the ethnic sentiments of his Qurayshi kinsmen, whom he called "the noblest and purest of the descendants of Ismail," Qusayy was able to capture the Ka'ba from his rival clans and declare himself "King of Mecca." Although he allowed the pilgrimage rituals to remain unchanged, he alone held the keys to the temple. As a result, he had sole authority to feed and provide water to the pilgrims, to preside at assemblies around the Ka'ba where marriage and circumcision rites were performed, and to hand out the war banners. As if to emphasize further the sanctuary's power to bestow authority, Qusayy divided Mecca into quarters, creating an outer and an inner ring of settlements. The closer one lived to the sanctuary, the greater one's power. Qusayy's house, it seems, was actually *attached* to the Ka'ba.

The significance of his proximity to the sanctuary was not lost on the Meccans. It would have been difficult to ignore the fact that the pilgrims who circumambulated the Ka'ba were also circumambulating Qusayy. And because the only way to enter the Ka'ba's inner shrine was through a door located inside Qusayy's house, no person could approach the gods in the sanctuary without first going through him. In this way, Qusayy bestowed upon himself both political and religious authority over the city. He was not just the King of Mecca, he was "the Keeper of the Keys." "His authority among his tribe of Quraysh, in his life and after his death, was like a religion which people followed," recounts Ibn Ishaq.

Qusayy's most important innovation was the establishment of what would become the foundation of Mecca's economy. He began by strengthening his city's position as the dominant place of worship in the Arabian Peninsula, collecting all the idols venerated by neighboring tribes—especially those situated on the sacred hills of Safah and Marwah—and transferring them to the Ka'ba. Henceforth, if one wanted to worship, say, the lover gods, Isaf and Na'ila, one could do so only at Mecca, and only after paying a toll to the Quraysh for the right to enter the sacred city. As Keeper of the Keys, Qusayy also maintained a monopoly over the buying and selling of goods and services to the pilgrims, which he in turn paid for by taxing the city's inhabitants and keeping the surplus for himself. In a few short years, Qusayy's system had made him, and those ruling clans of Quraysh who had managed to connect their fortunes with his, enormously wealthy. But there was even more profit to be made in Mecca.

Like all Semitic sanctuaries, the Ka'ba transformed the entire surrounding area into sacred ground, making the city of Mecca a neutral zone where fighting among tribes was prohibited and weapons were not allowed. The pilgrims who traveled to Mecca during the pilgrimage season were encouraged to take advantage of the peace and prosperity of the city by bringing with them merchandise to trade. To facilitate this, the great commercial fairs coincided with the pilgrimage cycle, and the rules for one complemented those for the other. Whether it was Qusayy's idea to begin collecting a tax on this trade is difficult to know. At this point, it is likely that the Quraysh acted only as stewards of the trade that took place in and around Mecca, collecting a small fee for assuring the safety of the caravans in what was a dangerous and unpatrolled region of the desert. What seems clear, however, is that a few generations after Qusayy, under the directive of his grandson and Muhammad's great-grandfather, Hashim, the Quraysh had managed to create a modest but lucrative trading zone in Mecca, one which relied almost entirely on the Ka'ba's pilgrimage cycle for its subsistence.

How expansive the trade in Mecca was is a matter of fierce debate among scholars. For years it was axiomatic to think of Mecca as the nexus of an international trade route that imported gold, silver, and spices from the southern ports of Yemen, then exported them to the Byzantine and Sasanian empires for a hefty profit. According to this view, which is confirmed by an overwhelming number of Arabic sources, the Quraysh presided over what would have been a natural trading outpost between southern and northern Arabia, a region whose prestige would have been greatly enhanced by the presence of the Ka'ba. Thus, Mecca was the financial center of western Arabia, according to Montgomery Watt, and trade was Mecca's *raison d'être*, in the words of Muhammad Shaban.

Recently, however, a number of scholars have questioned this view, primarily because not a single non-Arabic source has been discovered to corroborate the theory of Mecca as the hub of an international trade zone. "Of Quraysh and their trading center there is no mention at all, be it in the Greek, Latin, Syrian, Aramaic, Coptic, or other literature composed outside Arabia before the conquests," Patricia Crone writes in *Meccan Trade and the Rise of Islam.* "This silence is striking and significant."

Crone and others have argued that unlike the case in other firmly established trading centers like Petra and Palmyra, there are no tangible signs of amassed capital in pre-Islamic Mecca. And, despite the claims of the Arabic sources, both historical evidence and basic geographical sense clearly indicate that Mecca was not situated on any known trading route in the Arabian Peninsula. "Why should caravans have made a deep descent to the barren valley of Mecca when they could have stopped at Ta'if?" asks Crone.

Crone is correct. There was no reason either to travel to Mecca or, for that matter, to settle there. No reason, that is, but the Ka'ba.

There is no question that Mecca was out of the way. The natural trade route in the Hijaz lay east of the city; a stop in Mecca would have required a significant detour between Yemen and Syria, the primary transit for international trade in pre-Islamic Arabia. Certainly, Ta'if, which was situated near the trade route and which also had a sanctuary (dedicated to Allat), would have been a more natural stop along the way. But the city of Mecca was endowed with a special sanctity that went beyond the Ka'ba itself, by virtue of the presence of the sanctuary and the gods housed inside.

Unlike the other sanctuaries dotting the Arabian landscape—each dedicated to a local deity—the Ka'ba was unique in that it claimed to be a universal shrine. Every god in pre-Islamic Arabia was said to reside in this single sanctuary, which meant that regardless of their tribal beliefs, all peoples of the Arabian Peninsula felt a deep spiritual obligation not only to the Ka'ba, but also to the city that housed it and the tribe that preserved it. Crone's solution to the discrepancies between the Arabic and non-Arabic texts is to conclude that everything we know about the pre-Islamic Ka'ba, indeed everything we know about the Prophet Muhammad and the rise of Islam in seventh-century Arabia, is a complete fabrication created by Arab storytellers in the eighth and ninth centuries—a fiction containing not one kernel of sound historical evidence.

The truth is probably somewhere between Watt's "center of international commerce" theory and Crone's "fictional Muhammad" solution. The non-Arabic texts clearly disprove the notion that Mecca was the hub of an international trading zone. However, the overwhelming Arabic evidence to the contrary indicates that there was at least some measure of trade taking place in Mecca long before the rise of Islam. Even if the size and scope of this trade have been overstated by the Arabic sources, whose authors may have wanted to exaggerate the commercial expertise of their ancestors, it seems clear that the Meccans were engaged in what F. E. Peters calls an "internal trade-barter system," which was supplemented by a modest trading zone along the frontiers of the Syrian and Iraqi borders and which relied almost exclusively on the cycle of commercial fairs that, by design, coincided with the pilgrimage season in Mecca.

The point is that this trade, modest as it may have been, was wholly dependent on the Ka'ba; there was simply no other reason to be in Mecca. This was a desert wasteland that produced nothing. As Richard Bulliet notes in his wonderful book *The Camel and the Wheel*, "The only reason for Mecca to grow into a great trading center was that it was able somehow to force the trade under its control." Indeed, that is precisely what Mecca had managed to do. By inextricably linking the religious and economic life of the city, Qusayy and his descendants had developed an innovative religio-economic system that relied on control of the Ka'ba and its pilgrimage rites—rites in which nearly the whole of Arabia participated—to guarantee the economic, religious, and political supremacy of a single tribe, the Quraysh.

That is why the Abyssinians tried to destroy the Ka'ba in the Year of the Elephant. Having constructed their own pilgrimage center in Sana', near the prosperous commercial ports of Yemen, the Abyssinians set out to eliminate Mecca's sanctuary, not because the Ka'ba was a religious threat, but because it was an economic rival. Like the leaders of Ta'if, Mina, Ukaz, and nearly every other neighboring region, the Abyssinians would have loved to replicate Mecca's religio-economic system in their own territories and under their own authority. After all, if this system had made a loose confederation of clans like the Quraysh rich, it could make anyone rich.

Yet not everyone in Mecca benefited from the Quraysh's system. The strictures of Bedouin life naturally prevented the social and economic hierarchies that were so prevalent in sedentary societies like Mecca. The only way to survive in a community in which movement was the norm and material accumulation impractical was to maintain a strong sense of tribal solidarity by evenly sharing all available resources. The tribal ethic was therefore founded on the principle that every member had an essential function in maintaining the stability of the tribe, which was only as strong as its weakest members. This was not an ideal of social equality: the notion that every member of the tribe was of equal worth. Rather, the tribal ethic was meant to maintain a semblance of social egalitarianism so that regardless of one's position, every member could share in the social and economic rights and privileges that preserved the unity of the tribe.

In pre-Islamic Arabia, the responsibility for maintaining the tribal ethic fell upon the *Sayyid* or *Shaykh* of the tribe. Unanimously elected as "the first among equals," the Shaykh (the title means "one who bears the marks of old age") was the most highly respected member of his community, the figurehead who represented the strength and moral attributes of the tribe. Although it was a common belief that the qualities of leadership and nobility were inherent in certain families, the Shaykh was not a hereditary position; the Arabs had great disdain for the inherited reigns of the Byzantine and Sasanian kings. The only requirement for becoming a Shaykh, besides maturity, was to embody the ideals of *muruwah:* the code of tribal conduct that was composed of important Arab virtues like bravery, honor, hospitality, strength in battle, concern for justice, and, above all, an assiduous dedication to the collective good of the tribe.

Because the Arabs were wary of concentrating all the functions of leadership in a single individual, the Shaykh had little real executive authority. Every important decision was made through collective consultation with other individuals in the tribe who had equally important roles: the *Qa'id*, who acted as war leader; the *Kahin*, or cultic official; and the *Hakam*, who settled disputes. The Shaykh may occasionally have acted in one or more of these functions, but his primary responsibility was to maintain order within and between the tribes by assuring the protection of every member of his community, especially those who could not protect themselves: the poor and the weak, the young and the elderly, the orphan and the widow. Loyalty to the Shaykh was symbolized by an oath of allegiance called *bay'ah*, which was given to the *man*, not the office. If the Shaykh failed in his duty to adequately protect every member of his tribe, the oath would be withdrawn and another leader chosen to fill his place.

In a society with no concept of an absolute morality as dictated by a divine code of ethics—a Ten Commandments, if you will—the Shaykh had only one legal recourse for maintaining order in his tribe: the Law of Retribution. *Lex talionis* in Latin, the Law of Retribution is more popularly known as the somewhat crude concept of "an eye for an eye." Yet far from being a barbaric legal system, the Law of Retribution was actually meant to *limit* barbarism. Accordingly, an injury to a neighbor's eye confined retaliation to only an eye and nothing more; the theft of a neighbor's camel required payment of exactly one camel; killing a neighbor's son meant the execution of one's own son. To facilitate retribution, a pecuniary amount, known as "blood money," was established for all goods and assets, as well as for every member of society, and, in fact, for every part of an individual's body. In Muhammad's time, the life of a free man was worth about one hundred camels; the life of a free woman, fifty.

It was the Shaykh's responsibility to maintain peace and stability in his community by ensuring the proper retribution for all crimes committed within the tribe. Crimes committed against those outside the tribe were not only unpunished, they were not really crimes. Stealing, killing, or injuring another person was not considered a morally reprehensible act *per se*, and such acts were punished only if they weakened the stability of the tribe.

Occasionally, the sense of balance inherent in the Law of Retribution was skewed because of some logistical complication. For example, if a stolen camel turned out to be pregnant, would the thief owe the victim one camel or two? Because there was no formal law enforcement and no judicial system at all in tribal societies, in cases in which negotiation was required, the two sides would bring their arguments to a Hakam: any trusted, neutral party who acted as an arbiter in the dispute. After collecting a security from both sides to ensure that all parties would abide by his arbitration—which was, technically, unenforceable—the Hakam would make an authoritative legal declaration: "A pregnant camel is worth two camels." As the Hakam's arbitrations accumulated over time, they became the foundation of a normative legal tradition, or *Sunna*, that served as the tribe's legal code. In other words, never again was arbitration needed to decide the worth of a pregnant camel.

However, because each tribe had its own Hakams and its own Sunna, the laws and traditions of one tribe did not necessarily apply to another. It was often the case that an individual had no legal protection, no rights, and no social identity whatsoever outside his own tribe. How the pre-Islamic Arabs were able to maintain intertribal relations when there was technically nothing *morally* wrong with stealing from, injuring, or killing someone outside one's own tribe is a complicated matter. The tribes maintained relationships with one another through a complex network of alliances and affiliations. But the easy answer is that if someone from one tribe harmed a member of another, the injured tribe, if strong enough, could demand retribution. Consequently, it was the Shaykh's responsibility to ensure that neighboring tribes understood that any act of aggression against his people would be equally avenged. If he could not provide this service, he would no longer be the Shaykh.

The problem in Mecca was that the concentration of wealth in the hands of a few ruling families had not only altered the social and economic landscape of the city, it had effectively destroyed the tribal ethic. The sudden tide of personal wealth in Mecca had swept away tribal ideals of social egalitarianism. No longer was there any concern for the poor and marginalized; no longer was the tribe only as strong as its weakest members. The Shaykhs of Quraysh had become far more interested in maintaining the apparatus of trade than in caring for the dispossessed. How could the Law of Retribution function properly when one party in a dispute was so wealthy and so powerful as to be virtually untouchable? How could intertribal relations be maintained when the Quraysh's ever-expanding authority placed them essentially beyond reproach? It certainly didn't help matters that as Keepers of the Keys, the Quraysh's authority in Mecca was not just political or economic but also religious. Consider that the Hanifs, whom the traditions present as severely critical of the insatiable greed of their fellow Meccans, nevertheless maintained an unshakable loyalty to the Quraysh, whom they regarded as "the legitimate agents of the Abrahamic sacredness of Mecca and the Ka'ba."

With the demise of the tribal ethic, Meccan society became strictly stratified. At the top were the leaders of the ruling families of Quraysh. If one was fortunate enough to acquire enough capital to start a small business, one could take full advantage of the city's religio-economic system. But for most Meccans, this was simply not possible. Especially for those with no formal protection—such as orphans and widows, neither of whom had access to any kind of inheritance—the only option was to borrow money from the rich at exorbitant interest rates, which inevitably led to debt, which in turn led to crushing poverty and, ultimately, to slavery.

As an orphan, Muhammad must have understood all too well the difficulty of falling outside Mecca's religio-economic system. Fortunately for him, his uncle and new guardian, Abu Talib, was also the Shaykh of the Banu Hashim—a small, not very wealthy, yet prestigious clan within the mighty tribe of Quraysh. It was Abu Talib who kept Muhammad from falling into the debt and slavery that were the fate of so many orphans in Mecca by providing him with a home and the opportunity to eke out a living working for his caravan.

There is no question that Muhammad was good at his job. The traditions go to great lengths to emphasize his success as a skillful merchant who knew how to strike a lucrative deal. Despite his lowly status in Meccan society, he was widely known throughout the city as an upright and pious man. His nickname was *al-Amin*, "the trustworthy one," and he was on a few occasions chosen to serve as Hakam in small disputes.

Muhammad was also, it seems, a striking man. He is described as broad-chested, with a full beard and a hooked nose that gave him a stately appearance. Numerous accounts speak of his wide black eyes and the long thick hair he kept tied behind his ears in plaits. And yet, as honest or skilled as he may have been, by the turn of the seventh century, Muhammad was a twenty-five-year-old man, still unmarried, with no capital and no business of his own, who relied entirely on his uncle's generosity for his employment and his housing. In fact, his prospects were so depressingly low that when he asked for the hand of his uncle's daughter, Umm Hani, she rejected him outright for a more prosperous suitor.

Things changed for Muhammad when he attracted the attention of a remarkable forty-year-old widow named Khadija. Khadija was an enigma: a wealthy and respected female merchant in a society that treated women as chattel and prohibited them from inheriting the property of their husbands, Khadija had somehow managed to become one of the most respected members of Meccan society. She owned a thriving caravan business and, though advanced in age and with children of her own, was pursued by many men, most of whom would have loved to get their hands on her money.

According to Ibn Hisham, Khadija first met Muhammad when she hired him to lead one of her caravans. She had heard of his "truthfulness, reliability, and nobility of character," and decided to entrust him with a special expedition to Syria. Muhammad did not disappoint her. He returned from the trip with almost double the profits Khadija had expected, and she rewarded him with a proposal of marriage. Muhammad gratefully accepted.

His marriage to Khadija paved the way for Muhammad's acceptance at the highest levels of Meccan society and thoroughly initiated him into the religio-economic system of the city. By all accounts he was extremely successful in running his wife's business, rising in status and wealth until he was, while not part of the ruling élite, a member of what may be considered anachronistically "the middle class." He even owned his own slave.

Yet despite his success, Muhammad felt deeply conflicted by his dual status in Meccan society. On the one hand, he was renowned for his generosity and the evenhandedness with which he conducted his business. Although now a well-respected and relatively affluent merchant, he frequently went on solitary retreats of "self-justification" (the pagan practice of *tahannuth* mentioned in the previous chapter) in the mountains and glens surrounding the Meccan valley, and he regularly gave money and food to the poor in a religious charity ritual tied to the cult of the Ka'ba. On the other hand, he seemed to be acutely aware of his complicity in Mecca's religio-economic system, which exploited the city's unprotected masses in order to maintain the wealth and power of the élite. For fifteen years he struggled with the incongruity between his lifestyle and his beliefs; by his fortieth year, he was an intensely troubled man.

Then, one night in 610 C.E., as he was meditating on Mt. Hira during one of his religious retreats, Muhammad had an encounter that would change the world.

He sat alone in a cave, deep in meditation. Suddenly an invisible presence crushed him in its embrace. He struggled to break free but could not move. He was overwhelmed by darkness. The pressure in his chest increased until he could no longer breathe. He felt he was dying. As he surrendered his final breath, light and a terrifying voice washed over him "like the break of dawn."

"Recite!" the voice commanded.

"What shall I recite?" Muhammad gasped.

The invisible presence tightened its embrace. "Recite!"

"What shall I recite?" Muhammad asked again, his chest caving in.

Once more the presence tightened its grip and once more the voice repeated its command. Finally, at the moment when he thought he could bear no more, the pressure in his chest stopped, and in the silence that engulfed the cave, Muhammad *felt* these words stamped upon his heart:

> Recite in the name of your Lord who created,
> Created humanity from a clot of blood.
> Recite, for your Lord is the Most Generous One
> Who has taught by the pen;
> Taught humanity that which it did not know. (96:1–5)

This was Muhammad's burning bush: the moment in which he ceased being a Meccan businessman concerned with society's ills, and became what in the Abrahamic tradition is called *prophet*. Yet, like his great prophetic predecessors—Abraham, Moses, David, and Jesus—Muhammad would be something more.

Islam preaches the continual self-revelation of God from Adam down to all the prophets who have ever existed in all religions. These prophets are called *nabis* in Arabic, and they have been chosen to relay God's divine message to all humanity. But sometimes a *nabi* is given the extra burden of handing down sacred texts: Moses, who revealed the Torah; David, who composed the Psalms; Jesus, whose words inspired the Gospels. Such an individual is more than a mere prophet; he is God's messenger—a *rasul*. Thus, Muhammad, the merchant from Mecca, who over the course of the next twenty-three years will recite the entire text of the Quran (literally, "the Recitation"), would henceforth be known as *Rasul Allah:* "the Messenger of God."

What that first experience of Revelation was like for Muhammad is difficult to describe. The sources are vague, sometimes conflicting. Ibn Hisham states that Muhammad was sleeping when the Revelation first came to him like a dream, while al-Tabari claims the Prophet was standing when the Revelation dropped him to his knees; his shoulders trembled and he tried to crawl away. The command (*iqra*) that Muhammad heard in the cave is best understood as "recite" in al-Tabari's biography, but is clearly intended to mean "read" in Ibn Hisham's. In fact, according to one of Ibn Hisham's traditions, the first recitation was actually written on a magical brocade and placed in front of Muhammad to be read.

Muslim tradition has tended to focus on al-Tabari's definition of *iqra* ("recite"), mostly to emphasize the notion that the Prophet was illiterate, which some say is validated by the Quran's epithet for Muhammad: *an-nabi al-ummi*, traditionally understood as meaning "the unlettered Prophet." But while Muhammad's illiteracy may enhance the miracle of the Quran, there is no historical justification for it. As numerous scholars and Arab linguists have demonstrated, *an-nabi al-ummi* should more properly be understood as "the Prophet for the unlettered" (that is, the Scriptureless), a translation consistent both with the grammar of the sentence and with Muhammad's view that the Quran is the Revelation for a people without a sacred book: "We did not give [the Arabs] any previous books to study, nor sent them any previous Warners before you" (34:44).

The fact is that it would be highly unlikely that a successful merchant like Muhammad would have been unable to read and write the receipts of his own business. Obviously he was neither a scribe nor a scholar, and he in no way had the verbal prowess of a poet. But he must have been able to read and write basic Arabic—names, dates, goods, services—and, considering that many of his customers were Jews, he may even have had rudimentary skills in Aramaic.

The traditions also disagree about how old Muhammad was when the Revelation first came to him: some chroniclers say forty, others claim he was forty-three. Although there is no way to know definitively, Lawrence Conrad notes that it was a common belief among the ancient Arabs that "a man only reaches the peak of his physical and intellectual powers when he becomes forty years old." The Quran confirms this belief by equating manhood with the realization of the fortieth year of life (46:15). In other words, the ancient biographers may have been guessing when they attempted to calculate Muhammad's age at Mt. Hira, just as they were probably guessing when they figured the year of his birth.

Likewise, there is a great deal of confusion over the precise date of that first revelatory experience. It is cited as having occurred either on the fourteenth, seventeenth, eighteenth, or twenty-fourth day of the month of Ramadan. There is even some debate within the earliest community over exactly what the first recitation was: some chroniclers claim that God's first command to Muhammad was neither "recite" nor "read," but rather "arise and warn!"

Perhaps the reason the traditions are so vague and conflicting is that there was no single momentous revelatory event that initiated Muhammad's prophethood, but rather a series of smaller, indescribable supernatural experiences that climaxed in a final, violent encounter with the Divine. Aisha, who would become the Prophet's closest and most beloved companion, claimed that the first signs of prophethood occurred long before the experience at Mt. Hira. These signs came in the form of visions that assailed Muhammad in his dreams, and which were so disturbing that they made him increasingly seek solitude. "He liked nothing better than to be alone," Aisha recalled.

Muhammad's disturbing visions seem to have been accompanied by aural perceptions. Ibn Hisham records that when the Prophet set off to be alone in the "glens of Mecca," the stones and trees that he passed along the way would say, "Peace unto thee, O Apostle of Allah." When this happened, Muhammad "would turn to his right and left and look behind him and he would see naught but trees and stones." These aural and visual hallucinations continued right up to the moment in which he was called by God at Mt. Hira.

Obviously, no one but the prophet can describe the experience of prophecy, but it is neither irrational nor heretical to consider the attainment of prophetic consciousness to be a slowly evolving process. Did Jesus require the heavens to part and a dove to descend upon his head to affirm his messianic character, or had he understood for some time that he was being singled out by God for a divine mission? Did enlightenment suddenly burst like a flash of light upon Siddhartha while he sat under the Bodhi tree, as the event has so often been described, or was his enlightenment the result of a steadily developing conviction of the illusion of reality? Perhaps the Revelation came to Muhammad "like the break of dawn," as some traditions claim, or maybe he gradually became aware of his prophetic consciousness through a series of ineffable supernatural experiences. It is impossible to know. What seems certain, however, is that Muhammad, like all the prophets before him, wanted nothing to do with God's calling. So despondent was he about the experience that his first thought was to kill himself.

As far as Muhammad understood, only the Kahin, whom he despised as reprehensible charlatans ("I could not even look at them," he once exclaimed), received messages from the heavens. If his experience at Mt. Hira meant that he was himself becoming a Kahin, and that his colleagues in Mecca were now going to regard him as such, then he would rather be dead.

"Never shall Quraysh say this of me!" Muhammad swore. "I will go to the top of the mountain and throw myself down that I may kill myself and gain rest."

Muhammad was right to worry about being compared to a Kahin. What is impossible to discern in any translation of those first few verses of the Revelation is their exquisite poetic quality. That initial recitation, and those that immediately followed, were delivered in rhyming couplets which were very much like the ecstatic utterances of the Kahin. This would not have been unusual; after all, the Arabs were used to hearing the gods speak in poetry, which elevated their language to the realm of the divine. But much later, when Muhammad's message began to clash with the Meccan élite, his enemies would seize upon the similarities between the oracles of the Kahin and Muhammad's recitations, asking mockingly: "Should we abandon our gods for the sake of an insane poet?" (37:36).

The fact that there are dozens of verses in the Quran refuting the accusation that Muhammad was a Kahin indicates how important the issue was for the early Muslim community. As Muhammad's movement expanded throughout the region, the Revelation gradually became more prosaic and ceased to resemble the oracular style of the early verses. However, in the beginning, Muhammad knew exactly what would be said of him, and the thought of being considered a Kahin by his contemporaries was enough to bring him to the edge of suicide.

Eventually God relieved Muhammad's anxiety by assuring him of his sanity. But it is safe to say that if it were not for Khadija, Muhammad might have gone through with his plan to end it all, and history would have turned out quite differently.

"By her, God lightened the burden of His prophet," Ibn Hisham writes of the remarkable Khadija. "May God Almighty have mercy upon her!"

Still frightened and trembling from the experience in the cave, Muhammad made his way back home, where he crawled to his wife's side, crying "Wrap me up! Wrap me up!"

Khadija immediately threw a cloak over him and held him tightly in her arms until the trembling and convulsions stopped. Once he had calmed, Muhammad wept openly as he tried to explain what had happened to him. "Khadija," he said, "I think that I have gone mad."

"This cannot be, my dear," Khadija replied, stroking his hair. "God would not treat you thus since He knows your truthfulness, your great trustworthiness, your fine character, and your kindness."

But because Muhammad remained inconsolable, Khadija gathered her garments about her and sought out the only person she knew who would understand what had happened to her husband: her Christian cousin, Waraqa, the same Waraqa who had been one of the orig -

inal Hanifs before converting to Christianity. Waraqa was familiar enough with the Scriptures to recognize Muhammad's experience for what it was.

"He is a prophet of this people," Waraqa assured his cousin after hearing her story. "Bid him be of good heart."

Still Muhammad was unsure, particularly about what he was supposed to do now that he had been called by God. To make matters worse, when he needed assurance the most, God turned mute. That first revelatory experience on Mt. Hira was followed by a long period of silence, so that after a while even Khadija, who never doubted the truth of Muhammad's experience, began to question the meaning of it. "I think that your Lord must have come to hate you," she confessed to Muhammad.

Finally, when Muhammad was at his lowest, a second verse was sent down from heaven in the same painfully violent manner as the first, this one assuring Muhammad that, whether he liked it or not, he was now the Messenger of God:

> By the grace of your Lord, you are not a madman.
> Yours will be an unending reward;
> For you are a man of noble character.
> Soon, you shall see, and they shall see, who the madman is. (68:1–5)

Now Muhammad no longer had any choice but to "arise and warn."

THE EARLIEST VERSES that Muhammad revealed to the Meccans can be divided into two major themes, religious and social—though the same language was employed for both. First, in stunningly beautiful verse, Muhammad sang of the power and glory of the God who "cracked open the earth and caused to grow in it corn and grapes and clover and olives and dates and orchards dense with trees" (80:19). This was not the same powerful and distant High God with whom most people in Mecca were already familiar. This was a *good* God who deeply loved creation. This God was *ar-Rahman*, "the most merciful" (55:1); *al-Akram*, "the most generous" (96:3). As such, this was a God worthy of gratitude and worship. "How many favors from your Lord will you deny?" Muhammad asked his kinsmen.

Noticeably absent in these early verses about the power and good-ness of God is either an authoritative declaration of monotheism or a definitive critique of polytheism. In the beginning, Muhammad seemed more concerned with revealing what kind of god Allah was, not how many gods there were. Perhaps this is because, as previously mentioned, Muhammad was addressing a community that already possessed some measure of monotheistic—or at the very least, heno-theistic—tendencies. The Quraysh did not need to be told there was only one god; they'd heard that message many times before from the Jews, the Christians, and the Hanifs, and they did not necessarily dis-agree. At this point in his ministry, Muhammad had a far more urgent message.

That message—the second theme informing the bulk of Muham-mad's earliest recitations—dealt almost exclusively with the demise of the tribal ethic in Mecca. In the strongest terms, Muhammad decried the mistreatment and exploitation of the weak and unprotected. He called for an end to false contracts and the practice of usury that had made slaves of the poor. He spoke of the rights of the underprivileged and the oppressed, and made the astonishing claim that it was the duty of the rich and powerful to take care of them. "Do not oppress the orphan," the Quran commands, "and do not drive away the beggar" (93:9–10).

This was not friendly advice; it was a warning. God had seen the greed and wickedness of the Quraysh, and would tolerate it no longer.

Woe to every slanderer and backbiter
Who amasses wealth, hoarding it to himself.
Does he really think his wealth will make him immortal?
By no means! He will be cast into . . .
The fire kindled by God. (104:1–6)

More than anything else, Muhammad considered himself a warner carrying a message for those in his community who continued to abuse the orphan, who did not induce others to feed the needy, who prayed to the gods while remaining oblivious to their moral duties, and who withheld things of common use from others (107:1–7). His message was simple: the Day of Judgment was coming, when "the sky will be cleft asunder and the earth shall be leveled" (84:1–3), and those who did not "free the slave" or "feed others in times of famine" would be engulfed in fire (90:13–20).

This was a radical message, one that had never been heard before in Mecca. Muhammad was not yet establishing a new religion; he was calling for sweeping social reform. He was not yet preaching monotheism; he was demanding economic justice. And for this revolutionary and profoundly innovative message, he was more or less ignored.

This was partly Muhammad's fault. All of the traditions claim that, at first, Muhammad confined the Revelation to his closest friends and family members. The first person to accept his message was obviously Khadija, who from the moment she met him to the moment she died, remained by her husband, especially during those times when he was at his lowest. While there is a great deal of sectarian debate among Muslims as to who the second person to accept the message was, it is safe to assume it would have been Muhammad's cousin, Ali, who as Abu Talib's son had grown up in the same household as the Prophet and was the closest person to him after his wife.

Ali's acceptance came as a great relief to Muhammad, for he was not only Muhammad's cousin, he was also his closest ally: the man whom the Prophet repeatedly referred to as "brother." Ali would eventually mature into the most respected warrior in Islam. He would marry Muhammad's beloved daughter, Fatima, and provide the Prophet with his legendary grandsons, Hasan and Husayn. Considered the fount of esoteric knowledge and the father of Islamic metaphysics, Ali would one day inspire an entirely new sect in Islam. However, at the moment when he stood up as the first among the Banu Hashim to respond to the Prophet's call, he was only a thirteen-year-old boy.

Ali's conversion was promptly followed by the conversion of Muhammad's slave, Zayd, whom he naturally freed. Soon afterward, Abu Bakr, Muhammad's dear friend and a wealthy Qurayshi merchant, became a follower. A deeply loyal and fervently pious man, Abu

Bakr's first act after accepting Muhammad's message was to spend his wealth buying and freeing the slaves of his fellow merchants until he had almost nothing left. Through Abu Bakr, the message was dispersed throughout the city, for as Ibn Hisham testifies, he was not the sort to keep such things to himself, but "showed his faith openly and called others to God and his apostle."

One should, at this point, pause for a moment to consider several remarkable aspects of Muhammad's movement in Mecca. While his message had eventually reached nearly every sector of society—from the weak and unprotected whose rights he advocated, to the Meccan élite whom he preached against—the most surprising feature of his movement during those early years is that its followers consisted primarily of what Montgomery Watt has called "the most influential families in the most influential clans." These were young men, the majority under thirty years old, who felt the same discontent with Meccan society as Muhammad did. And yet, they were not all men: a great many of Muhammad's earliest followers were women, many of whom risked their lives in rejecting the traditions of their fathers, husbands, and brothers to join his movement.

Regardless, Muhammad's reticence during those first few years kept this a small group of about thirty to forty people who referred to themselves as Muhammad's *Companions*, for at this point, that was all they were. As far as everyone else in Mecca was concerned, Muhammad's message and his Companions were best ignored.

Both al-Tabari and Ibn Hisham state that even after Muhammad began preaching publicly, the Quraysh "did not withdraw from him or reject him in any way." Why would they? It was one thing to grow wealthy off the subjugation of the poor and the unprotected, but it was another matter entirely to defend such practices. Besides, there was nothing in Muhammad's message that directly threatened their way of life either religiously or financially. As long as Muhammad's movement did not affect the economic status quo, the Quraysh would have been happy to allow him and his Companions to continue praying in secret and meeting clandestinely to talk about their grievances.

Muhammad, however, was never one to be ignored.

IN 613, THREE years after the Revelation had begun, Muhammad's message underwent a dramatic transformation, one that is best summed up in the twofold profession of faith, or *shahadah*, that would henceforth define both the mission and principles of the movement:

There is no god but God, and Muhammad is God's Messenger.

From this point forward in Muhammad's ministry, the monotheism that had been implicit in the earliest recitations became the dominant theology behind what had thus far been primarily a social message. "Proclaim to them what you have been commanded," God demands, "and turn away from the polytheists" (15:94).

While it is commonly assumed that it was this new, uncompromising monotheism that ultimately brought the wrath of the Quraysh upon Muhammad and his small band of followers ("Does he make the gods one god?" the Quraysh are supposed to have asked. "This is indeed an astounding thing"), such a view fails to appreciate the profound social and economic consequences implied by this simple statement of faith.

It is important to bear in mind that the Quraysh were quite sophisticated with regard to religion. After all, they made their living off it. Polytheism, henotheism, monotheism, Christianity, Judaism, Zoroastrianism, Hanifism, paganism in all its varieties, the Quraysh had seen it all. It is difficult to believe they would have been shocked by Muhammad's monotheistic claims. Not only had the Hanifs been preaching the same thing for years, but the traditions list a number of other well-known prophetic figures living throughout the Arabian Peninsula who also preached monotheism. In fact, the early Muslims revered two of these "prophets"—Suwayd and Luqman—as Muhammad's predecessors. Luqman even has his own chapter in the Quran (31), in which he is called a man upon whom God had bestowed great wisdom. So, theologically speaking, Muhammad's assertion that "there is no god but God" would have been neither scandalous nor, for that matter, original in Mecca.

There are, however, two very important factors that distinguished Muhammad from the rest of his contemporaries, factors that would have enraged the Quraysh far more than his monotheistic beliefs. First, unlike Luqman and the Hanifs, Muhammad did not speak from his own authority. Nor were his recitations mediated by the Jinn, as was the case with the Kahins. On the contrary, what made Muhammad unique was his claim to be "the Messenger of God." He even went so far as to identify himself repeatedly with the Jewish and Christian prophets and messengers who had come before him, particularly with Abraham, whom all Meccans—pagan or otherwise—regarded as a divinely inspired prophet. Put simply, the difference between Muhammad and the Hanifs was that Muhammad was not just preaching "the religion of Abraham," Muhammad was the *new* Abraham (6:83–86; 21:51–93). And it was precisely this self-image that so greatly disturbed the Quraysh. For by proclaiming himself "the Messenger of God," Muhammad was blatantly transgressing the traditional Arab process through which power was granted. This was not authority that had been given to Muhammad as "the first among equals." Muhammad had no equals.

Second, as mentioned, the Hanif preachers may have attacked the polytheism and greed of their fellow Meccans, but they maintained a deep veneration for the Ka'ba and those in the community who acted as Keepers of the Keys. That would explain why the Hanifs appear to have been tolerated, for the most part, in Mecca, and why they never converted in great numbers to Muhammad's movement. But as a businessman and a merchant himself, Muhammad understood what the Hanifs could not: the only way to bring about radical social and economic reform in Mecca was to overturn the religio-economic system on which the city was built; and the only way to do that was to attack the very source of the Quraysh's wealth and prestige—the Ka'ba.

"There is no god but God" was, for Muhammad, far more than a profession of faith. This statement was a conscious and deliberate attack on both the Ka'ba and the sacred right of the Quraysh to manage it. And because the religious life and economic life of Mecca were inextricably linked, any attack on one was necessarily an attack on the other.

Certainly the shahadah contained an important theological innovation, but that innovation was not monotheism. With this simple profession of faith, Muhammad was declaring to Mecca that the God of the heavens and the earth required no intermediaries whatsoever, but could be accessed by anyone. Thus, the idols in the sanctuary, and indeed the sanctuary itself, insofar as it served as a repository for the gods, were utterly useless. And if the Ka'ba was useless, then there was no more reason for Mecca's supremacy as either the religious or the economic center of Arabia.

This message the Quraysh could not ignore, especially with the pilgrimage season fast approaching. They tried everything to silence Muhammad and his Companions. They went to Abu Talib for help, but the Shaykh of Hashim, though he would never accept Muhammad's message himself, refused to withdraw his protection from his nephew. They poured contempt on Muhammad and abused those of his Companions who did not have the good fortune of being protected by a Shaykh. They even offered Muhammad all the freedom, support, power, and money he wanted to continue his movement in peace, so long as he ceased insulting their forefathers, mocking their customs, dividing their families, and, above all, cursing the other gods in the sanctuary. But Muhammad refused, and as the time came for the pilgrims to gather once again at Mecca with their prayers and their merchandise, the anxiety of the Quraysh reached new heights.

The Quraysh knew that Muhammad intended to stand at the Ka'ba and deliver his message personally to the pilgrims gathering from all over the peninsula. And while this might not have been the first time a preacher had condemned the Quraysh and their practices, it was certainly the first time such condemnation was coming from a successful and well-known Qurayshi businessman—that is, "one of their own." Recognizing this as a threat that could not be tolerated, the Quraysh embarked on a strategy to preempt Muhammad's plan by sitting "on the paths which men take when they come to the fair" and warning everyone who passed that "a sorcerer, who has brought a message by which he separates a man from his father, or from his brother, or from his wife, or from his family," awaited them at the Ka'ba and should be ignored.

The Quraysh did not really believe that Muhammad was a sorcerer; they freely admitted that his recitations came with "no spitting and no knots," rituals that were apparently associated with sorcery. But they were absolutely earnest in their conviction that Muhammad was dividing the families of Mecca. Recall that in pre-Islamic Arabia, a person's social identity was derived solely from membership in the tribe, which necessarily entailed taking part in all tribal activities, especially those involving the tribal cult. However, conversion to Muhammad's movement meant not only changing one's faith, but also cutting oneself off from the activities of the tribe; in essence, removing oneself from the tribe.

This was a serious concern for the Quraysh, whose chief complaint against Muhammad (at least publicly) was neither his call for social and financial reform, nor his radical monotheism. Indeed, as Richard Bell has noted, in the whole of the Quran there exists not a single Qurayshi defense of polytheism that rests on the conviction of its truth. Rather, as indicated by their warnings to the pilgrims, the Quraysh seemed more disturbed with Muhammad's insistent derision of the rituals and traditional values of their forefathers, traditions upon which the social, religious, and economic foundation of the city rested, than they were by his message of monotheism.

Predictably, however, their warning to ignore "the sorcerer" standing at the Ka'ba only increased interest in Muhammad's message, so that by the time the pilgrimage cycle and the desert fairs were complete and the pilgrims had departed for their homes, Muhammad— the man who had so frightened the untouchable Quraysh—was talked about throughout Arabia.

After failing to silence Muhammad during the pilgrimage fair, the Quraysh decided to take a page out of the Prophet's book and attack Muhammad in the same way he had attacked them: economically. A boycott was placed not just on Muhammad and his Companions, but, in true tribal fashion, on Muhammad's entire clan. Henceforth, no one in Mecca was allowed to marry into, buy merchandise from, or sell goods (including food and water) to any member of the Banu Hashim, regardless of whether they were followers of Muhammad. The boycott was not an attempt by the Quraysh to starve the Companions out of Mecca; it was merely a way of demonstrating the consequences of removing oneself from the tribe. If Muhammad and his Companions wished to be separated from the social and religious activities of Mecca, then they must be prepared to be separated from its economy. After all, if religion and trade were inseparable in Mecca, no one could so brazenly deny the former and still expect to participate in the latter.

As intended, the boycott was devastating to the Companions, most of whom, including Muhammad, were still making their living from trade. In fact, the boycott was so destructive that it was protested by prominent members of the Quraysh who had rejected Muhammad but who could no longer bear to "eat food, drink drink, and wear clothes, while the Banu Hashim were perishing." After some months, the boycott was lifted, and the Banu Hashim were once again allowed to join in the commerce of the city. But just as he seemed to be regaining ground in Mecca, tragedy struck Muhammad in the form of the nearly simultaneous deaths of his uncle and protector, Abu Talib, and his wife and confidante, Khadija.

The significance of losing Abu Talib is obvious: Muhammad could no longer rely on his uncle's unwavering protection to keep him from harm. The new Shaykh of Banu Hashim, Abu Lahab, loathed Muhammad personally and made a formal withdrawal of his protection. The results were immediate. Muhammad was openly abused on the streets of Mecca. He could no longer preach or pray in public. When he tried to do so, one person poured dirt over his head; another threw a sheep's uterus at him.

The loss of Abu Talib may have placed Muhammad in a precarious situation, but the death of Khadija left him absolutely devastated. She was, after all, not only his wife, but also his support and comfort, the person who had lifted him out of his poverty, who had quite literally saved his life. In a polygamous society, in which both men and women were allowed an unlimited number of spouses, Muhammad's monogamous relationship with a woman fifteen years his elder was remarkable, to say the least. Maxime Rodinson's assertion that it is unlikely Muhammad would have felt any physical passion for Khadija, given her age, is both unsubstantiated and offensive. The loss of Abu Talib's protection was certainly demoralizing, if not detrimental to Muhammad's physical security. But returning home after one of his painfully violent revelatory experiences, or after suffering another indignity from the Quraysh—his head covered in dirt, his tunic defiled with blood—and not having Khadija there to wrap him in her cloak and hold him in her arms until the terror subsided must have been an unimaginable sorrow for the Prophet.

With the loss of both his physical and his emotional support, Muhammad could no longer remain in Mecca. Some time earlier, he had sent a small group of his followers—those without any form of protection in Meccan society—temporarily to Abyssinia, partly to seek asylum from its Christian emperor or "Negus," partly in an attempt to ally himself with one of the Quraysh's chief commercial rivals. But now Muhammad needed a permanent home where he and his Companions could be free from the unrestrained wrath of the Quraysh.

He tried Mecca's sister city, Ta'if, but its tribal leaders were not inclined to antagonize the Quraysh by giving refuge to their enemy. He visited the local fairs around Mecca—places where he must have been well known both as a merchant and as a troublemaker—but to no avail. Finally, the answer came in the form of an invitation from a small clan called the *Khazraj*, who lived in an agricultural oasis some two hundred fifty miles north of Mecca—a conglomeration of villages known collectively as Yathrib. Although Yathrib was a distant and totally foreign city, Muhammad had no choice but to accept the invitation and prepare his Companions to do the unthinkable: abandon their tribe and their families for an uncertain future in a place where they would be without protection.

The emigration to Yathrib occurred slowly and stealthily, with the Companions heading out toward the oasis a few at a time. By the time the Quraysh realized what was happening, only Muhammad, Abu Bakr, and Ali were left. Fearing that Muhammad was leaving Mecca to raise an army, the various clan Shaykhs decided to choose one man from each family, "a young, powerful, well-born, aristocratic warrior," who would sneak into Muhammad's house while he was asleep and simultaneously drive their swords into his body, thereby placing the responsibility for his death upon everyone in the tribe. But when the assassins arrived at Muhammad's house, they found Ali asleep in his bed pretending to be the Prophet. Having learned about the attempt on his life the night before, Muhammad and Abu Bakr had slipped out of the house through a window and fled the city.

The Quraysh were furious. They offered a massive bounty of a hundred she-camels to anyone who could find Muhammad and bring him back to Mecca. The unusually high reward attracted dozens of Bedouin tribesmen who combed the surrounding area night and day looking for the Prophet and his friend.

Meanwhile, Muhammad and Abu Bakr had taken cover in a cave not far from Mecca. For three days they hid from view, waiting for the hunt to subside and the Bedouin to return to their camps. On the third night, they carefully crept out of the cave and, making sure no one was following, mounted two camels brought to them by a sympathetic conspirator. They then quietly disappeared into the desert on their way to Yathrib.

It is a wonder—some would say a miracle—that this same man, who had been forced to sneak out of his home under cover of night to join the seventy or so followers anxiously awaiting him in a foreign land hundreds of miles away, would, in a few short years, return to the city of his birth, not covertly or in darkness, but in the full light of day, with ten thousand men trailing peacefully behind him; and the same people who once tried to murder him in his sleep would instead offer up to him both the sacred city and the keys to the Kaʻba—unconditionally and without a fight, like a consecrated sacrifice.

3. The City of the Prophet

THE FIRST MUSLIMS

IN THE EVENING, the sun in the desert is a glowing white orb set low in the sky. It dips into the horizon, and its light is eclipsed by the dunes, making them appear as heaving black swells in the distance. At the edge of Yathrib, a hedge of lofty palm trees forms a boundary separating the oasis from the advancing desert. Here, the small band of Companions wait—hands shading their eyes—staring out over the vast expanse for any sign of Muhammad. They've been standing at the edge of the desert for days and nights. What else can they do? Many of them have no homes in Yathrib. Most of their possessions were left behind in Mecca. Their journey was not a grand exodus through the desert, camels laden with goods. The *Hijra*, as the migration from Mecca to Yathrib is known, was a secret operation: daughters sneaking out of their fathers' homes at night, young men gathering whatever provisions they could carry on their backs for the arduous week-long journey through the barren wilderness. The few possessions they brought with them have become communal property; they will not last.

The problem is that the Companions—now more properly termed the Emigrants, or *Muhajirun* (literally, "those who have made the Hijra")—are primarily traders and merchants, but Yathrib is not a city built on trade; Yathrib is not a city at all. It is a loose federation of villages inhabited by farmers and orchardists, tillers of the earth. It is nothing like the bustling, prosperous city the Emigrants left behind. Even if they could transform themselves from traders to farmers, all the best agricultural lands in Yathrib are already occupied.

How are they to survive here except on the charity and goodwill of the *Ansar*, or "Helpers," that handful of Yathrib's villagers who have also accepted Muhammad's message and converted to his movement? And what is to happen to them now that they have abandoned the protection of the Quraysh? Will the most powerful tribe in Arabia simply allow them to leave Mecca without consequence? Have they really chosen to cast off their homes, their families, their very identities, all at the command of an extraordinary but untested prophet who is now nowhere to be found?

Just before the sun vanishes, two smoldering silhouettes are spotted in the desert, lurching toward Yathrib. A cry spreads among the Emigrants: "The Messenger is here! The Messenger has come!" The men jump up and run out to meet Muhammad and Abu Bakr as they cross into the oasis. The women join hands and dance in circles around the two men, their ululations rolling from house to house, announcing the Prophet's arrival.

Muhammad, parched and blistered from the journey, sits back in his saddle and lets the reins of his camel hang loose. A crowd gathers, offering food and water. A few of the Ansar struggle to grab hold of the camel's reins and steer it toward their villages. They shout, "Come, O Messenger of God, to a settlement which has many defenders and is well-provisioned and impregnable."

But Muhammad, not wishing to ally himself with any particular clan in Yathrib, refuses their offers. "Let go her reins," he commands.

The crowd backs off, and Muhammad's camel staggers forward a few more steps. It circles an abandoned burial ground now used for drying dates, then stops and kneels, lowering its neck for the Prophet to dismount. Of the owners of the land, Muhammad asks a price.

"We do not want money for it," the owners reply. "Only the reward we shall receive from God."

Grateful for their generosity, Muhammad orders the land to be leveled, the graves dug up, and the palm trees cut down for timber to build a modest home. He envisions a courtyard roofed in palm leaves, with living quarters made of wood and mud lining the walls. But this will be more than a home. This converted drying-ground and cemetery will serve as the first *masjid*, or mosque, of a new kind of community, one so revolutionary that many years later, when Muslim scholars seek to establish a distinctly Islamic calendar, they will begin not with the birth of the Prophet, nor with the onset of Revelation, but with the year Muhammad and his band of Emigrants came to this small federation of villages to start a new society. That year, 622 C.E., will forever be known as Year 1 A.H. (After Hijra); and the oasis that for centuries had been called Yathrib will henceforth be celebrated as *Medinat an-Nabi:* "The City of the Prophet," or more simply, Medina.

There exists an enduring mythology about Muhammad's time in the city that came to bear his name, a mythology that has defined the religion and politics of Islam for fourteen hundred years. It is in Medina that the Muslim community was born, and where Muhammad's Arab social reform movement transformed into a universal religious ideology.

"Muhammad in Medina" became the paradigm for the Arab empire that expanded throughout the Middle East after the Prophet's death, and the standard that every Islamic kingdom and sultanate struggled to meet during the Middle Ages. The Medinan ideal inspired the various Islamic revivalist movements of the eighteenth and nineteenth centuries, all of which strove to return to the original values of Muhammad's unadulterated community as a means to wrest control of Muslim lands from colonial rule (though they had radically different ideas about how to define those original values). And with the demise of colonialism in the twentieth century, it was the memory of Medina that launched the notion of the "Islamic state."

Today, Medina is simultaneously the archetype of Islamic democracy and the impetus for Islamic militancy. Islamic Modernists like the

Egyptian writer and political philosopher Ali Abd ar-Raziq (d. 1966) pointed to Muhammad's community in Medina as proof that Islam advocated the separation of religious and temporal power, while Muslim extremists in Afghanistan and Iran have used the same community to fashion various models of Islamic theocracy. In their struggle for equal rights, Muslim feminists have consistently drawn inspiration from the legal reforms Muhammad instituted in Medina, while at the same time, Muslim traditionalists have construed those same legal reforms as grounds for maintaining the subjugation of women in Islamic society. For some, Muhammad's actions in Medina serve as the model for Muslim-Jewish relations; for others, they demonstrate the insurmountable conflict that has always existed, and will always exist, between the two sons of Abraham. Yet regardless of whether one is labeled a Modernist or a Traditionalist, a reformist or a fundamentalist, a feminist or a chauvinist, all Muslims regard Medina as the model of Islamic perfection. Simply put, Medina is what Islam was meant to be.

As with all mythologies of this magnitude, it is often difficult to separate factual history from sacred history. Part of the problem is that the historical traditions dealing with Muhammad's time in Medina were written hundreds of years after the Prophet's death by Muslim historians who were keen to emphasize the universal recognition and immediate success of Muhammad's divine mission. Remember that Muhammad's biographers were living at a time in which the Muslim community had already become an enormously powerful empire. As a result, their accounts more often reflect the political and religious ideologies of ninth-century Damascus, or eleventh-century Baghdad, than of seventh-century Medina.

To understand what really happened in Medina and why, one must sift through these sources to uncover not the holy city that would become the capital of the Muslim community, but rather the remote desert oasis that nurtured and cultivated that community in its infancy. After all, long before there was a "City of the Prophet," there was only Yathrib.

YATHRIB IN THE seventh century was a thriving agricultural oasis thick with palm orchards and vast arable fields, most of which were dominated by some twenty Jewish clans of varying sizes. Unlike the Jews who had settled throughout western Arabia (the Hijaz), most of whom were immigrants from Palestine, Yathrib's Jews were mostly Arabs who had converted to Judaism. Apart from their religious designation as Jews, little differentiated them from their pagan neighbors. Like all Arabs, the Jews of Yathrib considered themselves first and foremost members of their own individual clans—each of which acted as a sovereign entity—rather than as a single community of Jews. And while a few Jewish clans may have had alliances with one another, even these in no way constituted a united Jewish tribe.

As the earliest settlers in the region, the Jews occupied Yathrib's most fertile agricultural lands, called "the Heights," quickly becoming masters of Arabia's most prized crop: dates. The Jews were also skilled jewelers, clothiers, arms makers, and vintners (Jewish wine was considered the best in the peninsula). But it was Yathrib's dates, coveted throughout the Hijaz, that had made them rich. As a matter of fact, five of the largest Jewish clans in the oasis—the Banu Thalabah, the Banu Hadl, the Banu Qurayza, the Banu Nadir, and the Banu Qaynuqa (who also controlled the city's sole market)—enjoyed an almost complete monopoly over Yathrib's economy.

By the time a number of Bedouin tribes gave up their nomadic existence and also settled in Yathrib, all the most fertile lands had already been claimed. What remained were the barely cultivable lots situated in a region termed "the Bottom." The competition over limited resources had not only created some conflict between the "pagan" (i.e., Arab) and Jewish clans, it had also resulted in a gradual decline of the Jews' authority and influence in Yathrib. For the most part, however, the two groups lived in relative peace through strategic tribal affiliations and economic alliances. The Jews regularly employed the Arabs to transport their dates to nearby markets (especially in Mecca), while the Arabs maintained a high esteem for the learning, craftsmanship, and heritage of their Jewish neighbors, who were, in the words of the Arab chronicler al-Waqidi, "a people of high lineage and of properties, whereas we were but an Arab tribe who did not possess any palm trees nor vineyards, being people of only sheep and camels."

The real conflict in the oasis was not between the Jews and Arabs, but among the Arabs themselves, and more specifically between its two largest Arab tribes: the *Aws* and the Khazraj, the tribe that had originally invited Muhammad and his followers to Yathrib. While the origins of this conflict have been lost to history, what seems clear is that the Law of Retribution, the purpose of which was to deter precisely this kind of ongoing tribal conflict, had failed to solve the long-standing quarrel. By the time Muhammad arrived in Yathrib, what had probably begun as a disagreement over limited resources had escalated into a bloody feud which had spilled over even to the Jewish clans, with the Banu Nadir and the Banu Qurayza supporting the Aws, and the Banu Qaynuqa siding with the Khazraj. In short, this conflict was splitting the oasis in two.

What the Aws and the Khazraj desperately needed was a Hakam, or arbiter. Not just any Hakam, but an authoritative, trustworthy, and neutral party who was totally unconnected with anyone in Yathrib, someone who had the power—better yet, the divine authority—to arbitrate between the two tribes. How fortunate, then, that the perfect man for the job was himself in desperate need of a place to live.

That Muhammad came to Yathrib as little more than the Hakam in the quarrel between the Aws and the Khazraj is certain. And yet the traditions seem to present Muhammad arriving in the oasis as the mighty prophet of a new and firmly established religion: the unchallenged leader of the whole of Yathrib. That view is partly the result of a famous document called the Constitution of Medina, which Muhammad may have drafted sometime after settling in the oasis. The document—often celebrated as the world's first written constitution—was a series of formal agreements of nonaggression among Muhammad, the newly arrived Emigrants, the Ansar in Medina who had converted to Muhammad's movement, and the rest of Yathrib's clans, both Jewish and pagan.

The Constitution is controversial, however, because it seems to assign to Muhammad unparalleled religious and political authority over the entire population of the oasis, including the Jews. It indicates that Muhammad had sole authority to arbitrate all disputes in Yathrib, not just that between the Aws and Khazraj. It declares him to be Yathrib's sole war leader (Qa'id) and unequivocally recognizes him as the Messenger of God. And while it implies that Muhammad's primary role was as "Shaykh" of his "clan" of Emigrants, it also clearly endows him with a privileged position over all other tribal and clan Shaykhs in Yathrib.

The problem lies in determining exactly when the Constitution of Medina was written. The traditional sources, including al-Tabari and Ibn Hisham, place its composition among the Prophet's first acts upon entering the oasis: that is, in 622 C.E. But that is highly unlikely, given Muhammad's weak position during those first few years in Yathrib. He was, after all, forced to flee Mecca and hunted throughout the Hijaz like a criminal. And, as Michael Lecker has shown, it was not until after the Battle of Badr in 624 (an event that will be discussed in the following chapter), and perhaps not even until 627—five years after the emigration (Hijra) to Yathrib—that the majority of the Aws tribe converted to Islam. Before then, few people outside the Ansar (which at that point consisted of only a handful of members of the Khazraj) would have known who Muhammad was, let alone have submitted to his authority. His movement represented the tiniest fraction of Yathrib's population; the Jews alone may have totaled in the thousands. When Muhammad arrived in the oasis, he had brought fewer than a hundred men, women, and children with him.

The Constitution of Medina may reflect several early pacts of nonaggression among Muhammad, the Arab clans, and their Jewish clients. It may even reproduce certain elements of Muhammad's arbitration between the Aws and the Khazraj. But there is simply no way it could have been completed as it has been preserved before 624 C.E. Only after the Battle of Badr could Muhammad have dreamed of the powers attributed to him by the Constitution of Medina; indeed, only after Badr could Yathrib even be thought of as Medina.

Muhammad's role during those first couple of years in Yathrib was very likely that of a Hakam—albeit a powerful and divinely inspired one—whose arbitration was restricted to the Aws and Khazraj, and whose authority as a Shaykh was confined to his own "clan" of Emigrants: one clan out of many; one Shaykh out of many. Muhammad's claim to be the Messenger of God would not have had to be either accepted or rejected for him to function properly in either of these two roles. Both the pagan Arabs and the Jews of Yathrib would have considered his prophetic character to be proof of his supernatural wisdom, especially since the ideal Hakam was almost always also the Kahin, or soothsayer, whose connection to the Divine was indispensable in especially difficult disputes like the one between the Aws and Khazraj.

Yet while the other inhabitants of Yathrib may have viewed Muhammad as little more than a Hakam and a Shaykh, that was not at all how his small band of followers saw him. To them, Muhammad was the Prophet/Lawgiver who spoke with the authority of the one God. As such, he had come to Yathrib to establish a new kind of socioreligious community, though how that community was to be organized, and who could be considered a member of it, had yet to be defined.

It may be tempting to call the members of this new community *Muslims* (literally, "those who submit" to God). But there is no reason to believe that this term was used to designate a distinct religious movement until many years later, perhaps not until the end of Muhammad's life. It would perhaps be more accurate to refer to Muhammad's followers by the same term the Quran uses: the *Ummah*. The problem with this term, however, is that no one is certain what it meant or where it came from. It may be derived from Arabic, Hebrew, or Aramaic; it may have meant "a community," "a nation," or "a people." A few scholars have suggested that *Ummah* may be derived from the Arabic word for "mother" (*umm*), and while this idea may be aesthetically pleasing, there is no linguistic evidence for it. To make matters more complicated, the word *Ummah* inexplicably ceases to be used in the Quran after 625 C.E., when it is replaced with the word *qawm*—Arabic for "tribe."

But there may be something to this change in terms. Despite its ingenuity, Muhammad's community was still an Arab institution based on Arab notions of tribal society. There was simply no alternative model of social organization in seventh-century Arabia, save for monarchy. Indeed, there are so many parallels between the early Muslim community and traditional tribal society that one is left with the distinct impression that, at least in Muhammad's mind, the Ummah was indeed a tribe, though a new and radically innovative one.

For one thing, the reference in the Constitution of Medina to Muhammad's role as Shaykh of his clan of Emigrants indicates that despite the Prophet's elevated status, his secular authority would have fallen well within the traditional paradigm of pre-Islamic tribal society. What is more, just as membership in the tribe obliged participation in the rituals and activities of the tribal cult, so did membership in Muhammad's community require ritual involvement in what could be termed its "tribal cult": in this case, the nascent religion of Islam. Public rituals like communal prayer, almsgiving, and collective fasting—the first three activities mandated by Islam—when combined with shared dietary regulations and purity requirements, functioned in the Ummah in much the same way that the activities of the tribal cult did in pagan societies: by providing a common social and religious identity that allowed one group to distinguish itself from another.

What made the Ummah a unique experiment in social organization was that in Yathrib, far away from the social and religious hegemony of the Quraysh, Muhammad finally had the opportunity to implement the reforms he had been preaching to no avail in Mecca. By enacting a series of radical religious, social, and economic reforms, he was able to establish a new kind of society, the likes of which had never before been seen in Arabia.

For instance, whereas power in the tribe was allocated to a number of figures, none of whom had any real executive authority, Muhammad instead united all the pre-Islamic positions of authority unto himself. He was not only the Shaykh of his community, but also its Hakam, its Qa'id, and, as the only legitimate connection to the Divine, its Kahin. His authority as Prophet/Lawgiver was absolute.

Also, while the only way to become a member of a tribe was to be born into it, anyone could join Muhammad's community simply by declaring, "There is no god but God, and Muhammad is God's Messenger." The shahadah, or profession of faith, was thus transformed in Yathrib from a theological statement with explicit social and political implications into a new version of the oath of allegiance, the bay'ah, which the tribe gave to its Shaykh. And because neither ethnicity nor culture nor race nor kinship had any significance to Muhammad, the Ummah, unlike a traditional tribe, had an almost unlimited capacity for growth through conversion.

The point is that one can refer to Muhammad's community in Yathrib as the Ummah, but only insofar as that term is understood to designate what the Orientalist explorer Bertram Thomas has called a "super-tribe," or what the historian Marshall Hodgson more accurately describes as a "neo-tribe": that is, a radically new kind of social organization, but one that was nonetheless based on the traditional Arab tribal paradigm.

As was the case with all tribal Shaykhs, Muhammad's primary function as head of the Ummah was to ensure the protection of every member in his community. This he did through the chief means at his disposal: the Law of Retribution. But while retribution was maintained as a legitimate response to injury, Muhammad urged believers toward forgiveness: "The retribution for an injury is an equal injury," the Quran states, "but those who forgive the injury and make reconciliation will be rewarded by God" (42:40). Likewise, the Constitution of Medina sanctions retribution as the principal deterrent for crime, but with the unprecedented stipulation that the entire community may be "solidly against [the criminal], and may do nothing except oppose him," a stark reversal of tribal tradition and a clear indication that Muhammad was already beginning to lay the foundations of a society built on moral rather than utilitarian principles. But this was only the beginning.

To further his egalitarian ideals, Muhammad equalized the blood-worth of every member of his community, so that no longer could one life be considered more or less valuable (pecuniarily speaking) than another. This was yet another innovation in the Arabian legal system, for while an injury to a victim's eye in pre-Islamic Arabia would have required an equal injury to the criminal's eye, no one would have considered a Shaykh's eye to be worth the same amount as an orphan's. But Muhammad changed all that, and not without seriously disrupting the social order. The traditions recount a particularly amusing story about an aristocratic tribesman named Jabalah ibn al-Ayham, an early follower of Muhammad, who was struck in the face by a humble man from the Muzaynah, a modest tribe in Arabia. Expecting that a stern penalty would be imposed on the lowly offender—one that would signify his inferior status in society—al-Ayham was shocked to learn that all he could expect as retribution was the opportunity to strike the humble man back. So outraged was he by this "injustice" that al-Ayham immediately abandoned Islam and became a Christian.

Nor did Muhammad's move toward egalitarianism end with reforming the Law of Retribution. In Yathrib, he categorically outlawed usury, the abuse of which was one of his chief complaints against the Meccan religio-economic system. To facilitate the new economy, he established his own market, which, unlike the one controlled by the Banu Qaynuqa, charged no tax on transactions and no interest on loans. While this tax-free market eventually became a point of conflict between Muhammad and the Banu Qaynuqa, the Prophet's move was not a means of antagonizing the wealthy and powerful Jewish tribe, but a further step toward alleviating the divide between the ridiculously wealthy and the absurdly poor.

Using his unquestioned religious authority, Muhammad instituted a mandatory tithe called *zakat*, which every member of the Ummah had to pay according to his or her means. Once collected, the money was then redistributed as alms to the community's neediest members. *Zakat* literally means "purification," and was not an act of charity but of religious devotion: benevolence and care for the poor were the first and most enduring virtues preached by Muhammad in Mecca. Piety, the Quran reminds believers, lies "not in turning your face East or West in prayer . . . but in distributing your wealth out of love for God to your needy kin; to the orphans, to the vagrants, and to the mendicants; it lies in freeing the slaves, in observing your devotions, and in giving alms to the poor" (2:177).

Perhaps nowhere was Muhammad's struggle for economic redistribution and social egalitarianism more evident than in the rights and privileges he bestowed upon the women in his community. Beginning with the unbiblical conviction that men and women were created together and simultaneously from a single cell (4:1; 7:189), the Quran goes to great lengths to emphasize the equality of the sexes in the eyes of God:

> God offers forgiveness and a great reward,
> For men who surrender to Him, and women who surrender to Him,
> For men who believe, and women who believe,
> For men who obey, and women who obey,
> For men who speak truth, and women who speak truth,

For men who persevere, and women who persevere,

For men who are humble, and women who are humble,

For men who give alms, and women who give alms,

For men who fast, and women who fast,

For men who are modest, and women who are modest,

For men who remember God, and women who remember God. (33:35)

At the same time, the Quran acknowledges that men and women have distinct and separate roles in society; it would have been preposterous to claim otherwise in seventh century Arabia. Thus, "men are to take care of women, because God has given them greater strength, and because men use their wealth to provide for them" (4:34).

With a few notable exceptions (like Khadija), women in pre-Islamic Arabia could neither own property nor inherit it from their husbands. Actually, a wife was herself considered property, and both she and her dowry would be inherited by the male heir of her deceased husband. If the male heir was uninterested in the widow, he could hand her over to his kin—a brother or a nephew—who could then marry her and take control of her dead husband's property. But if she was too old to marry again, or if no one was interested in her, she and her dowry would revert to the clan. The same was true for all female orphans, as well as those male orphans who, like Muhammad when his parents died, were considered too young to inherit property from their fathers.

However, Muhammad—who had benefited greatly from the wealth and stability provided by Khadija—strove to give women the opportunity to attain some level of equality and independence in society by amending Arabia's traditional marriage and inheritance laws in order to remove the obstacles that prohibited women from inheriting and maintaining their own wealth. While the exact changes Muhammad made to this tradition are far too complex to discuss in detail here, it is sufficient to note that women in the Ummah were, for the first time, given the right both to inherit the property of their husbands and to keep their dowries as their own personal property throughout their marriage. Muhammad also forbade a husband to touch his wife's dowry, forcing him instead to provide for his family from his own wealth. If the husband died, his wife would inherit a portion of his property; if he divorced her, the entire dowry was hers to take back to her family.

As one would expect, Muhammad's innovations did not sit well with the male members of his community. If women could no longer be considered property, men complained, not only would their wealth be drastically reduced, but their own meager inheritances would now have to be split with their sisters and daughters—members of the community who, they argued, did not share an equal burden with the men. Al-Tabari recounts how some of these men brought their grievances to Muhammad, asking, "How can one give the right of inheritance to women and children, who do not work and do not earn their living? Are they now going to inherit just like men who have worked to earn that money?"

Muhammad's response to these complaints was both unsympathetic and shockingly unyielding. "Those who disobey God and His Messenger, and who try to overstep the boundaries of this [inheritance] law will be thrown into Hell, where they will dwell forever, suffering the most shameful punishment" (4:14).

If Muhammad's male followers were disgruntled about the new inheritance laws, they must have been furious when, in a single revolutionary move, he both limited how many wives a man could marry and granted women the right to divorce their husbands.

In some ways, pre-Islamic Arabian custom was extraordinarily lax when it came to both marriage and divorce. In Bedouin societies, both men and women practiced polygamy and both had recourse to divorce: men simply by making a statement such as "I divorce you!" and women—who remained with their father's family during marriage—by turning their tent around so that its entrance would no longer be available to the husband when he came for a "visit." Because paternity was unimportant in Bedouin societies (lineage was passed primarily through the mother), it made no difference how many husbands a woman had or who fathered her children. However, in sedentary societies like Mecca, where the accumulation of wealth made inheritance and, therefore, paternity much more important, matrilineal society had gradually given way to a patrilineal one. As a result of this trend toward patriliny, women in sedentary societies were gradually stripped of both their right to divorce and their access to poly-andry (the practice of having more than one husband).

Although Muhammad's views on marriage seem far more influ-enced by Jewish tradition than by the traditions of pre-Islamic Arabia, he was still a product of Meccan society. So while he limited the rights of men to divorce their wives—forcing upon them a three-month rec-onciliation period before the statement of divorce could take effect—and while he provided women with the right to divorce their husbands if they feared "cruelty or ill-treatment" (4:128), he nonetheless con-solidated the move toward a patrilineal society by putting a definitive end to all polyandrous unions. Never again could a Muslim woman have more than one husband. Whether a Muslim man may have more than one wife (polygyny), however, remains a contested issue to this day.

On the one hand, Muhammad clearly accepted polygyny (within limits) as necessary for the survival of the Ummah, especially after war with the Quraysh resulted in hundreds of widows and orphans who had to be provided for and protected by the community. "Marry those women who are lawful for you, up to two, three, or four," the Quran states, *"but only if you can treat them all equally"* (4:3; emphasis added). On the other hand, the Quran makes it clear just a few verses later that monogamy is the preferred model of marriage when it asserts that "no matter how you try, *you will never be able to treat your wives equally"* (4:129; again, emphasis added). This seeming contradiction offers some insight into a dilemma that plagued the community during its early development. Essentially, while the individual believer was to strive for monogamy, the community that Muhammad was trying to build in Yathrib would have been doomed without polygyny.

For the vast majority of Muslims throughout the world, there is little doubt that the two verses cited above, when combined and con-sidered in their historical context, should be interpreted as rejecting polygamy in all its forms. And yet, there are still those Muslims, espe-cially in tribal societies like Saudi Arabia and Afghanistan, who justify their polygynous marriages, not necessarily by referring to the Quran, but by pointing to the example set by Muhammad, for whom neither the limitations on polygyny nor the preference for monogamy had any bearing.

After having lived a monogamous life with Khadija for more than twenty-five years, Muhammad, in the course of ten years in Yathrib, married nine different women. With very few exceptions, these marriages were not sexual unions but political ones. This is not to say that Muhammad was uninterested in sex; on the contrary, the traditions present him as a man with a robust and healthy libido. But as Shaykh of the Ummah, it was Muhammad's responsibility to forge links within and beyond his community through the only means at his disposal: marriage. Thus, his unions with Aisha and Hafsah linked him to the two most important and influential leaders of the early Muslim community—to Abu Bakr and Umar, respectively. His marriage to Umm Salamah a year later forged an important relationship with one of Mecca's most powerful clans, the Makhzum. His union with Sawdah—an elderly widow long past the age of marriage—served as an example to the Ummah to marry those women in need of financial support. His marriage to Rayhana, a Jew, linked him with the Jewish tribe of Banu Qurayza, while his marriage to Mariyah, a Christian and a Copt, created a significant political alliance with the Christian ruler of Egypt.

Nevertheless, for fourteen hundred years—from the medieval Popes of the Crusades to the Enlightenment philosophers of Europe to evangelical preachers in the United States—Muhammad's wives have been the source of numerous lurid attacks against the Prophet and the religion of Islam. In response, contemporary scholars—Muslim and non-Muslim alike—have done considerable work to defend Muhammad's marriages, especially his union with Aisha, who was nine years old when betrothed to the Prophet. While these scholars should be commended for their work in debunking the bigoted and ignorant critiques of anti-Islamic preachers and pundits, the fact is that Muhammad needs no defense on this point.

Like the great Jewish patriarchs Abraham and Jacob; like the prophets Moses and Hosea; like the Israelite kings Saul, David, and Solomon; and like nearly all of the Christian/Byzantine and Zoroastrian/Sasanian monarchs, *all* Shaykhs in Arabia—Muhammad included—had either multiple wives, multiple concubines, or both. In seventh-century Arabia, a Shaykh's power and authority was in large part determined by the size of his harem. And while Muhammad's union with a nine-year-old girl may be shocking to our modern sensibilities, his betrothal to Aisha was just that: a *betrothal*. Aisha did not consummate her marriage to Muhammad until after reaching puberty, which is when every girl in Arabia without exception became eligible for marriage. The most shocking aspect of Muhammad's marriages is not his ten years of polygamy in Yathrib, but his twenty-five years of monogamy in Mecca, something practically unheard of at the time. Indeed, if there is anything at all interesting or unusual about Muhammad's marriages, it is not how many wives he had, but rather the regulations that were imposed on them, specifically with regard to the veil.

Although long seen as the most distinctive emblem of Islam, the veil is, surprisingly, not enjoined upon Muslim women anywhere in the Quran. The tradition of veiling and seclusion (known together as *hijab*) was introduced into Arabia long before Muhammad, primarily through Arab contacts with Syria and Iran, where the hijab was a sign of social status. After all, only a woman who need not work in the fields could afford to remain secluded and veiled.

In the Ummah, there was no tradition of veiling until around 627 C.E., when the so-called "verse of hijab" suddenly descended upon the community. That verse, however, was addressed not to women in general, but exclusively to Muhammad's wives: "Believers, do not enter the Prophet's house . . . unless asked. And if you are invited . . . do not linger. And when you ask something from the Prophet's wives, do so from behind a hijab. This will assure the purity of your hearts as well as theirs" (33:53).

This restriction makes perfect sense when one recalls that Muhammad's house was also the community's mosque: the center of religious and social life in the Ummah. People were constantly coming in and out of this compound at all hours of the day. When delegations from other tribes came to speak with Muhammad, they would set up their tents for days at a time inside the open courtyard, just a few feet away from the apartments in which Muhammad's wives slept. And new emigrants who arrived in Yathrib would often stay within the mosque's walls until they could find suitable homes.

When Muhammad was little more than a tribal Shaykh, this constant commotion could be tolerated. But by the year 627, when he had become the supremely powerful leader of an increasingly expanding community, some kind of segregation had to be enforced to maintain the inviolability of his wives. Thus the tradition, borrowed from the upper classes of Iranian and Syrian women, of veiling and secluding the most important women in society from the peering eyes of everyone else.

That the veil applied solely to Muhammad's wives is further demonstrated by the fact that the term for donning the veil, *darabat al-hijab*, was used synonymously and interchangeably with "becoming Muhammad's wife." For this reason, during the Prophet's lifetime, no other women in the Ummah observed hijab. Of course, modesty was enjoined on both male and female believers, while women in particular were instructed to follow in the footsteps of the Prophet's wives and "draw their clothes around them a little to be recognized as believers and so that no harm will come to them" (33:59). More specifically, women should "guard their private parts . . . and drape a cover over their breasts" when in the presence of strange men (24:31–32; note that the word used for "cover" is *khamr* not *hijab*). However, as Leila Ahmed correctly observes, nowhere in the whole of the Quran is the term *hijab* applied to any woman other than the wives of Muhammad.

It is difficult to say with certainty when the veil was adopted by the rest of the Ummah, though it was most likely long after Muhammad's death. Muslim women probably began wearing the veil as a way to emulate the Prophet's wives, who were revered as "the Mothers of the Ummah." But the veil was neither compulsory nor, for that matter, widely adopted until generations after Muhammad's death, when a large body of male scriptural and legal scholars began using their religious and political authority to regain the dominance they had lost in society as a result of the Prophet's egalitarian reforms.

THE ERA IMMEDIATELY following Muhammad's death was, as will become evident, a tumultuous time for the Muslim community. The Ummah was growing and expanding in wealth and power at an astounding rate. A mere fifty years after his death, the tiny community that Muhammad had founded in Yathrib burst out of the Arabian

Peninsula and swallowed whole the massive Sasanian Empire of Iran. Fifty years after that, it had secured most of northwest India, absorbed all of North Africa, and reduced the Christian Byzantine Empire to little more than a deteriorating regional power. Fifty years after that, Islam began pushing its way into Europe through Spain and southern France.

As Muhammad's small community of Arab followers swelled into one of the largest empires the world has ever seen, it faced a growing number of legal and religious challenges that were not explicitly dealt with in the Quran. While Muhammad was still in their midst, these questions could simply be brought to him. But without the Prophet, it became progressively more difficult to ascertain God's will on issues that far exceeded the knowledge and experiences of a group of Arab tribesmen.

At first, the Ummah naturally turned to the early Companions for guidance and leadership. As the first generation of Muslims—the people who had walked and talked with the Prophet—the Companions had the authority to make legal and spiritual decisions by virtue of their direct knowledge of Muhammad's life and teachings. They were the living repositories of the *hadith:* oral anecdotes recalling the words and deeds of Muhammad.

The hadith, insofar as they addressed issues not dealt with in the Quran, would become an indispensable tool in the formation of Islamic law. However, in their earliest stages, the hadith were muddled and totally unregulated, making their authentication almost impossible. Worse, as the first generation of Companions passed on, the community had to rely increasingly on the reports that the second generation of Muslims (known as the *Tabiun*) had received from the first; when the second generation died, the community was yet another step removed from the actual words and deeds of the Prophet.

Thus, with each successive generation, the "chain of transmission," or *isnad,* that was supposed to authenticate the hadith grew longer and more convoluted, so that in less than two centuries after Muhammad's death, there were already some seven hundred thousand hadith being circulated throughout the Muslim lands, the great majority of which were unquestionably fabricated by individuals who sought to legitimize their own particular beliefs and practices by connecting them with the Prophet. After a few generations, almost any-thing could be given the status of hadith if one simply claimed to trace its transmission back to Muhammad. In fact, the Hungarian scholar Ignaz Goldziher has documented numerous hadith the transmitters of which claimed were derived from Muhammad but which were in real-ity verses from the Torah and Gospels, bits of rabbinic sayings, ancient Persian maxims, passages of Greek philosophy, Indian proverbs, and even an almost word-for-word reproduction of the Lord's Prayer. By the ninth century, when Islamic law was being fashioned, there were so many false hadith circulating through the community that Muslim legal scholars somewhat whimsically classified them into two cate-gories: lies told for material gain and lies told for ideological advantage.

In the ninth and tenth centuries, a concerted effort was made to sift through the massive accumulation of hadith in order to separate the reliable from the rest. Still, for hundreds of years, anyone who had the power and wealth necessary to influence public opinion on a particular issue—and who wanted to justify his own ideas about, say, the role of women in society—had only to refer to a hadith which he had heard from someone, who had heard it from someone else, who had heard it from a Companion, who had heard it from the Prophet.

It would be no exaggeration, therefore, to say that quite soon after Muhammad's death, those men who took upon themselves the task of interpreting God's will in the Quran and Muhammad's will in the hadith—men who were, coincidentally, among the most powerful and wealthy members of the Ummah—were not nearly as concerned with the accuracy of their reports or the objectivity of their exegesis as they were with regaining the financial and social dominance that the Prophet's reforms had taken from them. As Fatima Mernissi notes, one must always remember that behind every hadith lies the entrenched power struggles and conflicting interests that one would expect in a society "in which social mobility [and] geographical expansion [were] the order of the day."

Thus, when the Quran warned believers not to "pass on your wealth and property to the feeble-minded (*sufaha*)," the early Quranic commentators—all of them male—declared, despite the Quran's warnings on the subject, that "the *sufaha* are women and children . . . *and both of them must be excluded from inheritance*" (emphasis added).

When a wealthy and notable merchant from Basra named Abu Bakra (not to be confused with Abu Bakr) claimed, twenty-five years after Muhammad's death, that he once heard the Prophet say, "Those who entrust their affairs to a woman will never know prosperity," his authority as a Companion was unquestioned.

When Ibn Maja reported in his collection of hadith that the Prophet, in answer to a question about the rights a wife has over her husband, replied rather incredibly that her only right was to be given food "when you [yourself] have taken your food," and clothed "when you have clothed yourself," his opinion, though thoroughly against the demands of the Quran, went uncontested.

When Abu Said al-Khudri swore he had heard the Prophet tell a group of women, "I have not seen anyone more deficient in intelligence and religion than you," his memory was unchallenged, despite the fact that Muhammad's biographers present him as repeatedly asking for and following the advice of his wives, even in military matters.

And finally, when the celebrated Quranic commentator Fakhr ad-Din ar-Razi (1149–1209) interpreted the verse "[God] created spouses for you of your own kind so that you may have peace of mind through them" (30:21) as "proof that women were created like animals and plants and other useful things [and not for] worship and carrying the Divine commands . . . because the woman is weak, silly, and in one sense like a child," his commentary became (and still is) one of the most widely respected in the Muslim world.

This last point bears repeating. The fact is that for fourteen centuries, the science of Quranic commentary has been the exclusive domain of Muslim men. And because each one of these exegetes inevitably brings to the Quran his own ideology and his own preconceived notions, it should not be surprising to learn that certain verses have most often been read in their most misogynist interpretation. Consider, for example, how the following verse (4:34) regarding the obligations of men toward women has been rendered into English by two different but widely read contemporary translators of the Quran. The first is from the Princeton edition, translated by Ahmed Ali; the second is from Majid Fakhry's translation, published by New York University:

Men are the support of women [qawwamuna 'ala an-nisa] as God gives some more means than others, and because they spend of their wealth (to provide for them). . . . As for women you feel are averse, talk to them suasively; then leave them alone in bed (without molesting them) and go to bed with them (when they are willing).

Men are in charge of women, because Allah has made some of them excel the others, and because they spend some of their wealth. . . . And for those [women] that you fear might rebel, admonish them and abandon them in their beds and beat them [adribuhunna].

Because of the variability of the Arabic language, both of these translations are grammatically, syntactically, and definitionally correct. The phrase qawwamuna 'ala an-nisa can be understood as "watch over," "protect," "support," "attend to," "look after," or "be in charge of" women. The final word in the verse, adribuhunna, which Fakhry has rendered as "beat them," can equally mean "turn away from them," "go along with them," and, remarkably, even "have consensual intercourse with them." If religion is indeed interpretation, then which meaning one chooses to accept and follow depends on what one is trying to extract from the text: if one views the Quran as empowering women, then Ali's; if one looks to the Quran to justify violence against women, then Fakhry's.

Throughout Islamic history, there have been a number of women who have struggled to maintain their authority as both preservers of the hadith and interpreters of the Quran. Karima bint Ahmad (d. 1069) and Fatima bint Ali (d. 1087), for example, are regarded as two of the most important transmitters of the Prophet's traditions, while Zaynab bint al-Sha'ri (d. 1220) and Daqiqa bint Murshid (d. 1345), both textual scholars, occupied an eminent place in early Islamic scholarship. And it is hard to ignore the fact that nearly one sixth of all "reliable" hadith can be traced back to Muhammad's wife Aisha.

However, these women, celebrated as they are, were no match for the indisputable authority of early Companions like Umar, the young, brash member of the Quraysh élite who would eventually take over the leadership of the Muslim community after Muhammad's death. The Prophet had always admired Umar, not just for his physical prowess as a warrior, but for his impeccable moral virtue and the zeal with which he approached his devotion to God. In many ways, Umar was a simple, dignified, and devout man. But he also had a fiery temper and was prone to anger and violence, especially toward women. So infamous was he for his misogynist attitude that when he asked for the hand of Aisha's sister, he was flatly rebuffed because of his rough behavior toward women.

Umar's misogynist tendencies were apparent from the moment he ascended to the leadership of the Muslim community. He tried (unsuccessfully) to confine women to their homes and wanted to prevent them from attending worship at the mosque. He instituted segregated prayers and, in direct violation of the Prophet's example, forced women to be taught by male religious leaders. Incredibly, he forbade Muhammad's widows to perform the pilgrimage rites and instituted a series of severe penal ordinances aimed primarily at women. Chief among these was the stoning to death of adulterers, a punishment which has absolutely no foundation whatsoever in the Quran but which Umar justified by claiming it had originally been part of the Revelation and had somehow been left out of the authorized text. Of course, Umar never explained how it was possible for a verse such as this "accidentally" to have been left out of the Divine Revelation of God, but then again, he didn't have to. It was enough that he spoke with the authority of the Prophet.

There is no question that the Quran, like all holy scriptures, was deeply affected by the cultural norms of the society in which it was revealed—a society that, as we have seen, did not consider women to be equal members of the tribe. As a result, there are numerous verses in the Quran that, along with the Jewish and Christian scriptures, clearly reflect the subordinate position of women in the male-dominated societies of the ancient world. But that is precisely the point which the burgeoning Muslim feminist movement has been making over the last century. These women argue that the religious message of the Quran—a message of revolutionary social egalitarianism—must be separated from the cultural prejudices of seventh-century Arabia. And for the first time in history, they are incorporating their views into the male-dominated world of Quranic exegesis.

Throughout the Islamic world, a cadre of contemporary female textual scholars is reengaging the Quran from a perspective that has been sorely lacking in Islamic scholarship. Beginning with the notion that it is not the moral teachings of Islam but the social conditions of seventh-century Arabia and the rampant misogyny of many male Quranic exegetes that have been responsible for women's historically inferior status in Muslim society, these scholars are approaching the Quran free from the confines of traditional gender boundaries. Muslim feminists throughout the world have been laboring toward a more gender-neutral interpretation of the Quran and a more balanced application of Islamic law. The first English translation of the Quran by a woman, Laleh Bakhtiar, was recently published to critical acclaim in the United States and Europe, while a new batch of female imams and prayer leaders are now guiding Muslim congregations from Toronto to Shanghai. At the same time, there has been a steady rise in the number of female heads of state and political party leaders in Muslim-majority states, including Mame Madior Boye in Senegal, Tansu Çiller in Turkey, Kaqusha Jashari in Kosovo, Megawati Sukarnoputri in Indonesia, Nurul Izzah Anwar in Malaysia, Benazir Bhutto in Pakistan (who was tragically killed by a suicide bomber in 2007), and Khaleda Zia and Sheikh Hasina in Bangladesh. Over the last few years, the Islamic world has produced more female presidents and prime ministers than both Europe and North America combined.

Certainly, there are many Muslim-majority states where women still do not have the same legal rights as men; the same can be said about most developing countries in all parts of the world—Muslim or not. And no doubt the plight of women in places like Iran, Afghanistan, the Sudan, and Somalia is appalling and must be urgently addressed. But to use the experience of women in these countries to make broad generalizations about Islam's treatment of women would be grossly simplistic. Unfortunately, that is precisely what is happening throughout the Western world, where the image of the Muslim woman as indubitably oppressed and degraded by Islam not only persists but is being conceived of almost wholly through the singular symbol of the veil. In fact, it sometimes seems that for many in Europe and North America, the entirety of a Muslim woman's experience can be defined by a piece of cloth with which she may or may not choose to cover her hair.

This is not a new phenomenon, of course. Despite the fact that veiling is a custom among both men and women in countless cultures and across thousands of years, in the eyes of many in the West, the veil has long been viewed as the quintessential emblem of Islam's "otherness." Europeans in particular have been obsessed with the veil ever since the erotic travelogues of Orientalist writers such as Gustave Flaubert and Sir Richard Burton made a fetish of the Muslim woman as a kind of Oriental femme fatale. That image took on new life in the writings of European colonialists like Alfred, Lord Cromer, the British consul general to Egypt, for whom the veil was a symbol of the "degradation of women" and definitive proof that "Islam as a social system has been a complete failure." Never mind that the colonial gentleman was also the founder of the Men's League for Opposing Women's Suffrage in England. Cromer had no interest in the plight of Muslim women per se; the veil was, for him, an icon of the "backwardness of Islam," and the most visible justification for Europe's "civilizing mission" in the Middle East.

In the modern world, the veil has become a symbol not only of the objectification of Muslim women, but also of the wide chasm of values and mores that many insist separates Islam and the West. Hence, the recently enacted laws prohibiting Muslim women from donning certain versions of the hijab in France and in other parts of Europe. Supporters of such bans argue that the veil is an affront to the Enlightenment principles upon which Europe was founded. They claim the veil is, by definition, anathema to the concept of women's liberation. As the French president Nicolas Sarkozy said in signing the ban into law, "In our country, we cannot accept that women be prisoners behind a screen, cut off from all social life, deprived of all identity." Of course, at the heart of this argument is the profoundly misogynistic belief that no Muslim woman would freely choose to wear the veil, that she must be forced into her hijab by her husband or her father or by the societal restrictions placed on her by her religion—that, in fact, Muslim women are incapable of deciding for themselves what they should or should not wear, so it must fall to the state to decide for them.

This is not to argue, as so many liberal Muslim reformers have, that the veil is in reality a symbol of Muslim women's empowerment, an argument made famous by the distinguished Iranian political philosopher Ali Shariati (1933–77) in his celebrated book *Fatima Is Fatima*. For Shariati and others like him, the veil is not a symbol of female oppression but rather a sign of empowered defiance against the Western image of womanhood. But enlightened as this perspective may be, it is still tragically flawed by the fact that Shariati is describing something of which he has had no experience.

The truth is that the traditional image of the veiled Muslim woman as the sheltered and docile sexual property of her husband is just as misleading and simpleminded as the postmodernist image of the veil as the emblem of female freedom and empowerment from Western cultural hegemony. The veil may be neither or both of these things, but that is solely up to Muslim women to decide for themselves. Whatever sartorial choices a woman makes are hers and hers alone. It is neither a man's nor the state's place to define proper "womanhood" in Islam. Those who treat the Muslim woman not as an individual but as a symbol either of Islamic chastity or secular liberalism are guilty of the same sin: the objectification of women.

That, in essence, is the foundation of the so-called Muslim women's movement, which is predicated on the idea that it is male-dominated society, not Islam, which has been responsible for the suppression of women's rights in so many Muslim-majority states. For this reason, Muslim feminists throughout the world are advocating a return to the society Muhammad originally envisioned for his followers. Despite differences in culture, nationalities, and beliefs, these women believe that the lesson to be learned from the Prophet Muhammad and the unprecedented rights and privileges he bestowed upon women in Medina is that Islam is above all an egalitarian religion. The feminist's Medina is a society in which Muhammad designated women like Umm Waraqa as spiritual guides for the Ummah; in which the Prophet himself was sometimes publicly rebuked by his wives; in which women prayed and fought alongside men; in which women like Aisha and Umm Salamah acted not only as religious but also as political—and on at least one occasion military—leaders; and in which the call to gather for prayer, bellowed from the rooftop of Muhammad's house, brought men and women together to kneel side by side, *without division*, and be blessed as a single united community.

So successful was this revolutionary experiment in social egalitari-anism that from 622 to 624 C.E. the Ummah multiplied rapidly, both from the addition of new Ansar in Medina and from the influx of new Emigrants eager to join in what was taking place in the City of the Prophet. Though, in truth, this was still only Yathrib. It could not properly be called Medina until after Muhammad turned his attention away from his egalitarian reforms and back toward the sacred city of Mecca and the powerful tribe that held Arabia in its grip.

4. Fight in the Way of God

THE MEANING OF JIHAD

IN YATHRIB, THE Messenger of God is dreaming. He stands in a wide meadow. Cattle graze freely on the grass. There is something in his hand: a sword, unsheathed and glistening in the sun. A notch has been etched into the blade. War is approaching. But there is calm in the peaceful meadow, among the grazing beasts, in the warm light. Everything seems a good omen. Looking down at his body, he sees he is clad in an invulnerable coat of mail. There is nothing to worry about. Sword in hand, he faces the immeasurable horizon, tall and confident, waiting for the fight to come to him.

When he wakes, Muhammad understands at once the meaning of the dream: the Quraysh are coming. What he cannot know, however, is that they are at that moment charging toward Yathrib with three thousand heavily armed warriors and two hundred cavalrymen to put an end to Muhammad and his movement once and for all. As is the custom, the soldiers are trailed by a small group of women, bejeweled and dressed in their finest tunics.

The women are led by a powerful and enigmatic woman named Hind, the wife of Abu Sufyan, the new Shaykh of Quraysh. A year earlier, in 624 C.E., when the Quraysh first clashed with Muhammad and his followers at Badr, Hind's brother and father had both been killed by Muhammad's uncle, Hamzah. Now, as she trudges through the desert grasping the hem of her flowing white tunic in two clenched fists, Hind serves as a physical reminder of why the Quraysh are finally bringing the battle for control of Arabia directly to Muhammad's doorstep.

"Quench my thirst for vengeance," she shouts at the men marching in front of her, "and quench your own!"

Meanwhile, Yathrib buzzes with rumors of the impending attack. The Jewish clans, who want no part of this battle between Muhammad and Mecca, secure themselves inside their fortification, while the Ummah begin to frantically collect what weapons and provisions they can find in preparation for the siege. At dawn, the call to prayer draws the entire community to the mosque, where Muhammad calmly confirms the rumors.

It is true that the Quraysh are charging toward Yathrib, he announces; but rather than go out to meet them in battle, Muhammad reveals his plans to stay put and wait for their enemies to come to him. He is convinced that the coat of mail he wore in his dream represented Yathrib's invulnerable defenses. If the Quraysh were truly foolish enough to attack this oasis, he proclaims, then the men will fight them in the streets and alleyways, while the women and children hurl stones at them from atop the palm trees.

His followers are skeptical about Muhammad's plan. They remember well the beating they gave the Quraysh a year ago at Badr. Though ridiculously outnumbered, Muhammad's small band had inflicted heavy casualties on the mighty Meccan army, forcing them to retreat in utter humiliation. Surely they would destroy them again in battle.

"O Messenger of God," they declare, "lead us out to our enemies so that they may not think we are too cowardly and weak to face them."

Their response confuses Muhammad, who had assumed his dream to be a message from God. But the more his men urge him to go out and meet the enemy, the more he wavers. Even his most trusted advisers are divided about what to do. Finally, exasperated by the debate and knowing a decision must be made, Muhammad stands and orders his coat of mail to be brought to him. They will face the Quraysh in the open desert.

With just a few hundred men and a handful of women—including Aisha and Umm Salamah, who almost always accompany him into battle—Muhammad sets off toward a plain situated a few miles northwest of Yathrib called Uhud, where he has heard the Quraysh have stopped to camp and plan their attack. At Uhud, he makes his way down into a gorge and sets his own camp on the opposite side of a dry riverbed, not far from the Meccan army. From here, he can make out the Quraysh's tents. He takes stock of their massive numbers and superior weapons. His heart sinks when sees hundreds of their horses and camels grazing in a nearby pasture. His men have managed to round up only two horses; they have no camels.

Falling back, Muhammad orders his followers to make camp and wait for daybreak. In the morning, as the sky begins to redden, he leaps atop a horse and surveys his troops one final time. Among the men, he sees children armed with swords, some on their tiptoes trying to blend in. He angrily pulls them out of line and sends them home to their families, though a few manage to escape detection and return to fight. He then places his archers on top of a mountain near his flank, ordering them to "hold firm to your position, so that we will not be attacked from your direction." To the rest of his men he shouts his final instructions: "Let no one fight until I command him to fight!" Then, as if sensing he has somehow violated the omens in his dream, he puts on a second coat of mail and orders his army to attack.

Almost immediately, the Quraysh are put to flight. Muhammad's archers release a steady hail of arrows onto the battlefield, protecting his meager troops and forcing the Meccan army to retreat from their positions. But as the Quraysh pull back, the archers—in direct violation of Muhammad's orders not to move from their position—run down the mountain to claim the booty left behind by the retreating army. It does not take long for the Quraysh to regroup, and with his flank unguarded, the Prophet and his warriors are quickly surrounded. The battle becomes a slaughter.

The massive Meccan army makes quick work of Muhammad's forces on the ground. The bodies of the dead litter the battlefield. As the Quraysh draw closer, some of Muhammad's men form a tight circle to shield him from the advancing army and the volley of arrows raining down on all sides. One by one the men fall at his feet, their bodies riddled with arrows, until only one man is left. Then he falls.

Now alone, Muhammad kneels beside his dead warriors and continues to fire his arrows blindly at the Quraysh until the bow snaps in his hands. He is defenseless and seriously wounded: his jaw cracked, his teeth broken, his lip split, his forehead cut and covered in blood. For a moment, he considers summoning what strength he has left and charging the enemy, when suddenly one of his men—a hefty warrior named Abu Dujanah—runs onto the battlefield, catches hold of him, and drags him into the mouth of the gorge, where the last of the survivors have gathered to attend their wounds.

The Prophet's sudden disappearance from the battlefield launches a rumor that he has been killed, and ironically, this is exactly the reprieve Muhammad's men need. For with news of his death, the Quraysh halt their assault and the battle is over. As the remnants of Muhammad's army quietly creep back toward Yathrib—bloodied and humiliated—the victorious Abu Sufyan climbs atop a hill and, raising his bowed sword in the air, cries: "Be exalted, Hubal! Be exalted!"

Afterward, when a sense of calm has settled upon Uhud, Hind and the rest of the women of Quraysh roam the battlefield mutilating the bodies of the dead, a common practice in pre-Islamic Arabia. The women cut off the noses and ears of Muhammad's fallen warriors so as to fashion necklaces and anklets from them. But Hind has a more urgent purpose. She separates from the rest to search the gorge for the body of Muhammad's uncle, Hamzah—the man who had killed her father and brother at Badr. Finding him at last, she kneels beside his corpse, rips open his body, pulls out his liver with her bare hands, and bites into it, thus completing her vengeance against the Messenger of God.

* * *

Islam has so often been portrayed, even by contemporary scholars, as "a military religion, [with] fanatical warriors, engaged in spreading their faith and their law by armed might," to quote historian Bernard Lewis, that the image of the Muslim horde charging wildly into battle like a swarm of locusts has become one of the most enduring stereotypes in the Western world. "Islam was never really a religion of salvation," wrote the eminent sociologist Max Weber. "Islam is a warrior religion." It is a religion that Samuel Huntington has portrayed as steeped "in bloody borders."

This deep-rooted stereotype of Islam as a warrior religion has its origins in the papal propaganda of the Crusades, when Muslims were depicted as the soldiers of the Antichrist in blasphemous occupation of the Holy Lands (and, far more importantly, of the silk route to China). In the Middle Ages, while Muslim philosophers, scientists, and mathematicians were preserving the knowledge of the past and determining the scholarship of the future, a belligerent and deeply fractured Holy Roman Empire tried to distinguish itself from the Turks who were strangling it from all sides by labeling Islam "the religion of the sword," as though there were in that era an alternative means of territorial expansion besides war. And as the European colonialists of the eighteenth and nineteenth centuries systematically plundered the natural resources of the Middle East and North Africa, inadvertently creating a rabid political and religious backlash that would produce what is now popularly called "Islamic fundamentalism," the image of the dreaded Muslim warrior, "clad in a long robe and brandishing his scimitar, ready to slaughter any infidel that might come his way," became a widely popular literary cliché. It still is.

Today, the traditional image of the Muslim horde has been more or less replaced by a new image: the Islamic terrorist, strapped with explosives, ready to be martyred for God, eager to take as many innocent people as possible with him. What has not changed, however, is the notion that Islam is a religion whose adherents have been embroiled in a perpetual state of holy war, or *jihad*, from the time of Muhammad to this very day.

Yet the doctrine of jihad, like so many doctrines in Islam, was not fully developed as an ideological expression until long after Muhammad's death, when Muslim conquerors began absorbing the cultures and practices of the Near East. Islam, it must be remembered, was born in an era of grand empires and global conquests, a time in which the Byzantines and Sasanians—both theocratic kingdoms—were locked in a permanent state of religious war for territorial expansion. The Muslim armies that spread out of the Arabian Peninsula simply joined in the existing fracas; they neither created it nor defined it, though they quickly dominated it. Despite the common perception in the West, the Muslim conquerors did not force conversion upon the conquered peoples; indeed, they did not even encourage it. The fact is that the financial and social advantages of being an Arab Muslim in the eighth and ninth centuries were such that Islam quickly became an élite clique, which a non-Arab could join only through a complex process that involved becoming first the client of an Arab.

This was also an era in which religion and the state were one unified entity. With the exception of a few remarkable men and women, no Jew, Christian, Zoroastrian, or Muslim of this time would have considered his or her religion to be rooted in the personal confessional experiences of individuals. Quite the contrary. Your religion was your ethnicity, your culture, and your social identity; it defined your politics, your economics, and your ethics. More than anything else, your religion was your *citizenship*. Thus, the Holy Roman Empire had its officially sanctioned and legally enforced version of Christianity, just as the Sasanian Empire had its officially sanctioned and legally enforced version of Zoroastrianism. In the Indian subcontinent, Vaisnava kingdoms (devotees of Vishnu and his incarnations) vied with Saiva kingdoms (devotees of Shiva) for territorial control, while in China, Buddhist rulers fought Taoist rulers for political ascendancy. Throughout every one of these regions, but especially in the Near East, where religion explicitly sanctioned the state, territorial expansion was identical to religious proselytization. Thus, *every* religion was a "religion of the sword."

As the Muslim conquerors set about developing the meaning and function of war in Islam, they had at their disposal the highly developed and imperially sanctioned ideals of religious warfare as defined and practiced by the Sasanian and Byzantine empires. In fact, the term "holy war" originates not with Islam but with the Christian Crusaders who first used it to give theological legitimacy to what was in reality a battle for land and trade routes. "Holy war" was not a term used by Muslim conquerors, and it is in no way a proper definition of the word *jihad*. There are a host of words in Arabic that can be definitively translated as "war"; *jihad* is not one of them.

The word *jihad* literally means "a struggle," "a striving," or "a great effort." In its primary religious connotation (sometimes referred to as "the greater jihad"), it means the struggle of the soul to overcome the sinful obstacles that keep a person from God. This is why the word *jihad* is nearly always followed in the Quran by the phrase "in the way of God." However, because Islam considers this inward struggle for holiness and submission to be inseparable from the outward struggle for the welfare of humanity, *jihad* has more often been associated with its secondary connotation ("the lesser jihad"): that is, any exertion—military or otherwise—against oppression and tyranny. And while this definition of *jihad* has occasionally been manipulated by militants and extremists to give religious sanction to what are in actuality social and political agendas, that is not at all how Muhammad understood the term.

War, according to the Quran, is either just or unjust; it is *never* "holy." Indeed, *jihad* should best be understood as a primitive "just war theory": a theory born out of necessity and developed in the midst of a bloody and often chaotic war that erupted in 624 C.E. between Muhammad's small but growing community and the all-powerful, ever-present Quraysh.

※※※

STRANGELY, THE QURAYSH seemed at first to be completely untroubled by the success of Muhammad's community in Yathrib. Certainly they were aware of what was taking place. The Quraysh preserved their dominant position in Arabia by maintaining spies throughout the peninsula; nothing that could endanger their authority or threaten their profits would have passed their notice. But while they may have been concerned with the growing number of his followers, as long as they remained confined to Yathrib, Mecca was content to forget all about Muhammad. Muhammad, however, was not willing to forget about Mecca.

Perhaps the greatest transformation that occurred in Yathrib was not in the traditional tribal system but in the Prophet himself. As the Revelation evolved from general statements about the goodness and power of God to specific legal and civil rules for constructing and maintaining a righteous and egalitarian society, so too did Muhammad's prophetic consciousness evolve. No longer was his message to be addressed solely to "the mother of cities [Mecca] and those who dwell around it" (6:92). The dramatic success of the Ummah in Yathrib had convinced Muhammad that God was calling him to be more than just a warner to his "tribe and close kin" (26:214). He now understood his role as being "a mercy to all the creatures of the world" (21:107) and the Messenger "to all of humanity" (12:104; 81:27).

Of course, no matter how popular or successful his community became, it could never hope to expand beyond the borders of Yathrib if the religious, economic, and social center of Arabia continued to oppose it. Eventually, Muhammad would have to confront and, if possible, convert the Quraysh to his side. But first, he had to get their attention.

Having learned in Mecca that the only effective way to confront the Quraysh was through their pocketbooks, Muhammad made the extraordinarily bold decision of declaring Yathrib to be a sanctuary city (*haram*). This declaration—formalized in the Constitution of Medina—meant that Yathrib could now conceivably become both a religious pilgrimage site and a legitimate trading center (the two being almost inseparable in ancient Arabia). This was not merely a financial decision. By declaring Yathrib a sanctuary city, Muhammad was deliberately challenging Mecca's religious and economic hegemony over the peninsula. And just to make sure the Quraysh got the message, he sent his followers out into the desert to take part in the time-honored Arab tradition of caravan raiding.

In pre-Islamic Arabia, caravan raiding was a legitimate means for small clans to benefit from the wealth of larger ones. It was in no way considered stealing, and as long as no violence occurred and no blood was shed, there was no need for retribution. The raiding party would quickly descend on a caravan—usually at its rear—and carry off whatever they could get their hands on before being discovered. These periodic raids were certainly a nuisance for the caravan leaders, but in general they were considered part of the innate hazards of transporting large amounts of goods through a vast and unprotected desert.

Though small and sporadic at first, Muhammad's raids not only provided the Ummah with desperately needed supplies, they also effectively disrupted the trade flowing in and out of Mecca. It wasn't long before caravans entering the sacred city began complaining to the Quraysh that they no longer felt safe traveling through the region. A few caravans even chose to detour to Yathrib instead to take advantage of the security Muhammad and his men were assuring. Trade began to dwindle in Mecca, profits were lost, and Muhammad finally got the attention he was seeking.

In 624, a full year before the disastrous defeat at Uhud, Muhammad received news that a large caravan was making its way to Mecca from Palestine, the sheer size of which made it too tempting to ignore. Summoning a band of three hundred volunteers—mostly Emigrants— he set out to raid it. But as his group arrived outside the city of Badr, they were suddenly confronted by a thousand Qurayshi warriors. Muhammad's plans had been leaked to Mecca, and now the Quraysh were ready to give his small band of insurgents a lesson they would not forget.

For days the two armies surveyed each other from opposite sides of a sizable valley: the Quraysh arrayed in white tunics, straddling ornately painted horses and tall, brawny camels; the Ummah, dressed in rags and prepared for a raid, not a war. In truth, neither side seemed eager for a fight. The Quraysh probably assumed their overwhelming numbers would elicit immediate surrender or, at the very least, contrition. And Muhammad, who must have known that fighting the Quraysh under these circumstances would result not only in his own death, but in the end of the Ummah, was anxiously awaiting instructions from God.

"O God," he kept praying, "if this band of people perishes, you will no longer be worshipped."

There was something more to Muhammad's reluctance at Badr than fear of annihilation. Although he had known for some time that his message could not expand outside Arabia without the capitulation of the Quraysh, and while he must have recognized that such capitulation would not come without a fight, Muhammad understood that just as the Revelation had forever transformed the socioeconomic land-scape of pre-Islamic Arabia, so must it alter the methods and morals of pre-Islamic warfare.

It is not that Arabia was short on "rules of war." A host of regulations existed among the pagan tribes with regard to when and where fighting could take place. But for the most part these rules were meant to contain and limit fighting to ensure the tribe's survival, not to establish a code of conduct in warfare. In the same way that absolute morality did not play a significant role in tribal concepts of law and order, neither did it play a role in tribal notions of war and peace.

The doctrine of jihad, as it slowly developed in the Quran, was specifically meant to differentiate between pre-Islamic and Islamic notions of warfare, and to infuse the latter with what Mustansir Mir calls an "ideological-cum-ethical dimension" that, until that point, did not exist in the Arabian Peninsula. At the heart of the doctrine of jihad was the heretofore unrecognized distinction between combatant and noncombatant. Thus, the killing of women, children, monks, rabbis, the elderly, or any other noncombatant was absolutely forbidden under any circumstances. Muslim law eventually expanded on these prohibitions to outlaw the torture of prisoners of war; the mutilation of the dead; rape, molestation, or any kind of sexual violence during combat; the killing of diplomats; the wanton destruction of property; and the demolition of religious or medical institutions—regulations that, many centuries later, would be incorporated into the modern international laws of war.

But perhaps the most important innovation in the doctrine of jihad was its outright prohibition of all but strictly defensive wars. "Fight in the way of God those who fight you," the Quran says, "but do not begin hostilities; God does not like the aggressor" (2:190). Elsewhere the Quran is more explicit: "Permission to fight is given *only to those who have been oppressed* . . . who have been driven from their homes for saying, 'God is our Lord' " (22:39; emphasis added).

It is true that some verses in the Quran instruct Muhammad and his followers to "slay the polytheists wherever you confront them" (9:5); to "carry the struggle to the hypocrites who deny the faith" (9:73); and, especially, to "fight those who do not believe in God and the Last Day" (9:29). However, it must be understood that these verses were directed specifically at the Quraysh and their clandestine partisans in Yathrib—specifically named in the Quran as "the poly-theists" and "the hypocrites," respectively—with whom the Ummah was locked in a terrible war.

Nevertheless, these verses have long been used by Muslims and non-Muslims alike to suggest that Islam advocates fighting unbeliev-ers until they convert. But this is not a view that either the Quran or Muhammad endorsed. This view was put forth during the height of the Crusades, and partly in response to them, by later generations of Islamic legal scholars who developed what is now referred to as "the classical doctrine of jihad": a doctrine that, among other things, parti-tioned the world into two spheres, the House of Islam (*dar al-Islam*) and the House of War (*dar al-Harb*), with the former in constant pur-suit of the latter.

As the Crusades drew to a close and Rome's attention turned away from the Muslim menace and toward the Christian reform move-ments cropping up throughout Europe, the classical doctrine of jihad was vigorously challenged by a new generation of Muslim scholars. The most important of these scholars was Ibn Taymiyya (1263–1328), whose influence in shaping Muslim ideology is matched only by St. Augustine's influence in shaping Christianity. Ibn Taymiyya argued that the idea of killing nonbelievers who refused to convert to Islam— the foundation of the classical doctrine of jihad—not only defied the example of Muhammad but also violated one of the most important principles in the Quran: that "there can be no compulsion in religion" (2:256). Indeed, on this point the Quran is adamant. "The truth is from your Lord," it says; "believe it if you like, or do not" (18:29). The Quran also asks rhetorically, "Can you compel people to believe against their will?" (10:100). Obviously not; the Quran therefore commands believers to say to those who do not believe, "To you your religion; to me mine" (109:6).

Ibn Taymiyya's rejection of the classical doctrine of jihad fueled the works of a number of Muslim political and religious thinkers in the eighteenth and nineteenth centuries. In India, Sayyid Ahmed Khan (1817–98) used Ibn Taymiyya's argument to claim that jihad could not be properly applied to the struggle for independence against British occupation because the British had not suppressed the religious freedom of India's Muslim community—a Quranic requirement for sanctioning jihad (as one can imagine, this was an unpopular argument in colonial India). Chiragh Ali (1844–95), a protégé of Ahmed Khan and one of the first Muslim scholars to push Quranic scholarship toward rational contextualization, argued that the modern Muslim community could not take Muhammad's historical Ummah as a legitimate example of how and when to wage war, because that community developed in a time when, as mentioned, the whole of the known world was in a state of permanent conflict. Early in the twentieth century, the Egyptian reformer Mahmud Shaltut (1897–1963) used Chiragh Ali's contextualization of the Quran to show that Islam outlaws not only wars that are not made in direct response to aggression, but also those that are not officially sanctioned by a qualified Muslim jurist, or *mujtahid*.

Over the last century, however, and especially after the colonial experience gave birth to a new kind of Islamic radicalism in the Middle East, the classical doctrine of jihad has undergone a massive resurgence in the pulpits and classrooms of a few prominent Muslim intellectuals. In Iran, the Ayatollah Khomeini (1902–89) relied on a militant interpretation of jihad, first to energize the anti-imperialist revolution of 1979 and then to fuel his destructive eight year war with Iraq. It was Khomeini's vision of jihad as a weapon of war that helped found the Islamic militant group Hizbullah, whose tactical use of the suicide bomber launched an appalling new era of international terrorism.

In Saudi Arabia, Abdullah Yusuf Azzam (1941–89), professor of Islamic philosophy at King Abdulaziz University, used his influence among the country's disaffected youth to promote an uncompromisingly belligerent interpretation of jihad that, he argued, was incumbent on all Muslims. "Jihad and the rifle alone," Dr. Azzam proclaimed to his students. "No negotiations, no conferences, and no dialogues." Azzam's views laid the foundations for the Palestinian militant group Hamas, which adopted Hizbullah's tactics in their resis-tance against the Israeli occupation. His teachings had an exceptional impact on one student in particular: Osama bin Laden, who eventually put into practice his mentor's ideology by calling for a worldwide Muslim campaign of jihad against the West, thus launching a horrifying wave of terrorism that has resulted in the deaths of thousands of innocent people.

The bloody terror organization that Osama bin Laden ultimately founded, al-Qaeda, is but one manifestation of a much larger movement of militant Islamic puritanism commonly called Jihadism (*jahadiyyah*). What makes Jihadism unique—indeed, what gives the movement its name—is its radical reinterpretation of the concept of jihad. What has for centuries been defined as a collective duty that can be waged solely in defense of life, faith, and property has, in Jihadism, been transformed into a radically individualistic obligation, totally divorced from any institutional power. In the hands of al-Qaeda and like-minded Jihadist organizations around the world, jihad has become an *offensive* weapon, one that can be wielded against all perceived "enemies" of Islam, whether Muslim or not. In fact, a recent report by the Combating Terrorism Center at West Point found that between 2004 and 2006, Muslims accounted for 85 percent of the casualties from al-Qaeda attacks (between 2006 and 2008, that number surged to 98 percent!). Women, children, the elderly, the sick, the lame—these are all legitimate targets according to Jihadism, regardless of the Quran's clear prohibition against harming noncombatants. That is why, despite common perception in the West, the actions of Jihadist groups like al-Qaeda have been so roundly condemned not only by the vast majority of the world's Muslims, but even by other militant groups like the Palestinian Hamas or Lebanon's Hizbullah.

The fact is that nearly one out of five people in the world are Muslims. And while some of them may share bin Laden's grievances against the Western powers, very few share his interpretation of jihad. Indeed, despite the ways in which this doctrine has been manipulated to justify either personal prejudices or political ideologies, jihad is neither a universally recognized nor a unanimously defined concept in the Muslim world. It is true that the struggle against injustice and tyranny is incumbent on all Muslims. After all, if there was no one to stand up to despots and tyrants, then, as the Quran states, our "monasteries, churches, synagogues, and mosques—places where the name of God is honored—would all be razed to the ground" (22:40).

But it is nevertheless solely as a *defensive* response to oppression and injustice, and only within the clearly outlined rules of ethical conduct in battle, that the Quranic vision of jihad is to be understood. For if, as political theorist Michael Walzer claims, the determining factor of a "just war" is the establishment of specific regulations covering both *jus in bello* (justice *in* war) and *jus ad bellum* (justice *of* war), then there can be no better way to describe Muhammad's doctrine of jihad than as an ancient Arabian "just war" theory.

The Battle of Badr, in 624 C.E., became the first opportunity for Muhammad to put this theory of jihad into practice. As the days passed and the two armies steadily inched closer to each other, Muhammad refused to fight until attacked. Even as the fighting began—in traditional Arab fashion, with hand-to-hand combat between two or three individuals from both sides, at the end of which the field was cleared and another set of individuals chosen to fight— Muhammad remained on his knees, waiting for a message from God. It was Abu Bakr who, having had enough of the Prophet's indecisiveness, finally urged him to rise and take part in the battle that, despite Muhammad's reluctance, had already begun.

"O Prophet of God," Abu Bakr said, "do not call upon your Lord so much; for God will assuredly fulfill what he has promised you."

Muhammad agreed. Rising to his feet, he finally called upon his small band of followers to trust in God and advance in full against the enemy.

What followed was a fierce skirmish that the Italian historian Francesco Gabrieli has called "hardly more than a brawl." A brawl it may have been, but when the fighting stopped and the battlefield was cleared of bodies, there was little doubt as to who had come out on top. Astonishingly, Muhammad had lost only a dozen men, while the Quraysh were thoroughly routed. News of the Prophet's victory over the largest and most powerful tribe in Arabia reached Yathrib long before the victors did. The Ummah was ecstatic. The Battle of Badr proved that God had blessed the Messenger. There were rumors that angels had descended onto the battlefield to slay Muhammad's enemies. After Badr, Muhammad was no longer a mere Shaykh or a Hakam; he and his followers were now the new political power in the

Hijaz. And Yathrib was no longer just an agricultural oasis, but the seat of that power: the City of the Prophet. Medina.

Badr had essentially created two opposing groups in Arabia: those who favored Muhammad and those who remained loyal to the Quraysh. Sides were chosen. Clan representatives from throughout the peninsula flooded into Medina to ally themselves with Muhammad, while at the same time a rush of Qurayshi loyalists abandoned Medina for Mecca. Interestingly, many of these loyalists were Hanifs who had refused to convert to Muhammad's movement despite its connection to "the religion of Abraham," primarily because their Hanifism necessitated allegiance to the Ka'ba and its keepers, the Quraysh.

However, neither the "reverse migration" from Medina to Mecca nor the defection of the Hanifs troubled Muhammad. He was concerned with a far more urgent matter: there was a traitor in Medina. Someone had informed the Quraysh of his plans to raid the caravan. And while there were many possibilities, Muhammad's suspicions fell at once upon the Banu Qaynuqa, one of the largest and wealthiest Jewish clans in the oasis. Acting on his suspicions, he besieged the Qaynuqa fortification for fifteen days until the clan finally surrendered.

Muhammad's fears about the Banu Qaynuqa's treachery may not have been unfounded. Most of the Jewish clans in Medina had vital commercial links with the Quraysh and wanted no part in what they assumed would become a protracted war between the two cities. Muhammad's presence in the oasis had already made things financially difficult for them. The political alliance between the Arab tribes and an increasingly powerful Muhammad had drastically eroded the power and authority of Medina's Jewish clans. The Banu Qaynuqa suffered especially from the Prophet's tax-free market, which had eradicated their economic monopoly over Medina and greatly reduced their wealth. A war with Mecca would only have worsened the situation of Medina's Jewish clans by permanently severing their economic ties to the Quraysh, who were, after all, the primary consumers of their dates, wines, and arms. Despite the victory at Badr, there was still no reason to believe that Muhammad could actually conquer the Quraysh. Eventually the Meccans would regroup and return to defeat the Prophet. And when that happened, it would be imperative for the Jewish clans to make their loyalties to the Quraysh absolutely clear.

After Badr, Muhammad was likewise deeply concerned with clarifying loyalties, and it was for this reason that he cemented the agreements of mutual protection in the oasis by formalizing the Constitution of Medina. This document, which Moshe Gil aptly calls "an act of preparation for war," made clear that the defense of Medina—or at the very least the sharing of the cost of such a defense—was the common responsibility of every inhabitant. And while the Constitution clarified the absolute religious and social freedom of Medina's Jewish clans, stating "to the Jews their religion and to the Muslims their religion," it nevertheless fully expected them to provide aid to "whoever wars against the people of this document." In short, the Constitution of Medina provided the means through which Muhammad could ascertain who was and who was not on his side. Therefore, when he suspected that the Qaynuqa had betrayed their oath of mutual protection and shown themselves to be against him, he was quick to act.

According to Arab tradition, the penalty for treason was clearly defined: the men were to be killed, the women and children sold into slavery, and their property dispersed as booty. This is precisely what everyone in Medina assumed would happen to the Banu Qaynuqa, including the Qaynuqa themselves. They were shocked, therefore, when Muhammad rejected traditional law and decided instead to exile the clan from Medina, even going so far as to allow them to take most of their property with them. It was a magnanimous decision on Muhammad's part, one that was in many ways pressed upon him by his Medinan allies who did not wish to have the blood of their clients on their hands. But it was a decision he would be forced to make again a year later, after the disastrous defeat of his overconfident army at Uhud.

The Battle of Uhud crushed the morale of the Ummah. More importantly, it seemed to confirm the expectations of Medina's Jewish clans, who reasoned that it would only be a matter of time before the Quraysh were victorious over Muhammad. The Banu Nadir and the Banu Qurayza, the two most dominant Jewish clans left in the oasis,

were especially delighted by the outcome of Uhud. In fact, the Banu
Nadir, whose Shaykh had met secretly with the Quraysh's leader, Abu
Sufyan, before the battle, tried to capitalize on Muhammad's weakness
by assassinating him. But even before he had recovered from his battle
wounds, Muhammad discovered the plot and, just as he had done with
the Qaynuqa, rushed what was left of his battered army to besiege the
fortress of the Nadir. When the clan appealed to their fellow Jews for
help, the Shaykh of Banu Qurayza, Ka'b ibn Asad, made it clear they
were on their own. With this reply, the Nadir had no choice but to
surrender to Muhammad, but only on the condition that they be
given the same opportunity as the Banu Qaynuqa to lay down their
arms and leave Medina in peace. Again, to the utter disgust of his followers, many of whom had been seriously wounded in the battle,
Muhammad agreed. The Banu Nadir left Medina for Khaybar, taking
their wealth and property with them.

After Uhud, the skirmishes between Mecca and Medina continued for two more years. These were bloody times rife with secret
negotiations, clandestine assassinations, and horrific acts of violence
on both sides. Finally, in 627 C.E., the Quraysh, having tired of the
ongoing conflict, formed a massive coalition of Bedouin fighters and
headed one last time for Medina, hoping to put a definitive end to the
protracted war. This time, however, Muhammad decided to wait for
the Quraysh to come to him. In an innovative military tactic that
would be copied for centuries to come, he instructed his followers to
dig a trench around Medina, from inside which he was able to defend
the oasis indefinitely. After nearly a month of trying to overcome this
ingenious trench defense, the Quraysh and their large Bedouin coalition gave up and returned home, exhausted and out of supplies.

While this was far from a victory for Muhammad, he could not
have been displeased with the outcome, especially considering how
poorly the Battle of Uhud had gone. There wasn't much fighting; very
few people died on either side. In reality, not much happened. But the
Battle of the Trench, as it came to be known, is famous not for what
occurred during the fight, but for what happened afterward.

During the month-long siege, while the Medinan army struggled
to keep the Meccan invaders at bay, the Banu Qurayza—now the
largest Jewish clan in the oasis—openly and actively supported the

forces of the Quraysh, going so far as to provide them with weapons and supplies. Why the Qurayza would so openly have betrayed Muhammad is impossible to say. The brazenness with which they pursued negotiations with the Bedouin coalition—even while the battle was raging around them—indicates they may have thought this was the end of Muhammad's movement and wanted to be on the right side when the dust settled. Even if Muhammad won the battle, the Qurayza probably assumed that at worst they would be exiled from Medina like the Qaynuqa and the Nadir, the latter already thriving among the large Jewish population of Khaybar. But Muhammad's generosity had been pushed to its limit, and he was no longer in the mood for clemency.

For more than a month, he kept the Qurayza inside their fortress while he deliberated with his advisers about what to do. In the end, he turned to Arab tradition. This was a dispute; it could be settled only through the arbitration of a Hakam. But because this dispute involved Muhammad—who was obviously not a neutral party—the role of arbiter fell to Sa'd ibn Mu'adh, the Shaykh of the Aws.

On the surface, it seemed Sa'd was anything but a neutral party. After all, the Banu Qurayza were clients of the Aws and so, technically, fell under Sa'd's direct protection. This may have been why the Qurayza were so eager to accept him as Hakam. But when Sa'd came out of his tent, where he had been recovering from his battle wounds, his decision was the clearest sign yet that the old social order no longer applied.

"I pass judgment on them," Sa'd declared, "that their fighters shall be killed and their children [and wives] made captives and that their property shall be divided."

UNDERSTANDABLY, THE EXECUTION of the Banu Qurayza has received a great deal of scrutiny from scholars of all disciplines. Heinrich Graetz, writing in the nineteenth century, painted the event as a barbarous act of genocide reflecting Islam's inherently anti-Jewish sentiments. S. W. Baron's *Social and Religious History of the Jews* somewhat fantastically likened the Banu Qurayza to the rebels of Masada—the legendary Jews who heroically chose mass suicide over submission to the Romans in 72 C.E. Early in the twentieth century, a number of Orientalist scholars pointed to this episode in Islamic history as proof that Islam was a violent and backward religion. In his masterwork, *Muhammad and the Conquests of Islam*, Francesco Gabrieli claimed that Muhammad's execution of the Qurayza reaffirms "our consciousness as Christian and civilized men, that this God, or at least this aspect of Him, is not ours."

In response to these accusations, some Muslim scholars have done considerable research to prove that the execution of the Banu Qurayza never happened, at least not in the way it has been recorded. Both Barakat Ahmad and W. N. Arafat, for example, have noted that the story of the Qurayza is not only inconsistent with Quranic values and Islamic precedent, but is based upon highly dubious and contradictory accounts derived from Jewish chroniclers who wished to portray the Qurayza as heroic martyrs of God.

In recent years, contemporary scholars of Islam, arguing that Muhammad's actions cannot be judged according to our modern ethical standards, have striven to place the execution of the Qurayza in its historical context. Karen Armstrong, in her beautiful biography of the Prophet, notes that the massacre, while revolting to a contemporary audience, was neither illegal nor immoral according to the tribal ethic of the time. Likewise, Norman Stillman, in his *The Jews of Arab Lands*, argues that the fate of the Banu Qurayza was "not unusual according to the harsh rules of war during that period." Stillman goes on to write that the fact that no other Jewish clan in Medina either objected to Muhammad's actions or attempted to intervene in any way on behalf of the Qurayza is proof that the Jews themselves considered this event "a tribal and political affair of the traditional Arabian kind."

And yet, even Armstrong and Stillman continue to advocate the enduring view that the execution of the Qurayza, while understandable for historical and cultural reasons, was nonetheless the tragic result of a deeply rooted ideological conflict between the Muslims and Jews of Medina, a conflict that can still be observed in the modern Middle East. The Swedish scholar Tor Andrae most clearly encapsulates this view, arguing that the execution was the result of Muhammad's belief "that the Jews were the sworn enemies of Allah and His revelation. [Therefore] any mercy toward them was out of the question."

But Andrae's view, and the views of so many others who agree with him, is at best ignorant of Muslim history and religion and at worst bigoted and obtuse. The fact is that the execution of the Banu Qurayza, while undeniably a dreadful event, was neither an act of genocide nor part of some comprehensive anti-Jewish agenda on the part of Muhammad. And it most certainly was not the result of an entrenched and innate religious conflict between Islam and Judaism. Nothing could be further from the truth.

To begin with, the Banu Qurayza were not executed for being Jews. As Michael Lecker has demonstrated, a significant number of the Banu Kilab—*Arab* clients of the Qurayza who allied with them as an auxiliary force outside Medina—were also executed for treason. And while reports of the total number of men who were killed vary from 400 to 700 (depending on the source), the highest estimates still represent no more than a tiny fraction of the total population of Jews who resided in Medina and its environs. Even if one excludes the Qaynuqa and Nadir clans, thousands of Jews still remained in the oasis, living amicably alongside their Muslim neighbors for many years after the execution of the Qurayza. Only under the leadership of Umar near the end of the seventh century C.E. were the remaining Jewish clans in Medina expelled—peacefully—as part of a larger Islamization process throughout the Arabian Peninsula. Describing the death of only slightly more than one percent of Medina's Jewish population as a "genocidal act" is not only a preposterous exaggeration, it is an affront to the memory of those millions of Jews who truly have suffered the horrors of genocide.

Second, as scholars almost unanimously agree, the execution of the Banu Qurayza did not in any way set a precedent for future treatment of Jews in Islamic territories. On the contrary, Jews throve under Muslim rule, especially after Islam expanded into Byzantine lands, where Orthodox rulers routinely persecuted both Jews and non-Orthodox Christians for their religious beliefs, often forcing them to convert to Imperial Christianity under penalty of death. In contrast, Muslim law, which considers Jews and Christians "protected peoples" (*dhimmi*), neither required nor encouraged their conversion to Islam. (Pagans and polytheists, however, were often given a choice between conversion and death.)

Muslim persecution of the dhimmi was not only forbidden by Islamic law, it was in direct defiance of Muhammad's orders to his expanding armies never to trouble Jews in their practice of Judaism, and always to preserve the Christian institutions they encountered. Thus, when Umar ordered the demolition of a mosque in Damascus that had been illegally constructed by forcibly expropriating the house of a Jew, he was merely following the Prophet's warning that "he who wrongs a Jew or a Christian will have me as his accuser on the Day of Judgment."

In return for a special "protection tax" called *jizyah*, Muslim law allowed Jews and Christians both religious autonomy and the opportunity to share in the social and economic institutions of the Muslim world. Nowhere was this tolerance more evident than in medieval Spain—the supreme example of Muslim, Jewish, and Christian cooperation—where Jews especially were able to rise to the highest positions in society and government. Indeed, one of the most powerful men in all of Muslim Spain was a Jew named Hasdai ibn Shaprut, who for many decades served as the trusted vizier to the Caliph, Abd al-Rahman III. It is no wonder, then, that Jewish documents written during this period refer to Islam as "an act of God's mercy."

Of course, even in Muslim Spain there were periods of intolerance and religious persecution. Moreover, Islamic law did prohibit Jews and Christians from openly proselytizing their faith in public places. But, as Maria Menocal notes, such prohibitions affected Christians more than they did Jews, who have been historically disinclined toward both proselytizing and public displays of their religious rituals. This may explain why Christianity gradually disappeared in most of the Islamic lands, while Jewish communities increased and prospered. In any case, even during the most oppressive periods in Islamic history, Jews under Muslim rule received far better treatment and had far greater rights than when they were under Christian rule. It is no accident that a few months after Muslim Spain fell to Ferdinand's Christian armies in 1492, most of Spain's Jews were summarily expelled from the realm. The Inquisition took care of those who remained.

Finally, and most importantly, the execution of the Banu Qurayza was not, as it has so often been presented, reflective of an intrinsic religious conflict between Muhammad and the Jews. This theory, which is sometimes presented as an incontestable doctrine in both Islamic and Judaic studies, is founded on the belief that Muhammad, who considered his message to be a continuation of the Judeo-Christian prophetic tradition, came to Medina fully expecting the Jews to confirm his identity as a prophet. Supposedly, to facilitate the Jews' acceptance of his prophetic identity, Muhammad connected his community to theirs by adopting a number of Jewish rituals and practices. To his surprise, however, the Jews not only rejected him but strenuously argued against the authenticity of the Quran as divine revelation. Worried that the rejection of the Jews would somehow discredit his prophetic claims, Muhammad had no choice but to turn violently against them, separate his community from theirs, and, in the words of F. E. Peters, "refashion Islam as an alternative to Judaism."

There are two problems with this theory. First, it fails to appreciate Muhammad's own religious and political acumen. It is not as though the Prophet were an ignorant Bedouin worshipping the elements or bowing before slabs of stone. This was a man who, for nearly half a century, had lived in the religious capital of the Arabian Peninsula, where he was a sophisticated merchant with firm economic and cultural ties to both Jewish and Christian tribes. It would have been ridiculously naïve for Muhammad to assume that his prophetic mission would be "as obvious to the Jews as it was to him," to quote Montgomery Watt. He would need only have been familiar with the most rudimentary doctrine of Judaism to know that they would not have necessarily accepted his identity as one of their prophets. Certainly he was aware that the Jews did not recognize Jesus as a prophet; why would he have assumed they would recognize him as such?

But the most glaring problem with this theory is not how little credit it gives to Muhammad, but how much credit it gives to Medina's Jews. As mentioned, the Jewish clans in Medina—themselves Arab converts—were barely distinguishable from their pagan counterparts either culturally or, for that matter, religiously. This was not a particularly literate group. The Arabic sources describe Medina's Jewish clans as speaking a language of their own called *ratan*, which al-Tabari claims was Persian but which was probably a hybrid of Arabic and Aramaic. There is no evidence that they either spoke or understood Hebrew. Indeed, their knowledge of the Hebrew Scriptures was likely limited to just a few scrolls of law, some prayer books, and a handful of fragmentary Arabic translations of the Torah—what S. W. Baron refers to as a "garbled, oral tradition."

So limited was their knowledge of Judaism that some scholars do not believe them to have been genuinely Jewish. D. S. Margoliouth considers the Jews of Medina to have been little more than a loose band of monotheists—not unlike the Hanifs—who should more properly be termed "Rahmanists" (*Rahman* being an alternative title for Allah). While many disagree with Margoliouth's analysis, there are other reasons to question the extent to which Medina's Jewish clans would have identified themselves with the Jewish faith. Consider, for example, that by the sixth century C.E., there was, as noted by H. G. Reissener, complete agreement among Diaspora Jewish communities that a non-Israelite could be considered a Jew only if he was "a follower of the Mosaic Law . . . in accordance with the principles laid down in the Talmud." Such a restriction would immediately have ruled out Medina's Jewish clans, who were not Israelites, and who neither strictly observed Mosaic law nor seemed to have any real knowledge of the Talmud. Moreover, there is a conspicuous absence in Medina of what should be easily identifiable archeological evidence of a significant Jewish presence. According to Jonathan Reed, certain archeological indicators—such as the remnants of stone vessels, the ruins of immersion pools (*miqva'ot*), and the interment of ossuaries—*must* be present at a site in order to confirm the existence there of an established Jewish religious identity. As far as we know, none of these indicators have been unearthed in Medina.

Naturally, there are those who continue to assert the religious identity of Medina's Jewish clans. Gordon Newby, for example, thinks Medina's Jews may have comprised distinct communities with their own schools and books, though no archeological evidence exists to confirm this hypothesis. In any case, even Newby admits that with regard to their culture, ethics, and even their religion, Medina's Jews were not only quite different from other Jewish communities in the Arabian Peninsula, they were practically identical to Medina's pagan community, with whom they freely interacted and (against Mosaic law) frequently intermarried.

Simply put, the Jewish clans of Medina were in no way a religiously observant group; they may not even have been Jews, if Margoliouth and others are correct. So it is highly doubtful that they would have engaged in complex polemical debates with Muhammad over the Quran's correlation to Hebrew Scriptures that they neither could read, nor likely even owned.

The fact is that nothing Muhammad either said or did would necessarily have been objectionable to Medina's Jews. As Newby writes in *A History of the Jews of Arabia*, Islam and Judaism in seventh-century Arabia operated within "the same sphere of religious discourse," in that both shared the same religious characters, stories, and anecdotes, both discussed the same fundamental questions from similar perspectives, and both had nearly identical moral and ethical values. Where there was disagreement between the two faiths, Newby suggests it was "over interpretation of shared topics, not over two mutually exclusive views of the world." To quote S. D. Goiten, there was simply "nothing repugnant to the Jewish religion in Muhammad's preaching."

Even Muhammad's claim to be the Prophet and Apostle of God, on the model of the great Jewish patriarchs, would not necessarily have been unacceptable to Medina's Jews. Not only did his words and actions correspond perfectly to the widely accepted pattern of Arabian Jewish mysticism, but Muhammad was not even the only person in Medina making these kinds of prophetic claims. Medina was also the home of a Jewish mystic and Kohen named Ibn Sayyad, who, like Muhammad, wrapped himself in a prophetic mantle, recited divinely inspired messages from heaven, and called himself "the Apostle of God." Remarkably, not only did most of Medina's Jewish clans accept Ibn Sayyad's prophetic claims, but the sources depict Ibn Sayyad as openly acknowledging Muhammad as a fellow apostle and prophet.

It would be simplistic to argue that no polemical conflict existed between Muhammad and the Jews of his time. But this conflict had far more to do with political alliances and economic ties than with a theological debate over scripture. This was a conflict fueled primarily by tribal partnerships and tax-free markets, not religious zeal. And while Muhammad's biographers like to present him as debating theology with belligerent groups of "rabbis" who show "hostility to the apostle in envy, hatred, and malice, because God had chosen His apostle from the Arabs," the similarities in both the tone and manner of these events and the stories of the quarrels Jesus had with the Pharisees points to their function as literary *topoi*, not historical fact. Indeed, scholars have for centuries been aware of the intentional connection the early Muslims tried to draw between Jesus and Muhammad in an attempt to connect the mission and message of the two prophets.

Bear in mind, Muhammad's biographies were written at a time when the Jewish minority in the Muslim state was Islam's only remaining theological rival. It is not surprising, therefore, that Muslim historians and theologians would have buttressed their arguments against the rabbinical authorities of their time by planting their words in Muhammad's mouth. If Muhammad's biographies reveal anything at all, it is the anti-Jewish sentiments of the Prophet's biographers, not of the Prophet himself. To understand Muhammad's actual beliefs regarding the Jews and Christians of his time, one must look not to the words that chroniclers put into his mouth hundreds of years after his death, but rather to the words that God put into his mouth while he was alive.

The Quran, as a holy and revealed scripture, repeatedly reminds Muslims that what they are hearing is not a new message but the "confirmation of previous scriptures" (12:111). In fact, the Quran proposes the unprecedented notion that *all* revealed scriptures are derived from a single concealed book in heaven called the *Umm al-Kitab*, or "Mother of Books" (13:39). That means that as far as Muhammad understood, the Torah, the Gospels, and the Quran must be read as a single, cohesive narrative about humanity's relationship to God, in which the prophetic consciousness of one prophet is passed spiritually to the next: from Adam to Muhammad. For this reason, the Quran advises Muslims to say to the Jews and Christians:

> We believe in God, and in that which has been revealed to us, which is that
> which was revealed to Abraham and Ismail and
> Jacob and the tribes [of Israel], as well as that which the Lord
> revealed to Moses and to Jesus and to all the other Prophets.
> We make no distinction between any of them;
> we submit ourselves to God. (3:84)

Of course, Muslims believe that the Quran is the final revelation in this sequence of scriptures, just as they believe Muhammad to be "the Seal of the Prophets." But the Quran never claims to annul the previous scriptures, only to complete them. And while the notion of one scripture giving authenticity to others is, to say the least, a remarkable event in the history of religions, the concept of the Umm al-Kitab may indicate an even more profound principle.

As the Quran suggests over and over again, and as the Constitution of Medina explicitly affirms, Muhammad may have understood the concept of the Umm al-Kitab to mean not only that the Jews, Christians, and Muslims shared a single divine scripture but also that they constituted a single divine Ummah. As far as Muhammad was concerned, the Jews and the Christians were "People of the Book" (*ahl al-Kitab*), spiritual cousins who, as opposed to the pagans and polytheists of Arabia, worshipped the same God, read the same scriptures, and shared the same moral values as his Muslim community. Although each faith comprised its own distinct religious community (its own individual Ummah), together they formed one united Ummah, an extraordinary idea that Mohammed Bamyeh calls "monotheistic pluralism." Thus, the Quran promises that "all those who believe— the Jews, the Sabians, the Christians—*anyone who believes in God and the Last Days, and who does good deeds*, will have nothing to fear or regret" (5:69; emphasis added).

It was this conviction of the existence of a unified, monotheistic Ummah that led Muhammad to connect his community to the Jews, not that he felt the need to emulate the Jewish clans, nor that he wanted to facilitate their acceptance of him as a prophet. Muhammad aligned his community with the Jews in Medina because he considered them, as well as the Christians, to be part of his Ummah. Consequently, when he came to Medina, he made Jerusalem—the site of the Temple (long since destroyed) and the direction in which the Diaspora Jews turned during worship—the direction of prayer, or *qiblah*, for all Muslims. He imposed a mandatory fast upon his community, which was to take place annually on the tenth day (*Ashura*) of the first month of the Jewish calendar, the day more commonly known as Yom Kippur. He purposely set the day of Muslim congregation at noon on Friday so that it would coincide with, but not disrupt, Jewish preparations for the Sabbath. He adopted many of the Jewish dietary laws and purity requirements, and encouraged his followers to marry Jews, as he himself did (5:5–7).

And while it is true that after a few years, Muhammad both changed the *qiblah* from Jerusalem to Mecca, and set the annual fast at Ramadan (the month in which the Quran was first revealed) instead of Yom Kippur, these decisions should not be interpreted as "a break with the Jews," but as the maturing of Islam into its own independent religion. Despite the changes, Muhammad continued to encourage his followers to fast on Yom Kippur, and he never ceased to venerate Jerusalem as a holy city; indeed, after Mecca and Medina, Jerusalem is the most sacred city in the whole of the Muslim world. Moreover, the Prophet maintained most of the dietary, purity, and marriage restrictions he had adopted from the Jews. And until the day he died, Muhammad continued to engage in peaceful discourse—not theological debate—with the Jewish communities of Arabia, just as the Quran had commanded him to do: "Do not argue with the People of the Book—apart from those individuals who act unjustly toward you— unless it is in a fair way" (29:46). Muhammad's example must have had a lasting effect on his early followers: as Nabia Abbott has shown, throughout the first two centuries of Islam, Muslims regularly read the Torah alongside the Quran.

Certainly, Muhammad understood that there were distinct theological differences between Islam and the other Peoples of the Book. But he saw these differences as part of the divine plan of God, who could have created a single Ummah if he had wanted to but instead preferred that "every Ummah have its own Messenger" (10:47). Thus, to the Jews, God sent the Torah, "which contains guidance and light"; to the Christians, God sent Jesus, who "confirms the Torah"; and finally, to the Arabs, God sent the Quran, which "confirms the earlier revelations." In this way, the ideological differences among the Peoples of the Book is explained by the Quran as indicating God's desire to give each people its own "law and path and way of life" (5:42–48).

That being said, there were some theological differences that Muhammad considered to be intolerable innovations created by ignorance and error. Chief among these was the concept of the Trinity.

"God is one," the Quran states definitively. "God is eternal. He has neither begotten anyone, nor is he begotten of anyone" (112:1–3).

Yet this verse, and the many others like it in the Quran, is in no way a condemnation of Christianity *per se* but of Imperial Byzantine (Trinitarian) Orthodoxy, which, as noted, was neither the sole nor the dominant Christian position in the Arabian Peninsula. From the beginning of his ministry, Muhammad revered Jesus as the greatest of God's messengers. Much of the Gospel narrative is recounted in the Quran, though in a somewhat abridged version, including Jesus' virgin birth (3:47), his miracles (3:49), his identity as Messiah (3:45), and the expectation of his judgment over humanity at the end of time (4:159).

What the Quran does not accept, however, is the belief of those Orthodox Trinitarians who argued that Jesus was *himself* God. These Christians Muhammad did not even consider to be Peoples of the Book: "It is the unbeliever who says, 'God is the third of three,' " the Quran declares. "There is only God the One!" (5:73). It was Muhammad's belief that Orthodox Christians had corrupted the original message of Jesus, who the Quran contends never claimed divinity and never asked to be worshipped (5:116–18), but rather commanded his disciples to "worship God, who is my Lord and your Lord" (5:72).

At the same time, Muhammad lashed out at those Jews in Arabia who had "forsaken the community of Abraham" (2:130) and "who were trusted with the laws of the Torah, but who fail to observe them" (62:5). Again, this was not a condemnation of Judaism. The respect and reverence that Muhammad had for the great Jewish patriarchs is evidenced by the fact that almost every biblical prophet is mentioned in the Quran (Moses nearly one hundred and forty times!). Rather, Muhammad was addressing those Jews in the Arabian Peninsula—and only in the Arabian Peninsula—who had in both belief and practice "breached their covenant with God" (5:13). And, if the Jewish clans in Medina were any indication, there were many of them.

Muhammad's complaints in the Quran were not directed against the religions of Judaism and Christianity, which he considered to be nearly identical to Islam: "We believe in what has been revealed to us, just as we believe in what has been revealed to you [Jews and Christians]," the Quran says. "Our God and your God are the same; and it is to Him we submit" (29:46). His complaint was against those Jews and Christians he had encountered in Arabia who, in his opinion, had forsaken their covenant with God and perverted the teachings of the Torah and Gospels. These were unbelievers with whom the Quran warns Muslims not to ally themselves: "O believers, do not make friends with those who mock you and make fun of your faith. . . . Instead say to them: 'O People of the Book, why do you dislike us? Is it because we believe in God and in what has been sent down to us [the Quran], and what was sent down before that [the Torah and Gospels], while most of you are disobedient?' " (5:57–59).

The point is that when Muhammad reminded the Jews of Arabia of the "favors [God] bestowed on you, making you the most exalted nation in the world" (2:47), when he raged against the Christians for abandoning their faith and confounding the truth of their scriptures, when he complained that both groups "no longer follow the teachings of the Torah and the Gospel, and what has been revealed to them by their Lord" (5:66), he was merely following in the footsteps of the prophets who had come before him. He was, in other words, Isaiah calling his fellow Jews "a sinful nation, a people laden with iniquity, offspring of evildoers" (Isaiah 1:4); he was John the Baptist lashing out against "the brood of vipers" who assumed that their status as "sons of Abraham" would keep them safe from judgment (Luke 3:7–8); he was Jesus promising damnation for the hypocrites who "for the sake of tradition, have made void the word of God" (Matthew 15:6). After all, isn't this exactly the message a prophet is supposed to deliver?

It is no coincidence that just as they reversed many of Muhammad's social reforms aimed at empowering women, the Muslim scriptural and legal scholars of the following centuries rejected the notion that Jews and Christians were part of the Ummah, and instead designated both groups as unbelievers. These scholars reinterpreted the Revelation to declare that the Quran had superseded, rather than supplemented, the Torah and the Gospels, and called on Muslims to distinguish themselves from the People of the Book. This was largely an attempt to differentiate the nascent religion of Islam from other communities so it could establish its own religious independence, much as the early Christians gradually dissociated themselves from the Jewish practices and rituals that had given birth to their movement by demonizing the Jews as the killers of Jesus.

Nevertheless, the actions of these scriptural scholars were in direct defiance of Muhammad's example and the teachings of the Quran. For even though Muhammad recognized the theological differences that existed among the Peoples of the Book, he never called for a partitioning of the faiths. On the contrary, to those Jews who say "the Christians are wrong!" and to those Christians who say "the Jews are wrong!" (2:113), and to both groups who claim that "no one will go to heaven except the Jews and Christians" (2:111), Muhammad offered a compromise. "Let us come to an agreement on the things we hold in common," the Quran suggests: "that we worship none but God; that we make none God's equal; and that we take no other as lord except God" (3:64).

It is a tragedy that after fourteen hundred years, this simple compromise has yet to overcome the sometimes petty yet often binding ideological differences between the three faiths of Abraham.

AFTER THE BATTLE of the Trench, with Medina firmly in his control, Muhammad once again turned toward Mecca, not as the Messenger of God but as something the Quraysh in their role as Keepers of the Keys could not refuse: a pilgrim.

In 628, Muhammad unexpectedly announced that he was going to Mecca to perform the pilgrimage rites at the Ka'ba. Considering that he was in the middle of a bloody and protracted war with the Meccans, this was an absurd decision. He could not have thought the Quraysh, who had spent the past six years trying to kill him, would simply move out of the way while he and his followers circumambulated the sanctuary. But Muhammad remained undaunted. With more than a thousand of his followers marching behind him, he crossed the desert on his way to the city of his birth, shouting fearlessly along the way the pilgrim's chant: "Here I am, O Allah! Here I am!"

The sound of Muhammad and his followers, unarmed and dressed in pilgrim's clothes, loudly proclaiming their presence to their enemies, must have rung like a death knell in Mecca. Surely the end was near if this man could be so audacious as to think he could walk into the sacred city unmolested. The Quraysh, who rushed out to halt Muhammad before he could enter Mecca, were confounded. Meeting him just outside the city, in a place called Hudaybiyyah, they made one last attempt to preserve their control of Mecca by offering the Prophet a cease-fire, the conditions of which were so against Muhammad's interests that it must have appeared to the Muslims to be a joke.

The Treaty of Hudaybiyyah proposed that in return for his immediate withdrawal and the unconditional cessation of all caravan raids in the vicinity of Mecca, Muhammad would be allowed to return in the following pilgrimage season, when the sanctuary would be evacuated for a brief time so that he and his followers could perform the pilgrimage rites undisturbed. Adding insult to injury, Muhammad would be required to sign the treaty not as the Apostle of God but only as the tribal head of his community. Given Muhammad's rapidly growing position in the Hijaz, the treaty was preposterous; more than anything, it demonstrated the certainty of Mecca's impending defeat. Perhaps that is why Muhammad's followers, who sensed victory lingering only a few kilometers in front of them, were so incensed when the Prophet actually accepted the terms.

Umar—ever the impetuous one—could barely contain himself. He jumped up and went to Abu Bakr. "Abu Bakr," he asked, pointing to Muhammad, "is he not the Messenger of God?"

"Yes," Abu Bakr replied.

"And are we not Muslims?"

"Yes."

"And are they not polytheists?"

"Yes."

At this Umar shouted, "Then why should we grant what is detrimental to our religion?"

Abu Bakr, who probably felt the same way, replied with the only words in which he could take solace: "I bear witness that he is the Messenger of God."

It is difficult to say why Muhammad accepted the Treaty of Hudaybiyyah. He may have been hoping to regroup and wait for an opportune time to return and conquer Mecca by force. He may have been observing the Quranic mandate to "fight until oppression ends and God's law prevails. But if [the enemy] desists, then you must also cease hostilities" (2:193). Whatever the case, the decision to accept the cease-fire and return the following year turned out to be the most decisive moment in the battle between Mecca and Medina. For when ordinary Meccans saw the respect and devotion with which their supposed enemy and his band of "religious zealots" entered their city and circled the Ka'ba, there seemed little incentive to continue supporting the war. Indeed, a year after that pilgrimage, in 630 C.E., after Muhammad interpreted a skirmish between the Quraysh and some of his followers as a breach of the cease-fire, he marched once more toward Mecca, this time with ten thousand men behind him, only to find the city's inhabitants welcoming him with open arms.

After accepting Mecca's surrender, Muhammad declared a general amnesty for most of his enemies, including those he had fought in battle. Despite the fact that tribal law now made the Quraysh his slaves, Muhammad declared all of Mecca's inhabitants (including its slaves) to be free. Only six men and four women were put to death for various crimes, and no one was forced to convert to Islam, though everyone had to take an oath of allegiance never again to wage war against the Prophet. Among the last of the Quraysh to take that oath were its Shaykh, Abu Sufyan, and his wife, Hind, who, even as she formally converted to Islam, remained proudly defiant, barely masking her disgust with Muhammad and his "provincial" faith.

When this business was complete, the Prophet made his way to the Ka'ba. With the help of his cousin and son-in-law, Ali, he lifted the heavy veil covering the sanctuary door and entered the sacred interior. One by one, he carried the idols out before the assembled crowd and, raising them over his head, smashed them to the ground. The various depictions of gods and prophets, such as that of Abraham holding divining rods, were all washed away with Zamzam water; all, that is, except for the one of Jesus and his mother, Mary. This image the Prophet put his hands over reverently, saying, "Wash out all except what is beneath my hands."

Finally, Muhammad brought out the idol representing the great

Syrian god, Hubal. As Abu Sufyan watched, the Prophet unsheathed his sword and hacked the idol into pieces, forever ending the worship of pagan deities at Mecca. The remains of Hubal's statue Muhammad used as a doorstep leading up to the new, sanctified Ka'ba, the sanctuary that would henceforth be known as "the House of God," the seat of a wholly new and universal faith: Islam.

5. The Rightly Guided Ones

THE SUCCESSORS TO MUHAMMAD

A STIRRING AT THE rear of the congregation, and every head turns to see Muhammad emerge from Aisha's apartment to stand in the courtyard of the mosque just as the Friday prayers begin. It has been some time since anyone has seen him out of doors. Rumors about his health have been circulating throughout Medina for weeks. During his long absence, Abu Bakr has been leading the Friday services, while the rest of the Companions have kept busy leading expeditions, managing the state, dispensing the tithes, and instructing new converts in the ethics and rituals of the Muslim faith. No one would give voice to what everyone was thinking: the Messenger is dying; he may already be dead.

The year is 632 C.E. Two years have passed since Muhammad walked triumphantly into Mecca and cleansed the Ka'ba in the name of the one God. At that time, he was a robust man at the peak of his political and spiritual power, unquestionably the most dominant leader in Arabia. Ironically, the movement that had begun as an attempt to reclaim the tribal ethic of Arabia's nomadic past had, in many ways, struck the final dagger into the traditional tribal system. Soon there will be only the Muslim community, the enemies of the Muslim community (including the Byzantine and Sasanian empires), the client tribes of the Muslim community, and the dhimmi (Christians, Jews, and other non-Muslims, protected by the Muslim community). Yet despite the enormous power that accompanied his defeat of the Quraysh, Muhammad refused to replace the Meccan aristocracy with a Muslim monarchy; he would be the Keeper of the Keys, but he would not be the King of Mecca. Thus, once the administrative affairs had been settled and delegations—both military and diplomatic—dispatched to inform the rest of the Arab tribes of the new political order in the Arabian Peninsula, Muhammad did something completely unexpected: he went back home to Medina.

Muhammad's return to Medina was meant to acknowledge the Ansar, the "helpers" who had provided him with refuge and protection when no one else would. But it was also a statement to the entire community that while Mecca was now the heart of Islam, Medina would forever be its soul.

It is in Medina that deputations will gather from all over the Peninsula with their pledge that "there is no god but God" (though as we shall see, for many, this oath is addressed not so much to God as to Muhammad). It is in Medina that the pillars of the Muslim faith and the foundations of Muslim government will be constructed and debated. And it is in Medina that the Prophet will breathe his last.

But now, the sight of Muhammad standing at the entrance of the mosque, a smile wrinkling his bronzed face, dispels all those anxious rumors about his health. He looks lean, but surprisingly hearty for a man of his age. The long back hair he keeps twisted into plaits is thin and silver. His back bows a bit and his shoulders droop. But his face is as radiant as ever, and his eyes still smolder with the light of God.

When Abu Bakr catches sight of Muhammad shuffling between the seated bodies, grasping the shoulders of friends for support, he immediately rises from the *minbar*—the elevated seat that serves as the pulpit in mosques—to allow the Prophet to take his rightful place at the head of the congregation. But Muhammad signals to his old friend to remain seated and continue with the service. The prayers resume, and Muhammad finds a quiet corner in which to sit down. He wraps his cloak tightly around his body and watches his community pray together in the manner he had taught them to so many years ago: moving as one body and speaking with one voice.

He does not stay long. Before the congregation disperses, Muhammad stands and quietly makes his way out of the mosque and back to Aisha's room, where he collapses on the bed. Even this short trip to the mosque has weakened him. He has trouble catching his breath. He calls for his beloved wife.

When Aisha finally arrives, Muhammad is barely conscious. She quickly clears the room of people and drapes the doors for privacy. She sits beside her husband and places his head on her lap, gently stroking his long hair, whispering soothing words to him as his eyes flicker, then slowly close.

News of Muhammad's death spreads rapidly through Medina. For most, it is inconceivable that the Messenger of God could have died. Umar, for one, refuses to believe it. He is so distraught that he immediately runs to the mosque, where the community has gathered for news, and threatens to pummel anyone who dares say Muhammad is dead.

It is up to Abu Bakr to calm the situation. After seeing Muhammad's corpse with his own eyes, he too goes to the mosque. There, he sees Umar rambling incoherently about the Prophet still being alive. He only appears to be dead, Umar bellows. He has been taken to heaven, like Moses; he will return shortly.

"Gently, Umar," Abu Bakr says, stepping to the front of the mosque. "Be quiet!"

But Umar will not be silenced. In a firm voice, he warns those who have accepted Muhammad's death that they will have their hands and feet cut off for their disloyalty when the Prophet returns from heaven.

Finally, Abu Bakr can take no more. He raises his hands over the congregation and shouts over Umar, "O men, if anyone worships Muhammad, Muhammad is dead; if anyone worships God, God is alive, immortal!"

When Umar hears these words, he crumples to the ground and weeps.

* * *

Part of the reason for the community's anxiety over Muhammad's death was that he had done so little to prepare them for it. He had made no formal statement about who should replace him as leader of the Ummah; or even what kind of leader that person should be. Perhaps he was awaiting a Revelation that never came; perhaps he wanted the Ummah to decide for themselves who should succeed him. Or perhaps, as some were whispering, the Prophet *had* appointed a successor, someone whose rightful place at the head of the community was being obscured by the internecine power struggles already beginning to take place among the Muslim leadership.

Meanwhile, the Muslim community was growing and expanding faster than anyone could have imagined and was in serious danger of becoming unmanageable. Muhammad's death had only complicated matters, so that some client tribes were now openly rebelling against Muslim control and refusing to pay the tithe tax (*zakat*) to Medina. As far as these tribes were concerned, Muhammad's death, like the death of any Shaykh, had annulled their oath of allegiance and severed their responsibility to the Ummah.

Even more disconcerting, Muhammad's vision of a divinely inspired state was proving so popular that throughout the Arabian Peninsula other regions had begun to replicate it using their own indigenous leadership and their own native ideology. In Yemen, a man named al-Aswad, who claimed to receive divine messages from a god he called Rahman (an epithet for Allah), had set up his own state independent of Mecca and Medina. In eastern Arabia, another man, Maslama (or Musaylama), had so successfully imitated Muhammad's formula that he had already gathered thousands of followers in Yamama, which he had declared to be a sanctuary city. To contemporary scholars like Dale Eickelman, the sudden upsurge of these "false prophets" is an indication that Muhammad's movement had filled a definite social and religious vacuum in Arabia. But to the Muslims, they signaled a grave threat to the religious legitimacy and political stability of the Ummah.

And yet the greatest challenge facing the Muslim community after Muhammad's death was neither rebellious tribes nor false prophets, but rather the question of how to build a cohesive religious system out of the Prophet's words and deeds, the majority of which existed solely in the memories of the Companions. There is a tendency to think of Islam as having been both completed and perfected at the end of Muhammad's life. But while that may be true of the Revelation, which ended with the Prophet's last breath, it would be a mistake to think of Islam in 632 C.E. as being in any way a unified system of beliefs and practices; far from it. As with all great religions, it would take generations of theological development for what Ignaz Goldziher calls "the unfolding of Islamic thought, the fixing of the modalities of Islamic practice, [and] the establishment of Islamic institutions" to take shape.

This is not to say, as the controversial American historian John Wansbrough has famously argued, that Islam as we know it originated *outside* Arabia hundreds of years after the death of Muhammad (if such a person even existed). Wansbrough and his colleagues have done remarkable work in tracing the evolution of Islam as it developed in the Judeo-Christian sectarian milieu of seventh- to ninth-century Arabia and its environs. But Wansbrough's persistent exaggeration of the non-Arabic (mostly Hebrew) sources regarding early Islam, and his unnecessary disregard of the historical Muhammad, has too often made his arguments seem more like "a disguised polemic seeking to strip Islam and the Prophet of all but the minimum of originality," to quote R. B. Sarjeant.

Polemical arguments aside, there can be no doubt that Islam was still in the process of defining itself when Muhammad died. By 632, the Quran had neither been written down nor collected, let alone canonized. The religious ideals that would become the foundation of Islamic theology existed only in the most rudimentary form. The questions of proper ritual activity or correct legal and moral behavior were, at this point, barely regulated; they did not have to be. Whatever questions one had—whatever issue was raised either through internal conflict or as a result of foreign contact—any confusion whatsoever could simply be brought before the Prophet for a solution. But without Muhammad around to elucidate the will of God, the Ummah was left with the nearly impossible task of figuring out what the Prophet would have said about an issue or a problem.

Obviously, the first and most urgent concern was to choose someone to lead the Ummah in Muhammad's stead, someone who could maintain the community's stability and integrity in the face of its many internal and external challenges. Unfortunately, there was little consensus as to who that leader should be. The Ansar in Medina had already taken the initiative of choosing a leader from among themselves: a pious early Medinan convert named Sa'd ibn Ubayda, the Shaykh of the Khazraj. But while the Medinans may have thought their sheltering of the Prophet had given them a preeminent position within the Ummah, the Meccans, and especially the former Qurayshi aristocracy who still held sway in Mecca, would never submit to being ruled by a Medinan. Some members of the Ansar tried to offer a compromise by choosing co-leaders, one from Mecca and one from Medina, but that too was unacceptable to the Quraysh.

It quickly became clear that the only way to maintain both a sense of unity and some measure of historical continuity in the Ummah was to choose a member of the Quraysh to succeed Muhammad, specifically one of the Companions who had made the original Hijra to Medina in 622 (the Muhajirun). Muhammad's clan, the Banu Hashim—now dubbed the *ahl al-bayt*, or the "People of the House [of the Prophet]"—agreed that only a member of the Quraysh could lead the Ummah, though they believed the Prophet would have wanted one of them to succeed him. Indeed, quite a large number of Muslims were convinced that during his final pilgrimage to Mecca, Muhammad had publicly designated his cousin and son-in-law, Ali, to be his successor. According to traditions, on his way back to Medina, Muhammad had stopped at an oasis called Ghadir al-Khumm and declared, "Whoever has me as his patron, has Ali as his patron (*mawla*)." Yet there were perhaps an equal number of Muslims who not only denied the events at Ghadir al-Khumm but who also vehemently rejected the privileged status of the Banu Hashim as the "People of the House of the Prophet."

To settle matters once and for all, Abu Bakr, Umar, and a prominent Companion named Abu Ubayda met with a group of Ansar leaders for a traditional *shura*, or tribal consultation (actually, the three men "crashed" a shura that was already taking place among the Ansar). And while an enormous amount of ink has been spilled over this historic meeting, it is still not clear exactly who was present or what took place. The only thing about which scholars can be certain is that at its conclusion, Abu Bakr, spurred on by Umar and Abu

Ubayda, was selected to be the next leader of the Muslim community and given the apt but rather vague title *Khalifat Rasul Allah*, "the Successor to the Messenger of God"—Caliph, in English.

What made Abu Bakr's title so appropriate was that nobody was sure what it was supposed to mean. The Quran refers to both Adam and David as God's Caliphs (2:30; 38:26), meaning they served as God's "trustees" or "vice-regents" on earth, but this does not seem to be how Abu Bakr was viewed. Despite the arguments of Patricia Crone and Martin Hinds to the contrary, the evidence suggests that the Caliphate was not meant to be a position of great religious influence. Certainly, the Caliph would be responsible for upholding the institutions of the Muslim faith, but he would not play a significant role in defining religious practice. In other words, Abu Bakr would replace the Prophet as leader of the Ummah, but he would have no prophetic authority. Muhammad was dead; his status as Messenger died with him.

The deliberate ambiguity of his title was a great advantage for Abu Bakr and his immediate successors because it gave them the opportunity to define the position for themselves, something they would do in widely divergent ways. As far as Abu Bakr was concerned, the Caliphate was a *secular* position that closely resembled that of the traditional tribal Shaykh—"the first among equals"—though with the added responsibility of being the community's war leader (Qa'id) and chief judge (Hakam), both of which were positions inherited from Muhammad. However, even Abu Bakr's secular authority was severely limited. Like any Shaykh, he made most of his decisions through collective consultation and, throughout his Caliphate, he continued his activities as a merchant, occasionally supplementing his meager income by milking a neighbor's cow. Abu Bakr's chief responsibility, as he seemed to have understood it, was to maintain the unity and stability of the Ummah so that the Muslims under his care would be free to worship God in peace. But because the restriction of his authority to the secular realm kept him from defining exactly *how* one was to worship God, the door was opened for a new class of scholars called the *Ulama*, or "learned ones," who would take upon themselves the responsibility of guiding the Ummah on the straight path.

As we shall see, the Ulama would eventually fashion a comprehensive code of conduct meant to regulate every aspect of the believer's life. And while it would be a mistake to consider these religious clerics and scholastic theologians as constituting a single, monolithic tradition, the power of the Ulama and their influence in shaping the faith and practice of Islam cannot be overstated. Caliphs will come and go, and the Caliphate as a civil institution will rise and fall in strength, but the authority of the Ulama and the power of their religious institutions will only increase with time.

ABU BAKR WAS, in many ways, the perfect choice to succeed Muhammad. Nicknamed *as-Siddiq*, "the faithful one," he was a deeply pious and respected man, one of the first converts to Islam and Muhammad's dearest friend. The fact that he had taken over the Friday prayers during Muhammad's lengthy illness was, in the minds of many, proof that the Prophet would have blessed his succession.

As Caliph, Abu Bakr united the community under a single banner and initiated a time of military triumph and social concord that would become known in the Muslim world as the Golden Era of Islam. It was Abu Bakr and his immediate successors—the first four Caliphs who are collectively referred to as the *Rashidun*, the "Rightly Guided Ones"—who tended the seed Muhammad had planted in the Hijaz until it sprouted into a dominant and far-reaching empire. While the Ummah expanded into North Africa, the Indian subcontinent, and large swaths of Europe, the Rightly Guided Ones strove to keep the community rooted in the principles of Muhammad—the struggle for justice, the equality of all believers, care for the poor and marginalized—yet civil strife and the incessant power struggles of the early Companions ultimately split the community into competing factions and turned the Caliphate into that form of government most reviled by the ancient Arabs: absolute monarchy.

As with most sacred histories, however, the truth about the era of the Rightly Guided Ones is far more complicated than the traditions suggest. Indeed, the so-called Golden Era of Islam was anything but a time of religious concord and political harmony. From the moment Muhammad died, there arose dozens of conflicting ideas about everything from how to interpret the Prophet's words and deeds to who should do the interpreting, from whom to choose as leader of the community to how the community should be led. It was even unclear who could and could not be considered a member of the Ummah, or, for that matter, what one had to do to be saved.

Again, as is the case with all great religions, it was precisely the arguments, the discord, and the sometimes bloody conflicts that resulted from trying to discern God's will in the absence of God's prophet that gave birth to the varied and wonderfully diverse institutions of the Muslim faith. In fact, just as it may be more appropriate to refer to the movements that succeeded Jesus' death—from Peter's messianic Judaism to Paul's Hellenic religion of salvation to the Gnosticism of the Egyptians and the more mystical movements of the East—as "Christianities," so it may be more appropriate to refer to what followed Muhammad's death as "Islams," clumsy as that sounds. Of course, early Islam was not nearly as doctrinally divided as early Christianity. But it is nevertheless important to recognize both the political and (as will be discussed in the following chapter) the religious divisions within the early Muslim community that were so instrumental in defining and developing the faith.

To begin with, the selection of Abu Bakr as Caliph was by no means unanimous. By all accounts, only a handful of the most prominent Companions were present at the shura. The only other serious contender for the leadership of the Muslim community had not even been informed of the meeting until it was over. At the same time that Abu Bakr was accepting the oath of allegiance, or *bay'ah*, Ali was washing the Prophet's body, preparing him for burial. Muhammad's clan, the Banu Hashim, fumed, claiming that without Ali, the shura was not representative of the entire Ummah. Likewise, the Ansar from Medina, who considered both Ali and Muhammad to be as much Medinan as Meccan—in other words, "one of their own"—complained bitterly about Ali's exclusion. Both groups publicly refused to swear allegiance to the new Caliph.

Many in the Muslim leadership—especially Abu Bakr and Umar—justified Ali's exclusion on the grounds that he was too young to lead the Ummah, or that his succession would appear too much like hereditary kingship (*mulk*): arguments that Muslim scholars and historians are still repeating to this day. In the first volume of his *Islamic History*,

M. A. Shaban claims that Ali was never really a serious candidate for the first Caliphate because of the reluctance of the Arabs to entrust "young and untried men with great responsibility." Henri Lammens concurs, citing the Arabs' abhorrence of hereditary leadership to suggest that Ali could not legitimately have succeeded Muhammad. As a result, most scholars agree with Montgomery Watt that Abu Bakr was "the obvious [and only] choice for successor."

But these are unsatisfying arguments. First of all, Ali may have been young—he was thirty years old at Muhammad's death—but he was by no means "untried." As the first male convert and one of Islam's greatest warriors, Ali was widely recognized for both his spiritual maturity and his military prowess. In Medina, Ali acted as Muhammad's personal secretary and was his standard-bearer in a number of important battles. He was regularly placed in charge of the Ummah in Muhammad's absence and, as Moojan Momen observes, was the only individual free to come and go as he pleased in the Prophet's house. And no one in the community would have forgotten that only Ali was allowed to assist the Prophet in cleansing the Ka'ba for God.

The proof of Ali's qualifications, despite his age, rests in the fact that it was not only the Banu Hashim who pushed for his succession as Caliph. The Prophet's cousin and son-in-law was supported by the majority of the Ansar from both the Aws and the Khazraj (one of the few things about which the two feuding tribes agreed); the Abd Shams and the Abd Manaf, two powerful and influential clans of Quraysh; and a significant number of prominent Companions.

Secondly, as Wilferd Madelung remarks in his indispensable book *The Succession to Muhammad*, hereditary succession may have been repugnant to the Bedouin Arabs, but it was hardly uncommon among the aristocratic Quraysh. In fact, the Quraysh regularly chose members of their own families to succeed them in positions of authority because, as mentioned, it was a common belief that noble qualities were passed through the blood from one generation to the next. The Quran itself repeatedly affirms the importance of blood relations (2:177, 215), and endows Muhammad's family—the ahl al-bayt—with an eminent position in the Ummah, somewhat akin to that enjoyed by the families of the other prophets.

This is a vital point to bear in mind. Regardless of their opinions regarding Ali's qualifications, no Muslim could argue with the fact that a great many of the prophets and patriarchs of the Bible were succeeded by their kin: Abraham to Isaac and Ismail; Isaac to Jacob; Moses to Aaron; David to Solomon; and so on. Faced with this fact, opponents of the Banu Hashim claimed that, as the Seal of the Prophets, Muhammad could have no heir. But considering that the Quran goes to such great lengths to emphasize the congruence between Muhammad and his prophetic predecessors, and recognizing the numerous traditions that parallel Ali's relationship to Muhammad with Aaron's relationship to Moses, one would be hard pressed to ignore Ali's candidacy simply on the grounds that it violated the Arabs' distaste for hereditary leadership.

The truth is that Ali's deliberate exclusion from the shura that resulted in the selection of Abu Bakr was a result neither of his age nor of the Arab aversion for hereditary leadership. Ali was excluded because of a growing fear among the larger and wealthier clans of the Quraysh that allowing both prophethood and the Caliphate to rest in the hands of a single clan—especially the Banu Hashim—would too greatly alter the balance of power in the Ummah. Furthermore, there seemed to be some anxiety among certain members of the community, most notably Abu Bakr and Umar, that maintaining a prolonged hereditary leadership within Muhammad's clan would blur the distinction between the religious authority of the Prophet and the secular authority of the Caliph.

Whatever the justifications, Ali's proponents would not be silenced; so it was left to Umar to silence them himself. Having literally beaten the leader of the Ansar, Sa'd ibn Ubayda, into submission, Umar went to the house of Fatima, Ali's wife and Muhammad's daughter, and threatened to burn it down unless she and the rest of the Banu Hashim accepted the will of the shura. Fortunately, Abu Bakr restrained him at the last moment, but the message was clear: the Ummah was too unstable, and the political situation in Arabia too volatile, for this kind of open dissent to be tolerated. Ali agreed. For the sake of the community, he and his entire family surrendered their claim to leadership and solemnly swore allegiance to Abu Bakr, though it took another six months of cajoling for them to do so.

* * *

As turbulent as the succession to Muhammad may have been, there is one detail that should not be lost in the tumult and confusion that led to Abu Bakr's Caliphate. Implicit in the conflict over who should lead the Ummah was the unanimous conviction among all Muslims that some kind of popular sanction was required to approve the candidate. Certainly this was not a democratic process; Abu Bakr was appointed through the consultation of a select group of elders, not elected by the Ummah. But the great effort that the Companions went through to achieve some semblance of unanimity is proof that Abu Bakr's appointment would have been meaningless without the consensus of the entire community. Thus, upon becoming Caliph, Abu Bakr stood before the Ummah and humbly proclaimed, "Behold me, charged with the cares of the government. I am not the best among you. I need all your advice and help. If I do well, support me; if I make a mistake, counsel me. . . . As long as I obey God and the Prophet, obey me; if I neglect the laws of God and the Prophet, I have no right to your obedience."

From our privileged position, the succession to Muhammad may seem a chaotic affair full of intimidation and disorder: a rigged process, to say the least. But it was a process, nonetheless; and from the Nile to the Oxus and beyond, nowhere else had such an experiment in popular sovereignty even been imagined, let alone attempted.

ABU BAKR'S WAS a short but highly successful reign—only two and a half years. His principal achievement as Caliph was his military campaigns against the "false prophets" and those tribes who had ceased paying the tithe tax because, in true tribal fashion, they considered their oath of allegiance to have been made to Muhammad, the "Shaykh" of the Ummah. Consequently, these tribes assumed that Muhammad's death had annulled their pledge, meaning they no longer had to pay taxes to his "tribe." Recognizing that the defection of these tribes would greatly weaken the political stability of the Ummah and economically devastate the small Muslim régime in Medina, Abu Bakr sent his armies to deal ruthlessly with the rebels. The Riddah Wars, as these campaigns came to be known, sent a powerful message to the

Arab tribes that their pledge had been made not to any mortal Shaykh but to the immortal community of God, making its retraction both an act of treason against the Ummah and a sin against God.

The Riddah Wars represented Abu Bakr's conscious effort to maintain the unity of the Arabs under the eternal banner of Islam and the centralized authority of Medina, and thus to prevent Muhammad's community from dissolving back into the old tribal system. But these must not be mistaken for religious wars; the campaigns were intended to reinforce the purely political interests of Medina. Still, the Riddah Wars did have the regrettable consequence of permanently associating apostasy (denying one's faith) with treason (denying the central authority of the Caliph).

Because religious affiliation and citizenship were nearly identical terms in seventh-century Arabia, so therefore were apostasy and treason considered one and the same. However, the relationship between the two has endured in Islam, so that even today there are some Muslims who continue to make the unsubstantiated and un-Quranic assertion that the two sins—apostasy and treason—deserve the same punishment: death. It is this belief that has given the Ulama in some Muslim countries the authority to impose capital punishment on apostates, by whom they mean anyone who disagrees with their particular interpretation of Islam. This despite the fact that nowhere in the whole of the Quran is any earthly punishment proscribed for apostasy (such punishment, the Quran repeatedly insists, is reserved for God alone in the afterlife: 3:86–87; 4:137; 5:54; 16:106; 47:25–28; 73:11).

Abu Bakr is remembered for one other decision that he made as Caliph. Claiming once to have heard Muhammad say "We [the Prophets] do not have heirs. Whatever we leave is alms," the Caliph disinherited Ali and Fatima from Muhammad's property. Henceforth, the family of the Prophet was to be fed and clothed only through alms provided by the community. Given that there were no other witnesses to Muhammad's statement, this was a remarkable decision. But what makes the decision even more problematic is that Abu Bakr generously provided for Muhammad's wives by giving them the Prophet's house as a bequest. He even gave his own daughter, Aisha, some of Muhammad's former property in Medina.

Abu Bakr's actions are often interpreted as an attempt to enfeeble the Banu Hashim and strip the ahl al-bayt of their privileged status as Muhammad's kin. But it also seems likely that in both providing for Muhammad's wives and ensuring that their purity would remain inviolate, Abu Bakr was signaling to the community that it was Aisha and the rest of the "Mothers of the Faithful" who were truly the heirs of the Prophet.

Ali was stunned by Abu Bakr's decision, but he accepted his fate without argument. Fatima, on the other hand, was inconsolable. In the span of a few months she had lost her father, her inheritance, and her livelihood. She never spoke to Abu Bakr again, and when she died a short time later, Ali quietly buried her at night without bothering to inform the Caliph.

Scholars have long argued that there must have been some other motivation behind Abu Bakr's decision to disinherit Ali and strip Muhammad's clan of power. Indeed, throughout his short Caliphate, Abu Bakr seemed to do everything in his power to prevent Ali from ever attaining a position of authority in the Ummah, mostly because of his conviction that prophethood and Caliphate—that is, religious and secular authority—should not rest in a single clan, lest the two become indistinguishable. But to say that there was no personal animosity between Abu Bakr and Ali would be a lie. Even while Muhammad was alive, there was a great deal of friction between the two men, as evidenced by the infamous "affair of the necklace."

As the story goes, on the way home from a raid against the Banu al-Mustaliq, Aisha—who nearly always followed Muhammad regardless of whether he was going into battle or negotiating a treaty—was accidentally left behind at one of the campsites. She had slipped away to relieve herself, and in so doing she lost a necklace Muhammad had given her. While she searched for it, the caravan departed, assuming she was still in her litter; no one noticed her absence until the following morning. While the men scrambled about frantically, trying to figure out what to do about having lost Muhammad's beloved wife, a camel suddenly entered the camp carrying Aisha and a handsome young Arab (and childhood friend of hers) named Safwan ibn al-Mu'attal.

Safwan had stumbled upon Aisha in the desert and, despite her veil (the verse of the hijab had recently been revealed), he recognized her at once. "What has caused you to stay behind?" he asked.

Aisha did not answer; she would not violate her hijab.

Safwan understood her predicament but was not about to leave Muhammad's wife in the desert. He rode up to her and extended his hand. "Mount!" he said. "May God have mercy on you." Aisha hesitated for a moment, then mounted the camel. The two raced to catch up with the caravan, but did not make it to the next campsite until morning.

The sight of Muhammad's veiled wife clinging to Safwan atop the camel launched a wave of rumors throughout Medina. When the story first reached Muhammad, he reacted with uncertainty. He did not believe that anything had happened between Aisha and Safwan, but the scandal was starting to become disruptive. Already his enemies had produced some deliciously lewd verses about the event. As the days passed, he grew cold and distant toward his wife. When he asked her to repent to God so that the matter could be settled and forgiven, Aisha flew into a rage. "By God," she said, "I will never repent to God of that which you have spoken of." Offended and unapologetic, she stormed out of Muhammad's house and moved back in with her mother.

The absence of his beloved devastated Muhammad. One day he stood among the people and, clearly distraught, asked, "Why are some men hurting me regarding my family and saying falsehoods about them?"

Although most of his advisers were convinced of her guilt, they clambered over one another to praise Aisha's chastity. "We know nothing but good about [your wives]," they declared. Only Ali remained adamant that regardless of Aisha's guilt or innocence, the scandal was damaging enough to Muhammad's reputation to merit divorce. As one can imagine, this advice infuriated Aisha's father, Abu Bakr.

Eventually, Muhammad received a Revelation clearing Aisha of the adultery charges. Overjoyed, he rushed to his wife, crying, "Rejoice, Aisha! God has revealed your innocence."

Aisha, who, as all the traditions attest, was the only person who could get away with talking back to Muhammad, replied, "To God's praise and your blame!" Still, she was redeemed and the matter forgotten. But neither Aisha nor Abu Bakr ever forgave Ali.

The schism between the two men widened further when, without any consultation whatsoever, Abu Bakr decided to appoint Umar as his successor rather than call for another shura. There is only one plausible explanation for Abu Bakr's decision: a shura would have undoubtedly revived the debate over the rights of the family of the Prophet. Indeed, a shura might have led to the succession of Ali, who had, over the past two years, become increasingly popular. The support he already enjoyed from a number of influential clans and Companions could very well have led uncommitted clans to back his candidacy. Granted, the vested interests of the Quraysh aristocracy in maintaining the status quo would not have made Ali's selection certain. But had it come to a contest between the enormously popular Ali and the fiery, rigid, misogynistic Umar, the latter would not have been assured of victory. To avoid that outcome, Abu Bakr ignored both tribal tradition and Muslim precedent, and simply handpicked Umar, though, again, the new Caliph had to be approved by the consensus of the community.

As Caliph, Umar was exactly what Muhammad had always considered him to be: a brilliant and energetic leader. Tall, brawny, and completely bald, Umar was an intimidating presence who, when he walked, "towered above the people as though he were on horseback." A warrior at heart, he maintained the Caliphate as a secular position but emphasized his role as war leader by adopting the additional title *Amir al-Mu'manin*, "the Commander of the Faithful." His superior skills in battle led to the defeat of the Byzantine army in southern Syria in 634 and the capture of Damascus a year later. With the help of the oppressed Syrian Jewish community, whom he had freed from Byzantine control, Umar then devastated the Iranian forces at Qadisiyyah on his way to subduing the great Sasanian Empire. Egypt and Libya fell easily to Umar's army, as did Jerusalem: the crowning achievement of his military campaigns.

Surprisingly, however, Umar proved to be a far better diplomat than anyone could have imagined. Recognizing the importance of appeasing the non-Arab converts to Islam, who even in his time were beginning to outnumber the Arabs, the Caliph treated his vanquished enemies as equal members of the Ummah and strove to eliminate all ethnic differences between Arab and non-Arab (at this point, however, the latter still had to become a client of the former to convert to Islam). The wealth that poured into Medina as a result of his military victories was distributed proportionately to everyone in the community, including the children. Umar went out of his way to curb the power of the former Quraysh aristocracy and strengthened his central authority by appointing governors, or *amirs*, to administer the Muslim provinces both near and far. At the same time, he gave his amirs strict instructions to respect the existing traditions and mores of the provinces, and not to attempt any radical changes in the way the local peoples had been previously governed. He reorganized the taxation system, bringing immense prosperity to the Ummah, and created a standing army of trained soldiers who were garrisoned away from the provinces so as to not disturb the local communities.

Umar even tried to heal the rift with Ali by reaching out to the Banu Hashim. Though he refused to return Ali's inheritance, he did hand over Muhammad's estates in Medina as an endowment to be administered by Muhammad's kin. He connected himself to the Banu Hashim by marrying Ali's daughter, and encouraged Ali's participation in his government by regularly consulting him on important matters. In fact, Umar rarely did anything without consulting a cadre of influential Companions that he kept around him at all times. This may have been because he recognized that his position as Caliph, though sanctioned by the Ummah, had not been achieved through traditional means. He was therefore keen to avoid seeming despotic in his judgments, and was once quoted as saying, "If I am [a] king, it is a fearful thing."

Despite his attempts to reach out to the Banu Hashim, however, Umar continued to uphold, as a matter of religious dogma, the contention that prophethood and the Caliphate should not reside in the same clan. Indeed, acknowledging that contention and accepting Muhammad's statement about having no heirs became for Umar part of the oath of allegiance. Like Abu Bakr, Umar was convinced that such power in the Banu Hashim would be detrimental to the Muslim community. Nevertheless, he could not ignore Ali's rising popularity.

Not wishing to make the same mistake as Abu Bakr and so further alienate the Banu Hashim, Umar refused to handpick a successor, choosing instead to gather a traditional shura.

On his deathbed (he had been stabbed by a mad Persian slave named Firooz), Umar brought together the six leading candidates for the Caliphate, including, at last, Ali, and gave them three days to decide among themselves who would lead the community after his death. It was not long before only two men remained: Ali, the scion of the Banu Hashim, and a somewhat unremarkable septuagenarian named Uthman ibn Affan.

A wealthy member of the Umayyad clan—the clan of Muhammad's fiercest enemies, Abu Sufyan and Hind—Uthman was a Quraysh through and through. Although an early convert to Islam, he had never exhibited any leadership qualities; he was a merchant, not a warrior. Muhammad deeply loved Uthman, but never once entrusted him with leading a raid or an army on his behalf, something nearly every other man standing at the shura had done on more than one occasion. But it was precisely his inexperience and lack of political ambition that made Uthman such an attractive choice. He was, more than anything else, the perfect alternative to Ali: a prudent, reliable old man who would not rock the boat.

In the end, Ali and Uthman were each asked two questions by Abd al-Rahman, who, despite being Uthman's brother-in-law, had been selected as Hakam between the two men. First, would each man rule according to the principles of the Quran and the example of Muhammad? Both replied that they would. The second question was unexpected. Would each man, if selected Caliph, strictly follow the precedents set by the two previous Caliphs, Abu Bakr and Umar?

Not only was this a totally unprecedented requirement for leading the community, it was obviously meant to weed out one candidate in particular. For while Uthman remarked that he would follow the example of his predecessors in all his decisions as Caliph, Ali gave the men in the room a hard stare and answered flatly, "No." He would follow only God and his own judgment.

Ali's answer sealed the verdict. Uthman became the third Caliph, and in 644 C.E. was promptly endorsed by the Ummah.

THE BANU HASHIM had fumed when Ali was skipped over in favor of Abu Bakr. But Abu Bakr was a highly respected Muslim with impeccable credentials. The Hashim had been furious with Abu Bakr for ignoring Ali and simply choosing Umar as his successor. But, again, Umar was a strong leader and, without the proper channels, there was little they could do but voice their opposition. However, when Uthman was chosen as Caliph over Ali, the Banu Hashim had simply had enough.

It was perfectly clear to many in the community that Uthman's Caliphate was a deliberate attempt to accommodate the old Quraysh aristocracy, who were eager to regain their previous status as the elites of Arab society. With Uthman's selection, the House of Umayya was once again in charge of Arabia, just as it had been before Muhammad conquered it in the name of Islam. The irony of pledging allegiance to the clan of their former enemies was not lost on the members of Muhammad's clan. To make matters worse, rather than trying to heal the ever-widening rift in the community, Uthman only exacerbated the situation through his unabashed nepotism and inept leadership.

First, Uthman replaced nearly all of the existing amirs throughout the Muslim lands with members of his immediate family, as though signaling to everyone the preeminence of his clan. Then, he began dipping into the public treasury to dole out huge sums of money to his relatives. Finally, and most dramatically, he broke with tradition by giving himself the hitherto unthinkable title *Khalifat Allah:* "Successor to God," a title that Abu Bakr had explicitly rejected. To his many enemies, this decision was a sign of Uthman's self-aggrandizement. The Caliph, it seemed, was regarding himself not as the deputy of the Messenger, but as the representative of God on earth.

Uthman's actions made him a fiercely hated figure. Not only did the Banu Hashim and the Ansar in Medina turn against the Caliph, so did some of the Umayya's rival clans—the Banu Zuhra, the Banu Makhzum, and the Abd Shams—together with some of the most influential Companions, including Aisha and even Abd al-Rahman, Uthman's brother-in-law and the man who, as arbiter in the shura, had been instrumental in giving him the Caliphate in the first place. By the end of his rule, Uthman had made so many reckless decisions that not even his most significant accomplishment—the collection and canonization of the Quran—could enable him to escape the ire of the Muslim community.

In Muhammad's lifetime, the Quran was never collected in a single volume; in fact, it was never collected at all. As each individual recitation poured out of the Prophet's mouth, it was diligently memorized by a new class of scholars, personally instructed by Muhammad, called the *Qurra*, or Quran readers. Only the most important recitations—those dealing with legal issues—were ever written down, primarily on bits of bone, scraps of leather, and the ribs of palm leaves.

After the Prophet's death, the Qurra dispersed throughout the community as the authorized teachers of the Quran. But with the rapid growth of the Ummah and the passing of the first generation of Quran readers, certain deviations began to appear in the various recitations. These were mostly insignificant differences reflecting the local and cultural affinities of Muslim communities in Iraq, or Syria, or Egypt; they were immaterial to the meaning and message of the Quran. Nevertheless, the Medinan establishment became increasingly alarmed by these discrepancies, and so began plans to do what Muhammad had never bothered doing: to create a single, codified, uniform text of the Quran.

Some traditions claim that the Quran, in its present form, was collected by Abu Bakr during his Caliphate. This is Theodor Noeldeke's position, though even he admits that Abu Bakr's redaction had no real canonical authority. Most scholars, however, agree that it was Uthman who, in his capacity as the Successor to God, authorized a single universally binding text of the Quran in about 650 C.E. But in doing so, Uthman once again managed to alienate important members of the community when he decided to round up the variant collections of the Quran, bring them to Medina, and set fire to them.

This decision infuriated the leading Muslims of Iraq, Syria, and Egypt, not because they felt their Qurans were somehow better or more complete than Uthman's—as mentioned, the variations were quite inconsequential—but because they felt that Uthman was overstepping the bounds of his secular authority as Caliph. Uthman's response to their grievances was to brand as an unbeliever anyone who questioned the authority of the official collection.

Agitation against Uthman reached its peak in 655, with revolts breaking out throughout the Muslim lands against the Caliph's incompetent and often corrupt amirs. In Medina, Uthman was openly despised. Once, while leading the Friday prayers at the mosque, he was showered with stones hurled from the back of the congregation. A stone hit him in the forehead and he tumbled off the *minbar*, falling unconscious to the floor. Eventually the situation became so dire that a number of prominent Companions from Mecca banded together to beg the Caliph to recall his corrupt governors, cease his nepotism, and repent before the entire community. However, members of his own clan, and especially his influential and power-hungry cousin, Marwan, pressured Uthman not to look weak by humbling himself.

Things came to a violent end for Uthman a year later, when a massive delegation from Egypt, Basra, and Kufa marched to Medina to present their grievances directly to the Caliph. While refusing to receive the delegation personally, Uthman sent Ali to ask them to return to their homes with the promise that their grievances would be addressed.

What happened next is unclear; the sources are muddled and contradictory. Somehow, on their way back home, the Egyptian delegation intercepted a messenger en route to Uthman's representative in Egypt who carried with him an official letter demanding the immediate punishment of the rebel leaders for their insubordination. The letter was signed with the seal of the Caliph. Enraged, the delegation reversed course and returned to Medina, where, with the aid of the Basran and Kufan rebels, they laid siege to Uthman's home, trapping the Caliph inside.

Most historians are convinced that Uthman did not write that letter: he may have been a poor political leader, but he was not suicidal. He must have known the rebel leaders would not have accepted their punishment without a fight. Some scholars, like Leone Caetani, have blamed Ali for the letter, arguing that he wanted to depose Uthman and claim the Caliphate for himself; but this charge is totally unfounded. There may have been some hostility between the two men, and Ali may not have surrendered his aspirations for the Caliphate. But the fact is that Ali faithfully served as one of Uthman's most trusted advisers throughout his Caliphate and did everything in his power to appease the rebels. It was Ali, after all, who had persuaded them to go home in the first place. Even as the rebels were encircling Uthman's home, swords drawn, Ali maintained his support for the Caliph. Indeed, Ali's eldest son, Hasan, was among the handful of guards who continued to defend Uthman as the rebels charged into his home, while his second son, Husayn, transported water and food to the Caliph throughout the siege at great risk to his own life.

Most scholars agree that the true culprit was likely Marwan, who many in Uthman's own circle believed had written the letter. It was Marwan who had advised Uthman to deal harshly with the rebels when they first arrived with their grievances. It was Marwan's influence that kept Uthman from repenting of his more detrimental actions, like heaping riches upon his family from the public treasury. In fact, when the Companions criticized Uthman for precisely this kind of behavior, Marwan, who benefited most richly from Uthman's nepotism, drew his sword and threatened to kill the most respected members of the Ummah in the presence of the Prophet's successor.

Regardless of who wrote the letter, the Egyptian, Basran, and Kufan rebels—and nearly everyone else in Medina—believed that Uthman had, according to all customs, failed in his leadership and must, as a result, voluntarily step down as Caliph. He had, in one sense, forfeited his oath of allegiance as Shaykh of the Ummah, and violated Abu Bakr's declaration that if the Caliph neglects the laws of God and the Prophet, he has no right to obedience.

But there was also a small faction of Muslims who called for Uthman's abdication not on the grounds that he had forfeited his oath of allegiance, but because they believed that only a Caliph who was free from sin could be worthy to lead the holy community of God. This faction would come to be known as the *Kharijites*, and despite their small numbers, they and their uncompromising beliefs would soon play an important role in determining the fate of the Muslim community.

Even as nearly everyone had turned against him, Uthman still refused to give up power. As far as he understood, his position as Khalifat Allah had been bestowed upon him by God, not by man; only God could remove the mantle of leadership from him. However, as a pious Muslim, Uthman refused to attack the rebels who besieged him, hoping he could maintain control of the Caliphate without shedding Muslim blood. He therefore commanded his supporters not to fight, but to go home and wait for order to be restored naturally. But it was far too late for that.

The rebels, provoked by a scuffle outside Uthman's home, stormed into the Caliph's inner chamber, where they found him sitting on a cushion reading from the Quran that he himself had collected and codified. Ignored by the Companions and virtually unchallenged by the guards, the rebels asked him one final time to abdicate. When Uthman refused, the rebels drew their swords and plunged them into Uthman's chest. The Caliph fell forward upon the open Quran, his blood soaking into its gold-leafed pages.

THE CALIPH'S MURDER at the hands of fellow Muslims threw the Ummah into a state of pandemonium. With the rebels still in control of Medina, it was unclear what would happen next. There were more than a few Muslims in Mecca and Medina who would have leaped at the opportunity to succeed Uthman, including two of the most prominent Meccan Companions, Talha ibn Ubayd Allah and Zubayr ibn al-Awwam, both of whom had been singled out for their piety by Muhammad.

And, of course, there was Ali.

When he heard of Uthman's assassination, Ali was in the mosque praying. Sensing the chaos that would result, he quickly returned home to look after his family, and especially to find his son Hasan, who had stayed behind to try to protect Uthman. The following day, when a fragile peace had settled over the city, Ali returned to the mosque to find a substantial delegation of Muslims beseeching him to accept the oath of allegiance and become the next Caliph. For nearly a quarter of a century, Ali had been pursuing the Caliphate. But now that it was being handed to him, he refused to accept it.

Given the circumstances, Ali's reluctance was not surprising. If the demise of Uthman had proved anything, it was that some form of popular consent was still vital to maintaining the authority of the Caliphate. But with the rebels in control of Medina, Egypt and Iraq in revolt, Mecca calling for the Caliphate to be restored to the original vision of Abu Bakr and Umar, and Uthman's clan, the Banu Umayya, demanding immediate retribution for the Caliph's death, popular sanction would have been impossible to achieve. And yet there was still a very large and formidable contingent of Muslims whose unconditional support for Ali had not waned over the years. This faction consisted of members of the Ansar in Medina, Muhammad's clan, the Banu Hashim, some prominent clans of the Quraysh, a few leading Companions, and several large bodies of non-Arab Muslims (especially in Basra and Kufa) who together were loosely labeled *Shi'atu Ali*, the "Party of Ali": the *Shi'ah*.

Despite this support, it was not until his political rivals in Mecca, including Talha and Zubayr, promised to pledge him their allegiance that Ali finally succumbed and accepted the mantle of leadership. Insisting that the oath of allegiance be given publicly in the mosque and in the presence of the entire Medinan community, Ali ibn Abi Talib, cousin and son-in-law to the Prophet, finally took his place at the head of the Ummah. Significantly, Ali refused the title of Caliph, which he believed had been permanently tainted by Uthman. Instead, he opted for Umar's epithet, Amir al-Mu'manin, "Commander of the Faithful."

With the backing of his party, Ali restored order to Medina by announcing a general amnesty to all who had, in one way or another, played a role in Uthman's death. This was to be a time of forgiveness and reconciliation, not of retribution. The old tribal ways, Ali claimed, were over. He further appeased the rebellious territories by removing nearly all of Uthman's kin from their posts as amirs and filling the vacancies with qualified local leaders. Yet Ali's actions, especially his amnesty of the rebels, not only enraged the Banu Umayya, they paved the way for Aisha to rally support in Mecca against the new Caliph by pinning him with the responsibility for Uthman's murder.

Aisha did not really believe Ali was responsible for Uthman's death; even if she had, it is unlikely she would have cared. Aisha loathed Uthman and played a significant role in the rebellion against him. In fact, her brother, Muhammad, was instrumental in the Caliph's assassination. But having learned from her father, Abu Bakr, never to entrust Muhammad's clan with the Caliphate, lest the distinction between religious and political authority in the Ummah become confounded, Aisha saw Uthman's murder as a means to replace Ali with someone she considered more suitable for the position, most likely her close allies Talha or Zubayr. It was with the help of these two men that she organized a massive contingent of Meccans and, riding atop a camel, personally led them into battle against Ali's forces in Medina.

The Battle of the Camel, as it came to be known, was Islam's first experience of civil war, or *fitnah* (there would be many more over the next century and a half). In some ways, this conflict was the inevitable result, not just of the continuing antagonism between the factions of Ali and Aisha, but of a steadily evolving debate within the community over the role of the Caliph and the nature of the Ummah. Too often, this debate has been portrayed as strictly polarized between those who considered the Caliphate to be a purely secular position and those who believed it should encompass both the temporal and religious authority of the Prophet. But this simple dichotomy masks the diversity of religio-political views that existed in seventh- and eighth-century Arabia with regard to the nature and function of the Caliphate.

The astonishingly rapid expansion of Islam into what had to this point been considered the impregnable domains of the Byzantine and Sasanian empires was, for most Muslims, proof of God's divine favor. At the same time, the encounter with foreign peoples and governments was forcing these Muslims to reexamine the ideals that governed the political structure of the community. And while everyone agreed that the Ummah could remain united only under the authority of a single leader, there was still no consensus as to who that leader should be and almost no agreement as to how that leader should lead.

On the one hand, there were those Muslims, like Aisha and her faction, who, while recognizing the importance of building a community dedicated to the commandments of God, were nonetheless committed to maintaining the secular character of the Caliphate. This faction was referred to as the *Shi'atu Uthman*, "the party of Uthman," though one should remember that Aisha in no way considered herself as advancing the cause of Uthman, whom she considered to have blighted the Caliphate established by her father and his protégé, Umar.

On the other hand, there was the Banu Umayya, who, in light of Uthman's lengthy reign as Caliph, had fallen under the impression that the Caliphate was now the hereditary property of their clan. It was for this reason that, upon Uthman's death, his closest kin, Mu'awiyah, the governor, or amir, of Damascus and the scion of Umayya, decided to disregard the events taking place in Medina and instead begin plans to take over the Caliphate himself. In some ways, the *Shi'atu Mu'awiyah*, as this faction was called, represented the traditional ideal of tribal leadership, though Mu'awiyah himself seemed to be trying to steer the Ummah in the direction of the great empires of the Byzantines and Sasanians. No one was yet calling for the establishment of a Muslim kingdom, but it was becoming increasingly clear that the Ummah was now too large and too wealthy to maintain its unity according to the "neo-tribal" system established by Muhammad in Medina.

At the opposite end of the spectrum were the Shi'atu Ali, who were committed to preserving Muhammad's original vision of the Ummah, no matter the social or political consequences. Although it is true that some factions within this group thought the Caliphate should incorporate Muhammad's religious authority, it would be a mistake to consider this view the established *Shi'ite* position it would eventually become. At this point, there were no significant religious differences between the Shi'ah and the rest of the Muslim community, later called the Sunni, or "orthodox." The Party of Ali was nothing more than a political faction that maintained the right of Muhammad's clan to rule the community in Muhammad's stead.

However, there was a small faction within Ali's party who held the more extreme view that the Ummah was a divinely founded institution that could be run only by the most pious person in the community, irrespective of his tribe, lineage, or ancestry. Eventually called the Kharijites, this faction has already been cited for their justification of Uthman's murder on the grounds that he had broken the commands of God and rejected the example of the Prophet, making him no longer worthy of the Caliphate. Because the Kharijites stressed the need for a religious authority as Caliph, they are often credited with being the first Muslim theocrats. But this was a tiny, fractious group whose radically theocratic position was rejected by nearly every other faction vying for control of the Muslim community.

What makes the Kharijites so important to Islamic history, however, is that they represent the first self-conscious attempts at defining a distinctive Muslim identity. This was a group obsessed with establishing who could and could not be considered a Muslim. According to the Kharijites, anyone who disobeyed any of the Quranic prescriptions, or violated the example of the Prophet Muhammad in any way, was to be considered a *kafir*, or unbeliever, and immediately expelled from the Ummah.

Small as this group may have been, they made a lasting contribution to Muslim thought by arguing that salvation comes solely through membership in the Ummah, which they considered to be the charismatic and divine community of God. They divided all Muslims into two camps: the "People of Heaven," as the Kharijites referred to themselves, and the "People of Hell," by whom they meant everyone else. In this respect, the Kharijites can be considered the first Muslim "extremists," and although the group itself lasted only a couple of centuries, its austere doctrines were adopted by succeeding generations of extremists to give religious sanction to their political rebellions against both Muslim and non-Muslim governments.

One final issue: it is important to recognize that regardless of their views on the nature and function of the Caliphate, no Muslim in seventh-century Arabia would have recognized the distinction our modern societies make between the secular and religious. The primary philosophical difference between the Shi'atu Uthman and the Kharijites, for instance, was not whether but to what extent religion should play a role in the governing of the state. Thus, while the Shi'atu Ali, the Shi'atu Uthman, the Shi'atu Mu'awiyah, and the Kharijites were above all else *political* factions, all four of these groups were also described in more religiously oriented terms through the use of the word *din*, or "religion" (as in *din Ali*, *din Uthman*, etc.).

It is difficult to discern where Ali fit into this debate over the nature and function of the Caliphate because, as will shortly become apparent, he never had a chance to fully embrace the position. It seems clear from the decisions he made upon succeeding Uthman that Ali agreed with the Kharijite position that the Ummah was a divinely inspired community that could no longer abide either by the imperial ideals of the Shi'atu Mu'awiyah or by the neo-tribal precedents of Abu Bakr and Umar as envisioned by the Shi'atu Uthman. Whether Ali thought the Caliphate should fully encompass Muhammad's religious authority is another matter.

Ali was certainly no Kharijite. But he felt deeply his connection to the Prophet, whom he had known his entire life. The two men grew up together as brothers in the same household, and Ali rarely left Muhammad's side either as a child or as an adult. So it would have been understandable if Ali believed his relationship with Muhammad gave him both the religious and political qualities necessary to lead God's divine community on the path marked out by the Prophet. But this does not mean Ali considered himself to be divinely appointed to continue Muhammad's prophetic function, as his followers would eventually claim, nor does it mean he believed that the Caliphate should necessarily be a religious position.

Considering the cunning political maneuvering taking place around him, Ali's attempts to reshape the Caliphate into a position of religious piety, if not religious authority, seemed doomed from the start. Nevertheless, Ali was committed to uniting the Ummah under the banner of the ahl al-bayt and in accordance with Muhammad's egalitarian principles. Therefore, after his forces quickly over-whelmed Aisha's army at the Battle of the Camel—during which Talha and Zubayr were killed and Aisha seriously wounded by an arrow—rather than punish the rebels as Abu Bakr had done after the Riddah Wars, Ali rebuked, then pardoned Aisha and her entourage, allowing them to return to Mecca unmolested.

With Mecca and Medina finally subdued, Ali transferred his Caliphate to Kufa, in modern-day Iraq, so as to turn his attention to Mu'awiyah, who, as the son of Abu Sufyan and the cousin of Uthman, had appealed to the old tribal sentiments of his Qurayshi kinsmen in order to raise an army against Ali in retribution for Uthman's murder. In 657 C.E., Ali and his Kufan army met Mu'awiyah and his Syrian army at a place called Siffin. After a long and bloody battle, Ali's forces were on the verge of victory when, sensing defeat, Mu'awiyah ordered his army to raise copies of the Quran on their spears: a message signaling his desire to surrender for arbitration.

Most of Ali's army, and especially the Kharijite faction who had, to this point, remained loyal to him, pleaded with Ali to ignore the gesture and continue the battle until the rebels had been punished for their insubordination. But, though Ali sensed treachery on Mu'awiyah's part, he refused to ignore God's command that "if [the enemy] desists, then you must also cease hostilities" (2:193). Ordering his army to lay down their weapons, Ali accepted Mu'awiyah's surrender and called for a Hakam to settle the dispute between them.

This was a fatal decision. The arbitration that followed the Battle of Siffin declared Uthman's murder to have been unjust and worthy of retribution: a decision that, at least on the surface, seemed to justify Mu'awiyah's rebellion. However, far more ominous was the fact that the Kharijites considered Ali's decision to submit to arbitration rather than mete out God's justice upon the rebels to be a grave sin worthy of expulsion from the holy community. Crying "No judgment but God's," the Kharijites angrily abandoned Ali on the battlefield before the arbitration had even begun.

Ali barely had time to absorb the impact of the arbitration. After Siffin, he was reluctantly forced to send his army to deal with the Kharijites who had seceded from his party. No sooner had he subdued the Kharijites (in what was less a battle than a massacre) than he had to turn his attention back toward Mu'awiyah, who during the lengthy arbitration process had managed to reassemble his forces, capture Egypt, and, in 660 C.E., proclaim himself Caliph in Jerusalem. With his armies scattered and his supporters divided along ideological lines, Ali mustered what forces he had left and, the following year, prepared a final campaign against Mu'awiyah and the Syrian rebels.

The morning before the campaign was to begin, Ali entered the mosque in Kufa to pray. There he was met by Abd al-Rahman ibn 'Amr ibn Muljam, a Kharijite, who pushed his way through the crowded mosque, shouting, "Judgment belongs to God, Ali, not to you."

Drawing a poisoned sword, Ibn Muljam struck Ali on the head. It was a superficial wound, but the poison did its work. Two days later,

Ali died, and with him the dream of the Banu Hashim to unite the holy community of God under the single banner of the Prophet's family.

In a sermon delivered a few years before his assassination, Ali remarked that "a virtuous man is recognized by the good that is said about him and the praises which God has destined him to receive from others." These were prescient words, for Ali may have died, but he was not forgotten. For millions of Shi'ah throughout the world, Ali remains the model of Muslim piety: the light that illuminates the straight path to God. He is, in the words of Ali Shariati, "the best in speech . . . the best in worship . . . the best in faith."

It is this heroic vision of Ali that has been firmly planted in the hearts of those who refer to the person they believe to have been the sole successor to Muhammad not as the fourth Caliph, but as something else, something *more*.

Ali, the Shi'ah claim, was the first *Imam:* the Proof of God on Earth.

❧

THE CALIPHATE, WROTE Sir Thomas Arnold, "grew up without any pre-vision." This was an office that developed not so much through the conscious determination of the Rightly Guided Caliphs, but as the result of conditions that the Ummah encountered as it matured from a tiny community in the Hijaz to a vast empire stretching from the Atlas Mountains in West Africa to the eastern edges of the Indian subcontinent. It is not surprising, therefore, that disagreements over the function of the Caliphate and the nature of the Ummah ultimately tore the Muslim community apart, forever shattering any hope of preserving the unity and harmony that Muhammad had envisioned for his followers. Nor is it surprising that three of the first four leaders of Islam were killed by fellow Muslims, though it is important to recognize that both the rebels who murdered Uthman and the Kharijites who assassinated Ali were, like their spiritual successors among the Jihadists of today, far more concerned with maintaining their personal ideal of Muhammad's community than with protecting that community from external enemies.

After Ali's death, Mu'awiyah was able to seize absolute control of all the Muslim lands. Moving the capital from Kufa to Damascus, Mu'awiyah inaugurated the Umayyad Dynasty, completing the transformation of the Caliph into a king, and the Ummah into an empire. Mu'awiyah's Arab dynasty lasted a very short time, from 661 to 750 C.E. Ultimately, it was supplanted by the Abbasid Dynasty, which was carried to power with the help of the non-Arab (mostly Persian) converts who so greatly outnumbered the Arab élites. The Abbasids claimed descent from Muhammad's uncle al-Abbas and rallied support from the Shi'ite factions by moving their capital to Baghdad and massacring all the Umayya they could find. But the Shi'ah ultimately rejected Abbasid claims of legitimacy and, as a result, were ruthlessly persecuted by the new Caliphs.

While continuing to rule as secular kings, the Abbasid Caliphs embroiled themselves far more deeply in religious matters than had their Umayyad predecessors. As we shall see, the seventh Abbasid Caliph, al-Ma'mun (d. 833), even attempted to impose a measure of imperial orthodoxy upon the Muslims under his rule by launching a short-lived, and ultimately unsuccessful, religious inquisition against those Ulama who disagreed with his theological beliefs.

Although their dynasty lasted well into the eleventh century, the later Abbasid Caliphs were nothing more than figureheads who wielded no direct authority over the Muslim lands. Even Baghdad, their capital, was under the control of a Shi'ite conglomerate of aristocratic Iranian families called the Buyids, who from 932 to 1062 C.E. ran all affairs of state but still allowed the Abbasid Caliph to remain on his powerless throne. Meanwhile, in Cairo, the Fatimids (909–1171)—Shi'ites who claimed descent from Ali's wife and Muhammad's daughter, Fatima—established themselves as Baghdad's rivals, maintaining political control over everything from Tunisia to Palestine. And in Spain, a lone descendant of the Umayya, Abd al-Rahman, who had managed to escape from the massacre that took place in Syria, founded his own dynasty that not only lasted well into the fifteenth century but became the paradigm of Muslim-Jewish-Christian relations.

The Persian Buyid chiefs were eventually replaced by their own Turkic slave-guards who founded both the Ghaznavid Dynasty (977–1186), which claimed suzerainty over northeastern Iran, Afghanistan, and northern India, and the Saljuq Dynasty (1038–1194), which ruled most of the lands east of that. It was the Turks who, infiltrating the various sultanates as hired militia, managed many years later to reunite most of the Muslim lands under the single Caliphate of the Ottomans: the Sunni dynasty that ruled from their capital in Istanbul from 1453 until 1924, when the Ottoman Empire was dismantled and the Caliphate abolished.

There is no longer any such thing as a Caliph. With the rise of the modern nation-state in the Middle East, Muslims have been struggling to reconcile their dual identities as both citizens of independent sovereign states and members of a unified worldwide community. Some have argued, a few of them violently, that the Caliphate should be restored as the emblem of Muslim unity. These Muslims believe that the ideals of Islam and nationalism are "diametrically opposed to each other," to quote Mawlana Mawdudi, founder of the Pakistani sociopolitical movement *Jama'at-i Islami* (the Islamic Association). Consequently, Mawdudi and many others feel that the only legitimate Islamic state would be a world-state "in which the chains of racial and national prejudices would be dismantled."

The twentieth century has witnessed a transformation of the historic contest over the function of the Caliph and the nature of the Ummah into a debate over the proper way to combine the religious and social principles of Islam—as defined by Muhammad and developed by the Rightly Guided Ones—with modern ideals of constitutionalism and democratic rights. And yet, this contemporary debate remains deeply rooted in the same questions of religious and political authority with which the Ummah grappled during the first few centuries of Islam.

Thus, in 1934, the modernist reformer Ali Abd ar-Raziq (1888–1966) argued in his book *Islam and the Bases of Government* for the separation of religion and state in Egypt by drawing a clear distinction between the authority of the Prophet, which he believed was solely limited to his religious function as Messenger of God, and the purely secular function of the Caliphate, which was nothing more than a civil institution that all Muslims felt free to question, oppose, and even rise up against. Ar-Raziq claimed that the universality of Islam could be based only on its religious and moral principles, which have nothing to do with the political order of individual states.

Some years later, the Egyptian academic and activist Sayyid Qutb (1906–1966) countered ar-Raziq's argument by claiming that Muhammad's position in Medina encompassed both religious and political authority, making Islam a unity whose "theological beliefs [cannot be] divorced in nature or in objective from secular life." Therefore, the only legitimate Islamic state is that which addresses both the material and the moral needs of its citizens.

In the 1970s, the Ayatollah Ruhollah Khomeini applied a distinctly Shi'ite interpretation of Qutb's argument to assume control over a social revolution that was already under way against Iran's despotic American-backed monarchy. Appealing both to the historic sentiments of the country's Shi'ite majority and the democratic aspirations of its disaffected masses, Khomeini argued that only a supreme religious authority could manage the "social and political affairs of the people in the same way as the Prophet [had done]."

All three of these thinkers were, in one way or another, trying to restore some sense of unity to what has become a deeply fractured worldwide community of Muslims. Yet without either a centralized political authority (like a Caliph) or a centralized religious authority (like a Pope), the only institutions in the modern world that have had any measure of success in uniting the Muslim community under a single banner have been the religious institutions of the Ulama.

Throughout Islamic history, as Muslim dynasties tumbled over one another, Muslim kings were crowned and dethroned, and Islamic parliaments elected and dissolved, only the Ulama, in their capacity as the link to the traditions of the past, have managed to retain their self-imposed role as the leaders of Muslim society. As a result, over the past fourteen centuries, Islam as we know it has been almost exclusively defined by an extremely small, rigid, and often profoundly traditionalist group of men who, for better or worse, consider themselves to be the unyielding pillars upon which the religious, social, and political foundations of the religion rest. How they gained this authority, and what they have done with it, is perhaps the most important chapter in the story of Islam.

6. This Religion Is a Science

THE DEVELOPMENT OF ISLAMIC THEOLOGY AND LAW

THE INQUISITION BEGINS with a simple question: "Is the Quran created by God, or is it uncreated and coeternal with God?"

Sitting atop his throne of gleaming gold and precious gems, the young Abbasid Caliph, al-Mu'tasim (d. 842), remains apathetic as one by one "the learned men of God"—the Ulama—are dragged before him in shackles to answer the Inquisitor's question. If they admit the Quran is a *created* thing (the dominant theological position of those who are called "Rationalists"), they are free to return to their homes and continue their teaching. If, however, they still contend that the Quran is *uncreated* (the position of the so-called "Traditionalists"), they are flogged and thrown into prison.

The procession of Ulama continues for hours as al-Mu'tasim sits in silence, listening to theological arguments that he himself barely understands. He is bored and noticeably ill at ease. The controversy over whether the Quran was created by God or not holds no interest for him. He is a military commander, not a scholar. There are revolts to crush and battles to win throughout the Empire. And yet, here he must sit, flanked by his scarlet-robed viziers (themselves theologians, not soldiers), in command not of an army, but of an inquisition that was forced upon him by his older brother, the seventh Abbasid Caliph, al-Ma'mun.

"Stand together, all of you, and speak well of me if you can," al-Mu'tasim recalls his older brother muttering on his deathbed. "If you know of evil I have done, refrain from mentioning it, for I will be taken from among you [and judged] by what you say."

There is so much to say, al-Mu'tasim thinks, as yet another religious scholar is taken away to be tortured by his guards. Nevertheless—always dutiful, always loyal to his family—al-Mu'tasim remains silent, if only for the sake of his brother's immortal soul, and allows the next scholar to be dragged into his presence.

This one is a dark-skinned old man wearing a coarse white turban and filthy loincloth. His long beard is dyed with henna, which has bled onto his cheeks and chest. His face is bruised, his eyes blackened. He has been tortured already, and more than once. Like the rest, he is in chains. Yet he stands tall and faces the Caliph without fear. He has been here many times before to defend his position on the Quran against the former Caliph, al-Ma'mun. But this is the first time he has stood before al-Ma'mun's successor.

The weathered old man is forced to sit while his name is read to the court. When he is revealed to be none other than Ahmad ibn Hanbal—the immensely popular scholastic theologian and founder of the Traditionalist Hanbali school of law—al-Mu'tasim stiffens. Rising from his throne, he points an angry finger at his chief inquisitor, Ibn Abi Du'ad (another man forced upon him by his brother), and shouts, "Did you not allege that ibn Hanbal is a young man? Is this not a middle-aged Shaykh?"

The Inquisitor tries to calm al-Mu'tasim, explaining that the accused has already been questioned by al-Ma'mun on a number of occasions and, in light of his eminence, has been given many chances to reconsider his position with regard to the nature of the Quran.

However, he has rebuffed all attempts to make him compromise, insisting instead on maintaining his heretical position that the Quran, the Speech of God, is *one* with God.

Too exasperated to argue, al-Mu'tasim sits back down and allows his Inquisitor to commence the questioning. "Ahmad ibn Hanbal," Ibn Abi Du'ad begins, "do you regard the Quran to be created or uncreated?"

The Caliph leans forward, glaring at the old man, waiting for his answer. But, as he has done so many times before, Ibn Hanbal ignores the Inquisitor's question and instead replies with a slight smile, "I testify that there is no god but God."

Al-Mu'tasim sinks back into his throne, cursing his brother under his breath, while Ibn Hanbal is taken outside, suspended between two poles, and flogged.

Al-Ma'mun had become Caliph by laying siege to Baghdad—the capital of the Abbasid Caliphate—and killing his half-brother, al-Amin. But because al-Ma'mun and al-Amin had been designated co-Caliphs by their father, the infamous Harun al-Rashid (d. 809), al-Ma'mun was compelled to justify what was essentially an illegitimate usurpation of the Caliphate by claiming divine sanction. God had bestowed the Caliphate upon him, al-Ma'mun declared, and God must be obeyed.

None of this was new, of course; violent internecine conflict was a regular feature of all Muslim dynasties, and most usurpers are forced to legitimize their rule by asserting some kind of divine endorsement. The entire Abbasid Empire had excused their usurpation and indiscriminate massacre of the Umayyads by declaring themselves agents of God. But what made al-Ma'mun different from his predecessors was that he seemed honestly to believe that God had given him the Caliphate so that he could guide the Muslim community toward what he understood to be the correct interpretation of Islam.

"I am the rightly guided leader," he announced in a letter to the army, informing them of the new political and religious order in Baghdad and demanding absolute obedience to his divine guidance.

This was a startling statement. Ever since Mu'awiyah had transformed the Caliphate into a monarchy, the question of the Caliph's religious authority had been more or less settled: the Caliph ran the civil affairs of the community, while the Ulama guided the believers on the straight path to God. Certainly there were Caliphs who exercised religious influence over the Ummah. But none had ever dared to set themselves up as some sort of "Muslim Pope," demanding absolute religious obedience from the community. And yet, that is exactly what al-Ma'mun, who had always thought of himself as a religious scholar first and a political leader second, was seeking to do.

As a young boy, al-Ma'mun had been formally trained in the religious sciences and had distinguished himself as an expert in Islamic law and theology, especially in the Rationalist tradition (about which more will be said). When he became Caliph, he surrounded himself with like-minded Ulama, with whom he regularly debated matters pertaining to the attributes of God, the question of free will, and, most importantly, the nature of the Quran, which al-Ma'mun considered a created thing—wholly separate from God's essence.

Up until this time, al-Ma'mun's position with regard to the Quran was the minority opinion of the Ulama; most religious clerics believed the Quran to be coeternal with God. However, in the last year of his reign, the Caliph declared that henceforth, all teachers and scholars of religion had to conform to the doctrine that the Quran was created. Otherwise, they would no longer be allowed to teach.

Again, while the notion that the Caliph could have influence over religious issues was not new, this was the first time that a Caliph had made himself the exclusive arbiter of religious authority. It is impossible to say what would have happened had al-Ma'mun succeeded in his attempt at what Richard Bulliet has rightly called a "reformulation of [Caliphal] legitimacy." Quite likely, Islam would be a completely different religion today. The Caliphate might have become a Papacy; religious authority could have been centralized within the state, and an orthodox Muslim Church would have developed as a result.

But al-Ma'mun did not succeed. In fact, a few years later, under the Caliphate of al-Mu'tasim's son, al-Mutawakkil (d. 861), the Inquisition was repealed with the understanding that never again would the Caliph embroil himself so explicitly in religious affairs. Indeed, al-Mutawakkil swung the theological pendulum to the side of the Traditionalists by richly rewarding their Ulama and persecuting the very same Rationalists who had up until his reign enjoyed the favors of the court. By the reign of the Caliph al-Qadir (d. 1031), the vast majority of the Traditionalist Ulama, especially the influential Hanbalites, were united under a single doctrine.

Unshackled by the state, the Ulama were now free to ascend to a position of unquestioned religious authority in the Ummah, which they used not only to institutionalize their legal and theological opinions into distinct schools of thought but also to formulate a binding, comprehensive code of conduct called the *Shariah*, forever transforming Islam from a religion into an all-embracing way of life: one that the Ulama claimed sole authority to define. As the ninth-century legal scholar Malik ibn Anas, founder of the Maliki school of law, once quipped, "This religion is a science, so pay close attention to those from whom you learn it."

RELIGIONS BECOME INSTITUTIONS when the myths and rituals that once shaped their sacred histories are transformed into authoritative models of *orthodoxy* (the correct interpretation of myths) and *orthopraxy* (the correct interpretation of rituals), though one is often emphasized over the other. Christianity may be the supreme example of an "orthodoxic" religion; it is principally one's *beliefs*—expressed through creed—that make one a faithful Christian. On the opposite end of the spectrum is Judaism, a quintessentially "orthopraxic" religion, where it is principally one's *actions*—expressed through the Law—that make one an observant Jew. It is not that beliefs are irrelevant in Judaism, or actions unimportant in Christianity. Rather, it is that of the two religions, Judaism places far greater emphasis on orthopraxic behavior than does Christianity.

Like Judaism, Islam is primarily an orthopraxic religion, so much so that Wilfred Cantwell Smith has suggested translating the word *Sunni* as "orthoprax" rather than "orthodox." However, because the Ulama have tended to regard Islamic practice as informing Islamic theology, orthopraxy and orthodoxy are intimately bound together in Islam, meaning questions of theology, or *kalam*, are impossible to separate from questions of law, or *fiqh*.

For this reason, the Ulama often dismissed the practice of pure speculative theology as insignificant babble (*kalam* means "talking" or "speech," and Muslim theologians were often pejoratively referred to as *ahl al-kalam*, the "People of Talking"). What most concerned the Ulama from the first days of the Islamic expansion, especially as the Ummah became ever more widely dispersed and varied with regard to language and culture, was not so much theological arguments about the attributes of God (though, as we shall see, this would eventually become vigorously debated among scholars), but rather the formalization of specific ways to express faith through ritual. Their ultimate objective was to form strict guidelines that would establish exactly who was and who was not a Muslim. The result of their labors became what is now commonly known as the *Five Pillars of Islam*.

The Five Pillars constitute the principal ritual activities of the Muslim faith. Yet, as John Renard remarks, the Pillars are not meant to "reduce the spirit and life of a complex global community to a cluster of religious practices." More than anything, the Five Pillars are meant as a *metaphor* for Islam; they are a summary not just of what is required to be a member of the Ummah, but also of what it means to be a Muslim.

Contrary to perception, the Pillars are not oppressive obligations—quite the opposite. These are highly pragmatic rituals, in that the believer is responsible only for those tasks that he or she is able to perform. Nor are the Pillars mere perfunctory actions. The single most important factor in the performance of any Muslim ritual is the believer's intention, which must be consciously proclaimed before the ritual can begin. Ultimately, the Pillars are intended to be "a totality of actions," which, according to Mohamed A. Abu Ridah, are not merely "verbal and bodily, but, above all, mental and moral, performed according to certain conditions of conscious intention, of external and internal purity, presence of mind, humility and submissiveness of the heart, creating within the soul of the believer a real life of religious devotion and spirituality."

With the exception of the main Pillar, the *shahadah*, or profession of faith (which will be discussed last), these are all fundamentally communal activities. In fact, the primary purpose of the Five Pillars is to assist the believer in articulating, through actions, his or her membership in the Muslim community. The ancient Kharijite ideal of the Ummah as a charismatic and divinely inspired community through

which salvation is achieved has become the standard (orthodox) doctrine of the vast majority of Muslims in the world who, without a centralized religious authority and with no Church or standardized
religious hierarchy, view the community as the nucleus of the Muslim
faith.

Put simply, the community is the Church in Islam: the "bearer of
values," to use Montgomery Watt's oft-quoted phrase. The Ummah
confers meaning and purpose on the believer, whose national, ethnic,
racial, and sexual identity are and always will be subordinate to his or
her membership in the worldwide community of Muslims: a community not bound by any borders, geographic or temporal. Thus when
one fasts during the month of Ramadan or joins in the Friday prayers,
one does so with the knowledge that all Muslims—from the first days
of Muhammad's preaching until today, and in every part of the
world—fast and pray in precisely the same way, at precisely the same
time.

The first Pillar, and the first distinctly Muslim practice enacted by
Muhammad in Mecca, is *salat*, or ritual prayer. There are two kinds of
prayer in Islam: *du'a*, which refers to individual, informal communication between the believer and God; and *salat*, which is the ritualized,
obligatory prayer performed five times a day: sunrise, noon, after-
noon, sunset, and evening. *Salat*, which means "to bow, bend, or
stretch," is composed of a series of yogic movements that include
standing, bowing, rising, sitting, turning east and west, and falling
prostrate, all repeated in cycles (called *raka'ah*), and accompanied by
specific verses from the Quran.

As with all Muslim rituals, *salat* can begin only after the intention
to pray is voiced, and only while the Muslim faces toward Mecca, the
direction of prayer, or *qiblah*. Although salat can be performed individually as a means to purify and cleanse the soul, it is meant to be a
communal act that binds the Ummah as a single body. For this reason,
it is always preferable to perform salat in a place of assembly. Indeed,
one particular salat—the noon prayer on Fridays (*salat al-jum'a*)—
must be performed in the mosque, in the presence of the community.
And while five daily prayers may seem like a heavy burden, the obligation is suspended for the sick, those who are traveling, or anyone else

who is unable to perform them for any justifiable reason; if one wishes, missed salats can always be made up at a later time.

The second Pillar was also established in the early years of Muhammad's movement in Mecca. This is the paying of alms, or *zakat*. As previously explained, zakat is alms given as a tax to the community, which is then distributed to the poor to ensure their care and protection. It is not a voluntary tithe; it is a religious obligation. *Zakat* literally means "purification," and it is a reminder to all Muslims of their social and economic responsibilities to the Ummah. Of course, zakat is paid only by those who can afford to do so; otherwise, one would receive zakat.

As the Ummah developed into an empire, zakat transformed from an obligatory almsgiving to a sort of state tax levied on all Muslims (as mentioned earlier, non-Muslims, such as Christians and Jews, paid a wholly separate "protection tax" called *jizyah*). During the height of the Caliphate, it was common practice to use zakat to fund the army—a practice that caused an uproar from many in the Muslim community. With the end of the Caliphal period and the rise of the modern nation-state, Muslim governments increasingly took upon themselves the role of collecting and distributing zakat. Indeed, the payment of zakat, though deliberately differentiated from regular state taxes, has become mandatory in a number of Muslim countries including Pakistan, Libya, Yemen, and Saudi Arabia, the latter of which imposes zakat on both individuals and businesses. However, most Muslims continue the traditional practice of paying zakat individually to their local mosque or religious institution, which then distributes the funds to the neediest members of the community.

The third Pillar, the month-long Muslim fast (*sawm* in Arabic) which takes place during Ramadan, was not firmly instituted as a Muslim ritual until after the emigration to Medina. Considering that the concept of fasting was thoroughly foreign to the Bedouin experience—it would have been absurd to go voluntarily without food or water in a desert climate—there can be no doubt that Muhammad adopted this ritual from Arabia's Jews. The Quran admits as much when it states, "Fasting is prescribed for you, *just as it was prescribed for those before you*" (2:183; emphasis added). And al-Tabari notes that the first Muslim fast coincided with Yom Kippur; Muhammad specifically ordered his followers to fast with the Jews in commemoration of their flight from Egypt. Only later was the fast changed to Ramadan, the month in which Muslims believe the Quran was first revealed to Muhammad.

During the month of Ramadan, no one may eat, drink, or have sexual intercourse between sunup and sundown. Again, the chief purpose behind the ritual fast is to bind the community as one. It is a reminder of the suffering and poverty of those among them who go without food throughout the year. For this reason, Muslims who are not obliged to fast—the old and the sick, the pregnant and nursing, travelers, and those who perform heavy manual labor—are instead required by the Quran to feed the hungry (2:184). And while an entire month of fasting may sound like a grim experience, Ramadan is in actuality a time for both spiritual introspection and festive celebration. Friends, families, entire neighborhoods spend the long nights of the month breaking fast together, while the final night of Ramadan, *Eid al-Fitr*, is the most widely celebrated holiday in the whole of the Islamic world.

The fourth, and perhaps the most famous, Pillar is the annual Hajj pilgrimage to Mecca. All Muslims must, if possible, journey to Mecca at least once in their lives to take part in the sacred rites of the Ka'ba. Technically, the rites at the Ka'ba can be performed anytime in what is known as the "lesser pilgrimage," or *umra*. However, the Hajj itself takes place only during the last month of the lunar year, when the sacred city swells to accommodate the crowds of pilgrims like a "mother's uterus that miraculously makes room for its child," to quote the famed twelfth-century Spanish scholar and poet Ibn Jubayr.

Like their pagan counterparts, Muslim pilgrims travel to Mecca to experience the transformative effects of the Ka'ba. But unlike the pagan sanctuary, the Muslim Ka'ba is not a repository of the gods. Rather, it is a symbol for the living presence of the one and only God. The Ka'ba, it must be understood, has no architectural significance. It is a cube—the simplest form a building can take—veiled in black (which is no color) and rimmed with the word of God. It is not a temple in the traditional sense. It no longer has any intrinsic sanctity; it has been torn down and rebuilt a number of times. Though dubbed "the House of God," the Ka'ba houses nothing, save for a few Qurans and some ancient relics. Yet in its utter simplicity, the Ka'ba and the rites associated with it function as a communal meditation on the Oneness and Unity of God (a concept that will be more fully explored below).

The Hajj begins when the pilgrims cross the consecrated threshold of the Grand Mosque, which surrounds the Ka'ba, separating the sacred from the profane. To come into the presence of the sanctuary, pilgrims must rid themselves of their ordinary clothes and don the sanctified garments—two seamless white pieces of cloth for men; any similar plain garment for women—that signify a state of purity (*ihram*). The men shave their heads and trim their beards and nails; the women clip a few locks of hair.

Once this sanctified state has been reached, the intention to perform the rites is voiced, and the pilgrim embarks on the *tawaf*: the seven circumambulations of the sanctuary, which still function as the principal ritual of the pilgrimage. While in every corner of the world—from the farthest fringes of sub-Saharan Africa to the affluent suburbs of Chicago—Muslims face the Ka'ba in prayer, when they are gathered in Mecca, the Ka'ba becomes the axis of the world, and *every* direction is the direction of prayer. It is, one might say, the centrifugal force of praying in the presence of the sacred shrine that compels the worshipper to orbit the sanctuary.

When the circumambulations are complete, the pilgrim moves on to a series of rituals that, according to tradition, were established by Muhammad in the last year of his life. These include running back and forth between the twin hills, Safah and Marwah, to commemorate Hagar's search for water; traveling to Mt. Arafat (the refuge of Adam and Eve after they were exiled from Eden, and the site of Muhammad's final sermon); the stoning of three pillars at Mina, which represent the Devil; and finally, the sacrifice of sheep, cows, or lambs to mark the end of the pilgrimage (the meat is then distributed to the poor). When the rites are complete, the pilgrim removes the sanctified garments and reenters the world of the profane as a *Hajji;* the next time the garments are worn will be as a burial shroud.

The Hajj is the supreme communal event in Islam. It is the only major Muslim ritual in which men and women participate with no division between them. In the sanctified state, when every pilgrim is identically dressed, there is no longer any rank, or class, or status; there is no gender and no ethnic or racial identity: there is no identity whatsoever, save as Muslims. It was precisely this communal spirit that Malcolm X referred to when he wrote during his own pilgrimage, "I have never before seen sincere and true brotherhood practiced by all colors together."

These four rituals—communal prayer, the paying of alms, the fast of Ramadan, and the Hajj pilgrimage—provide meaning to the Muslim faith and unity to the Muslim community. Yet one could argue that the primary function of these four is to express the fifth and most important Pillar (and the only one requiring belief rather than action): the *shahadah*, or profession of faith, which initiates every convert into the Muslim faith.

"There is no god but God, and Muhammad is God's Messenger."

This deceptively simple statement is not only the basis for all articles of faith in Islam, it is in some ways the sum and total of Islamic theology. This is because the shahadah signifies recognition of an exceedingly complex theological doctrine known as *tawhid*.

The doctrine of tawhid is so central to the development of Islamic theology that "the Science of Kalam" (*'ilm al-kalam*) is synonymous with "the Science of Tawhid" (*'ilm al-tawhid*). But tawhid, which literally means "making one," implies more than just monotheism. True, there is only one God, but that is just the beginning. Tawhid means that God is Oneness. God is Unity: wholly indivisible, entirely unique, and utterly indefinable. God resembles nothing in either essence or attributes.

"Nothing is like Him," the mystic and scholar Abu Hamid al-Ghazali (1058–1111) wrote in his *Revival of the Religious Sciences*, "and He is not like anything." God is, as the Quran repeatedly reminds believers, "elevated"; God is "eminent." When Muslims cry *Allahu Akbar!* (literally, "God is greater!"), what they mean is not that God is greater than this or that, but that God is simply *greater*.

Obviously, human beings have no choice but to speak of God in human language, through human symbols and metaphors. Therefore, one can refer to God's attributes as embodying "Goodness" or

"Being," in the classical philosophical sense, but only with the recognition that these are meaningless terms when applied to God, who is neither substance nor accident. Indeed, tawhid suggests that God is beyond any description, beyond any human knowledge. "Imagination does not reach Him," stressed the Egyptian theologian al-Tahawi (d. 933), "and understanding does not comprehend Him." God is, in other words, wholly Other: the *Mysterium Tremendum*, to borrow Rudolph Otto's famous phrase.

Because tawhid insists that God is One, a group of Muslim mystics called the *Sufis* will claim that there can be nothing apart from God. God is, according to the Sufi master Ibn al-Arabi, the *only* being with real existence: the *only* reality. For al-Ghazali God is *al-Awwal*, "the First, before whom there is nothing," and *al-Akhir*, "the Last, after whom there is nothing." Al-Ghazali, it must be understood, is making neither an ontological nor a teleological argument for the existence of God; God is neither Thomas Aquinas's "First Cause," nor Aristotle's "Prime Mover." God is the *only* cause; God is movement itself.

If tawhid is the foundation of Islam, then its opposite, *shirk*, is Islam's greatest sin, for which some Muslims claim there can be no forgiveness (see the Quran 2:116). In its simplest definition, *shirk* means associating anything with God. But like tawhid, shirk is not so simple a concept. Polytheism is obviously shirk, but so is obscuring God's Oneness in any way. For Muslims, the Trinity is shirk, for God is nothing if not Unity. Any attempt to anthropomorphize God by endowing the Divine with human attributes, thereby limiting or restricting God's dominion, could be shirk. But shirk can also be defined as placing obstacles in the way of God, whether greed, or drink, or pride, or false piety, or any other grave sin that keeps the believer apart from God.

Ultimately, tawhid implies recognizing creation as a "universal unity," to quote Ali Shariati, without divisions into "this world and the hereafter, the natural and the supernatural, substance and meaning, spirit and body." In other words, the relationship between God and creation is like that between "light and the lamp that emits it." One God; one Creation. One God.

One God.

* * *

As the starting point for all doctrinal discussions in Islam, the Oneness and Unity of God clearly raise some theological problems. For example, if God is absolutely omnipotent, then is God also responsible for evil? Does humanity have the free will to choose between right and wrong, or are we all predetermined for either salvation or damnation? And how is one to interpret God's attributes—God's Knowledge, God's Power, and especially God's Speech as recorded in the Quran? Is the word of God *coexistent* with God, or is it a created thing, like nature and the cosmos? Does not an answer either way necessarily compromise Divine Unity?

Given the relationship between religion and politics in early Islam, it is not surprising that these distinctly theological questions also had important political implications. The Umayyad Caliphs, for instance, were eager to exploit the argument for God's determinate power to sanction their absolute authority over the Ummah. After all, if the Umayyads were the chosen deputies of God, then all of their actions were, in effect, decreed by God. This idea was adopted by the distinguished theologian Hasan al-Basra (642–728), who claimed that even a wicked Caliph must be obeyed, because he had been placed on the throne by God.

And yet, al-Basra was no predeterminist: his position on the Caliphate reflected his political quietism and his anti-Kharijite stance, not his theological views. Like the Qadarite school of theology with which he is often associated, al-Basra believed that God's foreknowledge of events did not necessarily correspond to predeterminism: God may know what one is going to do, but that does not mean God *forces* one to do it. Some theologians within the Qadarite school went one step further, to claim that God cannot know our actions until they occur, a notion that understandably offended the more traditionalist theologians, who believed the doctrine of tawhid necessitated the belief in God's determinate power. If the Creator and Creation are one, they argued, then how could humanity contradict the will of God?

But the "predeterminists" were themselves divided between those, like the radical sect of the Jahmites, who considered all human activities (including salvation) to be predetermined by God, and those, like the followers of the aforementioned legal scholar Ahmad ibn

Hanbal (780–855), who accepted God's absolute control over human affairs but still maintained humanity's responsibility for reacting positively or negatively to the circumstances predetermined by God.

By the ninth and tenth centuries, this debate over determinism and free will was loosely divided between two major strands of thought: the so-called "Rationalist position," most clearly represented by the Mu'tazilite school, and the "Traditionalist" position, dominated by the Ash'arite school. The Rationalist Ulama of the Mu'tazilah argued that God, while fundamentally indefinable, nevertheless exists within the framework of human reason. Challenging the notion that religious truth could be accessed only through divine revelation, the Mu'tazilah promulgated the doctrine that all theological arguments must adhere to the principles of rational thought. Even the interpretation of the Quran and the traditions, or Sunna, of the Prophet were, for the Rationalists, subordinate to human reason. As Abd al-Jabbar (d. 1024), the most influential Mu'tazilite theologian of his time, argued, the "truthfulness" of God's word cannot be based solely on God's Revelation, for that would be circular reasoning.

The Spanish philosopher and physician Ibn Rushd (1126–98), better known as Averroës in the West, pushed al-Jabbar's conception of truth to its limit by proposing a "two truths" theory of knowledge in which religion and philosophy are placed in opposition to each other. According to Ibn Rushd, religion simplifies the truth for the masses by resorting to easily recognizable signs and symbols, regardless of the doctrinal contradictions and rational incongruities that inevitably result from the formation and rigid interpretation of dogma. Philosophy, however, is *itself* truth; its purpose is merely to express reality through the faculty of human reason.

It is this commitment to what Binyamin Abrahamov calls "the overwhelming power of reason over revelation" that has led modern scholars to label the Mu'tazilah the first speculative theologians in Islam. And it was precisely this emphasis on the primacy of human reason that the Traditionalist Ulama of the Ash'arite school so strenuously opposed.

The Ash'ari argued that human reason, while certainly important, must nevertheless be subordinate to the Quran and the Sunna of the Prophet. If religious knowledge could be gained only through rational speculation, as the Mu'tazilah claimed, there would be no need for prophets and revelations; the result would be a confusion of theological diversity that would allow people to follow their own wills rather than the will of God. The Ash'ari considered reason to be unstable and changing, while the prophetic and scriptural traditions—especially as they were defined by the Traditionalist Ulama—were stable and fixed.

With regard to the question of free will, Rationalist theologians adopted and expanded the view that humanity was perfectly free to act in either goodness or evil, meaning that the responsibility for salvation rested directly in the hands of the believer. After all, it would be irrational for God to behave so unjustly as to will belief and unbelief upon humanity, then reward one and punish the other. Many Traditionalists rejected this argument on the grounds that it seemed to compel God to act in a rational, and therefore human, manner. This, according to the Ash'ari, was shirk. As the omnipotent creator of all things, God must be the progenitor "of the good and evil, of the little and the much, of what is outward and what is inward, of what is sweet and what is bitter, of what is liked and what is disliked, of what is fine and what is bad, of what is first and what is last," to quote the Hanbali creed, unquestionably the most influential of all Islamic schools of thought.

The Rationalist and Traditionalist theologians further differed in their interpretation of God's attributes. Both believed that God was eternal and unique, and both grudgingly acknowledged the anthropomorphic descriptions of God provided by the Quran. However, while most Rationalists interpreted these descriptions as merely figurative devices intended for poetical purposes, most Traditionalists rejected all symbolic interpretations of the Revelation, claiming that the Quran's references to God's hands and face, while not meant to be likened to human hands or faces, must nevertheless be read literally.

God has a face, argued Abu'l Hasan al-Ash'ari (873–935), founder of the Ash'arite school, because the Quran says so ("the face of your Lord will endure forever"; 55:27), and it is not our place to ask how or why. Indeed, the Ash'ari often responded to the rational incongruities and internal contradictions that resulted from their rigid interpretation of religious doctrine by cultivating a formula of *bila kayfa*, loosely translated as "Don't ask why."

This formula horrified the Rationalists, and especially scholars such as Ibn Sina (Avicenna in the West; 980–1037), who considered God's attributes—God's knowledge, speech, etc.—to be nothing more than "guideposts" that merely reflected the human mind's understanding of the Divine, not the Divine itself. The Rationalists argued that God's attributes could not possibly exist coeternally with God, but must be a part of creation. Assigning eternal attributes to God would, according to Wasil ibn Ata (d. 748), founder of the Mu'tazilite school, be tantamount to arguing for the existence of more than one eternal being.

The Traditionalist Ulama rejected Wasil's argument, countering that while God's attributes may be separate entities, they nevertheless inhere in God's essence and are, consequently, eternal. "His attributes are from eternity," claimed Abu Hanifah, the Traditionalist founder of the Hanafi school of law (the largest school of law in the modern Muslim world). "Whoever says they are created or originated . . . is an unbeliever."

Of course, when talking about the relationship between God's attributes and God's essence, both the Rationalists and the Traditionalists had one particularly significant attribute in mind: God's Speech; that is, the Quran.

A WONDERFUL STORY is told about the conversion of the Caliph Umar to Islam. Umar's fierce pride in his pagan ancestry and his tribal heritage initially led him to lash out violently against Muhammad and his followers. In fact, Umar had at one time planned to murder Muhammad in order to put an end to his disruptive movement. But as he was on his way to find the Prophet, a friend informed him that his own sister had accepted the new religion and was, at that moment, meeting with one of the believers in her home. Furious, Umar drew his sword and rushed to her house, determined to kill her for betraying their family and tribe. Before he could enter, however, he heard the sacred words of the Quran recited from within. The power and elegance of the recitation fixed him to the spot. He dropped his sword.

"How fine and noble is this speech!" he declared, his eyes filling with tears. And like Saul of Tarsus, who was struck blind by the vision of Jesus admonishing him to stop his persecution of the Christians, Umar was transformed by divine intervention: not because he saw God, but because he *heard* God.

It has been said that the medium through which humanity experiences "the miraculous" can alter dramatically according to time and place. In the age of Moses, for example, miracle was primarily experienced through magic. Moses was forced to prove his prophetic credentials by transforming a rod into a snake or, more spectacularly, by parting the Red Sea. By the time of Jesus, the experience of miracle had, for the most part, shifted to the field of medicine, which also included exorcism. The disciples may have believed Jesus to be the promised Messiah, but there is little doubt that the rest of Judea saw him as merely another wandering healer; almost everywhere Jesus went he was constantly challenged to demonstrate his prophetic identity, not by performing magical feats, but by healing the sick and the lame.

In Muhammad's time, the medium through which miracle was primarily experienced was neither magic nor medicine, but language. Predominantly oral societies like Muhammad's often viewed words as being infused with mystical power. The ancient Greek bard who sang of Odysseus' wanderings and the Indian poet who chanted the sacred verses of the *Ramayana* were more than mere storytellers; they were the mouthpieces of the gods. When at the start of each new year the Native American shaman recounts his tribe's creation myths, his words not only recall the past, they fashion the future. Communities that do not rely on written records tend to believe that the world is continuously re-created through their myths and rituals. In these societies, poets and bards are often priests and shamans; and poetry, as the artful manipulation of the common language, is thought to possess the divine authority necessary to express fundamental truths.

This was particularly true in pre-Islamic Arabia, where poets had an extraordinarily elevated status in society. As Michael Sells documents in *Desert Tracings*, at the start of each pilgrimage season, ancient Mecca's best poets had their verses embroidered in gold on expensive Egyptian cloth banners and suspended from the Ka'ba, not because their odes were of a religious nature (they were most often about the beauty and majesty of the poet's camel!), but because they possessed an intrinsic power that was naturally associated with the Divine. It was this same intrinsic divinity of words that led the Kahins to present their oracular pronouncements through poetry: it would have been inconceivable for the gods to speak in any other way.

Obviously, it is difficult for non-Arabic speakers to appreciate the exquisite quality of the Quran's language. But it may be sufficient to note that the Quran is widely recognized as the Arabic language at its poetic height. Indeed, in codifying the idiom and dialect of the Hijaz, the Quran essentially created the Arabic language. As a text, the Quran is more than the foundation of the Islamic religion; it is the source of Arabic grammar. It is to Arabic what Homer is to Greek, what Chaucer is to English: a snapshot of an evolving language, frozen forever in time.

As "the supreme Arab event," to quote Kenneth Cragg, the Quran is regarded by most Muslims as Muhammad's sole miracle. Like the prophets who came before him, Muhammad was repeatedly urged to prove his divine mission through miraculous acts. But whenever he was challenged in this way, he insisted that he was nothing more than a messenger, and his message was the only miracle he had to offer. And unlike the miracles of other prophets, which are confined to a particular age, Muhammad's miracle of the Quran would, in the words of the twelfth-century mystic Nadjm ad-Din Razi Daya (1177–1256), "remain until the end of the world."

Daya was appealing to a fundamental belief in Islam that in both speech and form, the Quran is incomparable to any other religious or secular writing the world has seen. Muhammad himself often challenged the pagan poets of his time to match the splendor of the Quran, saying, "If you are in doubt of what we have revealed . . . then bring [a verse] like it. But if you cannot—and indeed you cannot—then guard yourself against the Fire, whose fuel is men and stones" (2:23–24; also 16:101).

While the concept of the Umm al-Kitab ("the Mother of Books") means that the Quran is spiritually connected to other sacred scriptures, unlike the Torah and the Gospels—both of which consist of individual books written by many different writers over hundreds of years, conveying the experience of encountering the Divine in history—the Quran is considered to be direct revelation (*tanzil*), the actual words of God handed down through Muhammad, who was little more than a passive conduit. In purely literary terms, the Quran is God's dramatic monologue. It does not recount God's communion with humanity; it *is* God's communion with humanity. It does not reveal God's will; it reveals God's self. And if the doctrine of *tawhid* forbids any division in the Divine Unity, then the Quran is not just the Speech of God, it *is* God.

This was precisely what the Traditionalist Ulama argued. If God is eternal, then so are the divine attributes, which cannot be separated from God's self. This would make the Quran, as God's Speech, an eternal and uncreated thing. The Rationalist Ulama considered this to be an unreasonable point of view that would lead to a number of unsolvable theological problems (Does God speak Arabic? Is every copy of the Quran a copy of God?). The Rationalists argued instead that God's Speech *reflects* God but is not itself God.

Some members of the Ulama, such as Abu Hanifa, tried to bridge the debate between the Rationalists and Traditionalists by claiming that "our utterance of the Quran is created, our writing of it is created, our reciting of it is created, but the Quran [itself] is uncreated." Ibn Kullab (d. 855) agreed, arguing that the Traditionalists were right to consider the word of God as "one single thing in God," but only insofar as it is not made up of physical letters and words. Ibn Kullab's view was refined by Ibn Hazm (994–1064), who posited the existence of a "pre-revealed" Quran (as implied by the concept of Umm al-Kitab) in which "what is in the pages of the book is . . . an imitation of the [physical] Quran." Once again, however, it was the influential Ahmad ibn Hanbal who solidified the Traditionalist doctrine by claiming that what a Muslim reads between the physical covers of the Quran—its every word and letter—is itself the actual word of God: eternal and uncreated.

The debate between the Rationalist and the Traditionalist Ulama continued for a few hundred years, with each school alternating in influence, until the end of the thirteenth century, when, partly in response to al-Ma'mun's disastrous Inquisition, the Traditionalist position became the dominant position in Sunni Islam. Most Rationalists were branded as heretics, and their theories gradually lost influence in all the major schools of law and theology with the exception of the Shi'ite schools (discussed in the following chapter). And while the debate over the nature of the Quran continues to this day, the influence of the Traditionalist interpretation has led to a number of extraordinary theological and legal developments in Islam.

For instance, belief in the eternal, uncreated word of God has led to the widespread conviction among Muslims that the Quran cannot be translated from its original language. A translation into any other language would remove the direct speech of God, rendering it an interpretation of the Quran, not the Quran itself. As Islam spread from the Arabian Peninsula to the rest of the world, every convert—whether Arab, Persian, European, African, or Indian—had to learn the Arabic language in order to read Islam's sacred text. Even today, Muslims of every culture and ethnicity must read the Quran in Arabic, whether they understand it or not. The message of the Quran is vital to living a proper life as a Muslim, but it is the words themselves—the actual speech of the one and only God—that possess a spiritual power known as *baraka*.

While baraka can be experienced in a number of ways, it is most vividly encountered through Islam's unrivaled tradition of calligraphy. Partly because of the primacy of the word in Islam, and partly because of the religion's aversion to iconolatry and thus the figural arts, calligraphy has become the supreme artistic expression in the Muslim world. Yet Islamic calligraphy is more than just an art form; it is the visual representation of the eternal Quran, the symbol of God's living presence on earth.

The words of the Quran are inscribed on mosques, tombs, and prayer rugs in order to sanctify them. They are emblazoned on common objects like cups, bowls, and lamps, so that when one eats from a plate adorned with God's Speech, or lights a lamp with a Quranic verse etched into it, one is able to consume baraka, to be illuminated by it. In the same way that pre-Islamic poetry was thought to convey divine authority, so do the words of the Quran act as a talisman that transmits divine power. It is no wonder, then, that after the Ka'ba had been cleansed and rededicated, the pagan odes that had hung from the sanctuary were torn down and replaced by verses from the Quran, which still form a golden band around the sacred shrine.

Another way in which Muslims experience baraka is through the art, or rather the science, of Quranic recitation. As William Graham has observed, the early Muslim community undoubtedly understood the Quran to be an oral scripture that was intended to be spoken aloud in a community, not read quietly to oneself. Recall that the word "Quran" literally means "recitation," which is why so many passages begin with the command *qul*, or "say."

The early efforts of the Qurra, or Quran readers, to memorize and preserve the sacred scripture eventually led to the creation of a technical science of Quranic recitation called *tajwid*, with strict rules regulating when one is permitted to stop during a recitation and when it is forbidden to stop, when to prostrate oneself and when to rise, when to breathe and when not to take breath, which consonants to stress and how long to hold each vowel. Because Islam has tradition-ally been suspicious of the use of music in worship, for fear of compro-mising the divine nature of the text, a recitation can never be outright musical. However, the use of spontaneous melody is encouraged, and some contemporary Quranic reciters exhibit an extraordinary degree of musical virtuosity. Their recitals are akin to rock concerts at which thousands of boisterous listeners are encouraged to respond to the recitation by shouting their reactions—whether positive or nega-tive—at the performer on stage.

But it would not be entirely correct to call these recitations "con-certs," or even "performances." These are spiritual gatherings at which the reciter transmits the baraka of God's word to what is, in essence, a congregation. Because while the Quran may be God's dra-matic monologue, when read aloud, it is miraculously transformed into a dialogue between the Creator and Creation, a dialogue in which God is physically present.

By far the most significant development of the Traditionalist posi-tion regarding the eternal Quran can be observed in the science of Quranic exegesis. From the start, Muslims had an inordinately diffi-cult time interpreting the meaning and message of the Quran. As the direct speech of God, the Quran was recorded without interpretation or commentary, with little concern for chronology and almost no nar-rative. To assist them in their exegesis, the early Ulama divided the Revelation into two distinct periods—those verses revealed in Mecca and those revealed in Medina—thereby creating a loose chronology that helped clarify their interpretation of the text.

However, for the neophyte, the organization of the Quran can be baffling. The text that Uthman collected is divided into 114 chapters called *Surahs*, each containing a different number of verses or *ayahs*. With few exceptions, every Surah begins with the invocation of the *Basmallah:* "In the name of God, the Compassionate, the Merciful." Perhaps to emphasize the Quran's status as direct revelation, the Surahs are arranged neither chronologically nor thematically, but rather from the longest chapter to the shortest, the lone exception being the first and most important chapter, *Surah al-Fatiha:* the "Opening."

There are two distinct methods of interpreting the Quran. The first, *tafsir*, is primarily concerned with elucidating the literal meaning of the text, while the second, *ta'wil*, is more concerned with the hidden, esoteric meaning of the Quran. Tafsir answers questions of context and chronology, providing an easily understandable framework for Muslims to live a righteous life. Ta'wil delves into the concealed message of the text, which, because of its mystical nature, is comprehensible only to a select few. While both are considered equally valid approaches, the tension between tafsir and ta'wil is but one of the inevitable consequences of trying to interpret an eternal and uncreated scripture that is nevertheless firmly grounded in a specific historical context.

For the Rationalists, who rejected the notion of an uncreated Quran, the only reasonable method of exegesis was one that accounted for the temporal nature of the Revelation. For this reason, the Rationalists stressed the primacy of human reason in determining not just the essence of the Quran, but also its meaning and, most importantly, its historical context. To the Traditionalists, the eternal and uncreated nature of the Quran made it pointless to talk of historical context or original intent when interpreting it. The Quran has never changed and will never change; neither should its interpretation.

As one can imagine, the Traditionalist position had a profound influence on Quranic exegesis. First, it provided the orthodox Ulama with sole authority to interpret what was now widely considered to be a fixed and immutable text revealing the divine will of God. Second, because the eternal, uncreated Quran could not possibly be considered a product of Muhammad's society, historical context could not play any role in its interpretation. What was appropriate for Muhammad's community in the seventh century C.E. must be appropriate for all Muslim communities to come, regardless of the circumstances. This view of the Quran as static and unchanging became increasingly problematic as the Revelation gradually transformed from merely the principle of moral guidance in the Muslim community to the primary source of Islam's Sacred Law: the *Shariah*.

❧

CALLED "THE CORE and kernel of Islam" by Joseph Schacht, the Shariah was developed by the Ulama as the basis for the judgment of all actions in Islam as good or bad, to be rewarded or punished. More specifically, the Shariah recognizes five categories of behavior:

1) actions that are obligatory, in that their performance is rewarded and their omission punished;
2) actions that are meritorious, in that their performance may be rewarded, but their neglect is not punished;
3) actions that are neutral and indifferent;
4) actions that are considered reprehensible, though not necessarily punished; and
5) actions that are forbidden and punished.

These five categories are designed to demonstrate Islam's overarching concern with not only forbidding vice, but also actively promoting virtue.

As a comprehensive body of rules guiding the life of all Muslims, the Shariah is divided into two categories: regulations regarding religious duties, including the proper method of worship; and regulations of a purely juridical nature (though the two often overlap). In either case, the Shariah is meant to regulate only one's external actions; it has little to do with inner spirituality. As a result, those believers who subscribe to Islam's mystical traditions (the Sufis) tend to regard the Shariah as merely the starting point of righteousness; true faith, they say, requires moving beyond the law.

The moral provisions of the Shariah are made concrete through the discipline of *fiqh*, or Islamic jurisprudence, of which the Quran is its first and most important source. The problem, however, is that the Quran is not a book of laws. While there are some eighty or so verses that deal directly with legal issues—matters like inheritance and the status of women, in addition to a handful of penal prescriptions—the Quran makes no attempt whatsoever to establish a system of laws regulating the external behavior of the community, as the Torah does for the Jews. Thus, when dealing with the countless legal issues on which the Quran is silent, the Ulama turn to the traditions, or Sunna, of the Prophet.

The Sunna is composed of thousands upon thousands of stories, or hadith, that claim to recount Muhammad's words and deeds, as well as those of the earliest Companions. As discussed in Chapter 3, as these hadith were passed down from generation to generation, they became increasingly convoluted and inauthentic, so that after a while, nearly every legal or religious opinion—no matter how radical or eccentric—could be legitimated by the Prophet's authority. By the ninth century, the situation had gotten so out of hand that a group of legal scholars, working independently of one another, attempted to catalogue the most reliable hadith into authoritative collections, the most respected of which are the canons of Muhammad al-Bukhari (d. 870) and Muslim ibn al-Hajjaj (d. 875).

The primary criterion by which these collections were authenticated was the chain of transmission, or isnad, that often accompanied each hadith. Those hadith whose isnad could be traced to an early and reliable source were considered "sound" and accepted as authentic, while those that could not were considered "weak" and rejected. One major problem with this method, however, is that before the ninth century, when the collections were completed, a proper and complete isnad was by no means an essential element in the dissemination of a hadith. Joseph Schacht's extensive research on the development of the Shariah has shown how quite a large number of widely acknowledged hadith had their chains of transmission added conjecturally so as to make them appear more authentic. Hence Schacht's whimsical but accurate maxim: "the more perfect the isnad, the later the tradition."

But there is an even larger obstacle to using the Sunna of the

Prophet as a primary source of law. As rigorous as scholars like al-Bukhari and Ibn al-Hajjaj were in scrutinizing each hadith for the signs of correct transmission, the fact is that their method lacked any attempt at political or religious objectivity. The bulk of what are considered to be sound traditions were deemed so not because their isnads were particularly strong, but because they reflected the majority beliefs and practices of the community. In other words, the hadith were collected, and the Sunna developed, specifically to create a sense of Islamic orthodoxy and orthopraxy by legitimizing those beliefs and practices that were already widely accepted by the majority of the Ulama, and eliminating those that were not. While some hadith may in fact contain an authentic historical core that can be traced back to the Prophet and his earliest Companions, the truth is that the Sunna is a far better reflection of the opinions of the ninth-century Ulama than of the seventh-century Ummah. After all, to quote Jonathan Berkey, "It was not Muhammad himself who defined the Sunna, but rather a memory of him."

Reliable or not, the Sunna was grossly inadequate for addressing the myriad legal issues that arose as Islam expanded into an empire. A number of other sources had to be developed to cope with those concerns not expressly dealt with in the Quran and the Sunna. Chief among these was the use of analogical arguments, or *qiyas*, which allowed the Ulama to draw parallels between their community and Muhammad's when responding to new and unfamiliar legal dilemmas. Of course, analogies can be stretched only so far and, in any case, the Traditionalist-dominated schools of law were wary of placing too much emphasis on reasoning over Revelation. So while qiyas remained a vital tool in the development of the Shariah, the Ulama ultimately grew far more dependent on the fourth source of law: *ijma*, or "juridical consensus."

Relying on the Prophet's saying that "my community will never agree on an error," the Ulama posited that the unanimous consensus of the legal scholars of a particular age on a particular issue could create binding legal decisions, even if those decisions seemed to violate Quranic prescriptions (as was the case with the practice of stoning adulterers). Like the Sunna, ijma was developed specifically to create orthodoxy among the Muslim community. But more importantly, ijma served to consolidate the authority of the Ulama as the sole determiners of acceptable Muslim behavior and beliefs. Indeed, it was primarily through the use of ijma that the schools of law were formed.

Unfortunately, as these schools became firmly institutionalized in the Muslim world, so did their legal judgments, so that eventually the consensus of one generation of scholars became binding for successive generations, with the result that the Ulama gradually became less concerned with developing innovative solutions to contemporary legal problems and more occupied with what in Islam is referred to derisively as *taqlid*—the blind acceptance of juridical precedent.

One other major source of law must be mentioned. During the formative stages of the Shariah, it was commonly believed that when the Quran and the Sunna were silent on an issue, and if analogy and consensus had failed to deliver a solution, a qualified legal scholar could use his own independent juristic reasoning to issue a legal ruling, or *fatwa*, which could then be accepted or rejected by the community as they wished. Known as *ijtihad*, this was an absolutely vital source of the law until the end of the tenth century, when the Traditionalist Ulama, who at that time dominated nearly all the major schools of law, discouraged it as a legitimate tool of exegesis. The "closing of the gates of ijtihad," as this action has been called, signaled a major (albeit temporary) setback for those who held that religious truth, as long as it did not explicitly contradict the Revelation, could be discovered through human reason.

By the beginning of the eleventh century, what began as ad hoc gatherings of like-minded Ulama had become crystallized into legal institutions empowered with the binding authority of God's law. The modern Sunni world has four main schools. The Shafii School, which now dominates Southeast Asia, was founded on the principles of Muhammad ash-Shafii (d. 820), who held the Sunna to be the most important source of law. The Maliki School, which is primarily observed in West Africa, was founded by Malik ibn Anas (d. 795), who relied almost exclusively on the traditions of Medina in forming his opinions. The Hanafi School of Abu Hanifah (d. 767), which prevails across most of Central Asia and the Indian subcontinent, is by far the largest and most diverse legal tradition with regard to breadth of interpretation. And finally, the Hanbali School of Ahmad ibn Hanbal (d. 855), the most traditionalist of the legal schools, can be found in pockets throughout the Middle East, but tends to dominate ultraconservative countries like Saudi Arabia and Afghanistan. Added to this group is the Shi'ite school of law founded by Ja'far as-Sadiq (d. 765), which will be dealt with in the following chapter.

The Ulama associated with these schools entrenched themselves as the sole authority of acceptable Islamic behavior and the sole interpreters of acceptable Islamic beliefs. As these schools of thought gradually transformed into legal institutions, the diversity of ideas and freedom of opinion that characterized their early development gave way to rigid formalism, strict adherence to precedent, and an almost complete stultification of independent thought, so that even by the twelfth century, Muslim thinkers like al-Ghazali (himself a Traditionalist) began decrying the Ulama's assertion that "whoever does not know scholastic theology in the form [the Ulama] recognize and does not know the prescriptions of the Holy Law according to the proofs which they have adduced is an unbeliever." As we shall see, al-Ghazali's complaint against the Ulama is as applicable today as it was nine hundred years ago.

In the modern era, as questions of individual religious obligation have entered the political realm, the Ulama's ability to define the public discourse regarding correct behavior and belief has increased dramatically. They have even managed to broaden their audience by playing a far more active role in the political developments of the Middle East. In some Muslim countries, including Iran, Sudan, Saudi Arabia, and Nigeria, the Ulama exert direct political and legal control over the populations, while in most others, they indirectly influence the social and political spheres of society through their religious edicts, their legal rulings, and, most notably, their stewardship of Islam's religious schools, or *madrassas*, where generation after generation of young Muslims are often indoctrinated in a revival of Traditionalist orthodoxy, especially with regard to the static, literalist interpretation of the Quran and the divine, infallible nature of the Shariah. As one Pakistani teacher and scholar recently argued,

The Islamic law has not come into being the way conventional law has. It has not had to undergo the same process of evaluation as all the man-made laws have done. The case of the Islamic law is not that it began with a few rules that gradually multiplied or with rudimentary concepts refined by cultural process with the passage of time; nor did this law originate and grow along with the Islamic community.

As a matter of fact, that is *exactly* how the Shariah developed: "with rudimentary concepts refined by cultural process with the passage of time." This was a process influenced not only by local cultural practices but by both Talmudic and Roman law. With the exception of the Quran, every single source of Islamic law was the result of human, not divine, effort. The early schools of law understood this and so represented nothing more than trends of thought that existed within the Muslim community. The sources from which these schools formed their traditions, especially ijma, allowed for the evolution of thought. For this reason, the opinions of the Ulama—whether Rationalist or Traditionalist—were constantly adapting to contemporary situations, and the law itself was continually reinterpreted and reapplied as necessary.

Regardless, none of the legal decisions made by any of these schools of law were binding on individual Muslims. In fact, until the modern period, it was common for believers to switch their allegiance from one school to another at their pleasure, and there was nothing expressly prohibiting a Muslim from accepting Maliki doctrine on some issues and Hanafi doctrine on others. So it is simply unreasonable to consider what is so obviously the result of human labor, and so plainly subject to changing human biases, to be the infallible, unalterable, inflexible, and binding sacred law of God.

Even the most cursory analysis of the development of the Shariah demonstrates how both the law and the Revelation grew "along with the Islamic community." The Quran itself clearly indicates that while its message is eternal, it was revealed in response to very specific historical situations. The more Muhammad's community evolved, the more the Revelation changed to adapt to its needs. Indeed, during the twenty-two years of Muhammad's ministry, the Quran was in an almost constant state of flux, sometimes altering dramatically depending on where and when a verse was revealed, whether in Mecca or Medina, whether at the beginning or the end of Muhammad's life.

Occasionally, these changes led to what appear to be significant textual contradictions. For example, the Quran initially took a somewhat neutral stance on the drinking of wine and the practice of gambling, claiming that in both "there is great sin and some benefit for people, though the sin is greater than the benefit" (2:219). A few years later, another verse was revealed that, while still not prohibiting drinking and gambling, urged believers to refrain from gambling and not to "come to prayer while intoxicated" (4:43). Some time after that, however, the Quran explicitly outlawed both drinking and gambling, calling them "acts of Satan" and associating them with idolatry, the greatest sin (5:90). In this way, the previous verses, which condemned but did not forbid drinking and gambling, appear to have been abrogated by another, later verse, which unambiguously prohibited both.

Quranic scholars call this abrogation of one verse with another *naskh*, claiming that it demonstrates that God chose to introduce important sociological changes to Muhammad in stages, thereby allowing the Ummah to adjust gradually to the new moral ethos. But if naskh demonstrates anything, it is that while God may not change, the Revelation most certainly did, and without apology: "Whenever We abrogate a verse or cause it to be forgotten," the Quran says, "We exchange it with a better or similar one; don't you know that God can do anything?" (2:106; see also 16:101).

The Prophet himself sometimes openly suppressed or negated older verses, considering them to have been replaced by newer ones. That is because Muhammad did not consider the Quran to be a static Revelation, which may be why he never bothered to authorize its collection into a codified book. The Quran was for Muhammad a living scripture that consciously evolved alongside the Ummah, continually adapting itself to meet the specific needs of the developing community. In fact, an entire science of commentary called *asbab al-nuzul* ("the reasons for, or causes of Revelation") developed soon after Muhammad's death in order to determine the specific historical circumstances in which a certain verse was revealed. By tracking the changes in the Revelation, the early Quranic interpreters were able to create a helpful chronology of its verses. And what this chronology most clearly indicates is that God was rearing the Ummah like a loving parent, instructing it in stages and making alterations when necessary, from the first Revelation in 610 to the last in 632.

Of course, with Muhammad's death, the Revelation ceased. But that does not mean that the Ummah stopped evolving. On the contrary, the contemporary Muslim community—nearly a billion and a half strong—bears almost no resemblance to the small community of faith that Muhammad left behind in seventh century Arabia. While the Revelation may have ended, the Quran is still a living text and must be treated as such. The notion that historical context should play no role in the interpretation of the Quran—that what applied to Muhammad's community applies to all Muslim communities for all time—is simply an untenable position in every sense.

Nevertheless, the heirs of Traditionalism have managed to silence most critics of reform, even when that criticism has come from their own ranks. When in the 1990s Nasr Hamid Abu Zayd, a Muslim professor at Cairo University, argued that the Quran, while divinely revealed, was a cultural product of seventh-century Arabia, he was branded a heretic by the conservative-dominated Ulama of Egypt's famed al-Azhar University and forced to divorce his Muslim wife (the couple fled Egypt together). When Mahmoud Mohamed Taha (1909–85), the renowned Sudanese legal reformer, claimed that the Meccan and Medinan texts of the Quran differed so greatly from one another because they were addressed to very specific historical audiences and should be interpreted as such, he was executed.

As will become apparent, the debate over the nature and function of the Quran and the Shariah has in no way ended. Indeed, contemporary Muslim scholars such as Abdolkarim Soroush, Tariq Ramadan, Abdullahi An-Na'im, Amina Wadoud, Khaled Abou El Fadl, and many others have been vigorously pushing the Muslim community to reopen the gates of ijtihad and revive the rational exegesis of the Quran. Nevertheless, the dominance of the Traditionalist position continues to have devastating consequences for the development and progress of law and society in modern Islam.

The problem is that it is practically impossible to reconcile the Traditionalist view of the Shariah as a sacred and divinely revealed set of laws requiring no human interpretation or historical context with the requirements of a modern constitutional state, let alone the most minimum standards of democracy and human rights. The principal fallacy of the Traditionalist position lies not in the utterly false notion that the Shariah is a fixed and ahistorical legal code. As we have seen, there can be no question whatsoever that the Shariah was developed within a clear historical context, that it evolved in response to specific historical circumstances, and that it was privy to the same social, political, and economic factors that have influenced all legal codes in all cultures and in every part of the world. Anyone who claims otherwise is either wholly ignorant of Islamic history or simply delusional. No, the principal error of the Traditionalists is the intolerably heretical belief that a constantly changing and obviously man-made legal tradition built upon the wildly conflicting interpretations of half a dozen competing schools of law, each of which relies on drastically different textual and historical sources, should be treated as sacred and divine. Such a belief is, in a word, *shirk*.

There is absolutely nothing divine about the Shariah and in no way can it possibly be considered fixed and infallible. The argument that the Shariah derives its divine nature from its first and primary source, the Quran, falls flat when one recognizes that the Quran, unlike the Torah, is not a book of laws. The Quran is God's direct self-revelation to humanity. Certainly, it contains the moral framework for living a holy and righteous life as a Muslim. But it was never meant to function as a legal code, which is precisely why scholars had to rely so heavily on extra-Quranic sources like *ijma* (consensus), *qiyas* (analogy), *istislah* (which refers to the common good of the people), and *ijtihad* (independent juristic reasoning)—all of them, *by definition*, reliant on human judgment and historical context—in order to construct the Shariah in the first place. To say the Shariah is divine because the Quran is divine is akin to arguing that water and wine are the same, since water is a primary ingredient in wine.

So then, when it comes to incorporating the Shariah into its legal systems, a modern Islamic state has only three options. It can fully apply a Traditionalist understanding of Shariah to the state with no attempt either to modernize it or adapt it to contemporary norms of law and society, as Saudi Arabia and Afghanistan under the Taliban have done. It can accept the Traditionalist view of Shariah and declare it a legitimate source of civil law but choose to ignore it in all but the most obvious family, divorce, or inheritance cases, as Egypt and Pakistan do. Or it can attempt to fuse the traditional values of the Shariah with modern principles of constitutionalism and the rule of law through a comprehensive reform methodology that takes into account both its historical context and its evolution at the hands of human beings. Iraq's burgeoning democratic experiment notwithstanding, thus far only one Islamic state has seriously considered the latter option.

For more than thirty years, the Islamic Republic of Iran has been struggling to reconcile popular and divine sovereignty in an attempt to construct an Islamic state dedicated to pluralism, liberalism, and human rights yet founded upon a distinctly Islamic moral framework. It has been a difficult, violent, and hitherto unsuccessful endeavor, one that has been derailed both by external forces and by the corruption and ineptitude of the country's own religious and political authorities. Whether the Iranian experiment will ultimately prove successful remains to be seen. However, not since the Prophet Muhammad attempted to build a new kind of society in Medina has a more significant experiment in nation building been attempted.

Of course, Iran is a special case. The Iranian Islamic ideal is a patently Shi'ite one, and from their inception as a political movement with the aim of restoring the Caliphate to the family of the Prophet to their rise as a separate religious sect in Islam with its own distinct beliefs and practices, the Shi'ah have always done things differently.

7. In the Footsteps of Martyrs

FROM SHI'ISM TO KHOMEINISM

EARLY IN THE morning on the tenth day of the Islamic month of Muharram, in the sixty-first year of the Hijra (October 10, 680 C.E.), Husayn ibn Ali, grandson of the Prophet Muhammad and the *de facto* head of the Shi'atu Ali, steps out of his tent one last time to gaze across the vast, withered plane of Karbala at the massive Syrian army encircling his camp. These are the soldiers of the Umayyad Caliph, Yazid I, dispatched from Damascus weeks ago with orders to intercept Husayn and his party before they can reach the city of Kufa, where a brewing rebellion awaits his arrival.

For ten days the Syrian forces have besieged Husayn at Karbala. At first, they tried to storm the camp in a stampede of cavalry. But having anticipated the assault, Husayn had pitched his tents near a chain of hills, protecting his rear. He then dug a semicircular trench around three sides of his camp, filled the trench with wood, and ignited it. Gathering his men in the center of this crescent of fire,

Husayn ordered them to kneel in a tight formation with their lances pointing out, so that when the enemy horses neared, they would be forced by the flames to squeeze into the entrance of the trap.

This simple strategy allowed Husayn's tiny force to repel the thirty thousand soldiers of the Caliph for six long days. But on the seventh day, the Syrian army changed tactics. Rather than trying to storm the camp again, they shifted their lines to blockade the banks of the Euphrates, cutting off Husayn's supply of water.

Now the time for fighting is over. Sitting high atop their armored horses, the Caliph's soldiers make no move toward Husayn. Their swords are sheathed, their bows slung over their shoulders.

It has been three days since the canals stopped flowing into Husayn's camp; those few who haven't already lost their lives in battle are now slowly, painfully dying of thirst. The ground is littered with bodies, including those of Husayn's eighteen-year-old son, Ali Akbar, and his fourteen-year-old nephew, Qasim—the son of his elder brother, Hasan. Of the seventy-two companions who were to march with Husayn from Medina to Kufa in order to raise an army against Yazid, only the women and a few children remain, along with one other man: Husayn's sole surviving son, Ali, though he lies near death inside the women's tent. All the others are buried where they fell, their bodies wrapped in shrouds, their heads pointing toward Mecca. The wind stirs their shallow graves, carrying the stench of rot across the flat plain.

Alone, exhausted, and seriously wounded, Husayn collapses at the entrance to his tent. An arrowhead is lodged deep in his arm, his cheek pierced by a dart. He is parched and dizzy from loss of blood. Wiping the sweat from his eyes, he lowers his head and tries to ignore the wails of the women in the adjoining tent: they have just buried his infant son, who was struck in the neck by an arrow after Husayn carried him up a hill to beg the Syrian troops for water. Their anguish penetrates him deeper than any arrow could, but it also stiffens his resolve. There is now nothing left to do but finish the task for which he had set out from Medina. He must gather what strength he has left to lift himself off the ground. He must stand up and fight against the injustice and tyranny of the Caliph, even if it means sacrificing his life—especially if it means sacrificing his life.

Rising to his feet, he lifts his bloody hands to heaven and prays: "We are for God, and to God shall we return."

A Quran in one hand and a sword in the other, Husayn mounts his steed and tugs the horse's head to face the barricade of soldiers standing only a few hundred meters in front of him. With a swift kick to the horse's ribs, he launches himself ferociously at the enemy, swinging his sword left and right, all the while shouting, "Do you see how Fatima's son fights? Do you see how Ali's son fights? Do you see how the Banu Hashim fight despite three days of hunger and thirst?"

One by one, the Syrian riders perish by his sword, until their general, Shimr, orders the soldiers to regroup and surround Husayn from all sides. A swift blow from a lance knocks him off his horse. On the ground, he covers his head, writhing in pain as the horses trample his body. Husayn's sister, Zainab, rushes from the tent to come to his aid. But Husayn calls out to her to stay where she is. "Go back to the tent, sister," he shouts. "I am already undone."

Finally, Shimr orders the Syrian cavalry to pull back. As his soldiers round up the survivors from the camp, the general dismounts his horse and stands over Husayn's racked and broken body. "Make your confession," Shimr says. "It is time to cut your throat."

Husayn rolls over onto his back to face his executioner. "Forgive, O merciful Lord, the sins of my grandfather's people," he cries, "and grant me, bountifully, the key of the treasure of intercession . . ."

Before the Prophet's grandson can finish his prayer, Shimr lifts his sword in the air and swings the blade down in one swift motion, cleanly severing Husayn's head from his body. He raises the head on a lance to bring back to Damascus, where he will present it on a golden tray as a gift to the Umayyad Caliph.

After Ali's assassination in 661, the remnants of the Shi'atu Ali in Kufa selected his eldest son, Hasan, to succeed him as Caliph. But Kufa was a fractured and isolated city, and Ali's supporters were scattered and few in number. With Mu'awiyah having already declared himself Caliph in Jerusalem and the hegemony of Damascus stretching ever further over the Muslim lands, there was no way for Hasan's allies to compete with the Syrian army for control of the Muslim community.

Yet few as they may have been, the Shi'atu Ali were still an influential faction, particularly among the Iranians of the former Sasanian Empire, who saw in the ahl al-bayt an alternative to the ethnic Arab domination of the Umayyads, as well as among the populations of Mecca and Medina, where the memory of the Prophet was still fresh in the minds of those who, regardless of their political affiliation, could not help recognizing the grooves and shadows of Muhammad's features etched into the faces of his grandsons Hasan and Husayn. So when Hasan offered to come to terms with Mu'awiyah, proposing what amounted to a temporary cease-fire, Mu'awiyah was quick to accept.

Avoiding what would have been yet another civil war between the factions of the Banu Hashim and those of the Banu Umayya, the two men signed a treaty that handed the mantle of leadership to Mu'awiyah with the understanding that after his death the Caliphate would, at the very least, be decided by the consensus of the Muslim community, if not explicitly returned to Muhammad's family. The agreement benefited both men. It gave Hasan the opportunity to regroup the Shi'atu Ali without fear of annihilation at the hands of the Syrian army, and it offered Mu'awiyah the legitimacy he had been seeking since he first began pursuing the Caliphate.

With the capital of the Muslim community now firmly established in Damascus, Mu'awiyah launched a series of reforms meant to strengthen and centralize his authority as Caliph. He used the overwhelming might of his standing Syrian army to unite the troops scattered in garrison towns throughout the Muslim lands. He then forcibly resettled in distant villages those nomadic tribesmen who had never before considered themselves to be a part of the Ummah, thereby extending the grasp of his empire. He maintained his link to even the most remote Muslim provinces by reassigning his kinsmen—many of whom had been removed from their posts by Ali—as amirs, though he kept a tight leash on them to avoid the corruption and disorder that was so prevalent during his cousin Uthman's rule. Mu'awiyah's amirs secured their positions by diligently collecting taxes to send to Damascus, which the Caliph used to build a magnificent capital the likes of which had never before been imagined by any Arab tribe.

Although Mu'awiyah adopted Uthman's religiously oriented title, Khalifat Allah, and poured money into the institutions of the religious scholars and Quran reciters, he also set Umayyad precedent by not directly meddling in the theological and legal controversies of the Ulama. However, like his ancient ancestor, Qusayy, Mu'awiyah recognized the role of the Ka'ba in bestowing religious legitimacy to political rule. He therefore purchased from the Banu Hashim the right to care for the Meccan sanctuary and provide shelter and water to the pilgrims.

By centralizing his authority in Damascus and securing his position as Caliph with a mobile and highly disciplined army (not to mention a powerful naval fleet, which he used to conquer territories as distant as Sicily), Mu'awiyah managed to pull together the disparate regions of the Arab domain under his rule, ushering in a period of enormous expansion throughout the Muslim lands. But although he took great pains to style himself in both manner and conduct as an all-powerful tribal Shaykh, rather than as a Muslim king, there can be no question that Mu'awiyah's centralized and absolutist rule was deliberately meant to imitate the dynastic empires of the Byzantines and Sasanians. Hence, having completed the transformation of the Caliphate into a monarchy, Mu'awiyah did what any other king would do: he appointed his son, Yazid, to succeed him.

Considering his nearly wholesale slaughter of the Prophet's family at Karbala, it is not surprising that the traditions have been unkind to Yazid. Mu'awiyah's heir has been portrayed as a debauched, licentious drunkard more interested in playing with his pet monkey than in running the affairs of state. Although this may not be a fair depiction of the new Caliph, the fact is that Yazid's reputation was sealed from the moment he succeeded his father. For his succession marked the definitive end of the united community of God and the unambiguous commencement of the first Muslim—and distinctly Arab—empire.

This is why Kufa was in revolt. A garrison town teeming with freed slaves and non-Arab (mostly Iranian) Muslim soldiers, Kufa, which had served as the capital of Ali's brief and turbulent Caliphate, had become the locus of anti-Umayyad sentiment. That sentiment was perfectly embodied by the heterogeneous coalition of the Shi'atu Ali, who had little else in common save their hatred of the Banu Umayya and their belief that only the family of the Prophet could restore Islam to its original ideals of justice, piety, and egalitarianism.

As mentioned, the Shi'atu Ali first looked to Hasan, the eldest son of Ali and Fatima, to represent them as their new leader. But when Hasan died in 669—poisoned, his companions contended—their aspirations fell upon Ali's second son, Husayn. Unlike his older brother, who had a great distaste for politics and its machinations, Husayn was a natural leader who elicited fierce loyalty from his followers. After Hasan's death, the Shi'atu Ali pressured Husayn to rise up immediately against Mu'awiyah, pledging him their lives if necessary. But Husayn refused to violate his brother's treaty with the Caliph.

For eleven years, he bided his time in Medina, teaching, preaching, and preserving the legacy of his family while waiting for the Caliph to die. For eleven years he suffered the humiliation of having to sit through public cursings of his father, Ali, something Mu'awiyah had made obligatory from every pulpit in the Empire. Finally, in 680, Mu'awiyah passed away, and soon afterward, a message arrived from the Kufans begging Husayn to come to their city and take charge of their rebellion against the tyrant's son.

Although he had been awaiting this message for years, Husayn hesitated, knowing all too well the fickle and discordant nature of the Kufans and being unwilling to put his fate into their hands. He also recognized the futility of raising an army of Iraqi malcontents against the massive Syrian forces of the Caliph. At the same time, he could not ignore his duty as the Prophet's grandson to stand up against what he considered to be the oppression of his community at the hands of an illegitimate ruler.

Husayn's decision was made for him when Yazid, recognizing the threat he posed to his authority, summoned Husayn to appear before his amir, Walid, in Medina to pledge his allegiance to Damascus. However, when Husayn appeared before Walid and his aide, Marwan—the same Marwan who had so disastrously advised Uthman and who would eventually seize the Umayyad Caliphate for himself a few years later—he managed to put off his pledge by claiming that, as the representative of Muhammad's clan, he could better serve the Caliph if his allegiance were given in public. Walid agreed and let him go. But Marwan was not fooled.

"If Husayn is allowed to leave, you shall never recapture him," he told Walid. "Either ask him to swear allegiance now or have him killed."

Before Walid could act upon Marwan's advice, Husayn hastily gathered the members of his family and, along with a handful of supporters, headed off to Kufa. He never made it.

Having uncovered Husayn's plans to raise an army against him, Yazid sent his troops to Kufa to arrest and execute the leaders of the rebellion and to make sure the population of the city understood that any attempt to rally support for Husayn would be swiftly and mercilessly crushed. The threat worked. Long before Husayn and his followers were intercepted at Karbala, just a few kilometers south of Kufa, the insurrection had been quelled. Just as Husayn had predicted, the Kufans abandoned him to his fate. And yet, even after he had received news of the revolt's collapse, after he had been abandoned by those whom he came to lead, Husayn continued to march toward Kufa and certain death.

The events at Karbala sent shock waves through the Muslim lands. After the massacre, Yazid's troops made a point of parading the survivors, including Husayn's only remaining son, Ali—so ailing he had to be strapped to a camel—through the streets of Kufa as a cautionary message to Husayn's supporters. When Husayn's severed head was displayed to the crowd, the Kufans wailed and beat their breasts, cursing themselves for betraying the family of the Prophet. But even those factions who had strenuously opposed the leadership claims of the Banu Hashim were aghast at this demonstration of Caliphal might. This was, after all, the family of the Messenger of God, people said; how could they have been starved and massacred like animals?

Almost immediately, rebellion erupted throughout the Empire. The remaining Kharijite factions denounced Yazid as a heretic and set up their own separate régimes, one in Iran and one in the Arabian Peninsula. In Kufa, a brief yet bloody uprising to avenge the massacre at Karbala was instigated in the name of Muhammad ibn al-Hanafiyyah (the son of Ali but not of Fatima). In Mecca, Abd Allah ibn al-Zubayr— the son of the man who had, along with Talha, fought with Aisha against Ali at the Battle of the Camel—raised an army and declared himself Amir al-Mu'manin (Commander of the Faithful). The Ansar promptly followed Ibn al-Zubayr's example by declaring their independence from Damascus and selecting their own leader to represent them in Medina.

Yazid responded to these rebellions by turning his army loose. At his command the Syrian forces surrounded Mecca and Medina with massive catapults from which they indiscriminately launched fireballs at the inhabitants. In Mecca, the fires quickly spread to the Ka'ba, burning the sanctuary to the ground. When the flames finally subsided, both sacred cities lay in ruins. Medina immediately surrendered and pledged allegiance to Yazid. But it took another decade for the Umayyads, under the Caliphate of Abd al-Malik, to defeat the forces of Ibn al-Zubayr in Mecca once and for all and restore the absolute sovereignty of Damascus.

Meanwhile, unbeknownst to the Umayyad Caliphs, there was a subtler and far more significant revolution taking place in the Empire: a revolution not for political control but for control of the very essence of the Muslim faith. Four years after the events at Karbala, in 684 C.E., a small group of individuals from Kufa who called themselves the *tawwabun*, or Penitents, gathered at the site of the massacre—their faces blackened, their clothes torn—to mourn the death of Husayn and his family. This was an informal and unceremonious gathering meant not only as homage to Husayn but as an act of atonement for their failure to aid him against the Umayyad forces. The Penitents had assembled at Karbala to display their guilt publicly, and their communal act of mourning was a means of absolving themselves of their sins.

Although the notion of lamentation as atonement for sin was a common practice in most Mesopotamian religions, including Zoroastrianism, Judaism, Christianity, and Manichaeism, it was an unprecedented phenomenon in Islam. Indeed, the collective lamentations of the Penitents at Karbala were the first documented rituals of what would eventually become a wholly new religious tradition. Put simply, the memory of Karbala was slowly transforming the Shi'atu Ali from a political faction with the aim of restoring the leadership of the community to the family of the Prophet, into an utterly distinct religious sect in Islam: *Shi'ism*, a religion founded on the ideal of the righteous believer who, following in the footsteps of the martyrs at Karbala, willingly sacrifices himself in the struggle for justice against oppression.

WHAT SETS THE actions of the Penitents at Karbala apart in the history of religions is that they offer a glimpse into the ways in which ritual, rather than myth, can fashion a faith. This is a crucial point to bear in mind when discussing the development of Shi'ism. As Heinz Halm has noted, the Shi'ah are a community born not "by the profession of belief in dogma" but rather "through the process of performing the rituals" that sprang up around the Karbala myth. Only after these rituals had become formalized hundreds of years later did Shi'ite theologians reexamine and reinterpret them in order to lay the theological foundation for what was already a new religious movement.

Karbala became Shi'ism's Garden of Eden, with humanity's original sin being not disobedience to God, but unfaithfulness to God's moral principles. Just as the early Christians coped with Jesus' demoralizing death by reinterpreting the Crucifixion as a conscious and eternal decision of self-sacrifice, so also did the Shi'ah claim Husayn's martyrdom to have been both a conscious and an eternal decision. The Shi'ah claim that long before Husayn was born, the events of Karbala had been miraculously revealed to Adam, Noah, Abraham, Moses, Jesus, Muhammad, Ali, and Fatima. The Shi'ah noted that Husayn knew he could not defeat the Caliph, yet he deliberately chose to continue to Kufa in order to sacrifice himself for his principles and for all generations to come. Realizing that mere force of arms could not restore the vision of a united community under the rule of Muhammad's kin, Husayn had planned "a complete revolution in the consciousness of the Muslim community," to quote Husain Jafri. In fact, as the eminent Shi'ite theologian Shah Abdul Aziz has argued, Husayn's self-sacrifice was in reality the logical end to the story of Abraham's near-sacrifice of his firstborn son, Ismail—the sacrifice was not revoked but *postponed* until Karbala, when Husayn willingly fulfilled it. The Shi'ah thus regard Husayn's martyrdom as having completed the religion that Abraham initiated and Muhammad revealed to the Arabs.

Based on the way in which the events of Karbala were interpreted, there developed in Shi'ism a distinctly Islamic theology of atonement through sacrifice, something alien to orthodox, or Sunni, Islam. "A tear shed for Husayn washes away a hundred sins," the Shi'ah say. This concept, called '*aza*, or "mourning," achieved its full expression in the rites formalized by the Shi'ite authorities sometime around the mid-eighth century, and which to this day form the central rituals of the faith.

Every year, during the first ten days of the month of Muharram and culminating on the tenth day, or Ashura, the Shi'ah commemorate Husayn's martyrdom through lamentation assemblies, where stories of the martyrs are read by religious specialists called *zakirs*, and mourning processions, in which sacred objects belonging to Muhammad's family are carried through the neighborhoods. But perhaps the most famous rites of the Muharram ceremonies are the Shi'ite passion plays (*ta'ziyeh*), which dramatize in detail the events of Karbala, and the funereal processions (*matam*), in which participants either beat their breasts in a rhythmic, almost mantric act of contrition, or flog their backs with whips made of chains, all the while shouting out the names of Hasan and Husayn, until the streets are stained with their blood.

Despite appearances, the Shi'ite self-flagellation ceremonies have little in common with similar practices one finds in certain Christian monastic orders. This is not flagellation as a solitary act of pious self-mortification. Nor do these rituals correspond to the self-abnegation practices of some ascetic Hindu sects, for whom pain is a means of achieving a shift in consciousness. As nearly every objective observer of the Muharram ceremonies has documented, matam is meant to be a physically painless activity: an act of communal witnessing, not a means of scourging one's sins. It is not pain, but the voluntary shedding of blood and tears for Husayn that brings salvation. For this reason, in many large cities, where the Shi'ite funereal processions are frowned upon by both religious and political authorities, a vigorous campaign has been launched to replace the self-flagellation rituals with safe and supervised donations to mobile blood banks that trail behind the participants.

For the Shi'ah, the Muharram rituals signify a moral choice; they are a public statement that, in the words of one participant, "if we had been there at Karbala we would have stood with [Husayn] and shed our blood and died with him." Perhaps equally important, these rituals serve as an act of proselytizing. As another participant explained to David Pinault, "We do matam not just to commemorate Husayn but as a way of saying we are Shi'ites."

Most of the Sunni world condemns such acts of ritual devotion as *bid'a*, or "religious innovation," something strenuously opposed by all Sunni schools. But the Sunni are less offended by what the Muharram participants do than by what the rituals suggest: that paradise is awarded, according to the sixteenth-century Quranic scholar al-Kashifi, "to anyone who weeps for Husayn or who laments in company with those who weep for Husayn." Therein lies the principal difference between the Shi'ah and the Sunni. The Shi'ah believe that salvation requires the intercession of Muhammad, his son-in-law Ali, his grandsons Hasan and Husayn, and the rest of the Prophet's legitimate successors, the *Imams*, who not only serve as humanity's intercessors on the Last Days, but who further function as the eternal executors (*wali*) of the divine Revelation.

The word *Imam* has multiple connotations. In Sunni Islam, the imam is merely the person who stands at the head of the mosque and leads the congregation in prayer. While the Shi'ah sometimes employ this definition for their religious leaders as well, they also recognize a "fixed" number of Imams—the number of whom depends on the sect of Shi'ism—who, as the Prophet's legitimate successors, bear the responsibility of guarding and preserving Muhammad's divine message. Unlike the Caliph, who is a political leader designated, at least theoretically, by the consensus of the Muslim community, the Imam represents the spiritual authority of the Prophet Muhammad and is designated by God through the fact of his birth. While the Sunni Caliph can only claim to be Muhammad's vice-regent on earth, the Shi'ite Imam, though lacking any real political power, is endowed with the living spirit of the Prophet and, as such, is thought to possess a spiritual authority that sets him above any earthly ruler.

The existence of the Imam is essential, according to the preeminent Shi'ite theologian, Allamah Tabataba'i, because human beings

need the divine message to be elucidated for them—and not just elucidated, but preserved and renewed. Because human beings do not have
the capacity to attain knowledge of God on their own, the Imam
becomes a continuous necessity for all societies and in every era. So in
addition to the "fixed" number of Imams who succeeded Muhammad's earthly authority, there must also exist an "ever-present" or
"pre-existent" Imam who, as the eternal guardian of the Revelation,
functions as "the Proof of God on Earth." Thus, the first Imam was
neither Muhammad nor Ali but Adam. And while the functions of
Imam and prophet have occasionally existed in a single individual, the
difference between the two positions is primarily one of consciousness. A prophet, claim the Shi'ah, is someone who has, by the divine
will, become conscious of God's eternal message, which forever envel-
ops creation like a numinous ether we cannot escape, while the Imam
is someone who explicates that message for those who possess neither
the prophetic consciousness necessary to recognize it nor the power
of reason to understand it. Put another way, the prophet *transmits* the
Message of God, while the Imam *translates* it for human beings.

According to the Shi'ah, this relationship between prophet and
Imam can be observed throughout the history of prophecy. Abraham
may have been given the covenant by God, but it was Isaac and Ismail
who, as his Imams, fulfilled it; Moses may have revealed the divine
law, but it was Aaron who carried it into the Promised Land; Jesus
may have preached salvation, but it was Peter who built the Church.
In the same way, Muhammad, the Seal of the Prophets, may have
revealed God's message to the Arabs, but it was left to Ali, his legitimate successor, to execute it. Thus the Shi'ite profession of faith:

"There is no god but God, Muhammad is God's Messenger, and
Ali is God's Executor (*wali*)."

As the executor of God's will, the Imam is, like the Prophet, infallible and sinless, for as one Shi'ite theologian has argued, "sin would
destroy the validity of the call." Consequently, the Shi'ah developed
the view that the Imams were created not from dust, as other humans
were, but from eternal light. Furthermore, the Imams are said to preserve a secret esoteric knowledge handed down from Imam to Imam
in a mystical transfer of consciousness. This esoteric knowledge
includes the keeping of secret books, such as *The Book of Fatima*, which

recounts Gabriel's revelations to Fatima after Muhammad's death. The Imams also know the secret name of God and are the only ones who possess the spiritual guidance necessary to reveal the inner truth of the Muslim faith.

It is this spiritual guidance that gives the Imams sole authority to interpret the Quran. The Shi'ah believe the Quran contains within its pages two different messages meant for two different audiences. The Quran's explicit message (*zahir*) is obvious and accessible to all Muslims through the discipline of tafsir (traditional Quranic exegesis), referred to in the previous chapter. But only the Imam can correctly employ ta'wil (the hidden, secret meaning of the Quran) to uncover the Quran's implicit message (*batin*). And while the distinction between tafsir and ta'wil exists in Sunni Islam as well, the Shi'ah believe that because the Revelation emanates from sources beyond human comprehension, the *whole* of the Quran consists of symbols and allusions that only the Imam has the spiritual perfection to elucidate. In the words of the eighth Imam, Ali ar-Rida, only the person who can correspond the Quran's implicit verses to its explicit ones can claim "guidance to the right path."

The primacy of ta'wil in Shi'ism had great advantages for the early Shi'ah, who were eager to link themselves with Muhammad by uncovering scriptural references that would justify their distinctive beliefs and practices. Of course, this is a common tactic used by all sectarian movements that wish to connect themselves to their parent religion. The early Christians, for example, who were no more than Jews who believed that the Messiah had come, scoured the Hebrew Scriptures for allusions to Jesus so as to link their sect with Judaism and fit their Messiah into the numerous and often conflicting messianic prophecies of the Hebrew Scriptures. In the same way, the Shi'ah sifted through the Quran and found it replete with verses that, when properly interpreted through ta'wil, implicitly expressed the eternal truth of the Imamate. Consider the following extract from the Quran, known as "the Verse of Light":

God is the light of the Heavens and the Earth.
His light is like a niche in the wall in which there is a lamp,
The lamp is within a glass, and the glass is a glimmering star,

Lit with the oil of an olive tree—
A tree neither of the East nor of the West—
Whose oil glows though fire touches it not:
Light upon Light!
God guides to His Light whomever He will.
God gives examples to humanity,
And God has knowledge of everything. (24:35)

According to the sixth Imam, Ja'far as-Sadiq, these exquisitely wrought lines conceal a message from God to the Shi'ah. God's light, Ja'far claimed, is actually Muhammad; its containment in the glass, a reference to the prophetic knowledge that he passed on to Imam Ali, who "is neither a Jew [of the East] nor a Christian [of the West]." And just as the sacred oil glows without being touched by fire, so divine knowledge issues from the mouth of the Imam, "even if Muhammad had not spoken it."

"Light upon Light!" exclaims the Quran.

"Imam to Imam!" replied Ja'far.

The first of the "fixed" Imams to succeed Muhammad was obviously Ali, followed by his sons Hasan and Husayn, respectively. The fourth Imam was the only son of Husayn to have survived Karbala, Ali (also known as Zayn al-Abadin), who was eventually allowed to return to Medina after spending some years in captivity in Damascus. Ali Zayn al-Abadin was succeeded in 712 C.E. by his son Muhammad al-Baqir (who was four years old at the time of Karbala), though a small faction within the Shi'ah rejected al-Baqir as the fifth Imam and chose instead to follow another of al-Abadin's sons, Zayd ash-Shahid. This faction officially broke off from the main body of the Shi'ah and became known as the Zaydis.

The majority of the Shi'ah accepted the succession of al-Baqir, who then passed the Imamate to his son Ja'far as-Sadiq. As the sixth and most influential Imam, Ja'far formalized the Karbala rituals and established the principles of Shi'ism's main school of law. The Jafari school, as it is known, differentiates itself from Sunni schools of law, first by recognizing a different set of hadith, which include stories of the Imams as well as of Muhammad, and second by vigorously employing ijtihad, or independent juristic reasoning, as one of the primary sources of Shi'ite jurisprudence.

For years the Shi'ah were divided among themselves over the permissibility of the *mujtahid* (literally, one who employs ijtihad) to rely only on rational conjecture to issue authoritative legal decisions, or fatwas. The Akhbari school, for example, rejected the use of ijtihad altogether, requiring its Ulama to base their legal decisions solely on the traditions of the Prophet and the Imams. But it was the Akhbaris' rivals, the Usuli school, whose enthusiastic support for the use of ijtihad in the formation of Islamic jurisprudence made it the dominant school in Shi'ism. To this day, Shi'ite law maintains the conviction that "whatever is ordered by reason, is also ordered by religion," to quote the contemporary Shi'ite legal scholar Hossein Modarressi.

There are now so many mujtahids in the Shi'ite world that only those who have attained the very highest level of scholarship and who can boast the greatest number of disciples are still allowed to practice ijtihad. At the top of this order of mujtahids are the *ayatollahs* (the title means "the sign of God"), whose decisions are binding on their disciples. Only a handful of authoritative ayatollahs exist today—primarily in Iran and Iraq—but their religious and political authority over the Shi'ah is formidable. As we shall see, it was precisely this authority that allowed the Ayatollah Khomeini to impose his will upon the social, political, and economic forces that led to the Iranian Revolution in 1979.

Ja'far died in 757, allegedly from poisoning, though this claim has been made for every Imam who was not openly murdered by Sunni authorities. Before dying, Ja'far designated his eldest son Ismail as the seventh Imam. But Ismail died before his father, and was therefore replaced by Ja'far's second son, Musa al-Kazim. While the majority of the Shi'ah accepted Musa as the divinely guided leader of the community, there were those who were disturbed by this apparent "switching" of designations. Is not the Imam a divinely appointed position, they asked? How could Ja'far, the infallible Imam, have chosen the wrong successor? Ultimately, this faction was compelled by the force of their theology to argue that Ismail had not died, but gone into hiding, or "occultation," in a spiritual realm from which he would return at the end of time, not as Imam Ismail, but as the messianic restorer known in Islam as the *Mahdi*.

The followers of Ismail—called the Ismailis, or "Seveners," because they accept the existence of only seven Imams before the Mahdi—were not the first to promulgate the notion of a "Muslim messiah." The term *Mahdi* originally meant "one who guides divinely" and was regularly employed from the beginning of the Islamic era as an honorific title; Muhammad was called "Mahdi," as were Ali and his two sons, Hasan and Husayn. After the massacre at Karbala, both Abd Allah ibn al-Zubayr and Muhammad ibn al-Hanafiyyah were proclaimed the Mahdi during their unsuccessful revolts against the Umayyad Caliphate. However, the Ismailis were the first Islamic sect for whom belief in the Mahdi became the central tenet of faith. Even so, it was not until the majority Shi'ah—known as the "Twelvers" because they follow Musa's line down to the twelfth and final Imam—also adopted the doctrine of the Mahdi that a uniquely Islamic eschatology was developed centered on the "Hidden Imam" who had left this world for a transcendent realm from which he would return on the Day of Judgment to restore justice on earth.

Because there is no mention of the Mahdi in the Quran, Muslims looked to the hadith for insight into the second coming of the "Hidden Imam." As one would expect, these traditions differed greatly depending on geographical location and political affiliation. For instance, in Syria, where Umayyad loyalty dominated both religious and civil concerns, the hadith claimed that the Mahdi would be a member of the Quraysh, while in Kufa, the seat of Shi'ite aspirations, the hadith insisted that the Mahdi would be a direct descendant of Muhammad through his son-in-law, Ali; his first duty upon returning to earth would naturally be to avenge the massacre at Karbala. Some traditions predicted that the coming of the Mahdi will be portended by civil wars and false prophets, earthquakes and the abolition of Islamic law. According to the fourteenth-century historian and philosopher Ibn Khaldun, the Mahdi will either directly precede Jesus, or both messiahs will descend to earth together and join forces to kill the Antichrist.

As the doctrine of the Mahdi began to dominate Shi'ism, Sunni

religious scholars gradually distanced themselves from further speculation on the topic. Sunni schools of law openly criticized belief in the
Mahdi in an attempt to discourage what was fast becoming a politically disruptive theology. The fears of the Sunni establishment were
well warranted. The Abbasids overthrew the Umayyad Dynasty partly
by appealing to the messianic expectations of the Shi'ah. Indeed,
the first Abbasid ruler gave himself the messianic title *as-Saffah* ("the
Generous"). He was addressed as "The Mahdi of the Hashimis." The
second Abbasid Caliph gave himself the title *al-Mansur* (another messianic term for the Mahdi found primarily in Yemen), and the third
simply called himself "the Mahdi," explicitly identifying his rule with
that of the promised restorer.

After Imam Musa came Imam Rida, the eighth Imam, whose
tenure coincided with the Caliphate of the famed Abbasid leader
Harun al-Rashid. Imam Rida died in 817 C.E. and was succeeded by
his son Muhammad Taqi (sometimes called Imam Jawad). By this
point, the animosity between the Abbasid Caliphs (themselves Shi'ah)
and the Shi'ite Imams had become so great, owing to the Abbasids'
fear that the Imams could become political rivals, that the tenth and
eleventh Imams—Imam Hadi and Imam Askari, respectively—spent
nearly their entire Imamates locked away in Abbasid prisons. When
the twelfth and final Imam, Muhammad ibn Hasan, was born in
Samara in 868 C.E., the Shi'ah decided it would be better to spirit him
away and hide him from public view. Thus, the twelfth Imam, called
Imam Mahdi, went into occultation (*ghayba*), from which the Twelver
Shi'ah expect his return at the end of time to usher in an era of peace
and justice on earth.

With the Imam no longer present on earth, the Shi'ah settled into
a long period of political quietism and "cautionary dissimulation"
called *taqiyyah*. Because the exercise of direct political power necessarily entailed the usurpation of the Mahdi's divine authority, all governments were considered illegitimate pending his return. As a result, the
role of the Shi'ite Ulama was reduced to little more than representatives of the Mahdi, what the Iranian scholar Abdulaziz Sachedina has
termed "living isnads": human chains of transmission leading back to
the "Hidden Imam."

This is not to say that Shi'ite governments did not arise. In the year 1501, a sixteen-year-old amir named Ismail conquered Iran and installed himself as the first *Shah*, or King, of the Safavid Empire. Ismail proclaimed Twelver Shi'ism to be the official state religion of Iran and initiated a brutal jihad against Sunni Islam both within his land and in the neighboring Ottoman Empire. Ismail's jihad against the Sunnis ended a few years later at the hands of the Ottoman Sultan Salim I, and while that defeat may have halted the Shah's excursion into Ottoman territory, Iran itself was changed forever.

Shah Ismail was unmoved by arguments against the legitimacy of a Shi'ite state in the absence of the "Hidden Imam." Instead, he simply declared himself to be the long-awaited Mahdi, boldly crying out at his ascension, "I am very God, very God, very God!"

Soon after Ismail's Safavid Dynasty came to an end in the eighteenth century, Twelver Shi'ism, though remaining the "state religion" in Iran, reverted to its former political quietism, prompting the ayatollahs to cultivate once more the ideology of *taqiyyah* and to refrain from directly interfering in the administrations of the Qajar Dynasty, which succeeded the Safavids in the nineteenth century, and the Pahlavi Dynasty, which succeeded the Qajars in the twentieth.

All of that changed with the Ayatollah Khomeini.

※※※

ON A CHILLY February morning in 1979, hundreds of thousands of Iranians flooded the streets of Tehran to celebrate the end of the long, oppressive reign of Muhammad Reza Pahlavi, the last Shah of Iran. Among the crowd on that day were democrats, academics, and Western-educated intelligentsia, liberal and conservative religious clerics, bazaari merchants, feminists, communists, socialists, and Marxists, Muslims, Christians, and Jews, men, women, and children—all bound by their disdain for the despotic American-backed régime that had made life in Iran unbearable for so many people for so many years.

The crowd pumped their fists in the air, shouting "Death to the Shah!" and "Death to Tyranny!" Angry young men gathered throughout the city to burn American flags and chant anti-imperialist slogans against the superpower that had, a little more than two decades earlier, extinguished Iran's first attempt at democratic revolution. That revolution took place in 1953, when the same improbable coalition of intelligentsia, clerics, and bazaari merchants managed to topple Iran's monarchy, only to have it forcibly restored by the CIA a few months later.

"Death to America!" they shouted, their chants a warning to the American embassy in Tehran that *this* revolution would not be hindered, no matter the cost.

There was also on that day another, more singular contingent of demonstrators consisting mostly of bearded men and black-veiled women who marched through the streets shouting the names of the martyrs, Hasan and Husayn, and calling for the advent of the Last Days: the coming of the Mahdi. Almost to a person this raucous group displayed portraits and posters of the stern, brooding cleric who had over the last few years become the dominant voice of anti-imperialism in Iran: the Ayatollah Ruhollah Khomeini.

Born in 1902 to a respected family of Shi'ite clerics, Khomeini studied law and theology in the esteemed seminaries of Najaf and Qom. He quickly ascended to the heights of Shi'ism's enormously complex clerical hierarchy, becoming a mujtahid worthy of emulation at the extraordinarily young age of thirty-two, and an ayatollah soon after. Like most Iranians, Khomeini blamed Iran's weak-willed monarchy for allowing the country to be "the slaves of Britain one day, and America the next." However, unlike most of his fellow ayatollahs, who insisted on maintaining their traditional political quietism, Khomeini unabashedly injected his moral authority into the sociopolitical machinations of the state. His ruthless condemnations of the Shah and his repeated calls for the abolishment of the throne finally led to his arrest and exile in 1964.

Fifteen years later, in 1979, Khomeini returned to Iran, triumphant and determined to usher in a new era in the country's history—one that almost no one in the crowd could have predicted. Indeed, less than a year after his return from exile, Khomeini would ostracize, then execute his political and religious opponents—the same men and women who had brought this revolution to fruition—and replace the transitional government with his personal ideal of the Islamic state: a state in which he alone had final authority over all matters civil, legal, and religious.

But on that February morning, no one was calling Khomeini the

Faqih, "the Jurist": the title he would eventually give himself as Supreme Leader of the newly formed Islamic Republic of Iran. At that time, Khomeini had yet to unveil his plans for absolute clerical rule. Rather, amid the chants of "God, Quran, Khomeini," and the placards that declared the old ayatollah to be "the Light of Our Life," there was another title being bruited through the crowd like a secret that could not be contained. Khomeini, people were whispering, was the Mahdi; he had returned to Iran to restore Islam to its original state of perfection.

The reasons for the success of *Khomeinism*—the proper term for the religio-political philosophy that ultimately created the Islamic Republic of Iran—are numerous and too complicated to present here in detail. In many ways, the Iranian Revolution of 1979 was the inevitable conclusion of two previous popular revolutions—the Constitutional Revolution of 1905–11 and the Nationalist Revolution of 1953—both of which were suppressed by foreign governments (the first by the Russians and, to a lesser extent, the British; the second, as mentioned, by the United States) that wished to maintain their grip on Iran's natural resources. By the late 1970s, most Iranians had grown so weary of the corrupt and ineffectual rule of Iran's monarch, Muhammad Reza Pahlavi, that another revolution was unavoidable.

Faced with an almost total lack of political participation (the Shah had eliminated the country's party system and abolished its constitution), a reckless economic agenda that had fueled record inflation, a rapid and useless militarization, and a widespread loss of national and religious identity, the country's clergy, its intellectuals, the merchant class, and nearly every sociopolitical organization in Iran—from the communists to the feminists—put aside their ideological differences and joined together in an anti-imperialist, nationalist revolt against a corrupt monarchy. Despite the post-revolution propaganda, this was by no means a monolithic revolutionary movement initiated at the behest of the Ayatollah Khomeini with the aim of establishing an Islamic theocracy. On the contrary, there were dozens of diverse and sometimes conflicting voices raised against the Shah. Khomeini's, for better or worse, was merely the loudest.

Khomeini's genius, both as a politician and as a religious leader, was his recognition that in a country steeped in the faith and culture of Shi'ism, only the symbols and metaphors of Shi'ite Islam could provide a common language with which to mobilize the masses. Thus, in transforming Iran into his personal vision of theocratic rule, Khomeini turned to the best example history had made available to him: Ismail, the Safavid ruler who five hundred years earlier had created the first Shi'ite state by proclaiming himself the Mahdi.

Of course, Khomeini never likened himself to the Divine, nor did he ever explicitly claim the title of Mahdi—to have done so would have been political suicide. Rather, Khomeini consciously embraced the messianic charisma of the Mahdi, and allowed his followers to draw their own conclusions. Like all the Mahdis before him, Khomeini claimed descent from Imam Musa, and eagerly accepted the messianic title "Imam." He deliberately cast Iran's horrific eight-year war with Saddam Hussein's Iraq (1980–1988) as revenge for the massacre of Husayn and his family at Karbala, even though such vengeance was the exclusive right of the Mahdi. In fact, the thousands of Iranian children who were thrown onto the front lines of the war as human minesweepers wore "keys to paradise" around their necks and headbands emblazoned with the word *Karbala* to remind them that they were not fighting a war for territory, but walking in the footsteps of the martyrs.

By far the most overt connection Khomeini established between himself and the Mahdi was his doctrine of the *Valayat-e Faqih:* "the rule of the jurist." The particulars of this doctrine, in which popular and divine sovereignty are united in a single government, will be detailed in chapter 10. For now, it is sufficient to understand the basic outline of the doctrine and its place in Khomeini's political and religious ideology.

Khomeini argued that in the absence of the Mahdi, divine guidance could come only from the Hidden Imam's representatives on earth: that is, the ayatollahs. Khomeini was not the first Shi'ite theologian to have made this claim; the same idea was formulated at the turn of the twentieth century by politically minded clerics like Sheikh Fazlollah Nuri (one of Khomeini's ideological heroes) and the Ayatollah Kashani. But the Valayat-e Faqih proposed two startling modifications to traditional Shi'ite doctrine. First, it insisted that absolute authority be concentrated in the hands of a single cleric, instead of all qualified clerics. Second, it argued that, as the deputy of the Mahdi, the supreme cleric's authority was identical to that of the "Hidden Imam." In other words, Khomeini's guidance was, like the guidance of the Prophet and the twelve Imams, infallible and divinely inspired.

"When a mujtahid [a qualified jurist] who is just and learned stands up for the establishment and organization of the government," Khomeini wrote in his historic political treatise, *Islamic Government*, "he will enjoy all the rights in the affairs of the society that were enjoyed by the Prophet."

This was an astounding assertion and a radical religious innovation in Shi'ism. Countering long-held beliefs that the Shi'ah could be led only by the Mahdi when he returns from his occultation in the spiritual realm, Khomeini argued instead that it was the responsibility of the clerics to usher in the messianic era by establishing and governing the Mahdi's state for him. The Valayat-e Faqih proposed that in the absence of the "Hidden Imam," the Faqih—the Supreme Jurist and the country's "most learned cleric"—should have "the responsibility of transacting all the business and carrying out all the affairs with which the Imams were entrusted." And because he was the representative of the Mahdi on earth, the Faqih held "the same power as the Most Noble Messenger" and would also be entitled to absolute obedience from the people.

It is a sign of the great diversity of religious and political thought that exists in Shi'ism that most other ayatollahs in Iran—including his superiors, the Ayatollahs Boroujerdi and Shariatmadari—rejected Khomeini's doctrine of the Valayat-e Faqih, arguing that the responsibility of Muslim clerics in the modern world was to preserve the spiritual character of the Islamic state, not to run it directly. But what made Khomeini so alluring was his ability to couch his theology in the populist rhetoric of the time. He thus reached out to Iran's influential communist and Marxist factions by reformulating traditional Shi'ite ideology into a call for an uprising of the oppressed masses. He wooed the secular nationalists by lacing his speeches with allusions to Iran's mythic past, while purposely obscuring the details of his political philosophy. "We do not say that government must be in the hands of the Faqih," he claimed. "Rather we say that government must be run in accordance with God's laws for the welfare of the country." What he often failed to mention publicly was that such a state would not be feasible except, as he wrote, "with the supervision of the religious leaders."

Khomeini balked when his fellow ayatollahs objected that the Valayat-e Faqih merely replaced one form of tyranny with another. After all, Khomeini argued, the Faqih is no mere secular leader; he is the heir to the "Hidden Imam." As such, he does not administer divine justice, he *is* divine justice. Indeed, according to Khomeini, the Faqih is "not 'just' in the limited sense of social justice, but in the more rigorous and comprehensive sense that his quality of being just would be annulled if he were to utter a single lie."

Once his colleagues had been intimidated into silence and Iran's Shi'ite majority stirred into action, Khomeini was free to seize control of the transitional government. Before most Iranians knew what they had accepted, he had used his popular mandate to inject his theological beliefs into the political realm, transforming Iran into the Islamic Republic, and proclaiming himself the country's first Faqih: the supreme temporal and religious authority in Iran.

Three decades later, Khomeini's theory of "the rule of the jurist," or Valayat-e Faqih, is once again being challenged, not just by some of Iran's most senior religious figures, such as the Grand Ayatollahs Mir Mohammad Ruhani, Sayed Hassan Tabatabai-Qomi, Yusuf Sanei, and Hussein Ali Montazeri, the last of whom, before his death in 2010, famously declared that "even the Prophet did not have absolute Valayat-e Faqih." It is also being questioned by a new crop of young seminary students studying in the country's religious capitol, Qom. These future religious leaders have never been exposed to traditional (that is, pre-Khomeinist) Shi'ism. But they are keenly aware of the failure of the Valayat-e Faqih to usher in the "perfect state" promised by Ayatollah Khomeini. What's more, they are cognizant of the way in which Iran's politicized form of Shi'ism has perhaps irreparably damaged the perception that most Iranians—70 percent of whom are under the age of thirty and thus have no memory of prerevolutionary Iran—have of religion in general and Islam in particular.

However, by far the most significant challenge to Khomeinism has come from outside of Iran, in neighboring Iraq. The 2002

U.S.–led war to depose Saddam Hussein had the somewhat unexpected effect of liberating the other major Shi'ite school of law, in the holy Iraqi city of Najaf. Led by the Iranian-born Grand Ayatollah Ali al-Sistani, a man many consider to be the most senior ayatollah in the world, the Najaf school promulgates a more traditional, apolitical interpretation of Shi'ah Islam. Now that it has been freed from Saddam Hussein's brutal oppression, Najaf has begun spreading its influence across the border to Iran. Sistani's disciples have been flooding the seminaries of Qom, while Najaf itself has been admitting a steady stream of Iranian students eager to study a version of Shi'ah theology untainted by the political philosophy of Khomeini.

It may take a couple of generations before Shi'ism reverts to its pre-Khomeinist interpretation and the Shi'ite Ulama return to their roles as the moral, rather than the political, authorities of the Shi'ah community. Yet the reversal seems inevitable. After all, Shi'ism is a religion founded upon open debate and rational discourse. In its nearly fourteen-hundred-year history, no Shi'ite cleric has ever enjoyed unconditional authority over another Shi'ite cleric of equal learning. Nor has any cleric ever held sole interpretive powers over the meaning of the faith. The Shi'ah have always been free to follow the cleric of their choice, which is in part why Shi'ism has blossomed into such a wonderfully eclectic faith. It is also why so many Shi'ah both inside and outside Iran no longer view the Islamic Republic of Iran as the paradigm of the Islamic state, but rather as its corruption (though that argument must be reserved for another chapter).

The Ayatollah Khomeini died in 1989. Although he was a frail and sickly eighty-seven-year-old man, his death took much of the country by surprise. During the funeral his corpse was mobbed in the streets; the shroud in which he had been wrapped was torn to pieces and the fragments taken by mourners as relics. There even were those in Iran who refused to believe "the Imam" could have died. Some claimed he was not dead, but had only gone into hiding; he would return again.

Long before his messianic rise to power in Iran, however, Khomeini was a devoted disciple of the great mystics of Islam: the Sufis. In fact, as an idealistic university student, the young Ruhollah secretly filled his notebooks with astonishingly passionate verses describing his yearning to be united with God as a lover is united with his beloved.

"Oh, I desire a cup of wine from the Beloved's own hands," Khomeini wrote. "In whom can I confide this secret? Where am I to take my grief? I have yearned a lifetime to see the Beloved's face. I am a frenzied moth circling the flame, a wild rue seed pod roasting in the fire. See my stained cloak and this prayer rug of hypocrisy. Can I, one day, tear them to shreds at the tavern door?"

These may seem startling words for a future ayatollah. But to those familiar with the principles of Sufism, Islam's other major religious branch, they are not at all unfamiliar. For Sufis, Islam is neither law nor theology, neither creed nor ritual. Islam, according to Sufism, is merely the means through which the believer can destroy his ego so as to become one with the creator of the heavens and the earth.

8. Stain Your Prayer Rug with Wine

THE SUFI WAY

THIS IS THE legend of Layla and Majnun.

Once, a boy of exceeding beauty was born into the family of a noble Shaykh. He was named Kais, and as he matured it became obvious to all that he would one day become a source of great pride to his family and tribe. Even from a young age, his knowledge, his diligence, his learning, and his speech outshone that of all his peers. When he spoke, his tongue scattered pearls, and when he smiled, his cheeks were violet tulips awakening to the sun.

One day, Kais met a girl so lovely that he was instantly struck with a yearning he could not understand. Her name was Layla, meaning "night," and like the night, she was both dark and luminous. Her eyes were those of a gazelle, her lips two moist rose petals.

Layla too felt an emotion for Kais she could not comprehend. The two children were drowning in love, though in their youth they knew not what love was. It was as though love were a wine-bearer, filling the cups of their hearts to the brim; they drank whatever was poured for them and grew drunk without understanding why.

Kais and Layla kept their feelings secret as they roamed the alleyways and passages of the city's markets, close enough to steal a furtive glance and share a giggle, far enough not to arouse gossip. But a secret such as this cannot be contained, and a whisper is all it takes to topple a kingdom. "Kais and Layla are in love!" someone said on the street.

Layla's tribe was furious. Her father removed her from school and banned her from leaving her tent; her brothers vowed to ensnare Kais if he ever came near. But one cannot keep the baying hound away from the new moon.

Separated from his beloved, Kais wandered from stall to stall, from tent to tent, as if in a trance. Everywhere he went he sang of Layla's beauty, extolling her virtues to whoever crossed his path. The longer he went without seeing Layla, the more his love gave way to madness, so that soon people began pointing him out on the streets, saying, "Here comes the madman! Here comes the *majnun!*"

Kais was mad, it is true. But what is madness? Is it to be consumed by the flames of love? Is the moth mad to immolate itself in the fires of its desire? If so, then yes, Kais was mad. Kais was *Majnun*.

Clad in rags and stripped of his sanity, Majnun left the city and wandered aimlessly through the mountains and wastelands of the Hijaz, composing mournful odes to his absent beloved. He was homeless and tribeless, an exile from the land of happiness. Good and evil, right and wrong, no longer had any meaning for him. He was a lover; he knew nothing but love. He abandoned reason and lived as an outcast in the desert, his hair filthy and matted, his clothes tattered.

In his madness, Majnun came to the Ka'ba. Pushing through the crowd of pilgrims, he rushed at the sanctuary and hammered upon its doors, shouting, "O Lord, let my love grow! Let it blossom to perfection and endure. Let me drink from the wellspring of love until my thirst is quenched. Love is all I have, all I am, and all I ever want to be!"

The pilgrims were appalled. They watched as he fell to the ground, heaping dust on his head, cursing himself for the weakness of his passions.

Majnun's actions shamed his family and tribe, but he himself knew no shame. When he heard of Layla's arranged marriage to a man of untold wealth named Ibn Salam, Majnun lost all sense and reason. Tearing off his clothes, he crawled naked through the wilderness like an animal. He slept in ravines with the beasts of the desert, eating wild plants and drinking rainwater. He grew famous for his love. People from all over the land sought him out, sometimes sitting with him for hours as he spoke of his beloved Layla.

One day, while he was idly reciting his verses to a captive audience, a scrap of paper, borne by the wind, landed on his lap. On it were written two words: "Layla" and "Majnun." As the crowd watched, Majnun tore the paper in half. The half on which was written "Layla" he crumpled into a ball and threw over his shoulder; the half with his own name he kept for himself.

"What does this mean?" someone asked.

"Do you not realize that one name is better than two?" Majnun replied. "If only you knew the reality of love, you would see that when you scratch a lover, you find his beloved."

"But why throw away Layla's name and not your own?" asked another.

Majnun glowered at the man. "The name is a shell and nothing more. It is what the shell hides that counts. I am the shell and Layla is the pearl; I am the veil and she is the face beneath it."

The crowd, though they knew not the meaning of his words, were amazed by the sweetness of his tongue.

Meanwhile, trapped by the restrictions of her tribe and forced to marry a man she did not love, Layla was plunged into a lonely darkness. She suffered as deeply as Majnun but did not have his freedom. She too wanted to live with the beasts of the desert, to declare her love for Majnun from the tops of the mountains. But she was a prisoner in her own tent, and in her own heart. When one morning a traveling merchant brought her news of Majnun, Layla felt like a reed swaying in the wind, hollow and weightless.

"Without your radiance," the old man told her, "Majnun's soul is like the ocean in a winter's night, whipped up by a thousand storms. Like a man possessed, he roams the mountainside, screaming and shouting. And there is but one word on his lips: 'Layla.' "

"The blame is all mine," Layla cried, flinging curses on herself. "I am the one who has set fire to my lover's heart and reduced his being to ashes." Desperate, she removed the jewels from her earrings and handed them to the old merchant. "These are for you. Now go to Majnun and bring him here. I only want to see him, to look upon his face for a little while, to bathe in the light of his countenance for but a moment."

The old man agreed. For days he searched the desert for Majnun. When he finally found him, he relayed Layla's message. "Could you not bring yourself to break your vows of separation from the world to look upon her tearful face, just for a second?" he pleaded.

"Little does anyone understand me," Majnun thought. "Do they not realize that their idea of happiness is not mine? Do they not see that while it may be possible for them to have their wishes granted in this life, my longing is something else entirely, something that cannot be fulfilled while I remain in this transient world?"

But Majnun could not resist the opportunity to look upon the face of his beloved. Putting on a cloak, he followed the merchant to a palm grove and hid there while the old man left to fetch Layla.

As the merchant led her by the hand to the grove, to Majnun, Layla's entire body trembled. When no more than twenty paces separated her from her lover, she froze. The old man tugged on her arm, but Layla could not move.

"Noble sir," she pleaded, "this far but no farther. Even now I am like a burning candle; one step closer to the fire and I shall be consumed completely."

The old man left her and went to Majnun. Pulling him out of the palm grove, he brought the boy—his face drained of color, his eyes glass—under the moonlight and pointed him toward Layla. Majnun stumbled forward. Light from the stars peeked through the tops of the palm trees. There was a movement in the darkness, and suddenly, under the dome of heaven, Layla and Majnun faced each other.

It was only a moment: a rush of blood to the cheeks. The two lovers stared at one another, drunk with the wine of love. Yet though they were now close enough to touch, they knew that such wine could be tasted only in paradise. A breath, a sigh, a stifled cry, and Majnun turned and ran from the grove back into the desert, vanishing like a shadow into the night.

Years passed. The leaves on the palm trees lost their color. The flowers shed their petals in mourning. As the countryside turned yellow and wan and the gardens slowly withered, so did Layla. The light in her eyes dimmed, and with her final breath she breathed her lover's name.

When Majnun heard of the death of his beloved, he rushed back home and writhed in the dust of her grave. He lay down and pressed his body to the earth as though in prayer, but his parched lips could utter only one word: "Layla." Finally, he was released from his pain and longing. His soul broke free and he was no more.

Some say Majnun's body lay on top of Layla's grave for months; others say years. No one dared approach, for the grave was guarded night and day by the beasts of the desert. Even the vultures that swooped above the tomb would not touch Majnun. Eventually, all that remained of him was dust and bones. Only then did the animals abandon their master to lope back into the wilderness.

After the animals had gone and the dust of Majnun was swept away by the wind, a new headstone was fashioned for Layla's tomb. It read:

Two lovers lie in this one tomb
United forever in death's dark womb.
Faithful in separation, true in love:
May one tent house them in heaven above.

Sufism—the term given to Islam's immensely complex and infinitely diverse mystical tradition—is, as Reynold Nicholson long ago observed, fundamentally indefinable. Even the word *Sufi* provides little help in classifying this movement. The term *tasawwuf*, meaning "the state of being a Sufi," is without significance, referring as it probably does to the coarse wool garments, or *suf*, which the first Sufis wore as an emblem of their poverty and detachment from the world. Indeed, as a descriptive term, the word *Sufi* is practically interchangeable with the words *darvish* or *faqir*, meaning "mendicant" or "poor." Some have argued that *Sufi* is derived from the Arabic word *safwe*, meaning "elected," or *suffa*, meaning "purity," though both of these must be rejected on etymological grounds. Others have suggested that

Sufi is a corruption of the Greek word *sophia:* "wisdom." This is also unlikely, though there is a tempting symbolic connection between the two words. For if *sophia* is to be understood in its Aristotelian sense as "knowledge of ultimate things," then it is very much related to the term *Sufi,* just not linguistically.

As a religious movement, Sufism is characterized by a medley of divergent philosophical and religious trends, as though it were an empty caldron into which have been poured the principles of Christian monasticism and Hindu asceticism, along with a sprinkling of Buddhist and Tantric thought, a touch of Islamic Gnosticism and Neoplatonism, and finally, a few elements of Shi'ism, Manichaeism, and Central Asian shamanism thrown in for good measure. Such a hodgepodge of influences may frustrate scholarly analysis, but it also indicates how Sufism may have formed in its earliest stages.

The first Sufis were loosely affiliated and highly mobile individuals who traveled throughout the Muslim Empire seeking intimate knowledge of God. As these "wandering darvishes" grew in number, temporary boardinghouses were constructed in high traffic areas like Baghdad and Khurasan where the mendicants could gather together and share what they had learned during their spiritual journeys. By the eleventh century—around the same time that the Abbasids were actively persecuting the Shi'ah for their heterodox behavior—these boarding houses had become permanent structures resembling cloisters, a few of which gradually evolved into sophisticated schools, or *Orders,* of mysticism.

The Sufi Orders centered on a spiritual master who had withdrawn permanently from the Ummah to pursue the path of self-purification and inner enlightenment. Called *Shaykhs* in Arabic and *Pirs* in Persian (both of which mean "old man"), these Sufi masters were themselves the disciples of earlier, legendary masters whose unsystematic teachings they had collected so as to pass on to a new generation of disciples. As each disciple reached a level of spiritual maturity, he would then be charged with transmitting his master's words to his own pupils, and so on. It is therefore easy to see why Sufism appears like an eclectic recipe whose ingredients have been collected from a variety of sources over a long period of time. Of course, as the Sufi master Shaykh Fadhlalla Haeri teaches, "there is a big difference between merely collecting recipes and actually cooking and eating."

Like Shi'ism, Sufism began as a reactionary movement against both the Imperial Islam of the Muslim Dynasties and the rigid formalism of Islam's "orthodox" learned class, the Ulama. Both Shi'ism and Sufism vigorously employed ta'wil to uncover the hidden meaning of the Quran, both concentrated their spiritual activities on devotion to the Prophet Muhammad, and both developed cults of personality around saintly characters—whether Imams or Pirs.

But while the Shi'ah and Sufis existed in the same spiritual dimension and most certainly influenced each other, Sufism represents a rare anti-intellectual strain within Islam dedicated solely to esotericism and devotionalism. Also, unlike the Shi'ah, the Sufis were not interested in political power. Although they eventually entered the political realm, especially in the Indian subcontinent, the Sufi Pirs initially eschewed all temporal authority and completely removed themselves from the political and theological infighting that pervaded the Muslim community during its formative period. Instead, the Sufis strove toward asceticism and detachment from the Ummah and its worldly trappings through a life of simplicity and poverty. "If you cannot change the kings," the Sufis argued, "then change yourself."

In their rituals and practices, the Sufis sought the annihilation of the ego. And while this goal may be common to all mystical movements, there are a few important differences between Sufism and traditional ideals of mysticism. First, there exists in Islam a stringent anti-monasticism that permeates all aspects of the believer's life. Put simply, Islam is a communal religion. It abhors radical and reclusive individualism. One could argue that a Muslim who rejects the Ummah is like a Roman Catholic who denies the Apostolic Church: both are deliberately separating themselves from the source of their salvation. Although most Sufi masters withdrew from society, they were not monks; their disciples were artisans, chemists, and merchants who lived and worked in the real world. A true Sufi, Shaykh Haeri writes, "does not separate the inner from the outer," for when you "start by purifying your inner self, you end up being concerned with the outer and with society."

Secondly, the Quran categorically derides celibacy—another

common tradition in mysticism—as being against the command of God to "be fruitful and multiply." A significant portion of the Revelation is dedicated to the strengthening and preservation of the family, which in Islam is considered to be the model for the Ummah and a microcosm of all creation. In fact, the Quran repeatedly equates filial loyalty with fidelity to God (2:83; 4:36; 6:151; 31:14). So, while there were a few notable Sufi celibates—like the famed Rabia of Basra, who despite her legendary beauty rebuffed all suitors in order to give herself completely to God—celibacy never became a widespread phenomenon in Sufism.

But perhaps the most important difference between Sufism and traditional religious mysticism is that the latter tends to remain permanently attached to its "parent" religion, while Sufism, though born from Islam, treats its parent as a shell that must be cast off if one is to experience direct knowledge of God. Put another way, the formal religion of Islam is the prelude to Sufism, rather than its prominent motif. Islam, like all religions, can only claim to *point* humanity to God, whereas Sufism's goal is to *thrust* humanity toward God.

This does not mean that Sufism rejects Islam and its religious and legal requirements altogether. Despite the occasionally violent Shi'ite and Sunni accusations to the contrary, Sufis are Muslims. They pray as Muslims. They worship as Muslims. They use Muslim symbols and metaphors and follow Muslim creeds and rituals. To quote the esteemed Sufi Shaykh of the Rifa'i Order in Jerusalem, Muhammad ash-Shadhili, "If you want to walk in . . . the Way of the Prophet, you must be a real Muslim . . . one who gives everything to his God to be His slave."

That said, Sufis consider all orthodoxy, all traditional teachings, the law, theology, and the Five Pillars inadequate for attaining true knowledge of God. Even the Quran, which Sufis respect as the direct speech of God, lacks the capacity to shed light upon God's essence. As one Sufi master has argued, why spend time reading a love letter (by which he means the Quran) in the presence of the Beloved who wrote it?

Just as all journeys must have a beginning, so the Sufi path only originates with the "outer shell" of Islam. As the Sufi passes from one stage to another on the way to "self-annihilation" and unity with the

Divine, that shell must be gradually discarded, for, as Majnun said, "It is what the shell hides that counts." Sufis believe that reason and theology, creed and ritual, law and its commandments, all must be replaced in the soul of the enlightened person with the supreme virtue: love.

It is not surprising that most Muslims have historically regarded Sufism with suspicion. The Sufi assertion that human reason cannot fathom the Divine, that such knowledge can come only from intuitive perception of ultimate reality, naturally infuriated the religious authorities. It did not help matters that the Sufis rejected the Shariah as inapplicable to their search for the secret knowledge of the inner world. As noted, Islamic law is concerned with the external (*zahir*) nature of faith: it is quantitative; it can be regulated. But the internal (*batin*) cannot, and therefore represents a grave threat to the religious authorities. Worse, by detaching themselves from the Muslim community, the Sufis appeared to be creating their own Ummah, in which the Pirs replaced the Ulama as the sole religious authorities.

In rejecting the rigidity of the Shariah and its traditional interpretations, Sufism eagerly absorbed all manner of local beliefs and customs, and became immensely popular throughout those areas of the Muslim Empire that were not dominated by Arab majorities. In India, Sufism spread like fire as it enthusiastically syncretized anti-caste Muslim values with traditional Indian practices such as controlled breathing, sitting postures, and meditation. In Central Asia, a cadre of Persian Sufis developed a wholly new scriptural canon characterized by a rich panoply of poetry, songs, and Sufi literature, which, unlike the Quran, was written in the vernacular language and easily disseminated throughout the Empire.

This brief outline of Sufism's origins may clarify how the movement arose and spread, but it in no way explains what Sufism is. Nor could it. That is because Sufism is a religious movement that can only be described; it cannot be defined.

Consider the following parable originally composed by the greatest of all Sufi poets, Jalal ad-Din Rumi (d. 1273) and recounted by Idris Shah, the Grand Shaykh of Sardana:

A Persian, a Turk, an Arab, and a Greek were traveling to a distant land when they began arguing over how to spend the single coin they possessed among themselves. All four craved food, but the Persian wanted to spend the coin on *angur*; the Turk, on *uzum*; the Arab, on *inab*; and the Greek, on *stafil*. The argument became heated as each man insisted on having what he desired.

A linguist passing by overheard their quarrel. "Give the coin to me," he said. "I undertake to satisfy the desires of all of you."

Taking the coin, the linguist went to a nearby shop and bought four small bunches of grapes. He then returned to the men and gave them each a bunch.

"This is my *angur*!" cried the Persian.

"But this is what I call *uzum*," replied the Turk.

"You have brought me my *inab*," the Arab said.

"No! This in my language is *stafil*," said the Greek.

All of a sudden, the men realized that what each of them had desired was in fact the same thing, only they did not know how to express themselves to each other.

The four travelers represent humanity in its search for an inner spiritual need it cannot define and which it expresses in different ways. The linguist is the Sufi, who enlightens humanity to the fact that what it seeks (its religions), though called by different names, are in reality one identical thing. However—and this is the most important aspect of the parable—the linguist can offer the travelers only the grapes and nothing more. He cannot offer them wine, which is the *essence* of the fruit. In other words, human beings cannot be given the secret of ultimate reality, for such knowledge cannot be shared, but must be experienced through an arduous inner journey toward self-annihilation. As the transcendent Iranian poet, Saadi of Shiraz, wrote,

> I am a dreamer who is mute,
> And the people are deaf.
> I am unable to say,
> And they are unable to hear.

What is Sufism? It is the love of Majnun for Layla. It is "numberless waves, lapping and momentarily reflecting the sun—all from the same sea," according to the Sufi master Halki. It is the practice of "adopting every higher quality and leaving every lower quality," in the words of the "Patriarch of Sufism," Ibn Junayd (d. 910). The Sufi is "not Christian or Jew or Muslim," Rumi wrote. He is not of "any religion or cultural system . . . not from the East or the West, not out of the ocean or up from the ground, not natural or ethereal, not composed of elements at all . . . not an entity of this world or the next." He is, in Ishan Kaiser's description, "the actual temple of the fire worshipper; the priest of the Magian; the inner reality of the crossed-legged Brahmin meditating; the brush and the color of the artist."

Drunk without wine, sated without food, a king beneath a humble cloak, a treasure within a ruin, Sufism is to Islam what the heart is to the human being: its vital center, *the seat of its essence*. It is, in Majnun's words, "the pearl hidden in the shell, the face beneath the veil." Sufism is the secret, subtle reality concealed at the very depths of the Muslim faith, and only by mining those depths can one gain any understanding of this enigmatic sect.

❦

ONE SPRING MORNING in tenth-century Baghdad, the frenetic but scrupulously controlled markets of the capital city were thrown into a state of agitation when a raggedly dressed man named Husayn ibn Mansur al-Hallaj—one of the earliest and most renowned Sufi masters—burst onto the crowded square and exclaimed at the top of his voice, *Ana al-Haqq!* "I am the Truth!" by which he meant, "I am God!"

The market authorities were scandalized. They immediately arrested al-Hallaj and handed him over to the Ulama for judgment. The Ulama in Baghdad were already familiar with this controversial Sufi master. Although born a Zoroastrian into a priestly (*Magian*) family in southern Iran, al-Hallaj had converted to Islam and moved to the Abbasid capital of Baghdad at a fairly young age. An early disciple of the legendary Sufi Pir, Tustari (d. 896), he had matured into a charismatic preacher known for performing miraculous deeds and making outrageous statements. Called "the Nourisher" by his disciples, al-Hallaj first gained notoriety, not to mention the ire of the religious authorities, by claiming that the Hajj was an *internal* pilgrimage that a person of pure heart could perform anywhere. He further alienated the Ulama by focusing the bulk of his teachings on Jesus, whom he considered to be a "Hidden Sufi." For these declarations, he was condemned as a fanatic and a "secret Christian." But it was his intolerably heretical claim to have achieved unity with the Divine that made al-Hallaj the most famous, though by no means the only, Sufi martyr in history.

Although given numerous chances to recant during his eight years of imprisonment, al-Hallaj refused. Finally, the Abbasid Caliph al-Muqtadir, under pressure from the religious authorities, sentenced him to death. As a demonstration of the severity of his heresy, the Caliph had al-Hallaj tortured, flogged, mutilated, and crucified; his corpse was decapitated, his body dismembered, his remains burned, and the ashes scattered in the Tigris River.

What did al-Hallaj mean? Was he actually claiming to be God? If so, how can we reconcile Sufism as a legitimate sect of such a radically monotheistic and fervently iconoclastic religion as Islam?

Many prominent Sufis roundly condemned al-Hallaj. Al-Ghazali, perhaps the most important Muslim mystic in the history of Islam, referred to al-Hallaj in his eleventh-century masterpiece, *The Alchemy of Happiness*, as a "foolish babbler" whose death was "a greater benefit to the cause of true religion." Al-Ghazali did not criticize al-Hallaj for claiming to have achieved a level of spiritual unification with God in which his essence had merged with the essence of the Divine. What he and others objected to was the fact that al-Hallaj had publicly disclosed what was meant to be a secret.

Having spent his life striving to harmonize Islamic mysticism with Islamic orthodoxy (he was, incredibly, both a Sufi and a Traditionalist Ash'arite), al-Ghazali understood better than anyone that such esoteric knowledge must be revealed slowly and in stages. Just as "a child has no real knowledge of the attainments of an adult," and an unlettered adult "cannot understand the attainments of a learned man," so, al-Ghazali wrote in *Revival of the Religious Sciences*, not even a learned man can understand "the experiences of enlightened saints."

Al-Hallaj's offense was not the sacrilege of his startling declaration, but its imprudent disclosure to those who could not possibly understand what he meant. Sufi teaching can never be revealed to the unprepared or the spiritually immature. As al-Hujwiri (d. 1075) argued, it is all too easy for the uninitiated to "mistake the [Sufi's] intention, and repudiate not his real meaning, but a notion which they formed for themselves." Even al-Hallaj admitted that his experience of unity with God came after a long journey of inward reflection. "Your Spirit mixed with my Spirit *little by little,*" he wrote of God in his *Diwan,* "by turns, through reunions and abandons. And now I am Yourself. Your existence is my own, and it is also my will."

To understand where al-Hallaj ended on this inward journey, one must look back to where he began: at the first station on the long and arduous path of spiritual self-reflection that Sufis call the *tariqah:* the Way. The tariqah is the mystical journey that leads the Sufi away from the external reality of religion and toward the divine reality—the *only* reality of God. As with all journeys, the Way has an end, though it should not be imagined as a straight road leading to a fixed destination but rather as a majestic mountain whose peak conceals the presence of God. There are, of course, many paths to the summit—some better than others. But because every path eventually leads to the same destination, which path one takes is irrelevant. All that matters is to be on a path, to be constantly moving toward the top—one measured, controlled, and strictly supervised step at a time—passing diligently through specific "abodes and stations" along the Way, each of which is marked by an ineffable experience of spiritual evolution, until one finally reaches the end of the journey: that moment of enlightenment in which the veil of reality is stripped away, the ego obliterated, and the self utterly consumed by God.

By far the most famous parable describing the Sufi Way and the stations that a disciple must pass through on the journey toward self-annihilation was composed by the twelfth-century Iranian perfumer and alchemist Farid ad-Din Attar (d. 1230). In Attar's epic masterpiece, *The Conference of the Birds,* the birds of the world have gathered around the hoopoe (a mythical bird), who has been chosen by lot to guide them on a journey to see the *Simurgh:* King of the Birds. Before they can begin the journey, however, the birds must first declare their absolute obedience to the hoopoe, promising that

> Whatever he commands along the Way
> We must, without recalcitrance, obey.

The oath is necessary, the hoopoe explains, because the journey will be perilous and fraught with physical and emotional adversity, and only he knows the Way. Consequently, he must be followed without question, regardless of what he demands.

To reach the Simurgh, the birds will have to traverse seven treacherous valleys, each representing a station along the Way. The first is the Valley of the Quest, in which the birds must "renounce the world" and repent of their sins. This is followed by the Valley of Love, where each bird will be plunged into seas of fire "until his very being is enflamed." Next is the Valley of Mystery, where every bird must take a different path, for "There are so many roads, and each is fit / For that pilgrim who must follow it." In the Valley of Detachment, "all claims, all lust for meaning disappear," while in the Valley of Unity, the many are merged into one: "The oneness of diversity / Not oneness locked in singularity."

Upon reaching the sixth valley, the Valley of Bewilderment, the birds—weary and perplexed—break through the veil of traditional dualities and are suddenly confronted with the emptiness of their being. "I have no certain knowledge anymore," they weep in confusion.

> I doubt my doubt, doubt itself is unsure
> I love, but who is it for whom I sigh?
> Not Muslim, yet not heathen; who am I?

Finally, at the end of the journey, the birds arrive at the Valley of Nothingness, in which, stripped of their egos, they "put on the cloak that signifies oblivion" and become consumed by the spirit of the universe. Only when all seven valleys have been traversed, when the birds have learned to "destroy the mountain of the Self" and "give up the intellect for love," are they allowed to continue to the throne of the Simurgh.

Of the thousands of birds who began the journey with the hoopoe, only thirty make it to the end. With "hopeless hearts and tattered, trailing wings," these thirty birds are led into the presence of the Simurgh. Yet when they finally set their eyes upon him, they are astonished to see not the King of Birds they had expected, but rather *themselves. Simurgh* is the Persian word for "thirty birds"; and it is here, at the end of the Way, that the birds are confronted with the reality that although they have "struggled, wandered, traveled far," it is "themselves they sought" and "themselves they are." "I am the mirror set before your eyes," the Simurgh says. "And all who come before my splendor see / Themselves, their own unique reality."

Attar was a Sufi master who developed through his poetry and teachings the concept of "spiritual alchemy," in which the soul was treated like a transmutable base metal that must be rid of impurities before it can be restored to its original, pristine—one could say golden—state. Like most Sufis, Attar considered all souls to be receptacles for God's message. At the same time, he believed there exist varying degrees of receptivity in every individual depending on where he or she is on the Way.

During the first stages of the Way (where the great majority of humanity find themselves), the *nafs*, which is the self, the ego, the psyche, the "I"—however one chooses to define the "sum of individual egocentric tendencies"—remains the sole reality. As the disciple moves along the Way, he encounters the *ruh*, or Universal Spirit. The Quran refers to the ruh as "the breath of God" blown into Adam to give life to his body (15:29). In this sense, the ruh is equated with the divine, eternal, animating spirit that permeates creation—that is itself the essence of creation. The ruh is Pure Being. It is that which Hindus call *prana* and Taoists call *ch'i;* it is the ethereal force underlying the universe that Christian mystics refer to when they speak of the Holy Spirit.

In traditional Sufi doctrine, the ruh, or spirit of God, is locked in an eternal battle with the nafs, or the self, for possession of the heart— the *qalb*—which is not the seat of emotion (emotions, in most Muslim cultures, reside in the gut), but rather the vital center of human existence—"the seat of an essence that transcends individual form," in the words of Titus Burckhardt. In more familiar terms, the qalb is equivalent to the traditional Western notion of the soul as the driving force of the intellect.

An individual enters the final stages of the Way when the nafs begins to release its grip on the qalb, thus allowing the ruh—which is present in all humanity, but is cloaked in the veil of the self—to absorb the qalb as though it were a drop of dew plunged into a vast, endless sea. When this occurs, the individual achieves *fana:* ecstatic, intoxicating self-annihilation. This is the final station along the Sufi Way. It is here, at the end of the journey, when the individual has been stripped of his ego, that he becomes one with the Universal Spirit and achieves unity with the Divine.

Although the actual number of stations along the Way varies depending on the tradition (Attar's Order, for instance, acknowledged seven of them), Sufis are adamant that the steps must be taken one at a time. As Rumi wrote, "Before you can drink the fifth cup, you must have drunk the first four, each of them delicious." Furthermore, each station must be completed under the strict supervision of a Pir; only someone who has himself finished the journey can lead others along the path. "Do not travel through these stations without the company of a perfect master," warned the glorious Sufi poet Hafiz. "There is darkness. Beware of the danger of getting lost!"

The Pir is the "Sublime Elixir," the one who transmutes "the copper of seekers' hearts into pure gold, and cleanses their being," to quote the Sufi scholar Javad Nurbakhsh. Like the hoopoe, the Pir demands perfect submission from his disciples, who pledge him their loyalty in the form of a bay'ah, the oath of allegiance traditionally given to a Shaykh or a Caliph. Yet the Pir enjoys far greater authority than any Shaykh or Caliph ever could, for he is "the friend of God." The Pir is not just a spiritual guide; he is "the eyes through which God regards the world." In much of Sufi poetry the Pir is referred to as "the cosmic pole," or *qutb:* the axis around which the spiritual energy of the universe rotates. This concept is brought vividly to life by the famed Turkish Sufi Order of "Whirling Darvishes," who perform a spiritual, trance-inducing dance in which disciples mimic the movement of the cosmos by spinning in place, sometimes for hours at a time, while simultaneously orbiting the Pir, who becomes the center of their constructed universe.

As those who have completed the Way, Sufi Pirs are venerated as saints. The anniversaries of their deaths are holy days (termed *urs,*

Persian for "weddings," because in dying and leaving this world, the Pir is finally united with God). Their tombs are pilgrimage sites—especially for impoverished Muslims for whom the Hajj is unfeasible—where devotees gather with their oaths, petitions, and appeals for intercession. So great is the Pir's spiritual power—his *baraka*—that merely touching his tomb can heal a sick man of his illness or impart fertility to a barren woman. As with the majority of Sufi activities, these tombs are completely egalitarian with regard to sex, ethnicity, and even faith. Particularly in the Indian subcontinent, it is not unusual for Christians, Sikhs, Hindus, and Muslims to congregate in nearly equal numbers inside the mausoleums of Sufi saints.

By the sheer power of their spiritual charisma, the Pirs gather disciples in order to impart to them the esoteric knowledge Sufis call *erfan*. Like the Greek term *gnosis*, *erfan* refers to a heightened level of knowing in which one is able to intuit ultimate reality. However, erfan is a nonintellectual, nonrational knowing that, in the words of Shah Angha, the forty-second Pir of the Oveyssi Order, can be achieved only "through self-discipline and purification, in which case there is no need to become involved in the method of reasoning." Because the intellect cannot fathom the divine mystery, the Sufis believe that true understanding of the nature of the universe and humanity's place in it can be achieved only when reason has been abandoned for love.

Of all the principles that the Sufi disciple must integrate into his life, none is more important than the principle of love. Love is the foundation of Sufism. It is the language through which Sufism is most perfectly expressed and the sole avenue through which its ideals can be understood. The experience of love represents the most universal station on the Sufi Way, for it is love—not theology and certainly not the law—that engenders knowledge of God.

According to the Sufis, God's very essence—God's *substance*—is love. Love is the agent of creation. Sufism does not allow for the concept of creation *ex nihilo* because, before there was anything, there was love: that is, God loving God's self in a primordial state of unity. It was only when God desired to express this love to an "other" that humanity was created in the image of the Divine. Humanity, then, is God made manifest; it is God objectified through love.

When Sufis speak of their love for God, they are not referring

to the traditional Christian concept of *agape*, or spiritual love; quite
the opposite. This is a passionate, all-consuming, humiliating, self-
denying love. As with Majnun's love for Layla, Sufi love requires the
unconditional surrender to the Beloved's will, with no regard for one's
own well-being. This is love to the point of utter self-annihilation;
indeed, that is its very purpose. Love, according to Attar, is the fire
that obliterates the ego and purifies the soul, and the lover is he who
"flares and burns . . ."

> Whose face is fevered, who in frenzy yearns,
> Who knows no prudence, who will gladly send
> A hundred worlds toward their blazing end,
> Who knows of neither faith nor blasphemy,
> Who has no time for doubt or certainty,
> To whom both good and evil are the same,
> And who is neither, but a living flame.

Like most mystics, Sufis strive to eliminate the dichotomy between
subject and object in their worship. The goal is to create an inseparable
union between the individual and the Divine. In Sufism, this union is
most often expressed through the most vivid, most explicit sexual
imagery. Thus Hafiz wrote of God, "The scent of Your hair fulfills my
life, and the sweetness of Your lips has no counterpart."

Some of the most captivating use of sexual imagery in Sufism can
be found in the writings of the aforementioned Rabia of Basra
(717–801). Orphaned at a young age, Rabia became a slave and the sexual property of her master. Yet, she longed throughout her life to experience mystical union with God, sometimes going without sleep for
weeks at a time in order to fast, pray, and meditate on the movement of
the universe. It was during one of these nightly meditations that her
master first noticed a blinding nimbus of light shining above her head,
illuminating the entire house. Terrified, he immediately set Rabia free,
allowing her to go into the desert to pursue the Way. There, in the
wilderness, Rabia achieved fana, or self-annihilation, becoming the
first, though not the only, female Sufi master: a woman in whose presence the venerable scholar Hasan al-Basra admitted to feeling spiritually bankrupt.

Like her Christian counterpart, Teresa of Avila, Rabia's poetry betrays a profoundly intimate encounter with God:

You are my breath,
My hope,
My companion,
My craving,
My abundant wealth.
Without You—my Life, my Love—
I would never have wandered across these endless countries . . .
I look everywhere for Your love—
Then I am suddenly filled with it.
O Captain of my Heart,
Radiant Eye of Yearning in my breast,
I will never be free from You
As long as I live.
Be satisfied with me, Love,
And I am satisfied.

This intense longing for the Beloved, so prevalent in Rabia's verses, betrays an important aspect of the Sufi conception of love. Above all else, this is a love that must remain *unfulfilled*, as Majnun discovered in the palm orchard. After all, as Attar's birds realized on their journey to the Simurgh, one cannot begin the Way expecting to complete it; only a handful of individuals will reach the final destination and achieve unity with God. For this reason, the Sufi is often compared to the bride who sits on her marriage bed, "roses strewn on the cushions," yearning for the arrival of the Bridegroom, though she knows he may never come. And yet, the bride waits; she will wait forever, "dying from love," aching for the beloved, crying out with every breath, "Come to me! Come to me!" until she ceases to exist as a separate entity and becomes nothing more than a lover loving the Beloved in perfect union. As al-Hallaj wrote of his experience of unity with the Divine:

I am He whom I love, and He whom I love is I.
We are two spirits dwelling in one body,

If thou seest me, thou seest Him;
And if thou seest Him, thou seest us both.

If, then, the perfect love is unrequited love—the kind of love that expects nothing in return—then the perfect lover and the paradigm of love for Sufis is *Iblis*, or Satan, who began his existence as an angel in "the Way of devotion to the service of God," but who was cast out of God's presence for refusing to bow before Adam. Rumi illustrates in his "Apology of Iblis" that this refusal to obey God "arose from love of God, not from disobedience." After all, "all envy arises from love, for fear lest another become the companion of the Beloved."

Though cast into hell, never to see the face of God again, Iblis continues to yearn for his Beloved, who "rocked my cradle" and "found milk for me in my infancy." He will pine for God forever, crying out from the depths of hell, "I am mated by Him, mated by Him, mated by Him!"

If this somewhat flattering impression of the Devil is shocking to most Muslims, it is important to remember that that is precisely the point. As Attar claimed, "Love knows of neither faith nor blasphemy." Only by breaking through the veil of traditional dualities, which human beings have constructed in order to categorize proper moral and religious behavior, can one achieve fana. The Sufi knows no dualities, only unity. There is no good and evil, no light and dark; there is only God. This notion should not be confused with the Hindu principle of *maya* (the illusion of reality), or the Buddhist doctrine of *sunyata* (the emptiness of all things). For the Sufi, reality is neither emptiness nor illusion; reality is God. "Whichever way one turns, there is God," the Quran says; "God is all-pervading and all-knowing" (2:115). And because the doctrine of tawhid insists God is One, the Sufis argue, reality must also be One.

The atom, the sun, the galaxies, and the universe,
Are surely but names, images, and forms.
One they are in reality, and only one.

In traditional Western philosophy this concept of radical unity is often called *monism:* the notion that all things, despite their variety, can be reduced to a single unified "thing" in either space, time, essence, or quality. However, it is perhaps more appropriate to refer to the Sufi ideal of radical unity as *ahadiyyah*, or "oneness," to emphasize the theistic quality of this monistic ideal: *al-Ahad*, "the One," being the first and most important of God's ninety-nine beautiful names.

It is precisely this theistic monism that leads Sufis to reject traditional dualities, not because they eschew morally correct behavior, but because they accept only "the Existence of Oneness": that is, Divine Unity. Admittedly, this concept has led to a great deal of confusion about the true teachings of Sufism, especially in light of the actions of the so-called Drunken Sufis who blatantly violated Islamic law by publicly drinking, gambling, and womanizing as a means of overcoming the external aspects of religion. The nonexistence of traditional dualities is, however, usually demonstrated through metaphor. And the most common metaphor for doing so is that of drunkenness and debauchery, both of which have become dominant symbols in Sufi poetry for this self-annihilating and intoxicating love.

"I will take one hundred barrels of wine tonight," wrote Omar Khayyám in his superb *Rubáiyát*. "I will leave all reason and religion behind, and take the maidenhead of wine for mine." Khayyám's wine is spiritual wine—it represents "the grace of the Lord of the World"—and the Sufi is he who has rejected the traditional ideals of religious piety and moral behavior, who has fled "reason and the tangled web of the intellect," in order to fill the cup of his heart with the intoxicating wine of God's love. So says Hafiz: "Piety and moral goodness have naught to do with ecstasy; stain your prayer rug with wine!"

Once the veil of traditional dualities has been lifted, the ego obliterated, and the ruh allowed to absorb the qalb, the disciple finally achieves fana, which, as mentioned, is best translated as "ecstatic self-annihilation." It is here, at the end of the Way, that the truth of the Divine Unity of all creation is revealed and the Sufi realizes that, in the words of Shah Angha, "the brook, the river, the drop, the sea, the bubble, all in one voice say: Water we are, water."

By discarding his own qualities and attributes through a radical act of self-annihilation, the Sufi enters fully into the qualities and attributes of God. He does not *become* God, as fana is so often misunderstood by Sunni and Shi'ite Muslims; rather, the Sufi is *drowned* in

God, so that Creator and creation become one. This concept of Divine Unity is most keenly expressed by the great mystic and scholar Ibn al-Arabi (1165–1240), who reformulated the traditional Muslim profession of faith (*shahadah*) from "There is no god but God" to "There is no Being other than the Being of God; there is no Reality other than the Reality of God."

In Ibn al-Arabi's school of thought—a school so influential to the development of Sufism that this entire chapter could be devoted to it—humanity and the cosmos, as two separate but intimately connected constructions of the Universal Spirit, are like two mirrors reflecting one another. By employing ta'wil, Ibn al-Arabi reinterpreted the Quran's statement that God created humanity "from a single soul" (4:1) to mean that the universe itself is "as a single being." For al-Arabi, human beings are thus "an abridgment of the great cosmic book," and those few individuals who have "fully realized [their] essential oneness with the Divine Being," to quote Reynold Nicholson, are transformed into what al-Arabi terms "the Perfect Man" (also called "the Universal Man").

The Perfect Man is he for whom individuality is merely an external form, but whose inward reality conforms to the universe itself. He is "the copy of God," in the words of al-Arabi's greatest disciple, Abdul Karim al-Jili: he is the mirror in which the divine attributes are perfectly reflected; the medium through which God is made manifest.

Although Sufism considers all prophets and messengers, as well as the Imams and the Pirs, to be representatives of the Perfect Man, for Sufis the paradigm of this unique being is none other than the Prophet Muhammad himself. All Muslims look to the example of the Prophet (the *Imitatio Muhammadi*, if you will) to guide them on the straight path to God. But for the Sufi, Muhammad is more than just the "beautiful model" that the Quran calls him (33:21). Muhammad is the primordial light: the first of God's creations.

The concept of "the light of Muhammad" (*nur Muhammad*) reveals Sufism's deep Gnostic influences. In short, the Sufis understand Muhammad in the same way that many Christian Gnostics understood Jesus: as the eternal *logos*. Thus, Muhammad is, like Jesus in the words of John's Gospel, "the light shining in the darkness, though the darkness does not overcome it" (John 1:5); or to quote the Gospel of Thomas, he is "the light which is before all things."

Yet unlike Jesus in the Gnostic Gospels of John and Thomas, Muhammad is not to be understood as "God made flesh." "*God* is the light of the heavens and the earth," the Quran exclaims (24:35), meaning, as al-Ghazali argues in his *Niche of Lights*, that the *nur Muhammad* is, in reality, nothing more than the *reflection* of God's light. Indeed, Sufism often describes the relationship between God and Muhammad in terms of the relationship between the sun and the moon, in that the latter merely reflects the light of the former. The sun expresses power; it is *creative*. The moon expresses beauty; it is *responsive*. Thus, according to Inayat Khan, "the one who gives [God's] Message gives God's Knowledge, not his own. . . . Just [as] the moon's light is not its own." It is this unique impression of Muhammad that has led Sufis to refer to the Prophet not just as *Rasul Allah*, but also as *Dhikr Allah*: "the *remembrance* of God," though the term *dhikr* has many meanings in Sufism.

As one would expect, Sufi beliefs often resulted in bitter, sometimes violent persecution of their adherents at the hands of the religious authorities, who were deeply troubled by its antilaw, antiestablishment ideals. The Sufis were rarely welcomed in the mosques and so were forced to develop their own rituals and practices to assist them in breaking down the separation between the individual and the Divine. As a result, dhikr, as the physical act of remembering God, has become the central ritual activity for all Sufis, though the actual form and function of the dhikr varies drastically depending on the Order.

The most common form of dhikr is known as the "vocal dhikr," made popular through the rituals of the Qadiri Order, which exists primarily in Syria, Turkey, Central Asia, and parts of Africa. The Qadiri, who likely represent the first formally recognized tariqah in Sufism, center their dhikr activities on rhythmic and repetitive invocations of the shahadah or some other religious phrase. Often accompanied by strenuous breathing exercises and rapid movements of the head and torso (the disciples are usually sitting in a circle), these invocations are pronounced faster and faster until the phrase breaks down into meaningless, monosyllabic exhalations of breath, which naturally come to resemble the Arabic word *hu!* or "He," meaning God. By repeatedly invoking God through this physical act of remembrance, the disciple gradually strips himself of his ego so that he may be clothed instead in the attributes of God. In this way, the Qadiri claim, "the rememberer becomes the remembered."

Alongside the "vocal dhikr" of the Qadiri is the so-called "silent dhikr" popularized by the Order of the Naqshbandi. Considered the most traditional of the Sufi Orders, the Naqshbandi primarily comprised politically active pietists who traced their lineage back to Abu Bakr and who maintained strict adherence to the Shariah. The Naqshbandi's traditionalist brand of Sufism led them to reject music and dance in favor of more sober ritual activities like the silent dhikr, in which the names of God are repeated inwardly in an act of meditation, rather than aloud in an act of communion.

The silent dhikr does not exactly correspond to the meditation rituals found in, for example, Theravada Buddhism. However, the Naqshbandi, as well as a few other contemplative Sufi Orders, do practice something called *fikr*, which Ian Richard Netton correctly translates as "contemplation resulting in certitude of the divine." In any case, like the Qadiri, the Naqshbandi have only one goal in pursuing either dhikr or fikr: union with God.

Not all dhikrs involve recitation, either vocal or silent. In fact, the most widely recognized form of dhikr is the spiritual dance of Turkey's Mevlevi Order, founded by Rumi, and popularly known as the Whirling Darvishes. Some Sufis use the art of calligraphy as a form of dhikr, while in the Caucasus, where Sufism inherited many of the shamanistic practices of the ancient Indo-Europeans, dhikr tends to focus not so much on recitation or meditation, but rather on physical pain as a means to shock the disciple into a state of ecstasy. The Rifa'i Order in Macedonia, for example, is famous for its public acts of self-mutilation, in which disciples pierce themselves with spikes while in a trancelike state. In certain parts of Morocco, there are Sufis who practice dhikr through great feats of strength and stamina meant to separate them from the false reality of the material world.

There is another popular form of dhikr, primarily employed by the Chisti Order, who dominate the Indian subcontinent. The Chistis specialize in the use of music in their spiritual exercises. Their "remembrance of God" is best expressed through rapturous spiritual concerts called *sama'*, which Bruce Lawrence describes as "a dynamic dialogue between a human lover and the Divine Beloved."

Of course, music and dance—both of which tend to be frowned upon in traditional Islamic worship—have a long history in the Indian subcontinent, and part of the reason for the rapid spread of Sufism in India was the case with which it appropriated both into its worship ceremonies. In fact, early Chisti evangelists would often enter a town playing flutes or beating drums so as to gather a crowd, before launching into the tales of their Pirs. So the sama' is not only a means by which the Chistis experience the suprasensible world, it is also a valuable evangelical tool. And it is not unusual for the sama' to function as a political rally. Indeed, unlike most Sufi orders, which tend toward political quietism, Sufism in India has always been intertwined with the social and political machinations of the state, especially during the reign of the Mughal emperors (1526–1858), when, in exchange for providing spiritual prosperity and moral legitimacy to the Empire, a select number of Sufis enjoyed enormous influence over the government.

Perhaps the most influential of these "political Sufis" was the eighteenth-century writer and philosopher Shah Wali Allah (d. 1762). A fervent disciple of the traditionalist Naqshbandi Order, Wali Allah strove in his books and lectures to strip Sufism of its "foreign" influences (e.g., Neoplatonism, Persian mysticism, Hindu Vedantism) in order to restore it to what he considered to be an older, unadulterated form of Islamic mysticism, one inextricably bound to traditionalist Sunni orthodoxy. However, Wali Allah was far more interested in reasserting fundamental Islamic values in the social and economic spheres of the state than in merely purifying Sufism. As a result, his theo-political ideology, though interpreted in widely divergent ways, had a profound effect on succeeding generations of Muslim theologians and philosophers.

On the one hand, Wali Allah's emphasis on the resurgence of the Islamic sciences and his enlightened socioeconomic theories influenced Islamic modernists like Sayyid Ahmed Khan to form his Aligarh movement, an intellectual society dedicated not only to establishing a European educational system in India, but also to encouraging Muslim cooperation with the British colonialists who were just then beginning to take a more aggressive role in the political affairs of the Subcontinent.

On the other hand, Wali Allah's emphasis on orthodoxy sparked a number of so-called "puritan" movements in India, the most famous of which is the Deobandi School, whose students—*taliban* in Arabic—played an active role in opposing the British occupation of India, and whose ethnic Pashtun contingent would eventually seize control of Afghanistan in order to impose their radically orthodox theo-political philosophy upon the state (though that story must be reserved for another chapter).

Considering the tragic effects of the colonialist experience in India, it should be obvious which vision of Shah Wali Allah's theo-political views most successfully captured the imaginations of India's oppressed Muslim population. As will become apparent, throughout the colonized lands of the Middle East and North Africa, the voice of modernism and integration with the Enlightenment ideals of the European colonialists was consistently drowned out by the far louder and more aggressive voice of traditionalism and resistance to the insufferable yoke of imperialism. Thus, a new generation of Indian Muslims, born into a country that had become the exclusive financial property of the British Empire, no longer shared the popular Sufi sentiment that "if the world does not agree with you, you agree with the world." They instead preferred the version offered by the great mystical poet and philosopher Muhammad Iqbal (1877–1938)—a disciple of the Qadiri Order and a devotee of Wali Allah—who exclaimed, "If the world does not agree with you, *arise against it!*"

9. An Awakening in the East

THE RESPONSE TO COLONIALISM

DISPATCH FROM FREDERICK Cooper, Deputy Commissioner of Amritsar, to the Foreign Office in London, regarding the fate of the mutinous Sepoys (Bengali soldiers) at Lahore, India. First of August, 1857:

On the 30th of July, some 400 Sepoys from the 26th Native Infantry escaped from the prison camp at Mianmir, where by order of the Crown they had been assembled and disarmed to prevent them from possibly joining the Mohammedan rebels at Delhi. Being weakened and famished, the Sepoys were easily pursued to the banks of the Ravi, where some 150 of them were shot, mobbed backwards into the river, and drowned. The survivors floated across the river on pieces of wood until they reached the opposite shore, whereupon they gathered together like a brood of wild fowl, waiting to be captured. Had they tried to escape, a bloody struggle would have ensued. But Providence ordered otherwise. Indeed, everything nat-ural, artificial, and accidental combined to secure their fate.

The sun was setting in golden splendour; and as the doomed men, with joined palms, crowded down to the shore on the approach of our boats, their long shadows were flung athwart the gleaming waters. In utter despair, forty or fifty dashed into the stream; and the sowars [mounted Indian soldiers], being on the point of taking pot-shots at the heads of the swimmers, were given orders not to shoot. The mutineers were remarkably compliant. They were evidently possessed of a sudden and insane idea that they were going to be tried by court-martial, after some luxurious refreshment. In conse-quence, they submitted to being bound by a single man, and stocked like slaves into the holds of our boats.

By midnight, as the glorious moon came out through the clouds and reflected herself in myriad pools and streams, we had gathered 282 of the Bengali rebels. In the morning, a party of Sikhs arrived with a large supply of rope. But being as the trees were scarce, the rope was not used. A larger problem lay in dealing with the loyal Mohammedan troopers, who would surely not have stood by in silence as justice was meted out upon their rebellious co-religionists. As fortune would have it, the 1st of August was the anniversary of the great Mohammedan festival of Bukra Eid. A capital excuse was thus afforded to permit the Mohammedan horsemen to return to their homes to celebrate, while we Christians, unembarrassed by their presence and aided by the faithful Sikhs, might perform a cere-monial sacrifice of a different nature upon their brethren.

There remained one last difficulty, which was of sanitary con-sideration. But again, as fortune would have it, a deep dry well was discovered within one hundred yards of the police-station, furnish-ing a convenient solution as to how to dispose of the dishonoured soldiers.

At first light, the prisoners were bound together in groups of ten and brought out of their prisons. Believing they were about to be tried and their unwarranted grievances heard, the Sepoys were unusually docile. But when the shots began to ring in the still morn-ing air, and they suddenly discovered the real and awful fate that awaited them, they were filled with astonishment and rage.

The execution commenced uninterrupted until one of our men swooned away (he was the oldest of our firing-party), and a little respite was allowed. After we had shot some 237 of the Moham - medans, the district officer was informed that the remaining captives were apparently refusing to come out of the bastion, where they had been imprisoned temporarily in expectation of their execution. Anticipating a rush and resistance, preparations were made against their escape. The bastion was surrounded, the doors opened, and behold! Forty-five bodies, dead from fright, exhaustion, fatigue, heat, and partial suffocation, were dragged into the light. These dead, along with their executed comrades were thrown by the village sweepers into the well. Thus, within forty-eight hours of their escape, the entire 26th regiment was accounted for and disposed of.

To those of you fond of reading signs, we would point to the solitary golden cross still gleaming aloft on the summit of the Christian church in Delhi, whole and untouched; though the ball on which it rests is riddled with shots deliberately fired by the mutinous infidels of the town. The cross symbolically triumphant over a shattered globe! How the wisdom and heroism of our English soldiers seem like mere dross before the manifest and wondrous interposition of Almighty God in the cause of Christianity!

There were a number of reasons for what the British described as the Sepoy Mutiny, but which is now universally recognized as the Indian Revolt of 1857. The history that led to the revolt is clear enough. Under the auspices of the East India Company, which maintained a total monopoly over Indian markets, the British Empire had been the effective ruler of India since the mid-eighteenth century, though it was not until the last Mughal emperor, Bahadur Shah II, was forcefully deposed, in 1857, that it assumed direct control over the country. By then, the British had so effortlessly pressed their will on the enfeebled population that they were free to plunder the vast resources of the Subcontinent.

To keep Europe's industries running, the colonized lands were rushed toward modernization. European ideals of secularism, pluralism, individual liberties, human rights, and, to a far lesser degree, democracy—the wonderful legacy of the Enlightenment that had taken hundreds of years to evolve in Europe—were pressed upon the colonized lands with no attempt to render them in terms the indigenous population would either recognize or understand. Western technology was shared only insofar as it increased production. New cities were built instead of old cities being developed. Cheaply manufactured imports destroyed most local industries, and native markets had little choice but to focus almost exclusively on the economic needs of the colonial powers.

In return for the pillaging of their lands, the suppression of their independence, and the destruction of their local economies, the colonized peoples were to be given the gift of "civilization." Indeed, in every region to which Europeans laid claim, the colonialist project was presented in the guise of a "civilizing mission." As Cecil Rhodes, founder of the De Beers diamond company and at one time the virtual dictator of modern-day South Africa, famously declared, "We Britons are the first race in the world, and the more of the world we inhabit, the better it is for the human race."

Among the many problems with this so-called civilizing mission was that, well-intentioned as it may have been, it was often deliberately shadowed by a "Christianizing mission," the principal goal of which was, in the words of Sir Charles Trevelyan, Governor of Madras, "nothing short of the conversion of the natives to Christianity." In India, Christian evangelists were placed in the highest positions of government, including at all levels of the British Army. Charles Grant, the director of the East India Company (which until 1858 retained nearly all powers of government in the Indian Subcontinent), was himself an active Christian missionary who believed, along with most of his countrymen, that Britain had been granted dominion over India by God in order to rear it out of its heathen darkness and into the light of Christ. Nearly half of all schools in the Subcontinent were run by missionaries like Grant who received large amounts of aid from the British Empire to indoctrinate the natives into Christianity.

Not all colonialists agreed with Britain's missionary agenda. Lord Ellenborough, Governor General from 1842 to 1844, continually warned his countrymen that the imperial promotion of Christian evangelism was not only detrimental to the security of the Empire, it would likely lead to popular resentment and perhaps to open rebellion. Yet even Ellenborough would have agreed with Trevelyan, who argued that the Indian religion was "identified with so many gross immoralities and physical absurdities that it [would give] way at once before the light of European science."

The British conviction that the ancient foe of Christendom was in desperate need of civilization created a sense of inferiority and fear among India's Muslims, many of whom believed that their faith and culture were under attack. So while the annexation of native states, the dispossession of landowners, the disregard for the plight of the Indian peasantry, and the harsh revenue policies of the rapacious East India Company had formed a massive pyre of anger and resentment in India, in the end it was what Benjamin Disraeli called "the union of missionary enterprise with the political power of the Government" that struck the match of rebellion.

The fact is, the soldiers who launched the Indian Revolt in 1857 were not only angry at colonialist policies that had stripped their land of its natural resources, they were convinced, and rightly so, that the British Army was trying to convert them and their families forcibly to Christianity. It was enough that their commanding officer openly preached the Gospel to all his military classes, but when they discovered that their rifle cartridges had been greased with beef and pork fat, which would have contaminated both Hindus and Muslims, their greatest fears were confirmed. In an act of civil disobedience, a small group of soldiers refused to use the cartridges. Their British commanders responded by shackling them in chains and locking them in military prisons. Seeing this response as yet another indication of the colonialist mindset, the rest of the Bengali Army—some 150,000 soldiers—mutinied.

The soldiers quickly took control of Delhi and set up the deposed Mughal emperor, Bahadur Shah, as their leader. The octogenarian emperor released a written proclamation to the country, urging both the Hindu and Muslim populations to help him "liberate and protect the poor helpless people now groaning" under colonial rule. The proclamation reached every corner of India, and soon what had begun as a military mutiny among the Sepoy forces escalated into a joint Hindu-Muslim rebellion of the civilian population.

The British responded mercilessly and without restraint. To

subdue the uprising they were compelled, somewhat reluctantly, to unleash the full force of their colonial might. There were mass arrests throughout the country; demonstrators both young and old were beaten on the streets. Most major cities were ravaged. In Allahabad, British soldiers indiscriminately killed everyone in their path, leaving the dead bodies to rot in piles on the streets. Lucknow was sacked, Delhi practically razed. Approximately five hundred Sepoys of the 14th Native Infantry were massacred at Jhelam. In Benares, the bodies of civilian sympathizers were hung from the trees. Entire villages were looted, then set aflame. It took less than two years of carnage and plunder before full colonial control was restored. With the rebellion crushed and the East India Company dissolved, the administration of the Subcontinent became the direct responsibility of the Queen, who could now proudly proclaim that "the sun never sets on the British Empire."

The violence with which colonial control was reasserted in India forever shattered any illusions of British moral superiority. For most Muslims, Europe's civilizing mission in the Middle East was revealed for what it truly was: an ideology of political and economic dominance achieved through brutal military might. The ideals of the Enlightenment, which the British never tired of preaching, could no longer be separated from the repressive imperialist policies of the colonizing government. In short, India became the paradigm of the colonialist experiment gone awry.

Even so, a large number of Muslim intellectuals remained convinced that the adoption of European values, such as the rule of law and the pursuit of scientific progress, was the sole means of overcoming the rapid decline of Muslim civilization in the face of European imperialism. This group became known as the Modernists, and perhaps no intellectual better represented their reformist agenda than Sir Sayyid Ahmed Khan.

Born to a family of Mughal nobility, Sayyid Ahmed Khan was a devoted follower of the aforementioned Indian neo-mystic Shah Wali Allah, though by the mid-nineteenth century he had begun to distance himself from the puritanical overtones of an ideology that had already sparked a few anti-Hindu, anti-Sikh rebellions in India. During the Indian Revolt, Sir Sayyid worked as an administrator in the

East India Company and had witnessed for himself the gruesome revenge meted out by the British forces upon the rebellious population of Delhi. Although the experience did not deter him from remaining a loyal subject of the British Empire (as his knighthood suggests), he was nevertheless deeply pained over the plight of Indian Muslims after the collapse of the revolt. In particular, Sir Sayyid was worried about the way in which the revolt was being described by British authorities as "a long concocted Mohammedan conspiracy against British power," to quote Alexander Duff, Britain's leading missionary in India. Such beliefs had made the Muslim community the main target of government reprisals.

To combat this misperception, Sir Sayyid published his most famous work, *The Causes of the Indian Revolt*, which strove to explain to a British audience the reasons behind the events of 1857. This was not, he argued, a premeditated rebellion. It was the spontaneous result of a combination of social and economic grievances. That said, Sir Sayyid admitted that at the heart of the Indian Revolt was the widespread belief that the British were bent on converting the population to Christianity and forcing them to adopt European ways. This, according to Sir Sayyid, was surely a ludicrous notion. Despite the preponderance of evidence, he refused to accept the idea that the Queen's purpose in India was the conversion of its people. Sir Sayyid did, however, recognize that the mere *perception* that the colonialist project was a Christian war against Indian religions was enough to rouse the masses to revolt.

As a devout Indian Muslim and a loyal British subject, Sir Sayyid took upon himself the challenge of building a bridge between those two civilizations, so as to explain the culture, faith, and values of the one to the other. The problem as he saw it was that the Indians "did not understand what right the Government, whose subjects we are, had upon us, and what was our duty towards it." If only the goals and ideals of the British were explained to the indigenous population in a language they could understand, the Indians would become "not a burden but a boon to the community."

In 1877, Sayyid Ahmed Khan founded the Aligarh School, the primary goal of which was the revitalization of Islamic glory through modern European education. Sir Sayyid was convinced that if he could shine the light of European rationalism and scientific thought upon traditional Muslim beliefs and customs, the result would be an indigenous Islamic Enlightenment that would propel the Muslim world into the twentieth century. The Aligarh taught its students to throw off the shackles of the Ulama and their blind imitation (*taqlid*) of Islamic doctrine, for none of the problems facing Muslims in the modern world could be solved through their antiquated theology. The only hope for Islamic revival was the modernization of the Shariah; and the only way to achieve this was to take it out of the hands of the incompetent and irrelevant Ulama.

"What I acknowledge to be the original religion of Islam," Sir Sayyid claimed, "[is not the] religion which . . . the preachers have fashioned."

It was Sir Sayyid's Kashmiri protégé, Chiragh Ali (1844–95), who most succinctly outlined his mentor's argument for legal reform. Chiragh Ali was incensed at the way Islam had been portrayed by Europeans as "essentially rigid and inaccessible to change." The notion that its laws and customs are based "on a set of specific precepts which can neither be added to, nor taken from, nor modified to suit altered circumstances" is a fiction created by the Ulama to maintain their control over Muslims, Chiragh Ali said. He argued that the Shariah could not be considered a civil code of law because the only legitimate law in Islam is the Quran, which "does not interfere in political questions, nor does it lay down specific rules of conduct." Rather, the Quran teaches nothing more than "certain doctrines of religion and certain general rules of morality." It would be absurd, therefore, to regard Islamic law, which Chiragh Ali considered the product of the Ulama's imagination, to be "unalterable and unchangeable."

As one can imagine, the Ulama did not respond well to these charges of incompetence and irrelevance, and they used their influence over the population to fight with vehemence the Modernist vision of a new Islamic identity. Certainly, the Modernist cause was not helped by the fact that after the Indian Revolt it became increasingly difficult to separate the ideals of the European Enlightenment from its imperialist connotations. But it was the Modernist demand that the Shariah be withdrawn entirely from the civil sphere that caused the greatest concern among the Ulama. Religious scholars like

Mawlana Mawdudi, founder of the *Jama'at-i Islami* (the Islamic Association), countered the Aligarh platform by arguing that, far from
separating the religious and civil, Islam *requires* that "the law of God
should become the law by which people lead their lives."

Ironically, though Mawdudi was himself a fervent antinationalist,
his ideas were instrumental in providing the ideological foundation for
the creation of the world's first "Islamic state," Pakistan. Yet to understand how India's Muslim community progressed from the disastrous
aftermath of the Indian Revolt to the triumphant creation of their own
separate homeland in less than a hundred years requires a brief detour
through Egypt, where another group of Muslim reformists living
under colonial rule were on the verge of launching an awakening in the
East that would ripple through the whole of the Muslim world.

EGYPT AT THE turn of the nineteenth century had become, in the
words of William Welch, "an essential spoke in the imperial wheel" of
the British Empire. Unlike India, where the British held uncontested
and unconcealed control over every level of civic administration,
Egypt was allowed to maintain a façade of independence through the
hereditary reign of its utterly impotent viceroys, or *khedives*. Though
their fealty remained, in principle, to the Ottoman Empire, by the
nineteenth century the khedives were little more than subjects of the
British Empire. They were powerless to make any political or economic decisions in Egypt without the consent of their colonial masters. In exchange for a seemingly inexhaustible line of credit, which
they could never hope to repay, a succession of viceroys had gradually
settled into apathetic reigns characterized by unrestrained excess and
political indifference.

Meanwhile, Egypt was inundated with foreign workers, wealthy
investors, and middle-class Englishmen eager to stake their claims on
a country with few bureaucratic obstacles and unlimited opportunities
for advancement. To accommodate the rapid influx of Europeans,
entire cities were built on the outskirts of Cairo, far away from the
indigenous population. The foreigners quickly took charge of Egypt's
principal export of cotton. They built ports, railroads, and dams, all to
implement colonial control over the country's economy. With the

construction of their crowning achievement, the Suez Canal, Egypt's fate as Britain's most valuable colony was sealed.

To pay for these massive projects, taxes were increased, though they were already too high to be paid by the average Cairene, let alone by the expanding peasant class (the *fellaheen*) forced into the cities by the destruction of their local industries. Making matters worse, the khedives had been pressured into allowing the foreign élite unreasonable concessions, including exemption from all taxes except those levied on property, and total immunity from being tried in Egyptian courts.

Naturally, the iniquitous situation in Egypt led to widespread anticolonialist sentiment and sporadic uprisings, both of which were used by the British as further excuses to tighten their control over the population. The result was a government in staggering debt to European creditors and a disenfranchised population desperately in search of a common identity to unite them against the colonialist menace. By the middle of the century, the situation in Egypt was ripe for the Modernist message then being formed in India. That message would be brought to them by the man known as "the Awakener of the East"— Jamal ad-Din al-Afghani (1838–97).

Despite his name, al-Afghani was in fact not an Afghan. As his excellent translator, Nikki Keddie, has shown, al-Afghani was actually born and raised in Iran, where he received a traditional Shi'ite education in the Islamic sciences. Why he decided to pose alternately as a Sunni Muslim from Afghanistan or as a Turk from Istanbul is hard to say. In light of Shah Wali Allah's popular puritan movement, which had reached all corners of the Muslim world, al-Afghani may have considered it expedient to hide his Shi'ite identity so as to disseminate his reformist agenda more widely.

At the age of seventeen, al-Afghani left Iran for India to supplement his religious education with the so-called Western sciences. The year was 1856. Nearly two thirds of the Subcontinent was under the direct control of the British Empire. The economic policies of the East India Company and its various affiliates had allowed Britain to annex vast tracts of native-owned property. Regional rulers had been forcibly deposed and the peasantry stripped of their meager earnings. All through the country, rebellion was brewing.

At first, al-Afghani seemed unconcerned with the momentous

events taking place around him. As his earliest biographer, Salim al-Anhuri, notes, he was too engrossed in his academic studies to concern himself with the plight of the Indian population. But the following year, when Indian grievances erupted into open rebellion, al-Afghani was suddenly roused to action. The young man was traumatized not only by the violence with which the British reasserted their control, but by the hypocrisy they showed in preaching such exalted Enlightenment values while cruelly stifling Indian appeals for liberation and national sovereignty. His experiences in the Subcontinent engendered in his heart a lifelong loathing of the British and a single minded devotion to freeing the Muslim world from the yoke of European colonialism, which he considered to be the gravest threat to Islam.

Yet al-Afghani rarely spoke of Islam in religious terms. Perhaps his greatest contribution to Islamic political thought was his insistence that Islam, detached from its purely religious associations, could be used as a sociopolitical ideology to unite the whole of the Muslim world in solidarity against imperialism. Islam was for al-Afghani far more than law and theology; it was civilization. Indeed, it was a superior civilization because, as he argued, the intellectual foundations upon which the West was built had in fact been borrowed from Islam. Ideals such as social egalitarianism, popular sovereignty, and the pursuit and preservation of knowledge had their origins not in Christian Europe, but in the Ummah. It was Muhammad's revolutionary community that had introduced the concept of popular sanction over the ruling government while dissolving all ethnic boundaries between individuals and giving women and children unprecedented rights and privileges.

Al-Afghani agreed with Sayyid Ahmed Khan that the Ulama bore the responsibility for the decline of Islamic civilization. In their self-appointed role as the guardians of Islam, the Ulama had so stifled independent thought and scientific progress that even as Europe awakened to the Enlightenment, the Muslim world was still floundering in the Middle Ages. By forbidding rational dialogue about the limits of law and the meaning of scripture, the Ulama, whom al-Afghani likened to "a very narrow wick on top of which is a very small flame that neither lights its surroundings nor gives light to others," had become the true enemies of Islam.

But al-Afghani was no member of the Aligarh. In fact, he consid-

ered Sayyid Ahmed Khan a tool of the colonialist powers for his dot-
ing emulation of European ideals. As far as al-Afghani was concerned,
Europe's only advantages over Islamic civilization were its technological advancements and its economic prowess. Both of these attributes
would have to be developed in the Muslim world if Islam were to
regain its former glory. But the only way to achieve lasting social,
political, and economic reform in the region would be to contempo-
rize those enduring Islamic values that had founded the Muslim community. Merely imitating Europe, as Ahmed Khan would have
Muslims do, was a waste of time.

Al-Afghani's burgeoning political ideology was reinforced during
his tenure as a member of the Educational Council in the Ottoman
Empire. There, al-Afghani came into contact with a passionate group
of Turkish reformers dubbed the Young Ottomans. Led by a handful
of writers and academics, the most famous of whom was the brilliant
poet and playwright Namik Kemal (1840–88), the Young Ottomans
had developed an intriguing reformist agenda based on fusing Western democratic ideals with traditional Islamic principles. The result
was a supernationalist project, commonly referred to as *Pan-Islamism*,
whose principal goal was the encouragement of Muslim unity across
cultural, sectarian, and national boundaries, under the banner of a
single, centralized (and obviously Turkish) Caliphate—in other words,
the revival of the Ummah.

Al-Afghani enthusiastically embraced the philosophy of the
Young Ottomans, especially their call for the rebirth of the united
Muslim community—one that included Shi'ites and Sufis as equal
members—in order to combat European imperialism. In 1871, bol-
stered by his newfound faith in the prospects of Pan-Islamism, al-
Afghani went to Cairo—then as now the cultural capital of the
Muslim world—ostensibly to teach philosophy, logic, and theology,
but in truth to implant his vision of the Modernist agenda into the
political landscape of Egypt. It was in Cairo that he befriended a zealous young student named Muhammad Abdu (1845–1950), who would
become Egypt's most influential voice of Muslim reform.

Born a *fellah* in a small village on the Nile Delta, Abdu was an
extremely devout boy who by the age of twelve had memorized the
whole of the Quran. As a young disciple of the Shadhili Sufi Order, he

had excelled in his studies of the Islamic sciences, so much so that he was sent to al-Azhar University in Cairo to continue his education. But despite his piety and indefatigable intellect, Abdu immediately clashed with the rigid pedagogy and traditionalist teachings of al-Azhar's Ulama. At the same time, he was struck by the ways in which Europe's lofty principles were so blatantly contradicted by its colonialist agenda.

"We Egyptians," he wrote, "believed once in English liberalism and English sympathy; but we believe no longer, for facts are stronger than words. Your liberalness we see plainly is only for yourselves, and your sympathy with us is that of the wolf for the lamb which he designs to eat."

Disenchanted with his religious and political leaders, Abdu became an avid disciple of al-Afghani and, under his tutelage, published a number of books and tracts advocating a return to the unadulterated values of the *salafs* ("the pious forefathers") who founded the first Muslim community in Medina. Labeling himself a "neo-Mu'tazilite," Abdu called for the reopening of the gates of *ijtihad*, or independent reasoning. The only path to Muslim empowerment, he argued, was to liberate Islam from the iron grip of the Ulama and their traditionalist interpretation of the Shariah. Like Sir Sayyid, Abdu demanded that every man-made source of law—the Sunna, *ijma*, *qiyas*, and the like—must be subject to rational discourse. Even the holy Quran must be reopened to interpretation, questioning, and debate from all sectors of Muslim society. Muslims do not need the guidance of the Ulama to engage the sacred Revelation, Abdu argued; they must be free to experience the Quran on their own.

While Abdu did not believe that Islam need separate its religious ideals from the secular realm, he categorically rejected the possibility of placing secular powers in the hands of religious clerics, whom he deemed totally unqualified to lead the Muslim community into the new century. What was needed instead was a reinterpretation of traditional Islamic ideals so as to present modern democratic principles in terms that the average Muslim could easily recognize. Thus, Abdu redefined shura, or tribal consultation, as representative democracy; ijma, or consensus, as popular sovereignty; and *bay'ah*, or the oath of allegiance, as universal suffrage. According to this view, the Ummah was the nation, and its ruler the Caliph, whose sole function was to protect its members by serving the welfare of the community.

Together, al-Afghani and Muhammad Abdu founded the *Salafiyyah* movement, Egypt's version of the Modernist project. After al-Afghani's death, Abdu joined forces with his close friend and biographer, Rashid Rida (1865–1935), to push the Salafiyyah's reformist agenda to the forefront of Egyptian politics. Yet, despite its growing popularity throughout the region, the ideal of Pan-Islamism, which was at the heart of Abdu's reformist project, remained exceedingly difficult to implement.

The problem with Pan-Islamism was that the spiritual and intellectual diversity that had characterized the Muslim faith from the start made the prospects of achieving religious solidarity across sectarian lines highly unlikely. This was particularly true in light of the rising Islamic puritan movement, which sought to strip the religion of its cultural innovations. What is more, large and powerful groups of secular nationalists throughout the Middle East found the religious ideology behind the Salafiyyah movement to be incompatible with what they considered the principal goals of modernization: political independence, economic prosperity, and military might. Ironically, many of these secular nationalists were inspired by al-Afghani's brand of Islamic liberalism. In fact, Egypt's most influential nationalist, Sa'd Zaghlul (1859–1927), began his career as a disciple of Muhammad Abdu.

But while Zaghlul and his nationalist colleagues accepted the Salafiyyah's vision of "Islam as civilization," they rejected the argument that imperialism could be defeated through religious solidarity. One need only regard the petty squabbles of the Ulama to recognize the futility of the Pan-Islamist project, they argued. Rather, the nationalists sought to battle European colonialism through a secular countermovement that would replace the Salafiyyah's aspirations of religious unity with the more pragmatic goal of racial unity: in other words, *Pan-Arabism*.

Practically speaking, Pan-Arabism was deemed easier to achieve than Pan-Islamism. As one of its leading proponents, Sati al-Husri (1880–1968), reasoned, "Religion is a matter between the individual and God, while the fatherland is the concern of us all." Nevertheless, the Pan-Arabists considered their movement to be both political and religious because, in their view, Islam could not be divorced from its Arab roots. To quote the nationalist ideologue Abd al-Rahman al-Bazzaz, "The most glorious pages of Muslim history [are also] the pages of Arab history." Thus, while Pan-Arabists agreed with the Pan-Islamists that Muslims must return to the values of the original community in Medina, they defined that community as uniquely Arab. Muslim unity, it was claimed, could not be realized except through Arab unity, and Pan-Arabism was seen as "the practical step which must precede . . . Pan-Islamism."

Of course, the Pan-Arabists had a difficult time defining what exactly they meant by Arab unity. Despite their claims of racial solidarity, there is simply no such thing as a single Arab ethnicity. Egyptian Arabs had practically nothing in common with, say, Iraqi Arabs. The two countries did not even speak the same Arabic dialect. In any case, regardless of the Ummah's Arab roots, the fact is that at the beginning of the twentieth century, Arabs accounted for the tiniest fraction of the world's Muslim population—as little as 20 percent. In response to such obstacles some nationalists sought to connect themselves with the ancient cultures of their home countries. For example, Egyptian nationalists appealed to an imagined Pharaonic legacy, while Iraqi nationalists strove to return to their Mesopotamian heritage.

The Arab nationalists were given an unexpected boost at the end of the First World War, when the Ottoman Empire collapsed at the hands of Kemal Ataturk. The Caliphate that had, despite its declining powers, symbolized the spiritual unity of the Ummah for nearly fifteen centuries was suddenly replaced by a radically secular, ultranationalist Turkish republic. The Empire was broken up by the victors of the war, particularly Britain, into individual, semi-autonomous states. In Egypt, Britain seized the opportunity to sever all ties with the Turks, simply declaring itself the country's sole protector. The khedive was declared king of Egypt, though he was still a puppet of the colonialists.

With the Caliphate dismantled and Egypt firmly under British occupation, Pan-Islamism was discarded as a viable ideology for Muslim unification. And though Pan-Arabism was thus left as the principal voice of opposition to colonialism, it could no longer hope to extend beyond national boundaries. Muslims were being forced to identify themselves as citizens of nations, not members of a community. With Pan-Islamism waning and Pan-Arabism powerless as a political force, it was left to a new generation of Muslims, led by the charismatic young socialist Hasan al-Banna (1906–49), to revive not only Egyptian aspirations for liberty and independence but the aspirations of Muslims throughout the Middle East to shake free the chains of colonialism and Western imperialism.

Hasan al-Banna came to Cairo in 1923 to pursue a higher degree in education. Profoundly influenced by the mystical teachings of al-Ghazali, al-Banna had joined the Hasafiyyah Sufi Order at a young age in order to dedicate his life to preserving and renewing the traditions of his faith and culture. Later, as an ardent and bright university student, al-Banna devoured the works of al-Afghani and Muhammad Abdu, feeling, as they did, that the decline of Muslim civilization was the result not only of foreign influence, but of a lack of dedication on the part of Egyptians to the original principles of Islam preached by Muhammad in Medina.

In Cairo, al-Banna was struck by the depravity and rampant secularism that had gripped the city. Traditional Islamic ideals of egalitarianism and social justice had been swept aside by the unbridled greed of the country's political and religious élites, most of whom eagerly colluded with the British colonialists in exchange for wealth and status. Foreigners controlled all channels of government and maintained a monopoly over Egypt's economy. Cairo had become a virtual apartheid state where small pockets of tremendously wealthy Europeans and Westernized Egyptians ruled over millions of impoverished peasants who labored on their lands and cared for their estates.

Al-Banna appealed to the Ulama at Egypt's al-Azhar University, but found them to be as ineffectual and irrelevant as the Modernists had accused them of being. Yet he was convinced that the Modernist enterprise was misguided in its attempts to adopt what he called "the social principles on which the civilization of the Western nations has been built." Al-Banna also rejected the nationalist ideology of Pan-Arabism, considering nationalism to be the principal cause of the murderous world war that had just ended. In the end, al-Banna concluded that the only path to Muslim independence and self-empowerment lay in reconciling modern life with Islamic values—a process he referred to as "the Islamization of society."

In 1928, al-Banna carried his vision of Islamization to his first teaching post in the small village of Ismailiyyah, near the Suez Canal. If the Canal was the crowning achievement of the colonialist system in Egypt, Ismailiyyah represented the depths to which Arabs had sunk under that system. This was a region teeming with foreign soldiers and civilian workers who lived in luxurious gated communities that towered over the squalid and miserable neighborhoods of the local residents. Street signs were in English, cafés and restaurants segregated, and public spaces peppered with markers warning "no Arabs."

The iniquity and humiliation facing the residents in a region that was generating such colossal wealth for the British Empire enraged al-Banna. He began preaching his message of Islamization in parks and in restaurants, in coffee shops and in homes. The young and dispossessed, all those who felt betrayed by their feeble government and their ineffectual religious leaders, flocked to al-Banna and his simple message that "Islam is the answer." Eventually, what began as little more than an informal grassroots organization dedicated to changing the lives of people through social welfare was formalized into the world's first Islamic socialist movement.

"We are brothers in the service of Islam," al-Banna, then only twenty-two years old, announced at the first official meeting of his group, "hence we are *the Muslim Brothers*."

The influence of the Society of Muslim Brothers on the Islamic world can hardly be exaggerated. Al-Banna's Islamization project quickly spread to Syria, Jordan, Algeria, Tunisia, Palestine, Sudan, Iran, and Yemen. Islamic socialism proved to be infinitely more successful than either Pan-Islamism or Pan-Arabism in giving voice to Muslim grievances. The Muslim Brothers vigorously tackled issues that no one else would address. Matters such as the increase in Christian missionary activity in the Middle East, the rise of Zionism in Palestine, the poverty and political inferiority of Muslim peoples, and the opulence and autocracy of Arab monarchies were common themes in the Brothers' preaching.

Perhaps the most significant aspect of al-Banna's movement was that it represented the first modern attempt to present Islam as an all-encompassing religious, political, social, economic, and cultural system. Islam, in al-Banna's view, represented a universal ideology superior to all other systems of social organization the world had known. As such, it demanded a distinctly Islamic government—one that could properly address society's ills. Yet al-Banna did not believe it was his duty to impose this ideology on the current political system in Egypt. The Muslim Brothers was a socialist organization, not a political party: its principal concern was reconciling hearts and minds to God so as to alleviate human suffering, not bringing about a political revolution. True to his Sufi upbringing, al-Banna was convinced that the state could be reformed only by reforming the self.

Al-Banna's apolitical sentiments did not spare him the ire of the government. In 1949, at the behest of Egypt's khedive and undoubtedly with the encouragement of the colonialist leadership, al-Banna was assassinated. But while this act may have silenced the leader of the Muslim Brothers, it strengthened the Society itself, so that by the 1950s, it had become the most dominant voice of opposition in Egypt, boasting nearly half a million members. It therefore could not be ignored by the burgeoning anticolonialist, anti-imperialist rebellion that had been looming for years in the ranks of Egypt's armed forces.

On July 23, 1952, a group of disaffected military leaders who called themselves the Free Officer Corps launched a coup d'état against Egypt's inept monarchy and unilaterally declared the country free of colonial control. The coup was instigated by the head of the armed forces, General Muhammad Naguib. But everyone in Egypt knew that the real power behind the rebellion was Naguib's right-hand man, Colonel Gamal Abd al-Nasser.

Initially, the Muslim Brothers enthusiastically supported the Free Officers, primarily because Nasser had promised to implement their socialist agenda in postrevolutionary Egypt. The Society's leadership referred to the Free Officers as a "blessed movement" and helped maintain order and security in all the major cities in the aftermath of the coup. Nasser reciprocated their support by humbly going on a pilgrimage to al-Banna's tomb and even went so far as to invite the Muslim Brothers to join the new parliament, though they refused, for fear of sullying al-Banna's apolitical principles.

But as Nasser gradually implemented his nationalist agenda in Egypt, his authoritarian rule began to clash with the egalitarian values preached by the Muslim Brothers. In January of 1953, as part of Nasser's plan to consolidate his control over the government, all parties and political organizations were outlawed except the Muslim Brothers, whose support was still vital to his popularity with the people. The following year, however, when shots were fired at Nasser as he was delivering a speech in Alexandria, the opportunity to dismantle the Muslim Brothers finally presented itself. Blaming the attempt on his life on a conspiracy within the Society, Nasser outlawed the Muslim Brothers; its members were rounded up and imprisoned, its leaders tortured and executed.

In the dank, sadistic prisons of Nasser's Egypt, the Muslim Brothers fractured along ideological lines. For many members, it became painfully clear that the socialist vision of changing hearts to change society had failed. According to these Brothers, al-Banna's Islamization project could not be realized through acts of social welfare. If Nasser had taught them anything, it was that such lofty ideals could be enacted only by force. Postcolonial Egypt required a new vision of Islam and its role in the modern world, and the man who would provide that vision was, at the time, languishing in a prison cell in Cairo.

Poet, novelist, journalist, critic, and social activist Sayyid Qutb (1906–66) would come to be known as the father of Islamic radicalism. Born in Upper Egypt, he had, like al-Banna, moved to Cairo during the turbulent 1920s. After a brief stint in the Ministry of Education, Qutb traveled to the United States in 1948 to research its educational system. What he discovered was a nation committed to individual freedom, yet "devoid of human sympathy and responsibility . . . except under the force of law." He was disgusted by what he saw as the country's "materialistic attitude" and its "evil and fanatical racial discrimination," both of which he blamed on the West's compulsion to pull "religion apart from common life." Qutb was equally frightened at the rapid spread of Western cultural hegemony in the developing countries of the Middle East and North Africa, a phenomenon that the Iranian social critic Jalal Al-e Ahmad, Qutb's contemporary, dubbed *Gharbzadeghi*, or "Westoxification."

Upon his return to Cairo in 1950, Qutb joined the Muslim Brothers, seeing in the Society a fervent dedication to founding a socialist Islamic polity. He quickly ascended to a position of authority, heading the organization's propaganda department. After the revolution of 1952, Nasser asked Qutb to join his government, but Qutb refused, preferring to continue his social activities with the Brothers. That decision would have devastating consequences. After the attempt on Nasser's life, Qutb was one of countless Muslim Brothers who were arrested, brutally tortured, and tossed into prison to be forgotten.

In the solitary confines of his cell, Qutb had a revelation. "Preaching alone is not enough," he wrote in his revolutionary manifesto, *Milestones*, published in 1964, the year of his release. "Those who have usurped the authority of Allah and [who] are oppressing Allah's creatures are not going to give up their power merely through preaching."

Qutb shocked Muslims by claiming that they were still living in a state of Jahiliyyah—"the Time of Ignorance" that preceded the rise of Islam—in which decadent and corrupt human beings had seized for themselves one of God's greatest attributes, namely, sovereignty. Qutb agreed with al-Banna that society's inequities could be addressed only by asserting the superiority of Islam as a complete social, political, and economic system. However, unlike al-Banna, Qutb envisioned that process to be a cataclysmic, revolutionary event that could be brought about only through the establishment of an Islamic state. As he argued in *Milestones*, "setting up the kingdom of God on earth, and eliminating the kingdom of man, means taking power from the hands of its human usurpers and restoring it to God alone."

In Qutb's view, the Islamic state would not require a ruler, at least not a centralized executive power like a president or king. The only ruler would be God; the only law, the Shariah. Qutb's radicalized vision of political Islam completely transformed the landscape of the Middle East, giving rise to a new ideology called *Islamism*.

Not to be confused with Pan-Islamism, the supernationalist theory of Muslim unity under a single Caliph, Islamism is a nationalist ideology that calls for the creation of an Islamic state in which the sociopolitical order would be founded upon a distinctly Islamic moral framework. The Islamists argued that Islam is a comprehensive ideology that governs all aspects of the believer's life. As Qutb wrote, the fundamental concern of Islam is "to unify the realm of earth and the realm of heaven in one system." The primary condition for the realization of that system would be the adoption and implementation of the Shariah in the public sphere. Western secular values must be rejected in the Muslim world because Islam forbids its theological beliefs to be "divorced in nature or in objective from secular life and customs." All secular governments, therefore, including those run by Arabs like Nasser, must be replaced, by force if necessary, with a viable and morally accountable Islamic state.

In 1965, a year after he had been released from prison, Qutb was rearrested for the publication of *Milestones* and was hanged for treason. Meanwhile, those radicalized members of the Muslim Brothers who had managed to escape Nasser's wrath found refuge in the only place that would open its arms to them: Saudi Arabia, a country on the verge of an economic explosion that would transform its rough band of tribal leaders into the wealthiest men in the world—an astounding achievement for a kingdom founded upon an informal alliance between an insignificant tribal Shaykh and a barely literate religious zealot.

AT THE DAWN of the eighteenth century, around the time Europe was beginning to take notice of the vast natural resources waiting to be tapped across the Mediterranean, the sacred land that had given birth to Islam and reared it in its infancy fell under the nominal suzerainty of the Ottoman Empire, though the Caliph allowed the Sharif of Mecca—a descendant of the Prophet and heir to the Banu Hashim—to wield authority over the Arabian population. Yet neither Ottoman influence nor the Sharif's control extended far beyond western Arabia, the Hijaz. Throughout the vast, inaccessible deserts of eastern Arabia—a region called the *Najd*, whose austere and sterile landscape was matched by its stagnant religious and cultural development—there lived large numbers of autonomous tribes loyal to no one but themselves. Among these was a small clan of little account led by an ambitious Shaykh named Muhammad Ibn Saud (d. 1765).

While by no means a wealthy man, ibn Saud owned most of the cultivated lands in the tiny oasis town of Dariyah, which had been founded by his family. His position as Shaykh gave him exclusive control of the town's wells and primary trade routes. Although he maintained a small network of caravans, his finances were severely limited by his reach, which did not extend beyond the boundaries of the oasis. Still, Ibn Saud was a proud and ostentatious man, cut from the fabric of his ancient Arab ancestors, and fiercely dedicated to the protection of his family and clan. So when an itinerant preacher named Muhammad ibn Abd al-Wahhab (1703–66) arrived in his oasis looking for protection, he immediately seized the opportunity to create an alliance that would increase both his economic prosperity and his military might.

Born in the deserts of Najd to a devout Muslim family, Muhammad ibn Abd al-Wahhab displayed his religious zeal at a young age. Recognizing his talent for Quranic study, his father sent him to Medina to study with the disciples of Shah Wali Allah, who had only recently launched his campaign against Indian Sufism. Abd al-Wahhab was deeply influenced by Wali Allah's puritanical ideology. But it was not until he left Medina for Basra and experienced for himself the rich diversity of Shi'ism and Sufism in all its local variations that his anger at what he considered to be the adulteration of Islam transformed into a fanatical obsession to strip Islam of its "superstitious innovations" and restore it to its original Arab purity. Upon returning to the Arabian Peninsula, he embarked on a violent crusade to promote his radically puritanical sect of Islam, popularly known as *Wahhabism* (adherents prefer the term "Muwahiddun," meaning "Unitarians").

In truth, Wahhabi doctrine is little more than an overly simplified conception of tawhid. When the Wahhabi declares "There is no god but God," he means that God must be the sole object of religious devotion; any act of worship that involves any other entity whatsoever is considered shirk. For Abd al-Wahhab, this included the veneration of Pirs, the intercession of the Imams, the commemoration of most religious holidays, and all devotional acts that centered on the Prophet Muhammad. The Wahhabists sought to outlaw rituals like the Sufi dhikr or the Shi'ite matam or any other custom that had crept into Islam as it spread out of the tribal confines of the Arabian Peninsula to be absorbed by the disparate cultures of the Middle East, Central Asia, Europe, India, and Africa. In their place, Abd al-Wahhab instigated a strict implementation of the Shariah, free of all foreign influences and interpretations. As with al-Afghani, Muhammad Abdu, and the Pan-Islamists; Sa'd Zaghlul, Sati al-Husri, and the Pan-Arabists; Hasan al-Banna, the Muslim Brothers, and the Islamic socialists; and Sayyid Qutb, Mawlana Mawdudi, and the radical Islamists, Abd al-Wahhab called for a return to the unadulterated Muslim community established by Muhammad in Arabia. Yet Abd al-Wahhab's was an archaic and exclusivist vision of that original community, and any Muslims who did not share it—especially the Sufis and Shi'ah—were put to the sword.

As Hamid Algar has pointed out, had it not been for the extraordinary circumstances under which Wahhabism emerged, it would undoubtedly have "passed into history as a marginal and short-lived sectarian movement." Not only was this a spiritually and intellectually insignificant movement in a religion founded principally upon spiritualism and intellectualism, it was not even considered true orthodoxy by the majority of Sunni Muslims. Yet Wahhabism had two distinct advantages that would guarantee its place as the most important sectarian movement in Islam since the Penitents first gathered at Karbala a thousand years earlier. First, it had the good fortune to emerge in the sacred lands of the Arabian Peninsula, where it could lay claim to a powerful legacy of religious revivalism. Second, it benefited from a willing and eager patron who saw in its simple ideals the means of gaining unprecedented control over the entire Arabian Peninsula. That patron was Muhammad ibn Saud.

The facts of the alliance between Ibn Saud and Abd al-Wahhab have given way to legend. The two men first met as Abd al-Wahhab and his disciples were tearing through the Arabian Peninsula, demolishing tombs, cutting down sacred trees, and massacring any Muslim who did not accept their uncompromisingly puritanical vision of Islam. After being expelled from an oasis where they had received shelter (the horrified villagers demanded that Abd al-Wahhab leave after he publicly stoned a woman to death), they made their way toward the oasis of Dariyah and its Shaykh, Muhammad ibn Saud, who was more than happy to give Abd al-Wahhab and his holy warriors his unconditional protection.

"This oasis is yours," Ibn Saud promised; "do not fear your enemies."

Abd al-Wahhab replied with an unusual demand. "I want you to grant me an oath," he said, "that you will perform jihad against the unbelievers [non-Wahhabi Muslims]. In return you will be leader of the Muslim community, and I will be leader in religious matters."

Ibn Saud agreed, and an alliance was formed that would not only alter the course of Islamic history, it would change the geopolitical balance of the world. Abd al-Wahhab's holy warriors burst into the Hijaz, conquering Mecca and Medina and expelling the Sharif. Once established in the holy cities, they set about destroying the tombs of the Prophet and his Companions, including those pilgrimage sites that marked the birthplace of Muhammad and his family. They sacked the treasury of the Prophet's Mosque in Medina and set fire to every book they could find, save the Quran. They banned music and flowers from the sacred cities and outlawed the smoking of tobacco and the drinking of coffee. Under penalty of death, they forced the men to grow beards and the women to be veiled and secluded.

The Wahhabis purposely connected their movement with the first extremists in the Muslim world, the Kharijites, and like their fanatical predecessors, they focused their wrath inward against what they considered to be the failings of the Muslim community. With Arabia firmly under their control, they marched north to spread their message to the Sufi and Shi'ite infidels. In 1802, on the holy day of Ashura, they scaled the walls of Karbala and massacred two thousand Shi'ite worshippers as they celebrated the rituals of Muharram. In an uncontrolled rage, they smashed the tombs of Ali, Husayn, and the Imams, giving particular vent to their anger at the tomb of the Prophet's daughter, Fatima. With Karbala sacked, the Wahhabis turned north toward Mesopotamia and the heart of the Ottoman Empire. Only then did they get the attention of the Caliph.

In 1818, the Egyptian khedive, Muhammad Ali (1769–1849), at

the behest of the Ottoman Caliph, sent a massive contingent of heavily armed soldiers into the peninsula. The Egyptian army easily overwhelmed the ill-equipped and poorly trained Wahhabis. Mecca and Medina were once again placed under the care of the Sharif and the Wahhabists forcefully sent back into the Najd. By the time the Egyptian troops withdrew, the Saudis had learned a valuable lesson: they could not take on the Ottoman Empire on their own. They needed a far stronger alliance than the one they had with the Wahhabis.

The opportunity to form just such an alliance presented itself with the Anglo-Saudi Treaty in 1915. The British, who were eager to control the Persian Gulf, encouraged the Saudis to recapture the Arabian Peninsula from Ottoman control. To assist them in their rebellion, the British provided regular shipments of weapons and money. Under the command of Ibn Saud's heir Abd al-Aziz (1880–1953), the plan worked. At the close of the First World War, when the Ottoman Empire had been dismantled and the Caliphate abolished, ibn Saud reconquered Mecca and Medina and once again expelled the Sharif. After publicly executing forty thousand men and reimposing Wahhabism over the entire population, Abd al-Aziz ibn Saud renamed the Arabian Peninsula "the Kingdom of Saudi Arabia." The primitive tribe of the Najd and their puritanical allies had become the Wardens of the Sanctuary, the Keepers of the Keys.

Almost immediately, the sacred land where Muhammad had received the gift of revelation miraculously burst forth with another gift from God—oil—giving the tiny Saudi clan sudden dominion over the world's economy. They now felt it was up to them to respond to this blessing from God by spreading their puritanical doctrine to the rest of the world and purging the Muslim faith once and for all of its religious and ethnic diversity.

The Muslim Brothers arrived in Saudi Arabia at an opportune time. The Kingdom of Saudi Arabia remained the sole Muslim country in which the Ulama had not lost their grip over society. On the contrary, Saudi Arabia was both an utterly totalitarian and an uncompromisingly Wahhabist state. Here there was no debate between Modernists and Traditionalists; there was no debate whatsoever. Nationalism, Pan-Arabism, Pan-Islamism, Islamic socialism—none of these vibrant and influential movements had a significant voice in the Saudi kingdom. The only doctrine that was tolerated was Wahhabi doctrine; the only ideology, Islamic puritanism. Any deviation was violently suppressed.

No wonder the Saudi monarchy viewed Nasser's secular nationalism as a direct threat to their way of life. As the man who defied the West by nationalizing the Suez Canal, Nasser had achieved near-mythic status not only in the Muslim world but in most other third-world countries. In the Middle East, Nasser embodied the last gasp of Pan-Arabism. His Arab socialist vision, though failing miserably in Egypt, was regarded by many Muslims as the sole alternative to the spread of Westoxification. So great was his charisma, and so successful his brutal suppression of opposition, that by the 1960s, his authority was unchallenged in every sector of Egyptian society.

Hoping to curb Nasser's growing influence in the Muslim world, the Saudi monarchy opened its arms to the radicalized Muslim Brothers—not just those who had been exiled from Egypt, but also those from other secular Arab states like Syria and Iraq. The Saudis offered all the money, support, and security the Brothers needed to fight back against secular nationalism in their home countries. But the Muslim Brothers discovered more than shelter in Saudi Arabia. They discovered Wahhabism; and they were not alone. Hundreds of thousands of poor workers from all over the Muslim world began pouring into Saudi Arabia to work the oil fields. By the time they returned to their homes, they were fully indoctrinated in Saudi religiosity.

Religious adherence to the Saudi model became the prerequisite for receiving government subsidies and contracts. The vast sums the Saudis paid to various Muslim charities, the foundations they established, the mosques, universities, and primary schools they built—everything the Saudis did was inextricably linked to Wahhabism. In 1962, their missionary efforts gained momentum with the creation of the Muslim World League, whose primary goal was the spread of Wahhabi ideology to the rest of the world. This was, in effect, the new Islamic expansion, except that these tribal warriors did not need to leave the Arabian Peninsula to conquer their neighbors; their neighbors came to them. As Keepers of the Keys, the Saudis controlled the Hajj pilgrimage, to the chagrin of most Muslims who considered them little more than a crude band of unsophisticated puritans. With billions of dollars spent to modernize and expand the pilgrimage festivities so as to ensure maximum participation, nearly three million Muslims now inundate the bare Meccan valley every year.

Since the creation of the Muslim World League, the simplicity, certainty, and unconditional morality of Wahhabism have infiltrated every corner of the Muslim world. Thanks to Saudi evangelism, Wahhabi doctrine has dramatically affected the religio-political ideologies of the Muslim Brothers, Mawdudi's Islamic Association, the Palestinian Hamas, and Islamic Jihad, to name only a few groups. The Saudis have become the patrons of a new kind of Pan-Islamism: one based on the austere, uncompromising, and extremist ideology of "Islamic fundamentalism," which has become a powerful voice in deciding the future of the Islamic state.

Of course, the problem with fundamentalism is that it is by definition a reactionary movement; it cannot remain tied to power. The Saudi kingdom discovered this from the very beginning when, suddenly flush with money, Abd al-Aziz ibn Saud began using his newfound wealth to build a life befitting a king. Soon Saudi Arabia was awash in modern technology bought from the West. The elaborate process of extracting oil from the desert required the presence of hundreds of foreign nationals—mostly British and American—who brought to Arabia an unfamiliar yet alluring culture of materialism. So close was Abd al-Aziz to the British Empire that he was even knighted by the Queen. In short, the king had been Westoxified and, as a result, turned his back on the Wahhabi warriors—now dubbed the *Ikhwan*, or "brothers" (not to be confused with the Muslim Brothers)—who had helped place him in power.

In 1929, the Ikhwan, angered by the greed and corruption of the Saudi court, launched a rebellion in the city of al-Salba. They demanded that the king renounce his materialism and expel the foreign infidels from the holy land. In response, Abd al-Aziz sent an army to al-Salba and massacred the Ikhwan.

However, Saudi Arabia quickly discovered what the rest of the world would soon learn. Fundamentalism, in all religious traditions, is impervious to suppression. The more one tries to squelch it, the stronger it becomes. Counter it with cruelty, and it gains adherents. Kill its leaders, and they become martyrs. Respond with despotism, and it becomes the sole voice of opposition. Try to control it, and it will turn against you. Try to appease it, and it will take control.

When the Soviets invaded Afghanistan in 1979, the Saudi regime saw an opportunity to rid itself, however temporarily, of the holy warriors it had nurtured for nearly a century. With economic and military support from the United States and tactical training provided by Pakistan's Inter-Services Intelligence agency, the Saudis began funneling a steady stream of radical Islamic militants (known as the *Mujahadin*, or "those who make jihad") from Saudi Arabia and across the Middle East into Afghanistan, where they could be put to use battling the godless communists. The intention, as President Jimmy Carter's national security adviser, Zbigniew Brzezinski, famously put it, was to "give the USSR its own Vietnam" by keeping the Soviet army bogged down in an unwinnable war in hostile territory. The United States considered the Mujahadin to be an important ally in the Great Game being played out against the Soviet Union and, in fact, referred to these militants as "freedom fighters." President Ronald Reagan even compared them to America's founding fathers.

What no one considered at the time was the possibility that this ragtag band of international fighters would actually manage to defeat the Soviet Union. Not only did the Mujahadin expel the Soviet forces from Afghanistan, by abandoning their nationalist (read, *Islamist*) aspirations and joining together as a single united body in pursuit of a common cause, they gave birth to a new kind of *transnational* militant movement in the Islamic world called *Jihadism*.

Unlike Islamists, who remain committed to constructing an Islamic state either through political participation or through radical revolution, Jihadists envision a future where there would no longer be any states, Islamic or otherwise. The Jihadists want to create a world in which all the borders and boundaries that have fractured the Ummah into separate and distinct nation-states would be permanently erased. Their dream is to tear down the walls of culture, ethnicity, and nationality that divide the world's Muslims and to reunite the Ummah once again as a single global community, just as the Prophet Muhammad intended.

In some sense, Jihadism is merely a revival of Pan-Islamism, the now defunct notion of achieving religious unity among the world's

Muslim population. Except that the Islam preached by Jihadists is an ultra-conservative blend of Salafist activism and Wahhabi puritanism tinged with a radical reinterpretation of jihad as an offensive weapon with which they aspire to dominate the world. In true Kharijite fashion, Jihadists segregate all Muslims into "the People of Heaven" (themselves) and "the People of Hell" (everyone else). Anyone whose interpretation of scripture and observance of the Shariah does not correspond to the Jihadist model is considered a member of the latter group—apostates and infidels who must be expelled from the holy community of God.

The Jihadists initially burst onto the international scene in 1990, after Iraq's invasion of Kuwait. In response to the Saudi government's decision to invite the American military into the kingdom to repel the Iraqi forces, a small group of Jihadists turned against the Saudi royal family, accusing them of being corrupt degenerates who had sold the interests of the Muslim community to foreign powers. This group, headed by a Saudi exile named Osama bin Laden and an Egyptian dissident (and former Muslim Brotherhood member) named Ayman al-Zawahiri, formed an organization dubbed al-Qaeda ("the base" or "the fundamentals") that, ten years later, would turn its focus away from the corrupt leaders of the Arab and Muslim world—what the Jihadists term the "Near Enemy"—and toward the "Far Enemy," and the lone remaining superpower, the United States.

The attacks of 9/11 placed Jihadism squarely in America's crosshairs, launching the so-called war on terror and flooding the countries of the Middle East—from Afghanistan to Iraq and beyond—with hundreds of thousands of American military and civilian personnel whose mission is not only to root out and destroy Jihadist cells, but also to transform the entire Middle East into a more modern, more moderate, more democratic region. On the first point, the United States and its allies have had some measure of success. As an international terrorist organization, al-Qaeda has been severely crippled. Its founder has been killed; its leadership is on the run; its rank and file is nearly decimated. It may still maintain some operational control over Jihadist operations across the globe, but by no means does it possess the resources it enjoyed before 9/11. Far from inspiring a global Muslim uprising against the West, al-Qaeda's bloody actions and indiscriminate murder of women and children have turned overwhelming majorities of Muslims among all classes, ages, sects, and nations against both the organization and its ideology.

On the second objective—the democratization of the Middle East—the record of the United States and its allies has been disastrous. In fact, the ham-handed and hypocritical manner in which democracy has been promoted in the region, not to mention the religiously polarizing, "clash of civilizations" rhetoric that has accompanied America's democratization mission, has only further fueled the widespread belief among Muslims all over the world that the United States has become the new colonial power in the Middle East, that its true intention is neither to democratize nor to civilize but rather to Christianize the Islamic world.

And yet, as great a failure as the promotion of democracy in the Middle East has been thus far, the fact remains that only through genuine democratic reform can the appeal of Jihadism be undermined and the tide of Muslim militancy stemmed. As has been demonstrated by the wave of prodemocracy demonstrations that has swept across the Middle East and North Africa, the hope for peace and prosperity in the region lies in the creation of genuine, homegrown, and indigenous democratic societies. Indeed, the very future of Islam depends on it.

10. Slouching Toward Medina

THE QUEST FOR ISLAMIC DEMOCRACY

"IN THE NAME of God, the Compassionate, the Merciful," the IranAir pilot intones as our plane glides to a stop at Tehran's Mehrabad Airport. There is a nervous shifting in the seats around me. The women sit upright, adjusting their headscarves, making sure their ankles and wrists are properly covered, while their husbands rub the sleep from their eyes and begin gathering the belongings their children have scattered in the aisle.

I lift my head to look for the two or three faces I have been carefully observing since boarding the plane in London. They are the younger, single passengers on board, men and women who, like me, are in their late twenties or early thirties. They are dressed in ill-fitting clothes that look as though they were purchased in secondhand stores—awkward long-sleeved shirts; dull slacks; unadorned head scarves—all meant to appear as inoffensive as possible. I know this because this is precisely how I am dressed. When I catch their eyes, I can see a glint of the same anxiety that courses through my body. It is a mixture of fear and excitement. For many of us, this will be the first time we have set foot in the country of our birth since the revolution forced us from it as children.

As part of an effort to reach out to the massive Iranian Diaspora who fled to Europe and the United States in the early 1980s, the Iranian government had issued a tentative amnesty to all expatriates, announcing that they could return to Iran for brief visits—once a year and not to exceed three months—without fear of being detained or forced into completing their mandatory military duty. The response was immediate. Thousands of young Iranians began pouring into the country. Some had never known Iran except through the nostalgic tales of their parents. Others like me had been born in Iran but spirited away when we were still too young to make decisions of our own.

We disembark and slip into the steamy early morning. It is still dark, but already the airport is bursting with arrivals from Paris, Milan, Berlin, Los Angeles. A raucous crowd has gathered at passport control in nothing resembling a proper line. Babies scream. An unbearable odor of sweat and cigarette smoke wafts through the air. Elbows jab me from all sides. And suddenly I am flooded with memories of this very same airport many years ago; of linking arms with my family and shoving our way through a frantic mob, trying to leave Iran before the borders closed and the airplanes were grounded. I remember my mother crying out, "Don't lose your sister!" I can still hear the terrifying breathlessness of her voice, as though she was warning me that if I let go of my little sister's hand, she would be left behind. I gripped her fingers so tightly she began to cry, and dragged her roughly toward the gate, kicking at the knees around us to make way.

Two decades and four suffocatingly long hours later, I am finally at the passport window. I slip my documents through a slot in the glass to a young, lightly bearded man in broken spectacles. He flips through the pages absentmindedly while I prepare my well-rehearsed replies as to who I am and why I am here.

"What is your point of origin?" the agent asks wearily.

"The United States," I reply.

He stiffens and looks up at my face. I can tell we are the same age, though his tired eyes and his unshaven jowl make him appear much older. He is a child of the revolution; I am a fugitive—an apostate. He has spent his life surviving a history that I have spent my life studying from afar. All at once I feel overwhelmed. I can barely look at him when he asks, "Where have you been?" as all passport agents are required to do. I cannot help but sense the accusation in his question.

On the day the Ayatollah Khomeini returned to Iran, I took my four-year-old sister by the hand and, despite my mother's warning not to venture outdoors, led her out of our apartment in downtown Tehran to join the celebrations in the streets. It had been days since we had gone outside. The weeks preceding the Shah's exile and the Ayatollah's return had been violent ones. The schools were closed, most television and radio stations shut down, and our quiet neighborhood deserted. So when we looked out our window on that February morning and saw the euphoria in the streets, nothing could have kept us inside.

Filling a plastic pitcher with Tang and stealing two packages of Dixie cups from our mother's cupboard, my sister and I sneaked out to join the revelry. One by one we filled the cups and passed them out to the crowd. Strangers stopped to lift us up and kiss our cheeks. Handfuls of sweets were thrown from open windows. There was music and dancing everywhere. I wasn't really sure what we were celebrating, but I didn't care. I was swept up in the moment and enthralled by the strange words on everyone's lips—words I had heard before but which were still mystifying and unexplained: Freedom! Liberty! Democracy!

A few months later, the promise of those words seemed about to be fulfilled when Iran's provisional government drafted a constitution for the newly formed and thrillingly titled Islamic Republic of Iran. Under Khomeini's guidance, the constitution was a combination of third-world anti-imperialism mixed with the socioeconomic theories of legendary Iranian ideologues like Jalal Al-e Ahmad and Ali Shariati, the religio-political philosophies of Hasan al-Banna and Sayyid Qutb, and traditional Shi'ite populism. Its founding articles promised equality of the sexes, religious pluralism, social justice, freedom of speech, and the right to peaceful assembly—all the lofty principles the revolution had fought to attain—while simultaneously affirming the Islamic character of the new republic.

In some ways, Iran's new constitution did not differ markedly from the one written after the country's first anti-imperialist revolution in 1905, except that this constitution appeared to envisage *two* governments. The first, representing the sovereignty of the people, included a popularly elected executive heading a highly centralized state, a parliament charged with creating and debating laws, and an independent judiciary to interpret those laws. The second, representing the sovereignty of God, consisted of just one man: the Ayatollah Khomeini.

This was the Valayat-e Faqih ("the rule of the jurist") that Khomeini had been writing about furtively during his years of exile in Iraq and France. In theory, the Faqih, or Supreme Leader, is the most learned religious authority in the country, whose primary function is to ensure the Islamic quality of the state. Yet through the machinations of Iran's powerful clerical establishment, the Faqih was transformed from a symbolic moral authority into the supreme political authority in the state. The constitution provided the Faqih with the power to appoint the head of the judiciary, to be commander in chief of the army, to dismiss the president, and to veto all laws created by the parliament. Originally intended to reconcile popular and divine sovereignty, the Valayat-e Faqih had suddenly paved the way for the institutionalization of absolute clerical control.

Still, Iranians were too elated by their newfound independence, and too blinded by the conspiracy theories floating in the air about another attempt by the CIA and the U.S. embassy in Tehran to reestablish the Shah on his throne (just as they had done in 1953), to recognize the dire implications of the new constitution. Despite warnings from the provisional government and the vociferous arguments of Khomeini's rival ayatollahs, particularly the Ayatollah Shariatmadari (whom Khomeini eventually stripped of his religious credentials despite centuries of Shi'ite law forbidding such actions), the draft was approved in a national referendum by over 98 percent of the electorate.

By the time most Iranians realized what they had voted for, Saddam Hussein, encouraged by the United States and furnished with chemical and biological materials by the Centers for Disease Control and the Virginia-based company the American Type Culture Collection, launched an attack on Iranian soil. As happens in times of war, all dissenting voices were silenced in the interest of national security, and the dream that had given rise to revolution a year earlier gave way to the reality of an authoritarian state plagued by the gross ineptitude of a ruling clerical régime wielding unconditional religious and political authority.

The intention of the United States government in supporting Saddam Hussein during the Iran-Iraq war was to curb the spread of Iran's revolution, but it had the more disastrous effect of curbing its *evolution*. It was not until the end of the war in 1988 and the death of Khomeini a year later that the democratic ideals that had launched the Iranian Revolution a decade earlier were revived by a new generation of Iranians too young to remember the tyranny of the Shah yet old enough to realize that the present system was not what their parents had fought for. It was their discontent that fueled the activities of a handful of academics, politicians, activists, and theologians in Iran who initiated a reform movement, not to "secularize" the country but to refocus it on genuine Islamic values like pluralism, social justice, human rights, and above all, democracy. In the words of the Iranian political philosopher Abdolkarim Soroush, "We no longer claim that a genuinely religious government can be democratic, but that it cannot be otherwise."

The election of the reformist cleric Muhammad Khatami to the office of president in the late 1990s galvanized this movement, giving shape and substance to the premise that an indigenous democratic system could be founded upon a distinctly Islamic moral framework. Buoyed by this vision and emboldened by Khatami's reform agenda, hundreds of thousands of young Iranians began pouring onto the streets in 1999 to demand greater rights, including the right to peaceful assembly and a free press, in what became known around the world as the Tehran Spring.

Frightened by the awe-inspiring spectacle of people power in Iran (which, after all, is precisely what led to the creation of the Islamic Republic in the first place) and viewing the reform movement as a threat to the very existence of the state, the Iranian régime unleashed the full force of its security apparatus on the young protesters. In what has since become a familiar sight, the country's paramilitary forces (the dreaded *Basij*), under orders from the Revolutionary Guard, savagely suppressed popular demonstrations on the streets and in the universities, while reformist activists and Khatami's political allies were systematically silenced, arrested, and murdered. By 2005 and the election of Mahmoud Ahmadinejad to the office of president, the conservative forces in the Iranian government were once again ascendant. Analysts across the globe declared the reform movement in Iran to be dead and buried.

What few outsiders understood, however, is that the reformist message did not disappear or go underground. On the contrary, it dispersed and became absorbed into the political mainstream, so that by the end of the first decade of the new century, nearly all Iranians, regardless of their politics or piety, had adopted the reform movement's assertion that the democratic experiment that gave birth to the Islamic Republic of Iran in 1979 had been subverted and must be set right again. Thus, in the wake of the disputed elections that returned Ahmadinejad to power in 2009, despite widespread accusations of electoral fraud, a coalition of students, intellectuals, merchants, and religious leaders (the same coalition that had brought down the Shah thirty years earlier) once again took to the streets, this time under the banner of what became known as the Green Movement, not merely to protest a stolen election, but to revolt against the very nature of the Islamic Republic. And while the brutal response of the Iranian régime to this latest challenge seems to have temporarily quelled the popular protests that brought the country to a standstill, the government's actions have only further solidified the perception among the vast majority of the Iranian populace that the Islamic Republic, in its current iteration, is neither Islamic nor a republic.

Iran's previous attempts at democracy were thwarted by foreigners—the British and Russians in 1905–1911; the United States in 1953—whose interests were served by suppressing all democratic aspirations in the region. The revolution of 1979 was hijacked by the country's own clerical establishment, which used its moral authority to gain absolute power over the nascent state. The reform movement of the 1990s was quashed by a government deathly afraid of its own people and desperate to preserve its political power. The Green Movement's demand for greater human rights was overpowered by an increasingly militarized régime that has elevated its own survival over all other considerations. Yet the hundred-year quest in Iran to construct a truly indigenous democratic system that provides a place for religion in the public realm without subverting the will of the people continues to this day. In fact, it is a quest that is being replicated across the world, from Iraq and Pakistan to Turkey and Indonesia, from Tunisia and Egypt to Senegal and Bangladesh.

In the half century since the end of colonialism and the founding of the Islamic state, Islam has been invoked to legitimize and to overturn governments, to promote republicanism and defend authoritarianism, to justify monarchies, autocracies, oligarchies, and theocracies, and to foster terrorism, factionalism, and hostility. The question remains: Can Islam now be used to establish a genuinely liberal democracy in the Middle East and beyond? Can a modern Islamic state reconcile reason and Revelation to create a democratic society based on the ethical ideals established by the Prophet Muhammad in Medina fourteen centuries ago?

Not only can it do so, it must. Indeed, it is already doing so in a large number of Muslim-majority states. But it is a process that can be based only on Islamic values and customs. The principal lesson to be learned from both the failure of Europe's "civilizing mission" and the disaster of America's "democracy promotion" is that true democracy must be nurtured from within, founded upon familiar ideologies, and presented in a language that is both comprehensible and appealing to the indigenous population. For democracy to be effective and compelling in Muslim-majority states, it must balance the sometimes contentious relationship between faith and government that, as we have seen, has been the hallmark of political culture in Islam for centuries.

There are those in the West who argue that such a democratic system is impossible, that Islam is inherently opposed to democracy and that Muslim peoples are incapable of reconciling democratic and Islamic values. Such a view not only contradicts Islamic history (not to mention observable reality), it flies in the face of countless surveys that reveal overwhelming majorities throughout the Islamic world pining for democracy as "the best form of government." In fact, a 2006 Pew poll found that while the majority of the Western public thought democracy was "a Western way of doing things that would not work in most Muslim countries," pluralities or majorities in every single Muslim-majority country surveyed flatly rejected that argument and called for democracy to be immediately established, without conditions, in their own societies. It would seem, therefore, that the biggest obstacles in the path to creating a genuinely Islamic democracy are not only the Traditionalist Ulama or Jihadist terrorists, but, perhaps more destructively, those in the West who stubbornly refuse to recognize that democracy, if it is to be viable and enduring, can never be imported.

WITH THE END of the Second World War, a victorious yet financially devastated Britain, no longer able to bear the cost or justify the ideology of its colonial enterprise in India, finally granted to the greatest symbol of its imperialist ambitions—the jewel in the crown of its dwindling empire—its long-sought independence. On August 14, 1947, hundreds of years of colonial rule in India came to an end. Yet the day that C. E. Trevelyan predicted would be "the proudest monument of British benevolence," when, "endowed with [British] learning and political institutions," India would represent colonialism's greatest triumph, became the day in which the fractious population of the Subcontinent was violently partitioned along religious lines into a predominantly Hindu India and Muslim Pakistan.

In many ways, the partition of India was the inevitable result of three centuries of Britain's divide-and-rule policy. As the events of the Indian Revolt demonstrated, the British believed that the best way to curb nationalist sentiment was to classify the indigenous population not as Indians, but as Muslims, Hindus, Sikhs, Christians, etc. The categorization and separation of native peoples was a common tactic for maintaining colonial control over territories whose national boundaries had been arbitrarily drawn with little consideration for the ethnic, cultural, or religious makeup of the local inhabitants. The French went to great lengths to cultivate class divisions in Algeria, the Belgians promoted tribal factionalism in Rwanda, and the British fostered sectarian schisms in Iraq, all in a futile attempt to minimize nationalist tendencies and stymie united calls for independence. No wonder, then, that when the colonialists were finally expelled from these manufactured states, they left behind not only economic and political turmoil, but deeply divided populations with little common ground on which to construct a national identity.

The partition of India was not simply the result of an internal feud between Muslims and Hindus. Nor was it an isolated event. Indonesia's numerous secessionist movements, the bloody border disputes between Morocco and Algeria, the fifty-year civil war in Sudan between Arab northerners and Black African southerners, the partitioning of Palestine and the resulting cycle of violence, the warring ethnic factions in Iraq, and the genocide of nearly a million Tutsis at the hands of the Hutus in Rwanda, to name but a handful of cases, have all been in considerable measure a result of the decolonization process.

When Britain abandoned India with an overwhelming Hindu majority holding most of the economic, social, and political power in the country, the Muslim minority, educated by the British in the persuasive rhetoric of democracy, came to the conclusion that the only possible means of achieving autonomy was through Muslim self-determination. Hence, the birth of the Islamic state.

Yet beyond the call for self-determination, there was little else that India's Muslim community agreed upon with regard to the role of Islam in the state. For Muhammad Ali Jinnah, Pakistan's reluctant founder, Islam was merely the common heritage that could unite India's diverse Muslim population into a united state. Jinnah regarded Islam in the same way that Gandhi regarded Hinduism—as a unifying cultural symbol, not as a religio-political ideology. For Mawlana Mawdudi, Pakistan's ideological instigator, the state was merely the vehicle for the realization of Islamic law. Mawdudi regarded Islam as the antithesis to secular nationalism and believed Pakistan would be the first step toward the establishment of a Muslim world-state. While the Muslim League, Pakistan's largest political party, argued that the Islamic state must receive its mandate from its citizens, the Islamic Association, Pakistan's largest Islamist organization, countered that the state could be considered Islamic only if sovereignty rested solely in the hands of God.

In the wake of the chaos and bloodshed that followed the partition of India, as some seventeen million people—the largest human migration in history—fled across fractured borders in both directions, neither Jinnah's nor Mawdudi's vision of the Islamic state was realized. Despite the drafting of a constitution that envisioned a parliament elected to write the laws and a judiciary appointed to decide whether those laws were in accord with Islamic principles, Pakistan quickly gave way to military dictatorship at the hands of the army's commander in chief, Ayub Khan. Military rule lasted until 1972, when Zulfikar Ali Bhutto's platform of Islamic socialism made him Pakistan's first freely elected civilian ruler since partition. But Bhutto's socialist reforms, though popular with the people, were denounced as "un-Islamic" by extremist members of Pakistan's Muslim clergy, clearing the way for yet another military coup, this time by General Zia al-Haq. With the help of the religious authorities, Zia enacted a forced Islamization process in which Islam became both public morality and civil law. After Zia's death in 1988, a new wave of elections resulted in the reformist governments of Benazir Bhutto and Nawaz Sharif, both of whom expounded a more liberal ideal of Islam in order to tap into Pakistan's frustration with nearly a decade of brutal fundamentalism. But in 1999, after accusing the elected government of corruption, the head of Pakistan's army, Pervez Musharraf, imposed military dictatorship once again over the country. After another decade of military rule, Musharraf was forced to allow Benazir Bhutto and Nawaz Sharif, both of whom had been exiled from the country, to return to Pakistan, and then pressured to resign from the post of president in 2008. The assassination of Bhutto a few months after her return led to the assumption of the presidency by Bhutto's estranged husband, Ali Asif Zardari, whose tenuous grip on power has been repeatedly tested by a wave of attacks by Islamist militants centered in the North-West Frontier Province (or Khyber Pashtunkhwa) of Pakistan, who would like nothing more than to transform the country into a "Talibanized" state under their control.

All of this in a span of sixty years.

The experience of Pakistan serves as a reminder that the Islamic state is by no means a monolithic concept. Indeed, there are many countries in the Middle East that could be termed Islamic states, none of which have much in common with one another. Syria is an Arab dictatorship whose ruler serves at the pleasure of its all-powerful military. Jordan and Morocco are volatile kingdoms whose young mon-

archs have made timid steps toward democratization, though without
forfeiting their absolute rule. Iran is a authoritarian country run by a
corrupt clerical oligarchy committed to snuffing out any attempts at
democratic reform. Saudi Arabia is a fundamentalist theocracy that
claims its only constitution is the Quran and its only law the Shariah.
And yet not only do all of these countries view themselves as the realization of the Medinan ideal, they view each other as contemptible
desecrations of that ideal.

But if one were truly to rely on the Medinan ideal to define the
nature and function of the Islamic state, it would have to be characterized as nothing more than the nationalist manifestation of the
Ummah. At its most basic level, the Islamic state is one in which the
determination of values, the norms of behavior, and the formation of
laws are influenced by the mores and values of the Muslim-majority
population. At the same time, minority faiths would be protected
from harm and allowed complete social and political participation in
the community, just as they were in Medina. In the same way that the
Revelation was dictated by the needs of the Ummah, so would all legal
and moral considerations be determined by the citizens of the Islamic
state. For as Abu Bakr so wisely stated upon succeeding the Prophet,
Muslim allegiance is owed not to a president, prime minister, priest,
king, or any earthly authority, but to the community and to God. As
long as these criteria, which the Prophet established in Medina nearly
fourteen centuries ago and which the Rightly Guided Caliphs struggled in their own way to preserve, are satisfied, then what form the
Islamic state takes is irrelevant.

So, then, why not democracy?

Representative democracy may be the most successful social and
political experiment in the modern world. But it is an ever-evolving
experiment. These days there is a tendency to regard American
democracy as the model for all the world's democracies, and in some
ways this is true. The seeds of democracy may have been sown in
ancient Greece, but it is in American soil that they sprouted and flourished to achieve their full potential. Yet precisely for this reason, only
in America is American democracy possible; it cannot be isolated from
American traditions and values.

This is a fundamental fact that was thoroughly ignored by

President George W. Bush's "democracy promotion" agenda, which he vowed would form the foundation upon which relations between the United States and the Middle East would henceforth be based. Bush was ridiculed both at home and abroad for his quest to spread democracy in the Middle East; critics claimed it was little more than an excuse to wage unending war in the region. It was certainly not lost on the peoples of the Middle East that most of their dictators also happened to be America's closest allies in the region—in Egypt, Jordan, Saudi Arabia, and Morocco—all of whom had spent decades convincing the United States that even the slightest weakening of their dictatorial régimes would result in the immediate takeover of their countries by radical Islamists, a specious argument that the United Nations has dubbed a "legitimacy of blackmail." In any case, Bush's commitment to his florid talk about democracy was immediately seen as disingenuous and hypocritical once elections in Lebanon, Egypt, and Palestine did not go the way the United States had hoped and the democracy promotion agenda was shut down altogether.

Yet lost in the debate about America's true intentions in the Middle East was the fact that large majorities in every Muslim-majority state surveyed told pollsters they wanted to see their countries move toward greater democracy. A wave of democratic fervor across the Middle East created a renewed sense of hope for scores of people who had spent their lives in autocratic societies but who now looked forward to the possibility of having a say, even if in the most limited of ways, in their own political destinies. The Green Movement in Iran lit the fuse, employing new social media technologies like Twitter, Facebook, and YouTube to break the government's monopoly over the media and to demonstrate to the world their aspiration for freedom and liberty. The spark ignited in Iran quickly flashed across the region. In Tunisia, young protesters, fed up with their lack of political participation and economic opportunities, used the same social media tools to take to the streets and force the country's long-serving dictator to flee into exile. The fires of freedom then spread to Algeria and Yemen, and, perhaps most unexpectedly, to Egypt, where tens of thousands of young Egyptians poured onto the streets of Cairo, Suez, and Giza, demanding an end to the thirty-year rule of Hosni

Mubarak, a dictator who had used some sixty billion dollars in United States funds to create one of the most brutal, most repressive régimes in the Middle East. And the fire is still burning, threatening the other dictatorships in the region—Morocco, Jordan, Saudi Arabia, Libya, Syria—none of which are immune any longer to the simple notion that all peoples everywhere, regardless of their religious or cultural affiliations, must be free to decide for themselves who will speak for them, who will fight for them, who will lead them.

The fact is that the vast majority of the more than one billion Muslims in the world readily accept the fundamental principles of democracy. Thanks to the efforts of reformists and modernists throughout the Muslim world, most Muslims have already appropriated the language of democracy, recognizing traditional Islamic concepts like *shura,* or "consultation," as popular representation; *ijma,* or "consensus," as political participation; *bay'ah,* or "allegiance," as universal suffrage; and so on. One need only observe the massive demonstrations by democracy activists throughout the Islamic world to recognize how ideals such as constitutionalism, government accountability, pluralism, and human rights are widely accepted by Muslims throughout the world, even if most of the region's rulers refuse to implement them.

What is not necessarily accepted, however, is the distinctly Western notion that religion and the state should be entirely separate, that the foundation of a democratic society must be secularism. From the inception of the faith in seventh-century Arabia to the birth of the Islamic state in the twentieth, Islam has always endeavored to be more than mere religion. When the Prophet Muhammad created the first Islamic polity in Medina fourteen hundred years ago, he deliberately set the foundations for a comprehensive way of life meant to satisfy the social, spiritual, and material needs of the people, while at the same time fulfilling the will of God. In short, Islam is not just a faith; Islam is an *identity*. That is true of all religions. In the United States, polls show that some 70 percent of the population identifies itself as Christian. That does not mean that seven out of ten Americans go to church on Sundays, that seven out of ten Americans read the New Testament, that, in fact, seven out of ten Americans know anything at all about Christianity save that Jesus was born in a manger and died on a cross. No, the overwhelming majority of Americans who describe themselves as Christian are making a statement of identity, not a statement of belief. The same holds true for the overwhelming majority of Jews, Buddhists, Hindus, Jains, etc. Religion has always been more than a matter of beliefs and practices. It is, above all, a perspective, a mode of being. Religion encompasses one's culture, one's politics, one's very view of the world. This is particularly true of Islam, which, like all great religions, has been shaped not only by metaphysical concerns but also by the social, cultural, spiritual, and political milieu in which it finds itself.

This is not to suggest that Islam rejects the separation of "mosque and state." On the contrary, there are very few Muslim-majority countries in the world in which clerics exercise direct authority over the government. Those countries that have attempted such direct authority—Sudan, Nigeria, Afghanistan, and Iran—have been, without exception, devastating failures. Nevertheless, it is true that when it comes to religion the boundary between the public and private realm is far more fluid in Muslim-majority states than it is in the West. This is partly because, having originated in a tribal culture and been reared primarily in the communal societies of the Middle East and North Africa, Islam tends to eschew radical individualism, preferring to stress the needs of the community over the rights of the individual. Whatever the reasons may be, it is a fundamental and unavoidable fact that people in nearly all Muslim-majority states have repeatedly stated their desire for Islamic values and mores to have an influence over their countries' politics. And since a state can be considered democratic only insofar as it reflects its society, if the society is founded upon a particular set of values, then must not its government be also?

Admittedly, ever since September 11 it has been impossible to ask such questions without immediately conjuring up pictures of Afghanistan under the Taliban. In fact, the image of the Afghan woman enveloped in the *burqah* and subjugated to the whims of an ignorant band of misogynists has become the symbol of everything that is backward and wicked about the concept of Islamic governance, and such images are not easily supplanted by political philosophies.

Considering how often Islam has been used to rationalize the brutal policies of oppressive totalitarian régimes like the Taliban in

Afghanistan, the Wahhabists in Saudi Arabia, or the Faqih in Iran, it is hardly surprising that the term "Islamic democracy" provokes such skepticism in the West. Some of the most celebrated academics in the United States and Europe reject the notion outright, believing that the principles of democracy cannot be reconciled with fundamental Islamic values. When politicians speak of bringing democracy to the Middle East, they mean specifically an American secular democracy, not an indigenous Islamic one. And dictatorial régimes in the Middle East never seem to tire of preaching to the world that their brutally antidemocratic policies are justified because "fundamentalists" allow them but two possible options: despotism or theocracy. The problem with democracy from their point of view is that if people are allowed a choice, they may choose against their governments.

Ignoring for a moment the role these and so many other autocratic régimes in the Middle East have played in creating so-called fundamentalists in the first place, there exists a far more philosophical dispute in the Western world with regard to the concept of Islamic democracy: that is, that there can be no *a priori* moral framework in a modern democracy; that the foundation of a genuinely democratic society must be secularism. The problem with this argument, however, is that it not only fails to recognize the inherently moral foundation upon which a large number of modern democracies are built, it more importantly fails to appreciate the difference between *secularism* and *secularization*.

As the Protestant theologian Harvey Cox notes, secularization is the process by which "certain responsibilities pass from ecclesiastical to political authorities," whereas secularism is an ideology based on the eradication of religion from public life. Secularization implies a historical evolution in which society gradually frees itself from "religious control and closed metaphysical world-views." Secularism is itself a closed metaphysical world-view that, according to Cox, "functions very much like a new religion."

Turkey is a secular country in which outward signs of religiosity such as the *hijab* were, until quite recently, forcibly suppressed. With regard to ideological resolve, one could argue that little separates a secular country like Turkey from a religious country like Iran; both ideologize society. The United States, however, is a secularizing country, unapologetically founded on a Judeo-Christian—and more precisely Protestant—moral framework. As recognized nearly two hundred years ago by Alexis de Tocqueville, religion is the foundation of America's political system. It not only reflects American social values, it very often dictates them. One need only regard the language with which political issues like abortion rights and gay marriage are debated in Congress to recognize that religion is to this day an integral part of the American national identity and patently the moral foundation for its Constitution, its laws, and its national customs. Despite what schoolchildren read in their history books, the reality is that the separation of "church and state" is not so much the foundation of American government as it is the result of a two-hundred-forty-year secularization process based not upon secularism, but upon *pluralism*.

It is pluralism, not secularism, that defines democracy. A democratic state can be established upon any normative moral framework as long as pluralism remains the source of its legitimacy. England continues to maintain a national church whose religious head is also the country's sovereign and whose bishops serve in the upper house of Parliament. India was, until recently, governed by partisans of an élitist theology of Hindu Awakening (Hindutva) bent on applying an implausible but enormously successful vision of "true Hinduism" to the state. And yet, like the United States, these countries are considered democracies, not because they are secular but because they are, at least in theory, dedicated to pluralism.

Or consider the State of Israel, a country founded upon an exclusivist Jewish moral framework, which offers all the world's Jews—regardless of their nationality—immediate citizenship, providing them with a host of material benefits and privileges over its non-Jewish citizens; where the Orthodox rabbinical courts have jurisdiction over all matters relating to Judaism (including who is and who is not a Jew); where religious schools (yeshivas) are subsidized by the state, and marriages are religious rather than civil affairs (meaning no official will marry a Jew to a non-Jew); and where all new citizens, regardless of their religious affiliation, are required to take a loyalty oath affirming Israel's identity as a "Jewish state." By every definition of the term, Israel is a "Jewish democracy." Yet the very same people who praise Israel's reconciliation of Jewish and democratic ideals, despite the very obvious conflicts it has created both inside Israel and within the occupied Palestinian territories, reflexively deny that a similar reconciliation between Islamic and democratic ideals could be established in any Muslim-majority state. Never mind the enormously successful examples of precisely such a reconciliation in Turkey, Indonesia, Malaysia, Bangladesh, Senegal, etc., or the fact that nearly one-third of the world's Muslims already live in democratic states. Among certain critics of Islam, there can simply be no such thing as Islamic pluralism, no matter how much evidence exists to the contrary.

Yet, as we have seen, Islam has had a long commitment to religious pluralism. Muhammad's recognition of Jews and Christians as protected peoples (dhimmi), his belief in a common divine text from which all revealed scriptures are derived (the Umm al-Kitab), and his dream of establishing a single, united Ummah encompassing all three faiths of Abraham were startlingly revolutionary ideas in an era in which religion literally created borders between peoples. And despite the ways in which it has been interpreted by militants and fundamentalists who refuse to recognize its historical and cultural context, there are few scriptures in the great religions of the world that can match the reverence with which the Quran speaks of other religious traditions.

It is true that the Quran does not hold the same respect for polytheistic religions as it does for monotheistic ones. However, this is primarily a consequence of the fact that the Revelation was revealed during a protracted and bloody war with the "polytheistic" Quraysh. The truth is that the Quranic designation of "protected peoples" was highly flexible and was routinely tailored to match public policy. When Islam expanded into Iran and India, both dualist Zoroastrians and certain polytheistic Hindu sects were designated as dhimmi. And while the Quran does not allow any religion to violate core Muslim values, there is no country in the world that does not restrict the freedom of religion according to public morality. Pluralism implies religious tolerance, not unchecked religious freedom.

The foundation of Islamic pluralism can be summed up in one indisputable verse: "There can be no compulsion in religion" (2:256).

This means that the antiquated partitioning of the world into spheres of belief (*dar al-Islam*) and unbelief (*dar al-Harb*), which was first developed during the Crusades but which still maintains its grasp on the imaginations of Traditionalist theologians, is utterly unjustifiable. It also means that the ideology of those Islamic puritans like the Wahhabists who wish to return Islam to some imaginary ideal of original purity must be once and for all abandoned. Islam is and has always been a religion of diversity. The notion that there was once an original, unadulterated Islam that was shattered into heretical sects and schisms is a historical fiction. Both Shi'ism and Sufism in all their wonderful manifestations represent trends of thought that have existed from the very beginning of Islam, and both find their inspiration in the words and deeds of the Prophet. God may be One, but Islam most definitely is not.

Grounding an Islamic democracy in the ideals of pluralism is vital because religious pluralism is the first step toward building an effective human rights policy in the Middle East. Indeed, as Abdulaziz Sachedina notes, religious pluralism can function as "an active paradigm for a democratic, social pluralism in which people of diverse religious backgrounds are willing to form a community of global citizens." As with Islamic pluralism, the inspiration for an Islamic policy of human rights must be based on the Medinan ideal.

The revolutionary rights Muhammad gave to the marginalized members of his community have been exhaustively detailed in this book, as have the consistent efforts by Muhammad's religious and political inheritors to overturn those rights. Yet one need simply recall the Prophet's warning to those who questioned his egalitarian measures in Medina—"[They] will be thrown into Hell, where they will dwell forever, suffering from the most shameful punishment" (4:14)—to recognize that acknowledging human rights in Islam is not simply a means of protecting civil liberties, it is a fundamental religious duty.

Nevertheless, the Islamic vision of human rights is not a prescription for moral relativism, nor does it imply freedom from ethical restraint. Islam's quintessentially communal character necessitates that any human rights policy take into consideration the protection of the community over the autonomy of the individual. And while there may be some circumstances in which Islamic morality may force the rights of the community to prevail over the rights of the individual—for instance, with regard to Quranic commandments forbidding drinking or gambling—these and all other ethical issues must constantly be reevaluated so as to conform to the will of the community.

It must be understood that a respect for human rights, like pluralism, is a process that develops naturally within a democracy. Bear in mind that for approximately two hundred of America's two hundred forty years of existence, black American citizens were considered legally inferior to whites. Finally, neither human rights nor pluralism is the result of secularization, they are its root cause, meaning that any democratic society—Islamic or otherwise—dedicated to the principles of pluralism and human rights must dedicate itself to following the unavoidable path toward *political* secularization.

Therein lies the crux of the argument for Islamic democracy, which is not intended to be a "theo-democracy," but a democratic system founded upon an Islamic moral framework, devoted to preserving Islamic ideals of pluralism and human rights as they were first introduced in Medina, and open to the inevitable process of political secularization. Islam may eschew secularism, but there is nothing about fundamental Islamic values that opposes the process of political secularization. The separation of "church and state" of which America is so proud was established in Islam fourteen centuries ago, when it was decided that no Caliph would have religious authority over the community. Only the Prophet had both religious and temporal authority, and the Prophet is no longer among us. Hence, like the Caliphs, kings, and sultans of history's greatest Islamic civilizations, the leaders of an Islamic democracy can hold only civic responsibilities. Moreover, there can be no question as to where sovereignty in such a system would rest. A government of the people, by the people, and for the people can be established or demolished solely through the will of the people. After all, it is human beings who create laws, not God. Even laws based on divine scripture require human interpretation in order to be applied in the world. In any case, sovereignty necessitates the ability not just to make laws, but to enforce them. Save for the occasional plague, this is a power God rarely chooses to wield on earth.

Those who argue that a state cannot be considered Islamic unless sovereignty rests in the hands of God are in effect arguing that sovereignty should rest in the hands of the clergy. Because religion is, by definition, interpretation, sovereignty in a religious state would belong to those with the power to interpret religion. Yet for this very reason an Islamic democracy cannot be a religious state. Otherwise it would be an oligarchy, not a democracy.

From the time of the Prophet to the Rightly Guided Caliphs to the great empires and sultanates in Islamic history, there has never been a successful attempt to establish a monolithic interpretation of the meaning and significance of Islamic beliefs and practices. Indeed, until the founding of the Islamic Republic of Iran, no Islamic polity in the history of the world had ever been ruled by one individual's reading of scripture. This does not mean the religious authorities should have no influence on the state. Khomeini may have had a point when he asserted that those who spend their lives pursuing religion are the most qualified to interpret it. However, as with the Pope's role in Rome, such influence can be only moral, not political. The function of the clergy in an Islamic democracy is not to rule, but to preserve and, more important, to reflect the morality of the state. Again, because it is not religion, but the interpretation of religion that arbitrates morality, such interpretation must always be in accord with the consensus of the community.

It does mean, however, that Islam will necessarily play a role in defining what an indigenous democracy in many Muslim-majority states would look like, at least in the early stages. Those in Europe and North America who expect a secular, liberal democracy to arise fully formed in countries that have had little experience of anything other than authoritarian rule are living a fantasy. Even the most cursory study of Islamic history reveals the powerful role that Islam has had in shaping attitudes about government and politics among all Muslim peoples, whether on the left or the right. In Iran, for example, both the reformists and the hard-line conservatives rely on the same symbols, rhetoric, and language to fight either for democratic reform or for theocratic intransigence because both recognize the power that Islam has in mobilizing the masses. In fact, the reason that political opposition in the Middle East is so often religious in nature is not because opposition parties want to build a theocratic state but because it is the language of religion that holds the most currency with the Muslim community.

If democracy is to have a chance in many Muslim-majority states, religious factions must be encouraged to participate in the political process. This is particularly true with regard to moderate Islamist groups like the Muslim Brotherhood in Egypt, which has diligently transformed itself over the last decade into a legitimate political party. But even more extremist Islamist groups like Hizbullah in Lebanon and Hamas in Palestine must be brought into the political fold. It is true that there are those who have no interest in establishing anything other than an oppressive, archaic theocracy, and who pursue their theo-political ends through violence and terror. They must be opposed by all necessary measures. But when even legitimate religious opposition is discouraged or outlawed, the unfortunate result is that it becomes radicalized. That is what happened in Iran, when the Shah suppressed all clerical opposition to his despotic rule, only to see it radicalize into a wholly new brand of revolutionary Shi'ism that ultimately cast him from his throne and transformed Iran into the Islamic Republic.

No one doubts the potential danger in allowing religiously conservative groups a seat at the political table. And certainly, problems can arise when religion plays a role in the state; there will always be groups that will try to use their particular interpretation of religion to promote their own social and political agendas, though that is true of all democracies, especially America's. However, the real danger lies in stifling the political ambitions of such groups. For wherever legitimate Islamist opposition has been suppressed, militant groups and religious extremists have gained favor. Take the case of Algeria, where the rise of the ultra-violent Jihadist organization the Armed Algerian Group (GIA) was the direct result of the Algerian military's decision to ban political participation by the more moderate and accommodating Islamists of Islamic Salvation Front (FIS). Conversely, wherever moderate Islamist parties have been allowed to participate in politics and government, popular support for more extremist groups has diminished. In Turkey, for example, the political success of the Islamist Justice and Development Party (Adalet ve Kalkinma Partisi, or AKP) has sapped Turkey's more radical religious groups of their support among the masses. The simple fact is that democracy cannot take root in the Middle East and beyond without the participation of Islamists who are willing to play by the rules, to put down their weapons, and to pick up ballots instead.

Ultimately, an Islamic democracy must be concerned not with reconciling popular and divine sovereignty, but with reconciling "people's satisfaction with God's approval," to quote Abdolkarim Soroush. And if ever there is a conflict between the two, it must be the interpretation of Islam that yields to the reality of democracy, not the other way around. It has always been this way. From the very moment that God spoke the first word of Revelation to Muhammad—"Recite!"—the story of Islam has been in a constant state of evolution as it responds to the social, cultural, political, and temporal circumstances of those who are telling it. Now it must evolve once more. Because the fight for Islamic democracy is merely one front in a worldwide battle taking place within Islam, between those who seek to reconcile their faith and traditions with the realities of the modern world and those who react against those realities by reverting—sometimes violently—to the "fundamentals" of their faith.

Despite the tragedy of September 11 and the subsequent terrorist acts against Western targets throughout the world, despite the clash-of-civilizations mentality that has seized the globe and the clash-of-monotheisms reality underlying it, despite the blatant religious rhetoric resonating throughout the halls of governments, there is one thing that cannot be overemphasized. What is taking place now in Islam is an internal conflict between Muslims, not an external battle between Islam and the West. The West is merely a bystander—an unwary yet complicit casualty of a rivalry that is raging in Islam over who will write the next chapter in its story.

All great religions grapple with these issues, some more fiercely than others. One need only recall Europe's massively destructive Thirty Years' War (1618–1648) between the forces of the Protestant Union and those of the Catholic League to recognize the ferocity with which interreligious conflicts have been fought in Christian history. In many ways, the Thirty Years' War signaled the end of the Christian Reformation: perhaps the classic argument over who gets to decide the future of a faith. What followed that awful war—during which nearly half of the population of Germany perished—was a gradual progression in Christian theology from the doctrinal absolutism of the pre-Reformation era to the doctrinal pluralism of the early modern period and, ultimately, to the doctrinal relativism of the Enlightenment. This remarkable evolution in Christianity from its inception to its Reformation took fifteen vicious, bloody, and occasionally apocalyptic centuries.

Fourteen hundred years of rabid debate over what it means to be a Muslim; of passionate arguments over the interpretation of the Quran and the application of Islamic law; of trying to reconcile a fractured community through appeals to Divine Unity; of tribal feuds, crusades, and world wars—and Islam has finally begun its fifteenth century, and with it, the realization of its own long-awaited and hard-fought Reformation. Yet this is a reformation that is not going to be resolved in the deserts of the Arabian Peninsula, where the message of Islam was first introduced to the world, but in the developing capitals of the Islamic world— Tehran, Cairo, Damascus, and Jakarta—and in the cosmopolitan capitals of Europe and the United States—New York, London, Paris, and Berlin—where that message is being redefined by scores of first- and second-generation Muslim immigrants fed up with the dominance of Traditionalism and militancy in their faith. By merging the Islamic values of their ancestors with the democratic ideals of their new homes, these Muslims have formed what Tariq Ramadan, the Swiss-born intellectual and grandson of Hasan al-Banna, has termed the "mobilizing force" for the Islamic Reformation.

Like the reformations of the past, this will be a terrifying event, one that has already begun to engulf the world. But out of the ashes of cataclysm, a new chapter in the story of Islam is emerging. And while it remains to be seen who will write that chapter, even now a new revelation is at hand which, after centuries of stony sleep, has finally awoken and is slouching toward Medina to be born.

11 . Welcome to the Islamic Reformation

THE FUTURE OF ISLAM

IN THE HEART of the aged city of Cairo stands an institution as old and as triumphant as the city itself. For more than a millennium, the famed al-Azhar mosque and university has served as the locus of Sunni Islamic scholarship for millions of Muslims around the world. If there were such a thing as a Vatican in Islam, this would be it. Founded in 972 C.E. by the Caliphs of the Fatimid Dynasty, who claimed descent from the Prophet Muhammad's daughter, Fatima—nicknamed al-Zahra, or "the Radiant"—al-Azhar literally means *the most radiant*, and, indeed, one need only visit in the evening, when the sun sets behind its towering, mud-hued minarets, to see just how much brighter even than the stars in the hazy sky this blooming structure shines.

The campuses of al-Azhar sit beside the city's central bazaar, known as Khan el Khalili, whose cobblestone paths and labyrinthine walkways teem with local bargain hunters and weary tourists. In the summer months, when the raucous energy of Cairo becomes too much even for Cairenes to handle, men and women, young and old, Christian and Muslim huddle together in the cool, calming silence of al-Azhar's vast open courtyard. Barefoot old men sit on the marble floor, backs pressed against the crumbling columns, seeking shelter in the shade of the covered porticos. Young students cluster around the intricately carved inlets and corner coves of the main prayer hall, some here to study, most to gossip. On particularly hot days, the only movement in the entire complex belongs to the pigeons, and to the white-capped peasants in dusty, gray *galabiyas* who sweep the floors with dried-out husks of palm branches.

Everything within these hallowed walls, including the walls themselves, echoes with tradition. On my first visit to al-Azhar I asked an Egyptian friend how long the clerical institution had been in Cairo. "It has always been here," he replied.

He was not exaggerating. Egypt's modern capital may sit upon the detritus of half a dozen long-forgotten cities, but the city whose name in Arabic, al-Qahira, means "the Victorious"—the city of a thousand minarets that began as the seat of the Shi'ite Fatimid Empire and is now universally recognized as the cultural center of the Arab world—that city was constructed with al-Azhar as its backbone. In the twelfth century, when the inimitable Muslim warrior Saladin conquered and cleansed Egypt of Shi'ite imperial control, he stripped al-Azhar of funding and left it to ruin, only to have the institution rise out of the ashes of his Ayyubid Dynasty stronger than before. In the eighteenth century, Napoleon Bonaparte shelled al-Azhar into submission; his troops rode into the great mosque on horseback and sacked it, killing three thousand in the process. Three years later it was al-Azhar that led the uprising against the French, forcing Napoleon back to Europe in defeat. In the twentieth century, at the twilight of British colonial rule, al-Azhar's Ulama provided the theological basis for the strikes and boycotts that ultimately expelled the foreign invaders from Egypt. During the socialist revolution of Gamal Abd al-Nasser in the 1950s, al-Azhar first endorsed the ideals of Pan-Arabism, then turned against it when Nasser transformed the school into a secular university controlled by the state. In the post-revolutionary period, al-Azhar became a tool both to legitimize secular dictatorship and to foment the Islamist backlash against it. As the war on terror raged in neighboring Iraq and Afghanistan, al-Azhar served simultaneously as the bulwark against the West's "crusade against Islam," and the model of calm conservatism in the face of the zealous extremism that had gripped the country's youth.

It is the connection to what is spoken of with hushed reverence inside al-Azhar's walls as "tradition" that confers upon the institution and its scholars the authority to act as sole arbiters in all matters of faith and morality. Indeed, the entire foundation of the Ulama— whether here at al-Azhar or anywhere else in the world—is tied to their ability to regurgitate what has been said, written, or thought by men just like them who have sat in these very same classrooms studying the very same texts and commentaries for more than a thousand years.

In Shi'ism, religious authority is derived from the Ulama's spiritual link to the Prophet and the Imams. In Sunni Islam, religious authority is created solely through the Ulama's ability to be fully subsumed by tradition. Shi'ah authority is considered eternal and divinely inspired. Sunni authority is impermanent and anchored to the past. It is self-conferred, not divinely ordained. Like a Jewish rabbi, a Sunni cleric is a scholar, not a priest. His judgment is followed not because it carries the authority of God (it does not), but because the cleric's scholarship, his intimate knowledge of tradition, and his unbreakable bond with the past grant him special insight into God's will. Thus, if a rupture occurs that severs the Ulama's connection to the authority upon which it is built, if some social or political or religious crisis suddenly shakes the very foundations of Muslim society, then the entire institution begins to crumble.

There have been many such ruptures in the fourteen-hundred-year history of Islam: the death of the Prophet, the expansion into empire, the conflict with Europe, the Crusades, colonialism, the destruction of the Caliphate. Yet no previous rupture has had a greater impact on Islam's evolution, or so thoroughly breached the Ulama's bond with the past, than the Muslim encounter with modernity and globalization.

For fourteen centuries, the venerable scholars of al-Azhar and their cohorts in similar institutions around the world have claimed a total monopoly over the meaning and message of the Muslim faith. Everything from how to pray to when to fast, from how to dress to whom to marry, has been the sole prerogative of a group of learned old men cloistered inside dozens of clerical institutions and schools of law, whose self-appointed task it has been to divine the future of Islam by controlling its past. No longer.

Today, if a Muslim in Egypt wants legal or spiritual advice on how to live a righteous life, he or she is more likely to pass over the anti-quated scholarship provided by the stately Egyptian institution of al-Azhar for the television broadcasts of the wildly popular Egyptian televangelist Amr Khaled. Amr Khaled's weekly shows, through which he dispenses advice on religious and legal matters, are watched by tens of millions of young Muslims across the globe, from Jakarta to Detroit. His Facebook page has over two million fans. His YouTube channel boasts more than twenty-six million visits. His DVDs sell better than many Hollywood hits. In 2007, *Time* magazine named him the thirteenth most influential person in the world. He is without doubt one of the most prominent, most sought-after, most authoritative scholars of Islam on the planet.

Except that Amr Khaled is not a scholar. He is not a cleric. He has never studied at al-Azhar or, for that matter, at any recognized clerical institution. In fact, he has never studied Islam or Islamic law in any official capacity; he is an accountant. According to the strictures of Islamic law, he has no right to expound his theories on the meaning and interpretation of Islam. Nevertheless, through his ubiquitous television and Internet presence, Amr Khaled has utterly usurped the role traditionally reserved for the Ulama as the sole interpreters of Islam. And he is not alone. All over the world, a slew of self-styled preachers, spiritual gurus, academics, activists, and amateur intellectuals have begun actively redefining Islam by taking its interpretation out of the iron grip of the Ulama and seizing for themselves the power to dictate the future of this rapidly expanding and deeply fractured faith.

Welcome to the Islamic Reformation.

* * *

There is, admittedly, a great deal of religious and cultural baggage attached to the term *reformation*, which is why historians and scholars of religions so often shy away from using it. Beyond its obvious and unavoidable Christian and European connotations, for many the notion of a reformation necessarily implies something lacking or deficient, something requiring improvement or correction. But the term *reformation* contains no value judgment whatsoever. Stripped of its historical context, it signifies a universal religious phenomenon, one found in nearly all institutionalized religions. For however else one defines the Christian Reformation, it was, above all, an argument over who holds the authority to define faith: the individual or the institution. That argument ultimately led to the fracturing of Christianity into competing sects and schisms. But the underlying conflict of the Christian Reformation was by no means unique to either European or Christian history. On the contrary, the entire history of religions, and particularly of the so-called Western religions, can be viewed as a constant and sustained battle between institutions and individuals over religious authority. In times of social stress or political upheaval this ever-present conflict can explode onto the surface, often with catastrophic results.

That is what happened in the first century C.E., when a group of militant Jewish factions in Roman-occupied Palestine* began to vigorously challenge the authority of the Temple and its priestly hierarchy to define Judaism. What has been rightly called the "Jewish Reformation" ultimately led to the founding not only of Rabbinic Judaism, but also to a wholly new sect of Judaism called Christianity, sparked by a Jewish reformer whose principal message was that the authority to define the Jewish faith rests not with "the chief priests and the teachers of the law," but with every individual believer. (It should be noted that the Jewish Reformation also led to the destruction of Jerusalem and the expulsion of the Jews from the city.)

The reformation that gave birth to Christianity fractured it fifteen

---

* Palestine was the name given to the vast tract of land encompassing all of modern-day Israel/Palestine, as well as large parts of Jordan, Syria, and Lebanon during the Roman era.

centuries later when Martin Luther nailed his ninety-five theses to the door of All Saints' Church in Wittenberg. Of course, the Christian Reformation did not arise with Luther, nor was it simply due to widespread disaffection with the corruption of the Catholic Church. The Christian Reformation was the result of a long and gradual process that began as early as the fourteenth century, when a number of influential Church leaders, most notably John Wycliffe in England, Jan Hus in Bohemia, and Jean Gerson in France, began aggressively trying to reform the Church from within. Long before Luther entered the austere monastic order of the Augustinians, the Christian Humanists had launched a renaissance in medieval theology by insisting on bypassing the Latin Vulgate for the original languages of the Bible. Desiderius Erasmus, perhaps the most influential intellectual of the sixteenth century, had already foretold much of Protestant ideology with his 1516 edition of the New Testament, in which the Virgin became "gracious" rather than "full of grace," and John's apocalyptic cry in the Gospel of Matthew to "do penance" was deliberately transformed to "repent."

What separated Luther from Erasmus and the Humanists, and marked him in history as the instigator of the Christian Reformation, was that Luther had no interest in *reforming* the Catholic Church, which he viewed as the throne of the Antichrist. On the contrary, Luther wanted to tear down the Church, to take away its privilege as the sole agent of salvation and the sole authority on scripture. Hence his conception of *sola scriptura*, which emphatically stated that scriptural interpretation should rest, not in the hands of the Pope, but in the hands of individual believers.

That same reformation phenomenon, which forever altered the religions of Judaism and Christianity, has been taking place in Islam for nearly a century, ever since the era of European colonialism, under which some 90 percent of the world's Muslims lived throughout the nineteenth and early twentieth centuries. Unlike Judaism and Christianity, however, Islam has never had a single religious authority. There has never been a "Muslim Temple" or a "Muslim Pope"—that is, a centralized religious authority that claims the right to speak for the entire Muslim community. The Caliphate, it will be recalled, was a political not a religious position. Particularly in the Sunni tradition, which represents some 85 percent of the world's 1.5 billion Muslims, religious authority is not localized within a single individual or institution (not even in the preeminent al-Azhar). It is, instead, scattered among a host of competing clerical institutions and schools of law that, as demonstrated throughout this book, have maintained total control over the interpretation of Islam since the death of the Prophet Muhammad.

Yet over the last century—and especially since the destruction of the Caliphate, which, powerless as the institution may have become, nevertheless served as the embodiment of Muslim unity—a great many Muslims have been compelled to regard themselves less as members of a worldwide community of faith, than as citizens of individual nation-states. The result of this geopolitical fragmentation has been the almost total breakdown of the communal ideals upon which Islam was founded. For a while, the ideologies of Pan-Arabism and Pan-Islamism attempted to reunite the Muslim community across national boundaries. But as those ideologies collapsed, a new generation of Muslims came of age without any awareness of, or for that matter desire for, a unified Ummah. Meanwhile, the focus on modern schooling in many Muslim-majority states led to dramatic increases in literacy and education, shattering the Ulama's privilege as the "learned men" of Islam, even as widespread access to new ideas and sources of knowledge resulted in the gradual devaluation of the kind of institutional learning claimed by the Ulama as uniquely theirs. Add to this the rise of alternative forms of Muslim identity such as political Islam (Islamism), Islamic socialism, or even Jihadism—all predicated on the notion that the Ulama are to blame both for the decline of Islamic civilization and for the moral corruption of Muslim society—and the result is a kind of "democratization" of religious authority, as anyone with a significant platform and a loud enough voice can now claim for himself the rights and privileges once reserved solely for Islam's clerical class.

Part of the reason the Ulama have been able to maintain a monopoly on the interpretation of Islam is because, for the most part, they have been the only ones able to read Islam's scriptures and texts. Ever since the end of the seventh century C.E., when its verses were collected and canonized, the Quran has remained fixed in its original

Arabic because the Ulama insisted that a translation of the Holy Scripture into any other language would violate the divine nature of the text. To this day, non-Arabic versions of the Quran are considered *interpretations* of the Quran, not the Quran itself. This means that for most of the last fourteen centuries, some 80 percent of the world's Muslims, for whom Arabic is not a primary language, had to depend on the Ulama to define the meaning and message of their faith for them. (As one can imagine, such incontestable control over scripture has had a particularly negative effect on Muslim women, who have historically been even further removed from a text whose sole interpreters were, with two or three notable exceptions, strictly men.)

All of that is changing as the last century has witnessed the translation of the Quran into more languages than in the previous fourteen centuries combined. More and more Muslim laity, and especially women, are brushing aside centuries of clerical interpretation in favor of an individualized and unmediated reading of the Quran. Two Arabic terms have come to define this process: *tajdid*, which means "renewal," and *islah*, or "reform." Together these two terms signify a stripping away of centuries of accumulated clerical interpretation in favor of a return to the original founding texts of Islam. Indeed, one of the fastest-growing and most dynamic movements within Islam today is being led by an international community of Muslims, called *Quranists*, who reject all sources of authority in Islam—the hadith, the Sunna, the Shariah—save for the Quran.

If this idea sounds familiar, it is because scripture has always been the primary battleground in religious reformations. No reformation can succeed unless individuals are able to access the same texts that endow the institution with its power. Luther's concept of *sola scriptura*—the notion that all people should be able to interpret the Bible for themselves without the need for a papal mediator—would have been meaningless were it not for his translation of the New Testament from Latin (which only the clergy and the upper class intellectuals could read) to German, the language of the masses. Likewise, by taking upon themselves the authority to define the Quran and actively reinterpreting it according to their own evolving needs, these Muslim men and women are following in the footsteps of the great reformers of the past.

As a result of this remarkable, centuries-long process, Muslims all over the world have been galvanized by a familiar yet revolutionary idea that there need be no mediator between the believer and God, that all people have the ability to discern God's will for themselves, and that being bonded to the past does not necessarily qualify one to decide the future. Some have used this radical creed to develop wholly new interpretations of Islam that foster pluralism, individualism, modernism, and democracy; others have used it to propound an equally new ideal of Islam that calls for intolerance, bigotry, militancy, and perpetual war. Which of these interpretations is "true Islam" is an unanswerable question, since the rejection of institutional authority means that *all* interpretations of Islam must be considered equally authoritative. As Martin Luther quickly discovered, once individual believers are empowered to interpret religion for themselves, there can no longer be any constraints (institutional or otherwise) on how faith is construed. Just as the Christian Reformation opened the door to multiple, often conflicting, and sometimes baffling interpretations of Christianity, so has the Islamic Reformation created a number of wildly divergent and competing ideologies of Islam. What must be recognized, however, is that the peaceful, tolerant, and forward-leaning Islam of an Amr Khaled and the violent, intolerant, and backward-looking Islam of an Osama bin Laden are two competing and contradictory sides of the same reformation phenomenon, because both are founded upon the argument that the power to speak for Islam no longer belongs solely to the Ulama. For better or worse, that power now belongs to every single Muslim in the world.

A FEW KILOMETERS from the campuses of al-Azhar University, inside an unassuming office building in the rumbling business district of Dokki, about one hundred fifty full-time employees—most of them in their twenties and thirties—run an Internet site that has quickly become one of the most visited destinations on the Web. Islam-Online.net has, by some estimates, nearly one million daily visitors, the majority of them aged eighteen to twenty-four (it is also one of the most frequently visited sites on the Internet for Muslim women). Users can keep up with news and information from around the world, learn tips for maintaining health and well-being, debate Islamic law, discuss politics, arts, and culture, and communicate with like-minded Muslims from across the globe. But by far the biggest draw of Islam-Online is the site's popular and deeply controversial "fatwa bank."

It used to be that if a Muslim in Cairo wanted a fatwa, or religious edict, on a disputed topic, he had to sit at the feet of the venerable scholars of al-Azhar University, whose opinions on religious and social matters were essentially law. Today that Muslim can stay home and troll through IslamOnline's vast archive of new and previously published fatwas by a global assembly of *muftis* (scholars qualified to issue a fatwa) covering women's issues, health concerns, interfaith relations, money and business transactions, sports and games, war and peace, and every other topic imaginable. There is even a section on the site that provides ready-made fatwas linked to whatever the top news story of the day may be.

There are tens of thousands of fatwas to choose from on Islam-Online, nearly five thousand of them in English. Because the fatwas are collected from a wide array of sources, the user can access multiple, and often conflicting, fatwas on a single issue; one can simply decide which fatwa one likes best. If the desired fatwa is not found in the database, the employees at IslamOnline will happily connect the user to a live "cyber-mufti," who will chat with the supplicant in real time and issue a satisfactory fatwa in less than twenty-four hours. If the cyber-mufti's fatwa proves unsatisfactory, the user can simply switch his browser to one of IslamOnline's many competitors, such as Fatwa-Online.com, IslamismScope.net, Almultaka.net, Islam-QA.com (whose fatwas come in twelve languages), or AskImam.org—all of which provide their own unique (and also often contradictory) fatwa databases. If that still does not satisfy, there is always AmrKhaled.net, or the website of Iraq's Grand Ayatollah Ali al-Sistani (Sistani.org), or a thousand other sites run by a host of different clerical leaders, activists, academics, lay leaders, spiritual guides, intellectuals, and amateurs, any of whom can spread their influence beyond their local communities with a simple IP address. And because no centralized religious authority exists in Islam to determine which of these opinions is sound and which is not, the user can simply pick and choose whichever fatwa is most appealing from whomever he or she is drawn to most.

It is difficult to exaggerate the impact that the Internet has had, not just on Islam's evolution, but, more significantly, on the way religious authority in Islam has dispersed and become democratized. The only possible comparison one can make is to the invention of the printing press, for just as that technological advancement propelled Christian Europe inexorably toward the Reformation, making it possible for the leaders of the movement to share their ideas with an entire continent, so too has the Internet become the primary vehicle through which the Islamic Reformation is being realized. Ideas and opinions that used to take decades, even centuries, to spread across the borders of the Islamic world can now be accessed instantly and by anyone, simply with a click of a mouse. Millions of Muslims have unfettered access to the thoughts and teachings of acclaimed religious scholars and unknown amateur intellectuals alike, leading a prominent mufti at King Abdulaziz University in Saudi Arabia to lament, "Fatwas today have become something anyone can issue. This is very dangerous, and erroneous fatwas can bring total destruction."

The mufti may have a point. The Internet is a two-edged sword. It may be democratizing religious authority and spreading exciting new ideas, but it is also creating an environment in which highly individualized interpretations of Islam are battling one another online for the hearts and minds of Muslims. More significantly, the Internet has become a bastion for violent interpretations of Islam, and for Jihadism in particular, allowing militant preachers and propagandists to bypass the authority of the Ulama and communicate their anti-institutional message directly to Muslims across the world. And thanks to the relative anonymity of the Internet, it is often difficult to differentiate between the Ulama and the Jihadist, between the respected scholar and the dangerous dilettante.

But it is precisely for that reason that the Internet has become a principal source of spiritual guidance for a new generation of politically active, socially conscious, and globalized Muslim youth. The Internet—along with increased travel, satellite television, and a host of online social networks—has given these young Muslims a wholly new view of the world and, along with it, a healthy distrust of institutional authority, be it the government or the Ulama. In fact, for many, the two institutions are considered one and the same. After all, in almost every Muslim-majority country, the government exerts direct control over the Ulama, claiming custody over their leadership, choosing the Friday prayer leaders, and on occasion even writing their sermons for them. This has led to a widespread belief among many Muslims that the Ulama have been co-opted by the state and that their judgments on the important social, political, and religious issues of the day can no longer be trusted.

Such sentiments have been buoyed by the rapid influx of Muslim immigrants into Europe and North America, where individualism and the anti-institutional ethic are woven into the very fabric of society. A whole new generation of so-called westernized Muslims is seeking spiritual guidance not in the Grand Mosques of their parents (by some estimates, less than one-third of American Muslims go to mosques) but in smaller "garage mosques," student groups, spiritual circles, and Islamic centers, most of which are independent of traditional institutional leadership and totally divorced from the societal and cultural restraints of their homelands. True, the number of Muslims in Europe and North America is still relatively small. Despite the hysteria one so often hears about a creeping "Islamization" of the West, Muslims comprise only about 6 percent of the population in Europe and less than 2 percent of the population in the United States; demographers do not expect those percentages to climb much higher. Nevertheless, the freedom of speech and thought that they enjoy, and their greater access to new communication technologies through which they can spread their innovative views about contemporary Islam to the rest of the world, has given these "westernized" Muslims enormous influence over their coreligionists in Muslim-majority states.

What Muslims in Europe and North America do share with Muslims worldwide is that nearly three-quarters of them are under the age of thirty-five. In some parts of the world, most recently in Iran, Tunisia, Egypt, Algeria, and Yemen, this "Muslim youth bulge" has created restive populations who are fed up with their lack of political and economic opportunities and who are willing to rise up against their governments to demand their rights and privileges. Facebook, Twitter, and other social media platforms have provided this global youth population with a glimpse of a different world, of different opportunities and different social structures. Indeed, for many young

Muslims, the Internet is more than a means of communication and spiritual sustenance. It is the platform through which a new vision of the Ummah is being realized—a *virtual* Ummah, based not on creedal adherence or cultural affiliation, but on a shared sense of common interests, values, and concerns.

The same desire to recast religious authority and redefine the meaning and makeup of the Ummah is also what has drawn so many of these young Muslims to the militantly individualistic and radically anti-institutional version of Islam advocated by Jihadism. Jihadist leaders use the Internet to reach out to young Muslims who may feel a sense of social, economic, or religious alienation from their own communities, and to offer them an alternative source of community and identity, one whose aims and conclusions ironically hark back to those of the more radical reformers of the Christian Reformation. Bin Laden, in particular, used the Internet to present himself as a rival source of religious authority, issuing his own fatwas and expounding upon his own Quranic interpretations, even though, like Amr Khaled, he was not a cleric and had absolutely no seminary training of any kind.

Yet it is through their total disassociation with the clerical institutions that Jihadist leaders base their authority. Indeed, the entire Jihadist identity has been developed in direct opposition to the Ulama, which is why their leaders must also be viewed as walking in the footsteps of the great religious reformers of the past, particularly with the so-called radical reformers of the Christian Reformation, men like Hans Hut, Jacob Hutter, and Thomas Müntzer, who, in pushing the principle of religious individualism to its limits, called for the violent overthrow of the social order. In fact, bin Laden may have had more in common with mainstream Christian reformers like Martin Luther than many would like to admit. Luther may have advocated a similar anti-institutional reading of the scriptures and traditions of Christianity, but he also adamantly opposed any interpretation that challenged his. (He even went so far as to rank the different books of the Bible as more or less valuable depending on whether they agreed with his theology or not.) Nor was Luther hesitant to call for unrestrained violence against fellow reformers with whom he disagreed. During the Peasants' Revolt in 1525, led by Luther's rival Thomas

Müntzer, Luther not only aligned himself with the secular magistrates but publicly called for the mass murder of the peasants, writing "Let everyone who can, smite, slay and stab [them], secretly or openly, remembering that nothing can be so poisonous, hurtful, or devilish than a rebel." More than one hundred thousand peasants were massacred.

It is no wonder that the reform movement Luther is considered to have founded soon began to regard him as the problem and not the solution. By the middle of the sixteenth century, the Christian Reformation had more or less left Luther behind in favor of more populist movements like the Zwinglians in Switzerland, the Anabaptists in the Rhineland, and the Calvinists in Geneva, the latter of which quickly became the most dominant branch of Protestantism in western Europe. A similar process is now taking place in Islam, as Osama bin Laden and his Jihadist ideologues have been left behind by a movement they neither initiated nor led, yet brilliantly used to their advantage in promoting their religious and political agendas. An ideology that only ever appealed to a tiny fraction of the global Muslim movement has become even less tolerated over the last decade, as overwhelming majorities in nearly every Muslim-majority state have turned their backs on the Jihadist message.

But the reformation phenomenon that gave birth to Jihadism continues unabated. It has even begun to influence the very same clerical institutions against which it initially arose. A new class of so-called "dissident Ulama"—scholars and teachers who have declared independence from the accepted schools of law—has begun to gather large followings throughout the Islamic world. These Ulama have transformed themselves into something akin to itinerant preachers, creating a parallel authority structure at odds with the traditional clerical institutions. Meanwhile, the traditional institutions have themselves begun to re-exert some measure of influence and authority by adopting the same tactics as their reformist rivals. Call it a "counter-reformation," if you will. Al-Azhar has even begun its own television network that broadcasts in English, French, and Urdu (among other languages) as a means of combating the influence of popular preachers like Amr Khaled. Nearly every clerical institution in the world now has a significant online presence. There is a widespread recognition by the Ulama that its authority and reputation rest upon its ability to use new social media tools to engage young Muslims in discourse at their level and on their own terms. The result is a cacophony of voices from a variety of sources representing a veritable cornucopia of ideas, values, thoughts, and interpretations, many in conflict with one another, all claiming the right to define the future of what will soon become the largest religion in the world.

Reformations, as we know from Christian history, can be chaotic and bloody events. And the Islamic Reformation has some way to go before it is resolved. It may be too early to speculate about how the sense of radical individualism and anti-institutionalism that has seized Muslims across the world will influence Islam in the coming years. But one thing is certain: the past, and the idealized, perfected, and totally imaginary view of it wrought by those puritans and fundamentalists who strive to re-create it, is over. The next chapter in the story of Islam will be written solely by those willing to look forward, to confront whatever lies ahead, confident in the knowledge that the revolution launched by the Prophet Muhammad fourteen centuries ago to replace the archaic, rigid, and inequitable strictures of tribal society with a radically new vision of divine morality and social egalitarianism still continues to this day.

It took many years to cleanse Arabia of its "false idols." It will take many more to cleanse Islam of its new false idols—bigotry and fanaticism—worshipped by those who have replaced Muhammad's original vision of tolerance and unity with their own ideals of hatred and discord. But the cleansing is inevitable, and the tide of reform cannot be stopped. The Islamic Reformation is already here.

We are all living in it.

Glossary

ahadiyyah	Meaning "oneness," the Sufi ideal of Divine Unity
ahl/qawm	A people or tribe
ahl al-bayt	The family of the Prophet Muhammad
ahl al-Kitab	The "People of the Book"; usually referring to Jews and Christians (see *dhimmi*)
al-Qaeda	Wahhabist organization headed by Osama bin Laden
amir	A governor of a Muslim province
Ansar	The Helpers; members of Medina's clans who converted to Islam
asbab al-nuzul	The occasions for or causes of a particular verse being revealed to Muhammad
Ash'ari	Traditionalist school of Islamic theology
Ashura	The tenth day of the Islamic month of Muharram and the climax of the Shi'ite mourning ceremonies
Aws	Along with the Khazraj, one of the two main pagan Arab clans in Medina
ayah	A verse of the Quran
ayatollah	Meaning "sign of God"; other than Allamah, the highest level a Shi'ite cleric can achieve
baraka	Spiritual power

Basmallah	Invocation that opens most chapters (Surahs) of the Quran: "In the name of God, the Compassionate, the Merciful"
batin	The implicit, hidden message of the Quran
bay'ah	The oath of allegiance commonly given by the tribe to its Shaykh
bayt/banu	"House/sons," meaning clan
bid'a	Religious innovation
Caliph	The successor to Muhammad and the temporal leader of the Muslim community
Companions	The first generation of Muslims, those who accompanied Muhammad on the Hijra from Mecca to Yathrib (Medina); also called the Muhajirun
darvish	Meaning "beggar," a common term for Sufis
dhikr	Meaning "remembrance," the primary ritual in Sufism
dhimmi	Jews, Christians, and other non-Muslims considered "People of the Book" and protected by Islamic law
du'a	Informal prayer
erfan	Mystical knowledge
fana	The annihilation of the self that occurs when a Sufi has reached a state of spiritual enlightenment
Faqih	A Muslim jurist; the Supreme Leader of Iran
faqir	See *darvish*
fatwa	A legal declaration made by a qualified Muslim jurist
fikr	Mystical contemplation employed by certain Sufi Orders
fiqh	The study of Islamic jurisprudence
fitnah	Muslim civil war
hadith	Stories and anecdotes of the Prophet and his earliest companions
Hajj	The pilgrimage to Mecca
Hakam	An arbiter who settled disputes within and between tribes in pre-Islamic Arabia
Hanif	Pre-Islamic Arab monotheist
Hashim	The name of Muhammad's clan
henotheism	The belief in a single "High God," without the explicit rejection of other, lower gods
hijab	Muslim practice of veiling and seclusion of women

Hijaz	The region of western Arabia
Hijra	The emigration from Mecca to Yathrib (Medina) in 622 C.E.; year 1 A.H. (after Hijra) in the Islamic calendar
Iblis	The Devil (corruption of Latin *diabolus*); Satan
ijma	Traditionally, the consensus of the Ulama on a specific legal issue not covered by the Quran and hadith
ijtihad	The independent legal judgment of a qualified legal scholar, or mujtahid
Ikhwan	The Wahhabist holy warriors who helped the Saudis capture Arabia. Also a term for the Muslim Brothers.
Imam	In Shi'ism, the divinely inspired leader of the community
Islamism	An Islamic movement whose primary goal is the establishment of an Islamic polity
isnad	A chain of transmission meant to validate individual hadith
Jahiliyyah	The "Time of Ignorance" before the advent of Islam
jihad	A struggle or striving
Jinn	Imperceptible, salvable spirits, known as "genies" in the West
jizyah	Protection tax paid by the dhimmi
Ka'ba	The ancient sanctuary at Mecca that housed the tribal deities of the Hijaz before being cleansed by Muhammad and rededicated to Allah
kafir	An unbeliever
Kahin	A soothsayer or ecstatic poet in pre-Islamic Arabia who received inspirations from the Jinn
kalam	Islamic theology
Kharijites	Radical sect that broke off from Shi'ism during Ali's Caliphate
Khazraj	Along with the Aws, one of the two main pagan Arab clans in Medina, and the first clan to accept Muhammad's message
khedive	Egyptian monarchs under the suzerainty of the British Empire
madrassa	Islamic religious school
Mahdi	The "Hidden Imam," who is in occultation until the Last Days, when he will return to usher in a time of justice

matam	Self-flagellation rituals mourning the martyrdom of Husayn
Mujahadin	Muslim militants; literally, "those who wage jihad"
mujtahid	A Muslim jurist worthy of emulation and qualified to make authoritative legal declarations
muruwah	Pre-Islamic code of tribal conduct
Muslim Brothers	Islamic socialist organization founded by Hasan al-Banna in Egypt in 1928
Mu'tazilah	Rationalist school of Islamic theology
nabi	A prophet
nafs	Meaning "breath," the self or ego according to Sufism
Najd	The desert regions of eastern Arabia
naskh	The abrogation of one verse in the Quran by another
Pan-Arabism	Principle of racial unity among the world's Arab population
Pan-Islamism	Principle of religious unity among the world's Muslim population
Pir	A Sufi master (also known as Shaykh or Friend of Allah)
Qa'id	Pre-Islamic tribal war leader
qalb	The "heart," corresponding to the soul in Sufism
qiblah	The direction of prayer toward Mecca
qiyas	Analogical reasoning used as a source in the development of Islamic law
Quraysh	The rulers of Mecca in pre-Islamic Arabia
Qurra	The Quran readers who were the first to memorize, record, and disseminate the Revelation
qutb	The "cosmic pole" around which the universe rotates
Rashidun	The first four "Rightly Guided" Caliphs: Abu Bakr, Umar, Uthman, and Ali
rasul	A messenger
ruh	The Universal Spirit; the breath of God
Salafiyyah	Muslim reform movement begun in Egypt by Muhammad Abdu and Jamal ad-Din al-Afghani
salat	Ritual prayer performed five times a day at sunrise, noon, afternoon, sunset, and evening
sawm	Fasting

shahadah	The Muslim profession of faith: "There is no god but God, and Muhammad is God's Messenger."
Shariah	Islamic law whose primary sources are the Quran and hadith
Shaykh	The leader of the tribe or clan; also called Sayyid
Shi'ism	The largest sect in Islam, founded by the followers of Ali
shirk	To obscure the Oneness and Unity of God in any way
shura	A consultative assembly of tribal elders who chose the Shaykh in pre-Islamic Arabia
Sufism	The name given to the mystical traditions in Islam
Sunna	The traditions of the Prophet composed of the hadith
Sunni	The main or "orthodox" branch of Islam
Surah	A chapter of the Quran
Tabiun	The second generation of Muslims after the Companions
tafsir	Traditional Quranic exegesis
tahannuth	Pre-Islamic religious retreat
tajwid	The science of Quranic recitation
tanzil	Direct revelation handed down from God to Muhammad
taqiyyah	Cautionary dissimulation practiced by the Shi'ah
taqlid	Blind acceptance of juridical precedent
tariqah	The spiritual path or Way of the Sufi
tasawwuf	The state of being a Sufi
tawaf	The seven ritual circumambulations of the Ka'ba
tawhid	Meaning "making one," refers to God's Oneness and Unity
ta'wil	Textual exegesis of the Quran that focuses on the hidden, esoteric meaning of the text
ta'ziyeh	A public performance reenacting the martyrdom of Husayn at Karbala
topos	A conventional literary theme
Ulama	Islam's clerical establishment
Ummah	The name given to the Muslim community at Medina
Umm al-Kitab	"The Mother of Books," the heavenly source of all revealed scriptures
umra	The lesser pilgrimage at Mecca
Valayat-e Faqih	"The rule of the jurist"; the religio-political ideology founded by the Ayatollah Khomeini

Wahhabism   Puritanical sect of Islam founded by Muhammad ibn Abd al-Wahhab in Arabia

wali   The executor of God's divine message

zahir   The explicit message of the Quran

zakat   Mandatory alms given to the Muslim community and distributed to the poor

zakir   Shi'ite religious specialists who recite stories of the martyrs during the Muharram ceremonies

Zamzam   The well situated near the Ka'ba

Notes

Whenever possible, references to English translations of Arabic texts are provided for the convenience of Western readers.

Prologue: The Clash of Monotheisms

The Reverend Franklin Graham made his comments regarding Islam on November 16, 2002, while appearing on the *NBC Nightly News*. "We're not attacking Islam, but Islam has attacked us," he said. "The God of Islam is not the same God. He's not the son of God of the Christian or Judeo-Christian faith. It's a different God, and I believe it [Islam] is a very evil and wicked religion."

Ann Coulter's article "This Is War: We Should Invade Their Countries" was posted on *National Review Online* on September 13, 2001. Jerry Vines's speech was given at the annual Southern Baptist Convention, June 10, 2001. A text of James Inhofe's disturbing Senate address delivered on March 4, 2002, is available at the Middle East Information Center; see http://middleeastinfo.org/article316.html.

Barry Yeoman has written a wonderful article about undercover missionaries in the Muslim world, titled "The Stealth Crusade," in *Mother Jones* (May/June 2002).

1. The Sanctuary in the Desert

My description of the pagan Ka'ba relies on the writings of Ibn Hisham and al-Tabari, as well as *The Travels of Ali Bey al-Abbasi* as recounted in Michael Wolfe's excellent collection of pilgrimage accounts, *One Thousand Roads to Mecca* (1997). I also suggest F. E. Peters, *Mecca: A Literary History of the Muslim Holy Land* (1994). For the English translation of Ibn Hisham, see Alfred Guillaume's *The Life of Muhammad* (1955). For an English translation of al-Tabari, see the multivolume set edited by Ihsan Abbas et al., *The History of Al-Tabari* (1988).

The three hundred sixty gods in the sanctuary must be understood as a sacred, not a factual, number. Considering the small size of the Ka'ba, it is likely that most, if not all, the idols in Mecca were originally placed outside the sanctuary, near a semicircular region called the *Hijr*. For more on the role and function of the Hijr see Uri Rubin's article "The Ka'ba: Aspects of Its Ritual Function and Position in Pre-Islamic and Early Times," in *Jerusalem Studies in Arabic and Islam* (1986). In my opinion, the best text on the subject of sacred places is still Mircea Eliade's *The Sacred and the Profane* (1959); see also his *The Myth of the Eternal Return* (1954). The story of the "navel of the world" is treated in G. R. Hawting's brief article "We Were Not Ordered with Entering It but Only with Circumambulating It: *Hadith* and *Fiqh* on Entering the Kaaba," in *Bulletin of the School of Oriental and African Studies* (1984). What little we know about the Amir tribe's worship of dhu-Samawi is outlined in a brief article by Sheikh Ibrahim al-Qattan and Mahmud A. Ghul, "The Arabian Background of Monotheism in Islam," in *The Concept of Monotheism in Islam and Christianity*, edited by Hans Kochler (1982).

An excellent discussion of paganism in the Near East before the rise of Islam can be found in Jonathan P. Berkey, *The Formation of Islam* (2003). See also Robert G. Hoyland, *Arabia and the Arabs* (2001). For a more in-depth analysis of the various religious traditions that existed in the Arabian Peninsula before the rise of Islam, I suggest Joseph Henninger's brief article "Pre-Islamic Bedouin Religion" in *Studies on Islam*, edited by Martin Schwartz (1981). Despite his strict monotheism, Muhammad wholeheartedly accepted the Jinn and even gave them their own chapter in the Quran (Chapter 18). Muhammad may have equated the Jinn with some vague concept of angelology. Thus good Jinn are angels and bad Jinn, especially Iblis (Satan), who is often called a Jinn, are demons (see Quran 18:50).

An insightful discussion of the Ka'ba's Jewish influences can be found in G. R. Hawting's "The Origins of the Muslim Sanctuary at Mecca," in *Studies on the First Century of Islamic Studies*, edited by G.H.A. Juynboll (1982). That the traditions regarding the origins of the Ka'ba predate Islam is, I believe, definitively demonstrated by Uri Rubin's article "Hanafiyya and Ka'ba: An Enquiry into the Arabian Pre-Islamic Background of *din Ibrahim*," *Jerusalem Studies in Arabic and Islam* (1990). A closer inspection of the traditions surrounding the Black Stone makes it clear that this was a meteor that had fallen to earth. The Arab historian Ibn Sa'd states that when it was first discovered, "the black stone shone like the moon for the people of Mecca until the pollution of impure people caused it to go black." Jacob's dream can be found in Genesis 28:10–17. For more on the Jews in Arabia see Gordon Darnell Newby, *A History of the Jews of Arabia* (1988), especially pp. 49–55. For more on the relationship between the Kahin and Kohen, see applicable entries in *The Encyclopedia of Islam*.

Some examples of the Quran's use of explicit Christian imagery include its mention of the "trumpets" that will herald the Last Judgment (6:73; 18:99; 23:101; etc.), the fiery damnation awaiting sinners in hell (104:6–9), and the vision of paradise as a garden (2:25), though the latter may have its origins in Iranian religious traditions. A deeper study of this connection can be found in John Wansbrough, *Quranic Studies: Source and Methods of Scriptural Interpretation* (1977) and H.A.R. Gibb's regrettably titled but extremely informative book *Mohammedanism* (1970). For more general comments on the influence of Christianity in the Arabian Peninsula see Richard Bell, *The Origins of Islam in Its Christian Environment* (1968). The story of Baqura can be found in al-Tabari, p. 1135, and also in the chronicles of al-Azraqi as quoted in Peters, *Mecca*. Note that the Quranic claim that it was not Jesus, but another in his semblance, who was crucified echoes similar Monophysite, as well as Gnostic, beliefs regarding Jesus' divine nature. Some other tribes known to have converted to Christianity are the Taghlib, the Bakr ibn Wa'il, and the Banu Hanifa.

It is unclear exactly when Zarathustra preached his faith. Dates of the Prophet range from the purely mythical (8000 B.C.) to the eve of the Iranian Kingdom (seventh century B.C.). I believe the most logical date for the birth of Zoroastrianism is c. 1100–1000 B.C. See my article "Thus Sprang Zarathustra: A Brief Historiography on the Date of the Prophet of Zoroastrianism," in *Jusur* (1998–99). The influence of Zoroastrian eschatology can be seen quite clearly in Jewish apocalyptic movements such as that of the Essenes (or whoever is responsible for the Dead Sea Scrolls), who developed a complicated eschatology in which the sons of light battle the sons of darkness (both Zoroastrian terms) at the end times, ultimately ushering in the reign of the Teacher of Righteousness. For more on Zoroastrianism, I suggest Mary Boyce's comprehensive three-volume set *History of Zoroastrianism* (1996). Those with less time on their hands can try her abridgment, *Zoroastrians: Their Religious Beliefs and Practices* (2001), or alternatively, Farhang Mehr, *The Zoroastrian Tradition* (1991). Briefly, Mazdakism was a socioreligious movement founded by a Zoroastrian heretic named Mazdak, who emphasized equality and solidarity, primarily through the communal sharing of all goods and properties (including women). Manichaeism, the doctrine founded by the Prophet Mani, was a Gnostic religious movement heavily influenced by Zoroastrianism, Christianity, and Judaism which preached a complex, radical dualism between the forces of darkness/evil and the forces of light/good.

The story of Zayd and the Hanif can be found in Ibn Hisham, pp. 143–49. See also Jonathan Fueck, "The Originality of the Arabian Prophet," in *Studies on Islam*, ed. Schwartz (1981). The epitaphs of Khalid ibn Sinan and Qass ibn Sa'idah are quoted in Mohammed Bamyeh's truly indispensable book, *The Social Origins of Islam* (1999). For more on Abu Amir ar-Rahib and Abu Qais ibn al-Aslat, both of whom vigorously opposed Muhammad's Muslim community in Medina, see Rubin's "Hanafiyya and Ka'ba." Once again, Rubin definitively demonstrates that Hanifism existed before the rise of Islam, though other scholars, including Montgomery Watt, Patricia Crone, and John Wansbrough, disagree. Although it is obvious that Zayd's verses were put into his mouth by later Arab chroniclers, the content of his poetry nonetheless reveals what these Arabs thought Hanifism represented.

An analysis of the Zayd and Muhammad traditions can be found in M. J. Kister, "A Bag of Meat: A Study of an Early Hadith," *Bulletin of the School of Oriental and African Studies* (1968). The story I narrate here is an amalgamation of two of these traditions: one from folios 37b–38a in the Qarawiyun manuscript 727 and translated by Alfred Guillaume in "New Light on the Life of Muhammad," *Journal of Semitic Studies* (1960); the other recorded by al-Khargushi and translated by Kister. While the exact definition of *tahannuth* is still debated by scholars, Ibn Hisham and al-Tabari both indicate that this was a pagan religious practice connected in some way to the cult of the Ka'ba, which took place in the "edens," "valleys," and "mountains" of Mecca. For more on the subject see M. J. Kister, "*al-Tahannuth*: An Inquiry into the Meaning of a Term," *Bulletin of the School of Oriental and African Studies* (1968). F. E. Peters notes in *The Hajj* (1994) that the Arabic term for "erring" in verse 7 (*dalla*, meaning "misguided" or "astray") "leaves little doubt that the 'error' was not simply that Muhammad was confused but that he was immersed in the same reprehensible practices in which the Quraysh persisted even after God had sent the 'guidance' to them as well."

The rebuilding of the Ka'ba can be found in al-Tabari, pp. 1130–39. The traditions imply that Muhammad was somehow dragged into the process, though that
does not disprove Muhammad's full cooperation in the reconstruction of the pagan
sanctuary. A complete discussion of the date of the Abyssinian attack and the birth of
Muhammad is offered by Lawrence I. Conrad, "Abraha and Muhammad," *Bulletin
of the School of Oriental and African Studies* (1987). Muhammad's infancy narratives
can be found in Ibn Hisham, pp. 101–19, and in al-Tabari, pp. 1123–27.

2. The Keeper of the Keys

Rubin discusses Qusayy's religious innovations in "The Ka'ba." Mecca's geographical position on the north-south trade route is just one of the many issues analyzed by
Richard Bulliet in *The Camel and the Wheel* (1975). Those scholars who tend to
maintain the traditional view of Mecca's role as the dominant trading center in the
Hijaz include W. Montgomery Watt, *Muhammad at Mecca* (1953), and M. A. Shaban, *Islamic History: A New Interpretation* (1994). Patricia Crone's rejection of this
theory can be found in *Meccan Trade and the Rise of Islam* (1987). Peters's compromise comes from *Muhammad and the Origins of Islam* (1994), pp. 27, 74–75, and 93.
Those interested in Crone's theories regarding Muhammad and the rise of Islam
can see her books *Hagarism: The Making of the Islamic World* (1977) (coauthored with
M. A. Cook) and *God's Caliph: Religious Authority in the First Centuries of Islam* (1986)
(coauthored with Martin Hinds).

For the role and function of the Shaykh in pre-Islamic Arabia, see W. Montgomery Watt, *Islamic Political Thought* (1968). The role of the Hakam in developing
the normative legal tradition (Sunna) is most clearly described by Joseph Schacht,
An Introduction to Islamic Law (1998). The quote regarding the loyalty of the Hanifs
to the Quraysh is from Rubin, "The Hanafiyya and Ka'ba," p. 97. It is interesting to
note, by the way, that the protection of orphans and widows has always been the primary criterion for just rule. The great Babylonian king, Hammurabi, whose famous
stele represents the first written code of laws for governing society, states that he
conquered his enemies in order to give "justice to the orphan and the widow."

For more on the various meanings of *an-nabi al-ummi*, see Kenneth Cragg's
marvelous book on the history and meaning of the Quran, *The Event of the Qur'an*
(1971). Conrad's quote is from "Abraha and Muhammad," 374–75. For the narratives concerning Muhammad's first revelatory experience and his marriage to
Khadija, see Ibn Hisham, pp. 150–55, and al-Tabari, pp. 139–56.

As noted in the sixth chapter, the Quran is not chronologically organized, so it
is difficult to determine exactly which revelations came first. While there is a great
deal of disagreement, it is generally accepted that the two best compilations of the
earliest verses were completed individually by Theodor Noeldeke and Richard Bell.
Montgomery Watt has combined those verses about which both men agree to create
a list of what he considers to be the earliest verses in the Quran. I will not comment
on Watt's list, which most scholars accept, except to say that, whether it is a faultless
list or not, it provides a very good template of what the first message entailed. The
verses in Watt's list are taken from major sections of the following chapters: 96, 74,
106, 90, 93, 86, 80, 87, 84, 51, 52, 55; I would add to this list Noeldeke's inclusion of
104 and 107, which, because they indicate the presence of the first opposition to
Muhammad's message, may have been delivered right on the heels of the earliest
verses. See Watt's *Muhammad: Prophet and Statesman* (1974). Richard Bell provides a
four-column analysis of the Uthmanic and Egyptian chronologies, alongside
Noeldeke's and William Muir's, in his *Introduction to the Qur'an* (1953), pp. 110–14.

The names of Muhammad's earliest followers are listed in Ibn Hisham, pp. 159–65. Al-Tabari explicitly states that this group was "few in number." There is a disagreement between Sunnis and Shi'ites as to whether Abu Bakr or Ali was the first male convert, but this is an ideological argument. There can be no serious question that Ali, as the closest person to Muhammad at the time, was the first male convert to Islam. For the Qurayshi defense of polytheism see al-Tabari, p. 1175, and Richard Bell (1968), p. 55. The quotation regarding religion and trade in Mecca is from Muhammad Shaban, "Conversion to Early Islam," in *Conversion to Islam*, edited by Nehemia Levtzion (1979). For more on Luqman the Wise see *The Fables of Luqman*, edited by Reyes Carboneli (1965). Maxime Rodinson's book *Mohammad* (1971) offers an interesting, if outdated, perspective on the life of the Prophet. His comments about Muhammad's marriage to Khadija can be found on page 51. My physical description of Muhammad comes from the beautiful description of him written by Tirmidhi as quoted in Annemarie Schimmel, *And Muhammad Is His Messenger* (1985).

3. The City of the Prophet

Ibn Batuta provides what is probably the earliest description of the Prophet's mosque in his famous *Travels* (1958). There is evidence to suggest that Yathrib's inhabitants already referred to the oasis as Medina (the City) before Muhammad's arrival, though Muhammad's presence obviously changed the connotation of that name.

Ali Abd ar-Raziq's *Islam and the Bases of Government* is available in French as "L'Islam et les Bases du Pouvoir," translated by L. Bercher in *Revue des Etudes Islamiques*, VIII (1934). An English translation of important sections of the work can be found in *Islam in Transition*, edited by John J. Donohue and John L. Esposito (1982). Ahmed Rashid's *The Taliban* (2000) is the best introductory text on the history of the Taliban in Afghanistan.

The Banu Nadir and the Banu Qurayza, each of which consisted of several branches, may have had an alliance with each other. Together they were known as the Banu Darih. But like all tribal relationships, this was a political and economic affiliation and had nothing to do with their shared religious tradition. There is still debate over whether Yathrib's Jews were converts or immigrants. The majority of scholars believe them to be Arab converts and, as we shall see, the evidence seems to agree. For an outline of this argument see Watt, *Muhammad at Medina* (1956) and S. D. Goiten, *Jews and Arabs* (1970). Barakat Ahmad calculates the Jewish population of Yathrib to have been between 24,000 and 36,000 inhabitants in *Muhammad and the Jews: A Re-Examination* (1979); that may be a bit high.

For more on the brief period of Persian control over the region, as well as the division of Yathrib between the Jews and Arabs, see Peters, *Muhammad*; al-Waqidi's quote is from page 193 of Peters's text. See Michael Lecker, *Muslims, Jews, and Pagans: Studies on Early Islamic Medina* (1995) for a discussion of the late conversion of the Aws.

A full discussion of the controversy over the date and meaning of the Constitution of Medina can be found in Moshe Gil, "The Constitution of Medina: A Reconsideration," in *Israel Oriental Studies* (1974). For more on Muhammad's role as Shaykh of the Emigrants, see Watt, *Islamic Political Thought*. Watt also provides an English translation of the Constitution of Medina in his appendix, pp. 130–34.

For a further discussion of the origins of the word *Ummah*, I suggest the entry in *Encyclopedia of Islam*. Bertram Thomas's portrayal of the Ummah as a "super-tribe" is from *The Arabs* (1937); Marshall G. S. Hodgson's term "neo-tribe" is from *The Venture of Islam*, vol. 1 (1974). Anthony Black provides a valuable insight into the similarities between the purpose and function of rituals of the Ummah and the pagan tribes in *The History of Islamic Political Thought* (2001).

I am convinced that the *shahadah* was originally addressed not to God, but to Muhammad, because a great many of those who had proclaimed the *shahadah* (and thereby joined the Ummah) while Muhammad was alive considered their oaths to be annulled with the Prophet's death (according to tribal custom, the *bay'ah* never survived the death of the tribe's Shaykh). As we shall see in Chapter 5, the annulment of the *bay'ah* eventually led to the Riddah Wars. Incidentally, the word "Islam" to designate Muhammad's movement may not have been applied by the Prophet until his farewell pilgrimage: "Today I have perfected your religion, I have completed my blessings upon you, and I have approved Islam as your religion" (5:5).

There are many versions of the al-Ayham story. Mine is taken from Watt, *Muhammad at Medina*, p. 268. For more on Muhammad's market, see M. J. Kister, "The Market of the Prophet," *Journal of the Economic and Social History of the Orient* (1965).

There are, of course, two creation stories in Genesis. The first, which is derived from what is referred to as the Priestly tradition, can be found in the first chapter, in which God creates man and woman simultaneously. The second and better-known tradition of Adam and Eve is from the second chapter.

For Muhammad's reforms aimed at women and the reactions to them, see Fatima Mernissi, *The Veil and the Male Elite* (1991); al-Tabari's quote is taken from page 125 of Mernissi's book. How exactly the inheritance was to be divided between the male and female heirs can be found in the Quran 4:9–14, and is explained adequately by Watt in *Muhammad at Medina*, pp. 289–93. Watt also provides a valuable discussion of the transition from matriliny to patriliny in Meccan society on pp. 272–89. For more on the rules regarding the wife's dowry, see Hodgson (1974), p. 182. The traditions of pre-Islamic marriage and divorce, as well as the imposition of the veil, are dealt with in detail in Leila Ahmed's excellent book *Women and Gender in Islam* (1992).

Those interested in the issue of stoning as punishment for adultery should see my article "The Problem of Stoning in Islamic Law: An Argument for Reform," *UCLA Journal of Islamic and Near Eastern Law* (2005); also Ahmad Von Denffer, *Ulum Al-Qur'an* (1983), pp. 110–11. The punishment of stoning to death was actually derived from Hebrew law, where it was prescribed for a number of crimes including adultery (Deut. 22:13–21), blasphemy (Deut. 24:14), calling up spirits (Deut. 20:27), and disobeying one's parents (Deut. 21:18–21). The Quran establishes the punishment of lashes for the adulterer in one verse (24:2) and lifelong imprisonment in another (4:15–16). However, both Sahih al-Bukhari and Sahih al-Hajjaj claim that Muhammad had himself ordered stoning for adultery. But there is a great deal of confusion within these traditions. For instance, Abdullah ibn Aufa reports that Muhammad did indeed carry out stoning, but when asked whether Muhammad prescribed stoning before or after the Surah an-Nur, which clearly endorses lashes for the adulterer, Ibn Aufa replies that he did not know (al-Bukhari 8.824). For more on Umar's misogynist innovations, see Leila Ahmed (1992), pp. 60–61.

For the commentary on *sufaha* and Abu Bakra's hadith, see Mernissi, 126; 49 (also 45–46). The hadith on the rights of women is from Kitab al-Nikah, no. 1850; the Prophet's quote about women's deficiencies is from al-Bukhari, vol. 1, no. 304;

and ar-Razi's commentary is from his massive work *at-Tafsir al-Kabir*. (For Muhammad's consultation with Umm Salamah at Hudaybiyyah, see al-Tabari, p. 1550.) The origin of and problems with the hadith are dealt with well in Ignaz Goldziher, *Introduction to Islamic Theology and Law* (1981). Goldziher also outlines the remarkable contribution of female textual scholars in his brief article "Women in the Hadith Literature," in *Muslim Studies* (1977).

Lord Cromer's quote is from Leila Ahmed (1992), pp. 152–53. Ali Shariati's quote is from *Fatima Is Fatima* (1971), p. 136. Shirin Ebadi's quote is from the presentation speech by Professor Ole Danbolt Mjos, Chairman of the Norwegian Nobel Committee, and is available at http://www.payvand.com/news/03/dec/1065.html.

There are a number of excellent studies on the role of women in contemporary Muslim society. I recommend *Faith and Freedom*, edited by Mahnaz Afkhami (1995); *Islam, Gender, and Social Change*, edited by Yvonne Yazbeck Haddad and John L. Esposito (1998); *In the Eye of the Storm: Women in Post-Revolutionary Iran*, edited by Mahnaz Afkhami and Erika Friedl (1994); and Haideh Moghissi's *Feminism and Islamic Fundamentalism* (1999). See also my critique of Moghissi's text in *Iranian Studies* (2002).

4. Fight in the Way of God

The description of the Battle of Uhud that begins this chapter is drawn from the account in al-Tabari, pp. 1384–1427. Samuel Huntington's quote is from his article "The Clash of Civilizations?" in *Foreign Affairs* (Summer 1993), pp. 35. Bernard Lewis's quote can be found in Hilmi M. Zawati, *Is Jihad a Just War?* (2001), on p. 2; Zawati outlines the use of jihad as defensive war in pages 15–17, 41–45, and 107. Weber's quote is from Bryan S. Turner, *Weber and Islam: A Critical Study* (1974), p. 34. The quote about the scimitar-brandishing Arab warrior is from Rudolph Peters, *Islam and Colonialism: The Doctrine of Jihad in Modern History* (1979), p. 4.

For more on the use, function, and development of the doctrine of jihad, see Rudolph Peters's other work, *Jihad in Classical and Modern Islam* (1996); also *Jihad and Shahadat*, edited by Mehdi Abedi and Gary Legenhausen (1986), especially the definitions on pages 2 and 3; and Mustansir Mir's insightful article "Jihad in Islam," in *The Jihad and Its Times*, edited by Hadia Dajani-Shakeel and Ronald A. Messier (1991). Hadith forbidding the killing of women and children can be found in Sahih al-Hajjaj, nos. 4319 and 4320. For more on Vaisnava and Saiva traditions and the kingdoms they inspired, see Gavin Flood, *An Introduction to Hinduism* (1996).

The role of the Crusades in shaping Muslim ideas of jihad is discussed in Hadia Dajani-Shakeel's article "Perceptions of the Counter Crusade," in *The Jihad and Its Times*, pp. 41–70. Mustansir Mir's quote is on page 114. Those interested in the comparative ethics of war, as well as the doctrine of jihad as a just war theory, should see Michael Walzer, *Just and Unjust Wars* (1977) and John Kelsay, *Islam and War* (1993), especially pp. 57–76. Dr. Azzam's quote is from Peter L. Bergen, *Holy War, Inc.: Inside the Secret World of Osama bin Laden* (2001), p. 53. For Moulavi Chiragh Ali's views on jihad, see *A Critical Exposition of the Popular Jihad* (1976); Mahmud Shaltut's views are discussed in Kate Zabiri, *Mahmud Shaltut and Islamic Modernism* (1993). For the full report on the Muslim victims of al-Qaeda see Scott Helfstein, et al., "Deadly Vanguards: A Study of al-Qa'ida's Violence Against Muslims," Combating Terrorism Center at West Point, December 2009.

For more on Muhammad's enemies among the Hanif of Medina, see Uri Rubin, "Hanafiyya and Ka'ba," in *Jerusalem Studies in Arabic and Islam* (1990). Incidentally, Moshe Gil is almost alone in his conviction that the Constitution of

Medina did not originally include the Jews; see "The Constitution of Medina: A Reconsideration," in *Israel Oriental Studies* (1974), pp. 64–65. Otherwise, there is almost unanimous agreement among scholars that the document is authentic and that it included the Jews. For the traditions regarding the Banu Qurayza, see M. J. Kister, "The Massacre of the Banu Qurayza: A Reexamination of a Tradition," in *Jerusalem Studies in Arabic and Islam* (1986), and Hodgson (1974), p. 191. Kister puts the number at about four hundred. Ahmad estimates the number of Jews remaining in Medina to have been between 24,000 and 28,000. For the Jewish perspective see H. Graetz, *History of the Jews*, vol. 3 (1894); Salo Wittmayer Baron, *A Social and Religious History of the Jews*, vol. 3 (1964); and Francesco Gabrieli, *Muhammad and the Conquests of Islam* (1968): Gabrieli's quote regarding Badr is on page 68.

For Arab responses to the massacre of Banu Qurayza, see Ahmad (1976), pp. 76–94, and W. N. Arafat, "New Light on the Story of Banu Qurayza and the Jews of Medina," in *Journal of the Royal Asiatic Society* (1976). Tor Andrae's quote is from *Mohammad: The Man and His Faith* (1935), pp. 155–56.

For more objective studies on the massacre, see Karen Armstrong, *Muhammad* (1993), and Norman A. Stillman, *The Jews of Arab Lands* (1979). As the allies of the Qurayza, some members of the Aws asked Muhammad for leniency. It was for this reason that he chose one of their number as Hakam. However, after Sa'd's decision was made, there were no objections from the Aws, or from anyone else for that matter.

The story of the mosque demolished by Umar in Damascus is recounted in J. L. Porter, *Five Years in Damascus: With Travels and Researches in Palmyra, Lebanon, the Giant Cities of Bashan, and the Hauran* (1855). Muhammad's instructions to his armies are discussed in Ignaz Goldziher, *Introduction to Islamic Theology and Law*, pp. 33–36. Maria Menocal's excellent book *The Ornament of the World* (2002) describes the culture of religious tolerance founded by the Umayyads in medieval Spain. S. D. Goiten provides a more academic perspective on Jews under Muslim rule in *Jews and Arabs* (1970); his quotation is from page 63. Muhammad's quotation regarding the protection of Jews and Christians is taken from *The Shorter Encyclopedia of Islam*, p. 17. Peters's quote is from *Muhammad*, p. 203 (original italics); Watt's from *Muhammad at Medina* (1956), 195.

H. G. Reissener's views on the Jews of Medina are best described in "The Ummi Prophet and the Banu Israil," in *The Muslim World* (1949), while D. S. Margoliouth's views are discussed in his *The Relations Between Arabs and Israelites Prior to the Rise of Islam* (1924). For the Arabian Jews' knowledge of the Bible, see footnote 87 in S. W. Baron (1964), p. 261. Gordon Newby outlines the economic dominance of the Jewish clans in Yathrib in *A History of the Jews of Arabia* (1988), pp. 75–79 and 84–85. For a treatment of the relationship between Muhammad and the Jewish clans of Medina, see Hannah Rahman's excellent essay "The Conflicts Between the Prophet and the Opposition in Medina," in *Der Islam* (1985); also Moshe Gil, "The Medinan Opposition to the Prophet," in *Jerusalem Studies in Arabic and Islam* (1987), as well as his "Origin of the Jews of Yathrib," in *Jerusalem Studies in Arabic and Islam* (1984). The issue of archeology and Jewish identity is examined by Jonathan L. Reed in his *Archeology and the Galilean Jesus* (2000).

For a history of Ibn Sayyad, see David J. Halperin, "The Ibn Sayyad Traditions and the Legend of al-Dajjal," in *Journal of the American Oriental Society* (1976). Even though Ibn Sayyad may have accepted Muhammad's prophetic mission, Muhammad seems to have denied Ibn Sayyad's. In fact, Halperin shows how later Islamic tradition transformed Ibn Sayyad into an Antichrist figure. For the connection between Jesus and Muhammad, see Neal Robinson, *Christ in Islam and Christianity* (1991).

The break with the Jews and Christians is examined in M. J. Kister, "Do Not Assimilate Yourselves . . . ," in *Jerusalem Studies in Arabic and Islam* (1989). For more on Muhammad's monotheistic pluralism, see Mohammed Bamyeh, *The Social Origins of Islam* (1999), pp. 214–15. With the conquest of Persia, the Zoroastrians, who are given special mention in the Quran (22:17) and who have a "book" (the *Gathas*) which is older than both the Jewish and Christian texts, eventually become included in the *ahl al-Kitab*. Who the Sabians were is difficult to say. Apparently, some religious groups, including a few Christian and Hindu sects, eagerly took on the Sabian identity during the Muslim conquests in order to be counted as People of the Book and thus be considered dhimmi. Nabia Abbot's research on the early Muslim relations with the Jews can be found in *Studies in Arabic Literary Papyri*, vol. 2 (1967). The practice of reading the Torah was, according to Abbot, characteristic of "the early Muslims' preoccupation with non-Islamic thought and literature," especially the literature of the Peoples of the Book.

5. The Rightly Guided Ones

The story of Muhammad's death is derived from Ibn Hisham, trans. Guillaume, pp. 1012–13. Goldziher's quote is from *Introduction to Islamic Theology and Law*, pp. 31–32; see also his *Muslim Studies* (1971). John Wansbrough's theories can be found in the previously cited *Quranic Studies: Sources and Methods of Scriptural Interpretation* (1977), as well as *The Sectarian Milieu: Content and Composition of Islamic Salvation History* (1978). Sarjeant's review of Wansbrough's *Quranic Studies* and Cook and Crone's *Hagarism* is from the *Journal of the Royal Asiatic Society* (1978). Dale F. Eickelman provides a social anthropologist's perspective on the "false prophets" in "Musaylima," *Journal of Economic and Social History of the Orient* (1967). For more on the ahl al-bayt, see M. Sharon, "Ahl al-Bayt—People of the House," in *Jerusalem Studies in Arabic and Islam* (1986). It should be noted that Sharon considers the term *ahl al-bayt* to be a designation that was not formulated until the Umayyad period. While this may be true, the sentiment behind the term (that it gave the Banu Hashim a preeminent role in society) was thoroughly understood even before Muhammad's death. For the opposite view on the religious influence of the early Caliphate, see Patricia Crone and Martin Hinds, *God's Caliph: Religious Authority in the First Centuries of Islam* (1986).

By far the best analysis of the succession question is Wilferd Madelung's *The Succession to Muhammad* (1997). To say that this chapter relies on Professor Madelung's work would be an understatement. I also recommend Rafiq Zakaria's *The Struggle Within Islam* (1988); Abu Bakr's speech is from page 47. Zakaria also provides a valuable analysis of Umar's Caliphate on pages 48–53. See also M. A. Shaban's *Islamic History* (1994), pp. 16–19, and Moojan Momen's fabulous primer on Shi'ism, *An Introduction to Shi'i Islam* (1985), pp. 9–22; Momen notes that Ibn Hanbal records ten different traditions in which Ali is referred to as Muhammad's "Aaron," p. 325. Watt's quote is from *Muhammad: Prophet and Statesman*, p. 36.

Umar's physical description as well as his quote regarding kinghood is taken from the *New Encyclopedia of Islam*, edited by Cyril Glasse, p. 462. For the affair of the necklace see al-Tabari, pp. 1518–28. Though traditions claim that Umar was the first Caliph to use the title Amir al-Mu'manin, there is evidence to suggest that this title was used by Abu Bakr as well.

Noeldeke's excellent essay on the Quran can be found in the *Encyclopaedia*

Britannica, 9th ed., vol. 16 (1891); Caetani's article "Uthman and the Recension of the Koran" is from *The Muslim World* (1915). For examples of variant readings of the Quran that have survived, see Arthur Jeffery, "A Variant Text of the Fatiha," in *Muslim World* (1939). Once again, I am indebted in these pages to Wilferd Madelung's analysis of Uthman's assassination in *The Succession to Muhammad*, especially pages 78–140.

There are many books on the life and Caliphate of Ali. Particularly helpful to this section was Momen's *An Introduction to Shi'i Islam*, as well as S. Husain M. Jafri, *The Origins and Early Development of Shi'a Islam* (1979). See also Mohamad Jawad Chirri, *The Brother of the Prophet Mohammad* (1982). For more on the doctrine and history of the Kharijites, see Montgomery Watt, *The Formative Period of Islamic Thought*, pp. 9–37. Ali's quote is from *A Selection from "Nahjul Balagha,"* translated by Ali A. Behzadnia and Salwa Denny, p. 7. Ali was not the first to be called Imam; all four Caliphs shared that title, though with Ali, the title of Imam emphasizes his special relationship to the Prophet.

Sir Thomas W. Arnold's quote is from *The Caliphate* (1966), p. 10. For various views on the relationship between religion and politics in Islam, see Abu-l Ala (Mawlana) Mawdudi's *Nationalism and India* (1947), Abd ar-Raziq's previously cited *Islam and the Bases of Government*, Sayyid Qutb's *Social Justice in Islam* (1953), and Ruhollah Khomeini's *Islamic Government* (1979).

6. This Religion Is a Science

There are numerous accounts of the inquisition of Ahmad ibn Hanbal before al-Mu'tasim, most of which are compiled and brilliantly analyzed by Nimrod Hurvitz in *The Formation of Hanbalism: Piety into Power* (2002). For biographies of both Ibn Hanbal and al-Ma'mun, see Michael Cooperson, *Classical Arabic Biography: The Heirs of the Prophets in the Age of al-Ma'mun* (2000). I draw my physical description of Ibn Hanbal, as well as the deathbed quote of al-Ma'mun, from Cooperson's text. For more on the impact of the Inquisition, see Jonathan Berkey (2003), pp. 124–29, and Richard Bulliet, *Islam: The View from the Edge* (1994), pp. 115–27. The issue is also treated quite well by Patricia Crone in her newest work, *God's Rule: Government and Islam* (2004). Malik ibn Anas is quoted in Mernissi, p. 59.

Wilfred Cantwell Smith's description of Islamic orthodoxy is from his *Islam in Modern History* (1957), p. 20. For general treatments of the Five Pillars, see Mohamed A. Abu Ridah, "Monotheism in Islam: Interpretations and Social Manifestations," in *The Concept of Monotheism in Islam and Christianity*, edited by Hans Kochler (1982), and John Renard, *Seven Doors to Islam* (1996).

There is evidence (apart from the apocryphal story of Muhammad's ascension to heaven, when he negotiates the number of salats down from fifty to five) that the early tradition prescribed only three salats a day. The Quran says, "Hold the salat at the two ends of the day as well as at the ends of the night" (11:114). Eventually, two more salats must have been added, though no one is certain why or when. Ibn Jubayr's quote about Mecca and the Hajj is taken from his *Voyages* (1949–51). Malcolm X's quote is from *The Autobiography of Malcolm X* (1965).

Al-Ghazali's *The Ninety-nine Beautiful Names of God* has been translated into English by David B. Burrell and Nazih Daher (1970), while his *Revival of the Religious Sciences* has been translated into English by Nabih Amin Faris as *The Foundations of the Articles of Faith* (1963). Ali Shariati's reflections on tawhid can be found in his *On the Sociology of Islam* (1979).

The debate between the Traditionalists and the Rationalists is wonderfully illuminated in Binyamin Abrahamov's *Islamic Theology: Traditionalism and Rationalism* (1998). I also recommend the essays in *Religious Schools and Sects in Medieval Islam*, edited by Wilferd Madelung (1985), as well as Montgomery Watt's previously cited *The Formative Period of Islamic Thought*. The beliefs of the Mu'tazilah are discussed in detail by Richard S. Martin, Mark R. Woodward, and Dwi S. Atmaja in *Defenders of Reason in Islam* (1997), while the Ash'arite position is laid out in Richard McCarthy, *The Theology of the Ash'ari* (1953). Al-Tahawi's quote, as well as the creeds of Abu Hanifah, Ibn Hanbal, and al-Ash'ari, are all taken from Montgomery Watt's invaluable compilation, *Islamic Creeds: A Selection* (1994). See also George F. Hourani, *Islamic Rationalism: The Ethics of Abd al-Jabbar* (1971).

Excellent translations of Ibn Rushd include his commentary on Aristotle's *Metaphysics*, translated by Charles Genequand (1984); *The Epistle on the Possibility of Conjunction with the Active Intellect*, translated by Kalman P. Bland (1982); and *Averroes' Three Short Commentaries on Aristotle's "Topics," "Rhetoric," and "Poetics,"* translated by Charles E. Butterworth (1977). It is important to note that the two truth theory is a misnomer, because according to Ibn Rushd, philosophical truth is the *only* truth. For Ibn Sina, see his biography, *The Life of Ibn Sina*, translated by William E. Gohlman (1974), and his *Treatise on Logic*, translated by Farhang Zabeeh (1971).

For more on oral peoples, see Denise Lardner Carmody and John Tully Carmody, *Original Visions: The Religions of Oral Peoples* (1993). For the role of poets and poetry in the cult of the Ka'ba, see Michael Sells, *Desert Tracings: Six Classical Arabian Odes* (1989). Mohammed Bamyeh presents a wonderful discussion of the field of miracle in his chapter titled "The Discourse and the Path" in *The Social Origins of Islam*, pp. 115–40. My argument is completely indebted to his. See also Cragg, *The Event of the Qur'an*, p. 67. Daya's quote is from Annemarie Schimmel, *And Muhammad Is His Messenger* (1985), p. 67.

As will become apparent, there are some Muslims whose devotionalism has led to a number of apocryphal stories about the miraculous acts of Muhammad and his Companions. However, orthodox Islam flatly rejects these stories, considering Muhammad to be just an empty vessel through which the Quran was revealed—someone who should be emulated, but not worshipped like Christ. Incidentally, al-Tabari narrates a particularly strange account of Muhammad snapping his fingers to uproot a date tree and transport it to himself (p. 1146). But this story, like similar ones about Ali raising people from the dead or walking on water, were primarily apologetic in nature and meant to silence those critics who were accustomed to prophets doing tricks to prove their divine mission.

For a more comprehensive examination of the debate over the created Quran, I suggest Harry Austryn Wolfson, *The Philosophy of Kalam*, especially pages 235–78. My quotations of Ibn Hazm and Ibn Kullab are from Wolfson's text. For more on the role and function of baraka in Islamic calligraphy, see Seyyed Hossein Nasr, *Islamic Art and Spirituality* (1987). For general comments on baraka in the Quran, see the first chapter of John Renard, *Seven Doors to Islam* (1996). William Graham's insightful article "Qur'an as Spoken Word" can be found in *Approaches to Islam in Religious Studies*, edited by Richard C. Martin (2001). There are two kinds of Quranic recitation: *tajwid* (embellished) and *tartil* (measured). The latter is less musical and used primarily for worship. See Lois Ibsen al-Faruqi, "The Cantillation of the Qur'an," in *Asian Music* (1987), and Kristina Nelson, "Reciter and Listener: Some Factors Shaping the Mujawwad Style of Qur'anic Reciting," in *Ethnomusicology* (1987).

There are six collections of hadith that are considered canonical: al-Bukhari's; al-Hajjaj's; as-Sijistani's (d. 875); al-Tirmidhi's (d. 915); al-Nasa'i's (d. 915); and Ibn Maja's (d. 886). Added to this list is the Shi'ite compilation of Malik ibn Anas (d. 795), which was the first such collection to be written down. See Joseph Schacht, *Origins of Muhammadan Jurisprudence* (1950) and *An Introduction to Islamic Law* (1964). Schacht's quote is from "A Revaluation of Islamic Traditions," in the *Journal of the Royal Asiatic Society* (1949). See also Jonathan Berkey, *The Formation of Islam*, pp. 141–51. The Pakistani scholar is Abdul Qadir Oudah Shaheed, and his quote is from *Criminal Law of Islam* (1987), p. 13.

Mahmoud Taha's views on the Quran can be found in *The Second Message of Islam* (1996); see also Abdullahi an-Na'im, *Toward an Islamic Reformation* (1996). For Nasr Hamid Abu Zayd, see his brief article, "Divine Attributes in the Qur'an: Some Poetic Aspects," in *Islam and Modernity*, edited by John Cooper et al. (1998). Al-Ghazali's quote is from Zakaria's Appendix 1, page 303.

For more on *naskh* see Ahmad Von Denffer, *Ulum al-Qur'an: An Introduction to the Sciences of the Qur'an* (1983). There are scholars who reject the concept of *naskh* altogether; see Ahmad Hasan, *The Early Development of Islamic Jurisprudence* (1970), pp. 70–79. However, even Hasan recognizes the importance of historical context in interpreting the Quran.

7. In the Footsteps of Martyrs

My narrative of Karbala relies on Syed-Mohsen Naquvi, *The Tragedy of Karbala* (1992), and Lewis Pelly, *The Miracle Play of Hasan and Husain*, 2 vols. (1879). For the development and function of the Muharram ceremonies in Shi'ism, see Heinz Halm, *Shi'a Islam: From Religion to Revolution* (1997); Halm's quote is from page 41. See also the sociological works on the subject done by Vernon Schubel, *Religious Performance in Contemporary Islam* (1993), and David Pinault, *The Shi'ites* (1992), from which the two testimonials are taken (pp. 103–6). I also recommend Pinault's *The Horse of Karbala* (2001). Ehsan Yarshater traces the origins of lamentation rituals in "Ta'ziyeh and Pre-Islamic Mourning Rites" in *Ta'ziyeh: Ritual and Drama in Iran*, edited by Peter Chelowski (1979).

There are a few superb introductory texts on Shi'ism, including the previously cited Moojan Momen, *An Introduction to Shi'i Islam* (1985), and S. Husain M. Jafri, *The Origins and Early Development of Shi'a Islam* (1979). An English translation of Tabataba'i's work, *Shi'ite Islam*, by Seyyed Hossein Nasr (1977) is available. For Shi'ite conceptions of Shariah, see Hossein Modarressi, *An Introduction to Shi'i Law* (1984). The concept of the "pre-existent Imam" is discussed in great detail in Mohammad Ali Amir-Moezzi, *The Divine Guide in Early Shi'ism* (1994). For the Shi'ite view of the Quran, see Tabataba'i, *The Qur'an in Islam* (1987). Ja'far as-Sadiq's exegesis of the Verse of Light is taken from Helmut Gatje, *The Qur'an and Its Exegesis* (1976).

However, very few books deal adequately with the origins and evolution of the Mahdi in Islam. The books most useful to this study include Jassim M. Hussain, *The Occultation of the Twelfth Imam* (1982), and Abdulaziz Abdulhussein Sachedina, *Islamic Messianism* (1981). Sachedina also deals with the role of the Imam's deputies in *The Just Ruler in Shi'ite Islam* (1988).

Ibn Khaldun's seminal history *The Muqaddimah* is available in complete and abridged English translations by the eminent Islamist Franz Rosenthal. Those interested in an in-depth look at the machinations of the clerical establishment in Iran should see Roy Mottahedeh's marvelous book *The Mantle of the Prophet* (1985).

There are too many general histories of the Iranian Revolution to list, though I recommend Said Amir Arjomand's *The Turban for the Crown* (1988) and Charles Kurzman's *The Unthinkable Revolution in Iran* (2004). For a more contemporary perspective see Dariush Zaheri, *The Iranian Revolution: Then and Now* (2000). Sandra Mackey provides a delightful and readable account of Iranian history in *The Iranians* (1996).

For more on Khomeinism see Ervand Abrahamian, *Khomeinism: Essays on the Islamic Republic* (1993). For translations of Khomeini's writings into English see *Islamic Government* (1979); *Islam and Revolution* (1981); and *A Clarification of Questions* (1984). Khomeini's reinterpretation of Shi'ism is severely criticized by Mohammad Manzoor Nomani in *Khomeini, Iranian, Revolution, and the Shi'ite Faith* (1988). Khomeini's poem is from Baqer Moin's biography titled *Khomeini: Life of the Ayatollah* (1999).

8. Stain Your Prayer Rug with Wine

There are a number of exquisite English translations of Nizami's *The Legend of Layla and Majnun*, including Colin Turner's (1970), R. Gelpke's (1966), and James Atkinson's lovely verse rendition (1968). Mine is a loose combination of the three along with my own translation of the Persian text. See also the critical analysis of the poem by Ali Asghar Seyed-Gohrab, *Layli and Majnun: Love, Madness and Mystic Longing in Nizami's Epic Romance* (2003). For a discussion of the early development of Sufism I suggest Shaykh Fadhlalla Haeri, *The Elements of Sufism* (1990) and Julian Baldick, *Mystical Islam* (1989). Baldick provides a useful analysis of the various religious and cultural influences on Sufism and also explores the meanings of the term. R. A. Nicholson's texts include *The Mystics of Islam* (1914) and *Studies in Islamic Mysticism* (1921). Two of Idris Shah's many invaluable texts on Sufism are *The Sufis* (1964) and *The Way of the Sufi* (1969). See also Martin Lings, *What Is Sufism?* (1993); Inayat Khan, *The Unity of Religious Ideals* (1929); Ian Richard Netton, *Sufi Ritual* (2000); Nasrollah Pourjavady and Peter Wilson, *Kings of Love* (1978); J. Spencer Trimingham, *The Sufi Orders in Islam* (1971); Carl Ernst, *Teachings of Sufism* (1999); and Titus Burckhardt, *An Introduction to Sufi Doctrine* (1976).

For the teachings of Shaykh Muhammad al-Jamal ar-Rafa'i ash-Shadhili, see his *Music of the Soul* (1994). The historical and theological relationship between Shi'ism and Sufism is outlined in Kamil M. al-Shaibi, *Sufism and Shi'ism* (1991). Finally, there exists a helpful though not easily digested series of *Sufi Essays* by Seyyed Hossein Nasr (1972).

Al-Ghazali's *The Alchemy of Happiness* is translated by Claud Field (1980), while *The Niche of Lights* is translated by David Buchman (1998). For more on al-Ghazali's philosophy see Montgomery Watt, *The Faith and Practice of al-Ghazali* (1953). Al-Hujwiri's *The Revelation of the Mystery* is translated by Reynold Nicholson (1911). Without question the best translation of Farid ad-Din Attar's *The Conference of the Birds* is by Afkham Darbandi and Dick Davis (1984). The Persian scholar and Sufi Javad Nurbakhsh delves into the relationship between teacher and taught in his short tract *Master and Disciple in Sufism* (1977). On the stations along the Way, see Shaykh Abd al-Khaliq al-Shabrawi, *The Degrees of the Soul* (1997), and Abu'l Qasim al-Qushayri, *Sufi Book of Spiritual Ascent*, translated by Rabia Harris (1997). Al-Hallaj's *Kitab al-Tawasin* is available only in a French translation by the great scholar of Sufism, Louis Massignon (1913). Massignon's *Essay on the Origins of the Technical Language of Islamic Mysticism* (1997) is a helpful tool for those students already familiar with the rudiments of Sufism.

The concept of monism in Sufism is discussed at length by Molana Salaheddin Ali Nader Shah Angha in *The Fragrance of Sufism* (1996). Ibn al-Arabi's *Fusus al-Hikam* is available in English as *The Wisdom of the Prophets* (1975). For more on Rabia and other Sufi women, see Camille Adams Helminski, *Women of Sufism* (2003), and Margaret Smith, *Rabi'a the Mystic and Her Fellow-Saints in Islam* (1928). Rabia's poems are nicely collected and translated by Charles Upton in *Doorkeeper of the Heart: Versions of Rabi'a* (1988).

The best translations of Rumi include Colman Barks, *The Essential Rumi* (1995), and the two-volume *Mystical Poems of Rumi* translated by A. J. Arberry (1968); see also Reynold Nicholson's *Rumi: Poet and Mystic* (1950). For more on Rumi's life see Annemarie Schimmel, *I Am Wind, You Are Fire: The Life and Works of Rumi* (1992). For Hafiz see Nahid Angha, *Selections* (1991) and *Ecstasy* (1998). General treatises on Sufi poetry include Ali Asani and Kamal Abdel-Malek, *Celebrating Muhammad* (1995), and J.T.P. de Bruijn, *Persian Sufi Poetry* (1997).

With regard to Sufism in India I suggest Muhammad Mujeeb, *Indian Muslims* (1967) and Carl W. Ernst, *Eternal Garden: Mysticism, History, and Politics at a South Asian Sufi Center* (1992). See also Bruce Lawrence, "The Early Chisti Approach to Sama'," in *Islamic Societies and Culture: Essays in Honor of Professor Aziz Ahmad*, edited by Milton Israel and N. K. Wagle (1983).

Iqbal's quote is from Ali Shariati's commentary, *Iqbal: Manifestations of the Islamic Spirit* (1991). See also Muhammad Iqbal, *The Reconstruction of Religious Thought in Islam* (1960).

9. An Awakening in the East

Frederick Cooper's description of the execution of the 26th Native Infantry is excerpted in Edward J. Thompson, *The Other Side of the Medal* (1925), though for historical context and literary enhancement I have had to add a little bit to Cooper's account and rearrange the order of his narrative. Trevelyan's comment to the House of Commons is quoted in Thomas R. Metcalf, *The Aftermath of Revolt* (1964); see also C. E. Trevelyan, *On the Education of the People of India* (1838). Benjamin Disraeli and Alexander Duff are both quoted in Ainslee T. Embree's collection *1857 in India* (1963). Bahadur Shah's appeal to the Indian people is from the Azimgarh Proclamation, printed in Charles Ball, *The History of the Indian Mutiny* (1860). For firsthand accounts of the British response to the Indian Revolt see C. G. Griffiths, *Siege of Delhi* (1912), and W. H. Russell, *My Indian Diary* (1957). Cecil Rhodes's description and quote are from *The Columbia Encyclopedia*, 6th ed., 2001.

For Sir Sayyid Ahmed Khan's writings and views see his *The Causes of the Indian Revolt* (1873), and his "Lecture on Islam," excerpted in Christian W. Troll, *Sayyid Ahmed Khan: A Reinterpretation of Muslim Theology* (1978). For more on the Aligarh, see *The Aligarh Movement: Basic Documents, 1864–1898*, collected by Shan Muhammad (1978). Moulavi Chiragh Ali's quote is from *The Proposed Political, Legal, and Social Reforms in the Ottoman Empire and Other Mohammadan States* (1883). For more on Abu-l Ala (Mawlana) Mawdudi see *Nationalism and Islam* (1947) and *The Islamic Movement* (1984).

For texts on colonialism in Egypt, see Joel Gordon, *Nasser's Blessed Movement* (1992); Juan R. I. Cole, *Colonialism and Revolution in the Middle East* (1993); and William Welch, *No Country for a Gentleman* (1988). Al-Afghani's life and works are analyzed in Nikki R. Keddie, *Sayyid Jamal al-Din "al-Afghani": A Political Biography* (1972); M. A. Zaki Badawi, *The Reformers of Egypt* (1979); and Charles C. Adams, *Islam and Modernism in Egypt* (1933). For Muhammad Abdu, see Osman Amin,

Muhammad 'Abduh (1953), and Malcolm H. Kerr, *Islamic Reform: The Political and Legal Theories of Muhammad 'Abduh and Rashid Rida* (1966). For Hasan al-Banna I suggest his *Memoirs of Hasan al-Banna Shaheed* (1981) as well as Richard P. Mitchell, *Society of the Muslim Brothers* (1969) and *Pioneers of Islamic Revival*, edited by Ali Rahnema (1995).

Good texts on Pan-Arabism include Sylvia G. Haim's collection *Arab Nationalism* (1962); Nissim Rejwan, *Arabs Face the Modern World* (1998); Abd al-Rahman al-Bazzaz, *Islam and Nationalism* (1952); Michael Doran, *Pan-Arabism Before Nasser* (1999); and Taha Husayn, *The Future of Culture in Egypt* (1954).

For Sayyid Qutb see his masterpiece, *Milestones* (1993), and his *Social Justice in Islam*, translated by William Shepard as *Sayyid Qutb and Islamic Activism* (1996). See also Jalal-e Ahmad, *Gharbzadeghi* (1997).

Saudi Arabia's history is recounted in Madawi al-Rasheed, *A History of Saudi Arabia* (2003). For Wahhabism I suggest Hamid Algar's short introduction *Wahhabism: A Critical Essay* (2002). It should be noted that Wahhabis prefer to call themselves *ahl al-tawhid*, or *al-Muwahhidun*.

A few words are needed about the meaning and function of fundamentalism in Islam. The term "fundamentalism" was first coined in the early twentieth century to describe a burgeoning movement among Protestants in the United States who were reacting to the rapid modernization and secularization of American society by reasserting the fundamentals of Christianity. Chief among these was a belief in the literal interpretation of the Bible—an idea that had passed out of favor with the ascendance of scientific theories such as evolution, which tended to treat biblical claims of historicity with mocking contempt. Considering the fact that all Muslims believe in the "literal" quality of the Quran—which is, after all, the direct speech of God—it makes little sense to refer to Muslim extremists or militants as "fundamentalists." Nor is this a proper term for those Islamists like Sayyid Qutb whose goal is the establishment of an Islamic polity. Nevertheless, because the term "Islamic fundamentalism" has become so common that it has even slipped into Persian and Arabic (where its literal translations are, somewhat appropriately, "bigot" in Arabic and "backward" in Persian), I will continue to use it in this book—but not to describe politicized Islam. That movement will be called "Islamism," its proper name. "Islamic fundamentalism," in contrast, refers to the radically ultra-conservative and puritanical ideology most clearly represented in the Muslim world by Wahhabism.

There are few better general introductions to the history of political Islam than Gilles Kepel's *Jihad: The Trail of Political Islam* (2002) and *The War for Muslim Minds* (2004). See also Anthony Shadid, *The Legacy of the Prophet* (2002). Osama bin Laden's quote is from an interview he gave to ABC reporter John Miller in May 1998.

For more on the creation and evolution of Jihadism see Reza Aslan, *Beyond Fundamentalism* (2010).

According to a 2005 Gallup International poll, 78 percent of people in the Middle East considered democracy "the best form of government." See http://www.voice-of-the-people.net/. The 2006 Pew poll can be found here: http://pewglobal.org/2006/06/22/the-great-divide-how-westerners-and-muslims-view-each-other/.

10. Slouching Toward Medina

There were two draft constitutions after the revolution in 1979. The first draft, which did not give the clerics an important role in the government, was, ironically, rejected by Iran's leftist parties. The second draft, completed in November by a seventy-three-member Assembly of Experts, revamped the original documents to establish clerical domination of the state.

The activities of the CDC and the American Type Culture Collection before and during the Iran-Iraq war have been documented by declassified government papers. See "Report: U.S. Supplied the Kinds of Germs Iraq Later Used for Biological Weapons," in *USA Today*, September 30, 2002.

For more on the Taliban see Ahmed Rashid, *The Taliban* (2000). Harvey Cox's *The Secular City* (1966) is essential reading for all students of religion and politics; see also Will Herberg, *Protestant, Catholic, Jew* (1955).

Abdulaziz Sachedina's *The Islamic Roots of Democratic Pluralism* (2001) is an excellent discussion of Islamic pluralism. While there are few books by Abdolkarim Soroush in English, a collection of his essential writings has been compiled and translated by Mahmoud and Ahmad Sadri under the title *Reason, Freedom, and Democracy in Islam: Essential Writings of Abdolkarim Soroush* (2002). The quotation is from his acceptance speech for the "Muslim Democrat of the Year" award given by the Center for the Study of Islam and Democracy in Washington, D.C., in 2004.

11. Welcome to the Islamic Reformation

"Ruptures" is a term I've taken from Muhammad Qasem Zaman's book *The Ulama in Contemporary Islam: Custodians of Change* (Princeton: Princeton University Press, 2002).

For a close look at the inner workings of IslamOnline.net see Bettina Gräf, "IslamOnline.net: Independent, Interactive, Popular," *Arab Media and Society* 4 (2008), http://www.arabmediasociety.com/index.php?article=576&printarticle. See also Jens Kutscher's presentation to the 30th Deutscher Orientalistentag, "Online Fatwas and their Relevance to the European Union," Freiburg, September 24–28, 2007, http://orient.ruf.uni-freiburg.de/dotpub/kutscher.pdf.

The Sheikh Abduallah bin Beh quote is from Rasha Elass, "Scholar Condemns 'Fatwa Piracy,'" *The National* (September 17, 2008), http://www.thenational.ae/news/uae-news/scholar-condemns-fatwa-piracy.

For more on Luther and the Christian Reformation see Diarmade MacCulloch's magisterial work, *The Reformation: A History* (New York: Viking, 2004).

A 2010 survey by the Pew Research Center showed that more than nine in ten Muslims in Lebanon (94 percent) express negative opinions of al-Qaeda, as do majorities of Muslims in Turkey (74 percent), Egypt (72 percent), Jordan (62 percent), and Indonesia (56 percent). See http://pewglobal.org/2010/12/02/muslims-around-the-world-divided-on-hamas-and-hezbollah/.

Works Consulted

Books

Abbott, Nabia. *Studies in Arabic Literary Papyri*. Chicago, 1957–72.

Abd al-Rahman al-Bazzaz. *Islam and Nationalism*. Baghdad, 1952.

Abedi, Mehdi, and Gary Legenhausen, eds. *Jihad and Shahadat*. Houston, 1986.

Abrahamian, Ervand. *Khomeinism: Essays on the Islamic Republic*. Berkeley, 1993.

Abrahamov, Binyamin. *Islamic Theology: Traditionalism and Rationalism*. Edinburgh, 1998.

Adams, Charles C. *Islam and Modernism in Egypt*. London, 1933.

Ahmad, Barakat. *Muhammad and the Jews: A Re-Examination*. New Delhi, 1979.

Ahmad, Jalal-e. *Gharbzadeghi*. California, 1997.

Ahmed, Leila. *Women and Gender in Islam*. New Haven, 1992.

Ahmed, Rashid. *The Taliban*. New Haven, 2000.

al-Banna, Hasan. *Memoirs of Hasan al-Banna Shaheed*. Karachi, 1981.

Algar, Hamid. *Wahhabism: A Critical Essay*. New York, 2002.

al-Ghazali. *The Alchemy of Happiness*. London, 1980.

———. *The Foundations of the Articles of Faith*. Lahore, 1963.

———. *The Niche of Lights*. Utah, 1998.

———. *The Ninety-nine Beautiful Names of God*. Nigeria, 1970.

al-Rasheed, Madawi. *A History of Saudi Arabia*. Cambridge, 2003.

al-Shaibi, Kamil M. *Sufism and Shi'ism*. Great Britain, 1991.

al-Tabari, Abu Ja'far Muhammad. *The History of al-Tabari*, ed. Ihsan Abbas et al. New York, 1988.

Amin, Osman. *Muhammad 'Abduh*. Washington, D.C., 1953.

Andrae, Tor. *Mohammed: The Man and His Faith*. New York, 1960

Angha, Molana Salaheddin Ali Nader Shah. *The Fragrance of Sufism*. Lanham, 1996.

Angha, Nahid. *Ecstasy*. California, 1998.

———. *Selections*. California, 1991.

An-Na'im, Abdullahi. *Toward an Islamic Reformation*. Syracuse, 1990.

Arjomand, Said Amir. *The Turban for the Crown*. New York, 1988.

Armstrong, Karen. *Muhammad*. San Francisco, 1992.

Asani, Ali, and Kamal Abdel-Malek. *Celebrating Muhammad*. South Carolina, 1995.

Ash-Shabrawi, Abd al-Khaliq. *The Degrees of the Soul*. London, 1997.

Attar, Farid ad-Din. *The Conference of the Birds*. New York, 1984.

Badawi, M. A. Zaki. *The Reformers of Egypt*. London, 1979.

Baldick, Julian. *Mystical Islam*. New York, 1989.

Ball, Charles. *The History of the Indian Mutiny*. London, 1860.

Bamyeh, Mohammed A. *The Social Origins of Islam*. Minneapolis, 1999.

Baqer, Moin. *Khomeini: Life of the Ayatollah*. New York, 1999.

Barks, Colman. *The Essential Rumi*. San Francisco, 1995.

Baron, Salo Wittmayer. *A Social and Religious History of the Jews* (3 vols.). New York, 1964.

Bell, Richard. *The Origin of Islam in Its Christian Environment*. London,1968.

Bergen, Peter L. *Holy War, Inc.: Inside the Secret World of Osama bin Laden*. New York, 2001.

Berkey, Jonathan P. *The Formation of Islam*. Cambridge, 2003.

Black, Anthony. *The History of Islamic Political Thought*. New York, 2001.

Boyce, Mary. *History of Zoroastrianism* (3 vols.). Leiden, 1996.

———. *Zoroastrians: Their Religious Beliefs and Practices*. New York, 2001.

Bulliet, Richard. *The Camel and the Wheel*. Cambridge, 1975.

———. *Islam: The View from the Edge*. New York, 1994.

Burckhardt, Titus. *An Introduction to Sufi Doctrine*. Wellingsborough, 1976.

Chelowski, Peter. *Ta'ziyeh: Ritual and Drama in Iran*. New York, 1979.

Cole, Juan R. I. *Colonialism and Revolution in the Middle East*. Princeton, 1993.

Cooper, John, et al., eds. *Islam and Modernity*. London, 1998.

Cooperson, Michael. *Classical Arabic Biography*. Cambridge, 2000.

Cox, Harvey. *The Secular City*. New York, 1966.

Cragg, Kenneth. *The Event of the Qur'an*. Oxford, 1971.

———. *God's Rule: Government and Islam*. New York, 2004.

———. *Readings in the Qur'an*. London, 1988.

Crone, Patricia. *Meccan Trade and the Rise of Islam*. New Jersey, 1987.

——— and M. A. Cook. *Hagarism: The Making of the Islamic World*. Cambridge, 1977.

——— and Martin Hinds. *God's Caliph: Religious Authority in the First Centuries of Islam*. Cambridge, 1986.

Dajani-Shakeel, Hadia, and Ronald A. Messier, eds. *The Jihad and Its Times*. Ann Arbor, 1991.

de Bruijn, J.T.P. *Persian Sufi Poetry*. Surrey, 1997.

de Tocqueville, Alexis. *Democracy in America*. New York, 1969.

Donohue, John J., and John L. Esposito, eds. *Islam in Transition*. New York, 1982.

Doran, Michael. *Pan-Arabism Before Nasser*. Oxford, 1999.

Eliade, Mircea. *The Myth of the Eternal Return*. Princeton, 1954.

———. *The Sacred and the Profane*. San Diego,1959.

Embree, Ainslee. *1857 in India*. Boston, 1963.

Ernst, Carl. *Eternal Garden: Mysticism, History, and Politics at a South Asian Sufi Center*. New York, 1992.

———. *Teachings of Sufism*. Boston, 1999.

Esposito, John L., and John O. Voll. *Makers of Contemporary Islam*. New York, 2001.

Gabrieli, Francesco. *Muhammad and the Conquests of Islam*. New York, 1968.

Gatje, Helmut. *The Qur'an and Its Exegesis*. Berkeley, 1976.

Gelpke, R. *Layla and Majnun*. London, 1966.

Gibb, H.A.R. *Mohammedanism*. London, 1970.

Goiten, S. D. *Jews and Arabs*. New York, 1970.

Goldziher, Ignaz. *Introduction to Islamic Theology and Law*. Princeton, 1981.

———. *Muslim Studies* (2 vols.). Albany, 1977.

Graetz, Heinrich. *History of the Jews* (3 vols.). Philadelphia, 1894.

Griffiths, C. G. *Siege of Delhi*. London, 1912.

Haeri, Shaykh Fadhlalla. *The Elements of Sufism*. Great Britain, 1990.

Haim, Sylvia G., ed. *Arab Nationalism*. Berkeley, 1962.

Halm, Heinz. *Shi'a Islam: From Religion to Revolution*. Princeton, 1997.

Helminski, Camille Adams. *Women of Sufism*. Boston, 2003.

Herberg, Will. *Protestant, Catholic, Jew*. New York, 1955.

Hodgson, Marshall G. S. *The Venture of Islam*. Chicago, 1974.

Hourani, George. *Islamic Rationalism*. Oxford, 1971.

Hoyland, Robert G. *Arabia and the Arabs*. New York, 2001.

Hurvitz, Nimrod. *The Formation of Hanbalism: Piety into Power*. London, 2002.

Ibn Batuta. *The Travels of Ibn Batuta*. Cambridge, 1958.

Ibn Hisham. *The Life of Muhammad*. Oxford, 1955.

Ibn Rushd. *Commentary on Aristotle's Metaphysics*. Leiden, 1984.

———. *The Epistle on the Possibility of Conjunction with the Active Intellect*. New York, 1982.

———. *Three Short Commentaries on Aristotle's "Topics," "Rhetoric," and "Poetics."* Albany, 1977.

Ibn Sina. *The Life of Ibn Sina*. Albany, 1974.

———. *Treatise on Logic*. The Hague, 1971.

Israel, Milton, and N. K. Wagle, eds. *Islamic Societies and Culture: Essays in Honor of Professor Aziz Ahmad*. New Delhi, 1983.

Jafri, S. Husain M. *Origins and Early Development of Shi'a Islam*. London, 1978.

Juynboll, G.H.A., ed. *Studies on the First Century of Islamic Studies*. Carbondale and Edwardsville, Ill., 1982.

Keddie, Nikki R. *Sayyid Jamal al-Din "al-Afghani": A Political Biography*. Berkeley, 1972.

Kelsay, John. *Islam and War*. Kentucky, 1993.

Kepel, Gilles. *Jihad: The Trail of Political Islam*. Cambridge, 2002.

———. *The War for Muslim Minds: Islam and the West*. Cambridge, 2004.

Kerr, Malcolm H. *Islamic Reform: The Political and Legal Theories of Muhammad 'Abduh and Rashid Rida*. Berkeley, 1966.

Khan, Inayat. *The Unity of Religious Ideals*. London, 1929.

Khan, Sayyid Ahmed. *The Causes of the Indian Revolt*. Benares, 1873.

Khomeini, Ruhollah. *A Clarification of Questions*. Boulder, 1984.

———. *Islam and Revolution*. Berkeley, 1981.

———. *Islamic Government*. New York, 1979.

Kochler, Hans. *The Concept of Monotheism in Islam and Christianity*. Austria, 1982.

Lammens, Henri. *Islam: Beliefs and Institutions*. London, 1968.

Lecker, Michael. *Muslims, Jews, and Pagans: Studies on Early Islamic Medina*. Leiden, 1995.

Lings, Martin. *What Is Sufism?* Cambridge, 1993.

Mackey, Sandra. *The Iranians*. New York, 1996.

Madelung, Wilferd. *Religious Schools and Sects in Medieval Islam*. London, 1985.

———. *The Succession to Muhammad*. Cambridge, 1997.

Margoliouth, D. S. *The Relations Between Arabs and Israelites Prior to the Rise of Islam*. London, 1924.

Martin, Richard. *Approaches to Islam in Religious Studies*. Oxford, 2001.

Martin, Richard, et al. *Defenders of Reason in Islam*. Oxford, 1997.

Massignon, Louis. *Essay on the Origins of the Technical Language of Islamic Mysticism*. Bloomington, Ind., 1997.

Mawdudi, Abu-l Ala (Mawlana). *Nationalism and India*. Lahore, 1947.

———. *The Islamic Movement*. London, 1984.

McCarthy, Richard. *The Theology of the Ash'ari*. Beirut, 1953.

Mehr, Farhang. *The Zoroastrian Tradition*. Amherst, Mass., 1991.

Menocal, Maria Rosa. *Ornament of the World*. New York, 2002.

Mernissi, Fatima. *The Veil and the Male Elite*. Cambridge, 1991.

Metcalf, Thomas. *The Aftermath of Revolt*. Princeton, 1964.

Mitchell, Richard P. *Society of the Muslim Brothers*. New York, 1969.

Momen, Moojan. *An Introduction to Shi'i Islam*. New Haven, 1985.

Mottahadeh, Roy. *The Mantle of the Prophet*. New York, 1985.

Naquvi, M. A. *The Tragedy of Karbala*. Princeton, 1992.

Nasr, Seyyed Hossein. *Islamic Art and Spirituality*. New York, 1987.

———. *Sufi Essays*. London, 1972.

Netton, Ian Richard. *Sufi Ritual*. Surrey, 2000.

Newby, Gordon Darnell. *A History of the Jews of Arabia*. South Carolina, 1988.

Nicholson, R. A. *The Mystics of Islam*. London, 1914.

———. *Studies in Islamic Mysticism*. Cambridge, 1921.

Nicholson, Reynolds. *Rumi: Poet and Mystic*. London, 1978.

Nurbakhsh, Javad. *Master and Disciple in Sufism*. Tehran, 1977.

Peters, F. E. *Mecca: A Literary History of the Muslim Holy Land*. New Jersey, 1994.

———. *The Hajj*. New Jersey, 1994.

———. *Muhammad and the Origins of Islam*. New York, 1994.

Peters, Rudolph. *Islam and Colonialism: The Doctrine of Jihad in Modern History*. The Hague, 1979.

———. *Jihad in Classical and Modern Islam*. Princeton, 1996.

Pinault, David. *The Horse of Karbala*. New York, 2001.

———. *The Shiites*. New York, 1992.

Pourjavady, Nasrollah, and Peter Wilson. *Kings of Love*. Tehran, 1978.

Qutb, Sayyid. *Milestones*. Indianapolis, 1993.

———. *Social Justice in Islam*. Leiden, 1953.

Rahnema, Ali, ed. *Pioneers of Islamic Revival*. London, 1995.

Rashid, Ahmed. *The Taliban*. New Haven, 2000.

Rejwan, Nissim. *Arabs Face the Modern World*. Florida, 1998.

Renard, John. *Seven Doors to Islam*. Berkeley, 1996.

Robinson, Neal. *Christ in Islam and Christianity*. London, 1991.

Rodinson, Maxime. *Mohammad*. New York, 1971.

Rumi, Jalal al-Din. *Mystical Poems of Rumi* (2 vols.). Chicago, 1968.

———. *Rumi: Poet and Mystic*. London, 1950.

Russell, W. H. *My Indian Diary*. London, 1957.

Sachedina, Abdulaziz Abdulhussein. *Islamic Messianism*. Albany, 1981.

———. *The Islamic Roots of Democratic Pluralism*. Oxford, 2001.

———. *The Just Ruler in Shi'ite Islam*. New York, 1988.

Schacht, Joseph. *An Introduction to Islamic Law*. Oxford, 1998.

———. *Origins of Muhammadan Jurisprudence*. Oxford, 1950.

Schimmel, Annemarie. *And Muhammad Is His Messenger*. Chapel Hill, N.C., 1985.

——— —. *I Am Wind, You Are Fire: The Life and Works of Rumi*. Boston, 1992.

Schubel, Vernon. *Religious Performance in Contemporary Islam*. Columbia, 1993.

Schwartz, Martin. *Studies on Islam*. New York, 1981.

Sells, Michael. *Desert Tracings: Six Classical Arabian Odes*. Connecticut, 1989.

Shaban, M. A. *Islamic History: A New Interpretation*. Cambridge, 1994.

Shah, Idris. *The Sufis*. New York, 1964.

———. *The Way of the Sufi*. New York, 1969.

Shariati, Ali. *Fatima Is Fatima*. Tehran, 1971.

———. *Iqbal: Manifestations of the Islamic Spirit*. New Mexico, 1991.

Smith, Margaret. *Rabi'a the Mystic and Her Fellow-Saints in Islam*. Cambridge, 1928.

Smith, Wilfred Cantwell. *Islam in Modern History*. Princeton, 1957.

Soroush, Abdolkarim. *Reason, Freedom, and Democracy*. New York, 2000.

Stillman, Norman A. *The Jews of Arab Lands*. Philadelphia, 1979.

Tabataba'i, Muhammad H. *Qur'an in Islam*. London, 1988.

———. *Shi'ite Islam*. New York, 1979.

Taha, Mahmoud. *The Second Message of Islam*. Syracuse, 1987.

Thompson, Edward J. *The Other Side of the Medal*. London, 1925.

Trevelyan, C. E. *On the Education of the People of India*. Hyderabad, 1838.

Trimingham, J. Spencer. *The Sufi Orders in Islam*. Oxford, 1971.

Troll, Christian W. *Sayyid Ahmed Khan: A Reinterpretation of Muslim Theology*. New Delhi, 1978.

Turner, Bryan S. *Weber and Islam: A Critical Study*. London, 1974.

Von Denffer, Ahmad. *Ulum al-Quran: An Introduction to the Sciences of the Qur'an*. Leicester, 1983.

Wadud, Amina. *Qur'an and Woman: Rereading the Sacred Text from a Woman's Perspective*. New York, 1999.

Walzer, Michael. *Just and Unjust Wars*. New York, 1977.

Wansbrough, John. *Qurunic Studies: Sources and Methods of Scriptural Interpretation*. Oxford, 1977.

———. *The Sectarian Milieu. Content and Composition of Islamic Salvation History*. Oxford, 1978.

Watt, W. Montgomery. *The Faith and Practice of al-Ghazali*. London, 1953.

———. *Islamic Creeds*. Edinburgh, 1994.

———. *Islamic Political Thought*. Edinburgh, 1968.

———. *Muhammad at Mecca*. London, 1953.

———. *Muhammad at Medina*. Oxford, 1956.

———. *Muhammad: Prophet and Statesman*. London, 1961.

Welch, William M. *No Country for a Gentleman*. New York, 1988.

Wolfson, Harry Austryn. *The Philosophy of Kalam*. Cambridge, 1976.

Zabiri, Kate. *Mahmud Shaltut and Islamic Modernism*. New York, 1993.

Zaheri, Dariush. *The Iranian Revolution: Then and Now*. Boulder, Colo., 2000.

Zakaria, Rafiq. *The Struggle Within Islam: The Conflict Between Religion and Politics*. London, 1989.

Zawati, Hilmi M. *Is Jihad a Just War?* Lewiston, Me., 2001.

Articles

Abbot, Freedland. "The Jihad of Sayyid Ahmad Shahid," *Muslim World* (1962) 216–22.

al-Faruqi, Lois Ibsen. "The Cantillation of the Qur'an," *Asian Music* 19:1 (1987) 2–23.

Arafat, W. N. "New Light on the Story of Banu Qurayza and the Jews of Medina," *Journal of the Royal Asiatic Society* (1976) 100–107.

Aslan, Reza. "The Problem of Stoning in the Islamic Penal Code: An Argument for Reform," *Journal of Islamic & Near Eastern Law* 3 (2004).

———. "Thus Sprang Zarathustra: A Brief Historiography on the Date of the Prophet of Zoroastrianism," *Jusur: Journal of Middle Eastern Studies* 14 (1998–99) 21–34.

Caetani, Leone. "Uthman and the Recension of the Koran," *The Muslim World* 5 (1915) 380–90.

Conrad, Lawrence I. "Abraha and Muhammad," *Bulletin of the School of Oriental and African Studies* 50 (1987) 225–40.

Gil, Moshe. "The Constitution of Medina: A Reconsideration," *Israel Oriental Studies* 6 (1974) 44–65.

———. "The Medinan Opposition to the Prophet," *Jerusalem Studies in Arabic and Islam* 10 (1987) 65–96.

————. "Origin of the Jews of Yathrib," *Jerusalem Studies in Arabic and Islam* 4 (1984) 203–24.

Guillaume, Alfred. "New Light on the Life of Muhammad," *Journal of Semitic Studies* (1960) 27–59.

Halperin, David. "The Ibn Sayyad Traditions and the Legend of al-Dajjal," *Journal of the American Oriental Society* 96 (1976) 213–25.

Hawting, G. R. "We Were Not Ordered with Entering It but Only with Circumambulating It: *Hadith* and *Fiqh* on Entering the Kaaba," *Bulletin of the School of Oriental and African Studies* 47 (1984) 228–42.

Huntington, Samuel. "The Clash of Civilizations," *Foreign Affairs* 72:3 (Summer 1993) 22–49.

Kister, M. J. "*al-Tahannuth:* An Inquiry into the Meaning of a Term," *Bulletin of the School of Oriental and African Studies* 30 (1968) 223–36.

————. " 'A Bag of Meat:' A Study of an Early Hadith," *Bulletin of the School of Oriental and African Studies* 31 (1968) 267–75.

————. "Do Not Assimilate Yourselves . . . ," *Jerusalem Studies in Arabic and Islam* 12 (1989) 321–71.

————. "The Market of the Prophet," *Journal of the Economic and Social History of the Orient* 8 (1965) 272–76.

————. "The Massacre of the Banu Qurayza: A Reexamination of a Tradition," *Jerusalem Studies in Arabic and Islam* 8 (1986) 61–96.

Nelson, Kristina. "Reciter and Listener: Some Factors Shaping the Mujawwad Style of Qur'anic Reciting," *Ethnomusicology* (Spring/Summer 1987) 41–47.

Rahman, Hannah. "The Conflicts Between the Prophet and the Opposition in Medina," *Der Islam* 62 (1985) 260–97.

Reissener, H. G. "The Ummi Prophet and the Banu Israil," *The Muslim World* 39 (1949).

Rubin, Uri. "Hanafiyya and Ka'ba: An Enquiry into the Arabian Pre-Islamic Background of *din Ibrahim,*" *Jerusalem Studies in Arabic and Islam* 13 (1990) 85–112.

————. "The Ka'ba: Aspects of Its Ritual Function and Position in Pre-Islamic and Early Times," *Jerusalem Studies in Arabic and Islam* 8 (1986) 97–131.

Select Dictionaries and Encyclopedias

A Dictionary of Buddhism. Damien Keown, ed. Oxford, 2003.

The Encyclopedia of Gods. Michael Jordan, ed. Great Britain, 1992.

The Encyclopedia of Indo-European Culture. J. P. Mallory and D. Q. Adams, eds. New York, 1997.

The Encyclopedia of Islam (11 vols.). H.A.R. Gibb et al., eds. Leiden, 1986.

The Encyclopedia of Religion (16 vols.). Mircea Eliade et al., eds. New York, 1987.

The Encyclopedia of World Mythology and Legend. Anthony S. Mercatante, ed. New York, 1988.

The Encyclopedia of World Religions. Wendy Doniger, ed. Springfield, Mass., 1999.

The New Encyclopedia of Islam. Cyril Glasse, ed. Walnut Creek, Calif., 2002.

The Oxford Dictionary of World Religions. John Bowker, ed. Oxford, 1997.

The Oxford Encyclopedia of the Modern Islamic World. John L. Esposito, ed. Oxford, 1995.

Index

DR. REZA ASLAN is an internationally acclaimed writer and scholar of religions. His first book, *No god but God: The Origins, Evolution, and Future of Islam,* was an international bestseller. Shortlisted for the *Guadian* First Book Award, it has been translated into thirteen languages and was named by Blackwells as one of the hundred most important books of the last decade. He is also the author of *How to Win a Cosmic War: Confronting Radical Religion,* as well as the editor of *Tablet & Pen: Literary Landscapes from the Modern Middle East.* Born in Iran, he now lives in Los Angeles, where he is associate professor of creative writing at the University of California, Riverside.

About the Type

The text of this book was set in Janson, a typeface designed in about 1690 by Nicholas Kis, a Hungarian living in Amsterdam, and for many years mistakenly attributed to the Dutch printer Anton Janson. In 1991 the matrices became the property of the Stempel Foundry in Frankfurt. It is an old-style book face of excellent clarity and sharpness. Janson serifs are concave and splayed; the contrast between thick and thin strokes is marked.